The impact of Alexander's conquest

Subjects, conquered and chroniclers

UAH MONOGRAFÍAS
HUMANIDADES 88

The impact of Alexander's conquest

Subjects, conquered and chroniclers

M. Mendoza & B. Antela-Bernárdez (eds.)

Universidad de Alcalá

EDITORIAL
UNIVERSIDAD DE ALCALÁ

La colección de Monografías de Humanidades de la Editorial de la Universidad de Alcalá ha sido distinguida con el Sello de Calidad en Edición Académica - Academic Publishing Quality (CEA-APQ).

Calidad en Edición Académica
Academic Publishing Quality

Plaza de San Diego, s/n
28801 Alcalá de Henares
www.uah.es

I.S.B.N.:978-84-18979-19-4
Depósito legal: M-11199-2022

Composición: Solana e Hijos, A. G., S.A.U.
Impresión y encuadernación: Solana e Hijos, A.G., S.A.U.

Impreso en España

CONTENTS

Introduction

Living in a changing world is a challenging task. The events and historical development of the XXth Century, and as far as we can see, their continuity in our own XXIst Century, have driven Humankind to face its hardest age. Nevertheless, History is usually very helpful when we try to look for examples and ideas to confront our own reality. In this way, Antiquity is like a mirror to review our own worries and to find solutions, perspectives, and even some hope in order to gain a critical and deeper understanding of our days.

Alexander the Great has had a great impact from his own times on in the way that any thinker, past and present, has observed the contemporary facts and problems. From the Hellenistic Monarchies, based on Macedonian notions of Royalty, and the Roman Emperors to Christian and Islamic authors to the ages of the Renaissance, the Illustration or even the Colonialist West and Nazi Germany, we can trace the usings and impact of Alexander's conquest and the potential evaluation that every epoch did about his figure and his campaigns. Nevertheless, at least from Western eyes, Alexander had been usually adopted as a precedent of the Western hegemony and rule over the world. Not many voices have critically stressed and challenged this standard view of the young Macedonian king. However, nowadays, research has included this deeper reflection, avoiding celebrating Alexander's harshness and mistreatment of the conquered population. From Eddy's *The King is Dead* (1961) and Bosworth's unapologetic portrait of Alexander to more recent approaches by Pierre Briant, Alexander has been the object of a deep reappraisal. Modern historiography about Alexander, although frequently it still commends his ability and skills as commander and conqueror, seems to be going through a slow change of direction in order to get a better and wide picture of what the Macedonian conquest really meant to many people in Asia and Greece, and how expensive and bitter was the price to be paid for being part of the glorious tale of Alexander.

While writing these lines, we knew about a new book by the brilliant master Waldemar Heckel titled *In the Path of Conquest: Resistance to Alexander the Great* (2020), which pays attention to this range of topics. Good news, indeed, because the very stressed historical character Alexander deserves to be understood not just as a model or an ancient *exemplum* in the style of those by of Plutarch or Valerius Maximus, or as a gentle ruler and a romantic knight, like Tarn and his enormous amount of unconscious followers still do, but also as a bloodthirsty commander and a brutal leader who imposed his rule by force, in the Macedonian manner (rather than in the Greek one) to almost half the population of the 'known world'.

The following pages are a collection of works from different authors but with a common starting point. In December 2017, answering the open call from the organizer, Borja Antela-Bernárdez, many of the best international researchers on Alexander the Great met in Barcelona, within the classrooms and seminars of the Autonomous University, to face the difficult task of questioning Alexander and discuss the impact of the Macedonian conquest. This book is the result of those nice days of sharing ideas and confronting opinions with critical views. Some of the original participants, like Joseph Roisman, Tim Howe, Olga Palagia, Christian Djurslev, or Stephen Harrison, among others, have not been able to contribute to this book, for different reasons, but they are still part of this book.

These are, nowadays, challenging times for every one of us. But during the darker hours, we like to remember the beautiful moments we all shared, while talks, discussions, or meals took place, and we can still feel the nice atmosphere we all created, and the friendship that arose among many of us. This kind of friendly ties is the best nourishment for research and life itself, in its fullest form. Indeed, we dedicate this collection to all our friends from those days, with the hope that criticism of any kind of imperialism and violence can be discussed, analysed and freely expressed from academia in order to help people around the globe to improve our own world.

The Editors

Contributors

Mario Agudo Villanueva is a journalist and MBA at the University of Deusto and EAE. He has combined his professional career in mass media with research and divulgation works in the field of history, with several publications in specialised magazines, both academic and general (*National Geographic, Muy Historia, Desperta Ferro*). He has been director of publications such as *ROMÁNICO* and *Mediterráneo Antiguo*, as well as a regular contributor to radio spaces such as *Ser Historia*. He is currently on the editorial board of *Karanos. Bulletin of Ancient Macedonian Studies*. He is the author of the books *Palmira. La ciudad reencontrada* (Confluencias, 2016), *Macedonia. La cuna de Alejandro Magno* (Dstoria, 2016), *Atenas. El lejano eco de las piedras* (Confluencias, 2018) y *El bestiario de las catedrales. Animales y seres fantásticos del mundo antiguo al medievo cristiano* (Almuzara, 2019).

Manuel Albaladejo Vivero studied Laws at the Complutense University of Madrid, and History at the University of Alcalá. He received his PhD in Ancient History at Alcalá in 2003 with a thesis on India and Ethiopia in ancient Greek literature. He has enjoyed two postdoc fellowships at Freiburg University –one of them awarded by the Alexander von Humboldt Foundation. His main fields of research are India in Antiquity, the historical geography of the ancient world, and travels and navigation in the Classical world. Currently, he is Lecturer of Ancient History at the University of Valencia.

Eran Almagor is the author of many studies on Plutarch and other Greek writers of the Roman imperial period (Strabo, Josephus). His interests include Hellenistic history, the history of the Achaemenid Empire and its image in Greek literature (especially in Herodotus and Ctesias), Plutarch's works (mainly the *Lives*), and the modern reception of Antiquity, particularly in popular culture. He is the author of *Plutarch and the* Persica (Edinburgh University Press, 2018), and is co-editor of *Ancient Ethnography: New Approaches* (Bloomsbury, 2013) and *The Reception of Ancient Virtues and Vices in Modern Popular Culture* (Brill, 2017).

Borja Antela-Bernárdez is a Full Lecturer of Ancient Greek History at the Autonomous University of Barcelona (since 2005). From his PhD Thesis about Alexander and the Greeks on (published in 2005), he has written a lot about Alexander the Great, but also on other topics of research, such as Modern Historiography on Alexander and the Hellenistic World, the place of Athens in the First Mithridatic War, Gender and Ancient Greek History (mainly Hellenistic-Late Roman Republic periods), and Classical Reception in Cinema. Lately, he also has been writting about Theory of History and how alternative pedagogy should approach history from imagination and emotions (thoughts published in *Historia Viva*, 2019). Director of the journal *Karanos. Bulletin of Ancient Macedonian Studies*, IP of the Project *History of Conflict in Antiquity* (funded by the Catalonian Research Council), and Coordinator of the Master of the Mediterranean Sea (UOC-UAB-UAH), he is in his forties, and he usually says that he strongly believes in a better world.

Chiara Di Serio is a postdoctoral research affiliate of the Center for Religious Studies at the Central European University. She received a long training at the Roman School of History of Religions at the University of Rome *La Sapienza*. In February 2020 she defended her PhD dissertation focused on the apocryphal correspondence between Alexander the Great and Dindimus, head of the Brahmans. Her research interests concern the Graeco-Roman ethnographic literature on Eastern countries and peoples, specifically on India and its inhabitants. She is currently carrying out a research project on the narratives about the Indian «naked philosophers» from Antiquity to the Middle Ages.

Adolfo J. Domínguez Monedero is Professor of Ancient History at the Autonomous University of Madrid. Among the lines of research that he is developing in recent times is the study of the History of Macedonia and Epirus. Results of it are his book *Alejandro, Rey de Macedonia y de Asia* (Sílex, 2013) and the edition of the collective volume *Politics, Territory and Identity in Ancient Epirus* (ETS, 2018). He is a corresponding member of the German Archaeological Institute and a corresponding Academic of the Royal Academy of History.

Francisco Javier Gómez Espelosín is a Professor of Ancient History at the University of Alcalá. He is a specialist in the ancient Greek world, with particular attention and dedication to subjects related to Greek historiography and geography, to the Greek vision of other peripheral cultures and to the figure of Alexander. His most recent book is *Geografías de los exótico. Los griegos y otras culturas*. He is the author of articles in specialised journals, both Spanish and international, as well as of several chapters in collective works (Síntesis, 2019). He is also the translator of authors such as Apianus, Strabo, the Paradoxographers and Greek travel literature. He has managed research projects as IP funded by the Spanish Research Ministry. With other Spanish and foreign colleagues, he is a Founder Member GAHIA (International Society for the Study of Geography and Historiography in Antiquity) and Corresponding Academic of the Spanish Royal Academy of History.

Marc Mendoza completed his PhD with a dissertation focused on cases of irreligious behaviour during Alexander's reign. His main research fields so far have been Alexander the Great, the Diadochi and early Hellenistic Central Asia, but he has also published papers on Achaemenid deportations, modern reception and Catalan historiography. He is the secretary of Karanos: Bulletin of Ancient Macedonian Studies and, in the recent years, has published books like *La irreligiosidad de Alejandro* (Universidad de Alcalá, 2019) and edited collective volumes such as *Stranger Things. Fantasy in Antiquity* (Projekt Verlag, 2021). He is currently an Associate Lecturer at the University of Lleida.

Antonio Ignacio Molina Marín is a Doctor in Ancient History for the University of Murcia and an honorary researcher at the University of Alcalá de Henares. He has made stays as a visiting professor at the Universities of Exeter (England) and Santa Clara (USA). He is currently a member of the editorial board of the journal *Karanos: Bulletin of Ancient Macedonian Studies*. Among his most important publications are *Geographica: ciencia del espacio y tradición narrativa de Homero a Cosmas Indicopleustes* (University of Murcia, 2011), *Alejandro Magno: Apotheosis y paideia* (Editorial Académica Española, 2012) and *Alejandro Magno (1916-2015)*: *Un siglo de estudios sobre Macedonia antigua* (Pórtico, 2018). His main lines of research are Macedonia, Alexander the Great, the ruler cult, and the Greco-Roman geographical thought.

Jaakkojuhani Peltonen is a researcher at Tampere University. After defending his thesis, Peltonen has been as a visiting fellow at King's College London (2018-2020). In 2019 Routledge published his book *Alexander the Great in the Roman Empire, 150 BC to AD 600*. He has also been co-editor of a volume on the justification of war in history. Peltonen has contributed to *Brill's Companion to the Reception of Alexander the Great* and *Gender* and *Memory, and Identity in the Roman World*. His special interests include reception of Alexander the Great, conceptions of masculinity and ideology of war in ancient Rome.

Guendalina D. M. Taietti has a Bachelor in Classical Philology and a Masters in Ancient History from the University of Pavia (Italy), and a PhD in Classics from the University of Liverpool (UK). Her research focusses on ancient Macedon, the Hellenistic period, animals across Eastern and Western Classics, and the Greek Alexander Receptions. Taietti is passionate about teaching and getting to know new cultures; as a result, she has taught Classics in several countries, such as Greece, the UK, and China.

One King
to rule them all

Alexander the Great and the Macedonian Kingship

Guendalina D. M. Taietti
(University of Liverpool)

The paper addresses the big theme of the nature of Macedonian kingship specifically through three exhibits: the Philippi decree,[1] the Kalindoia dedication[2] and the Opis mutiny. I will consider Alexander the Great's role and actions as an Argead king and seek to assess to what extent Alexander followed the path drawn by his predecessors for issues concerning domestic and foreign policy, and how he altered Macedonian monarchy in the wake of his father Philip II's reforms. Finally, with this paper, I also aim at evaluating the impact that the Persian campaign had on the kingdom of Macedon from both a social and an institutional perspective.

Epigraphical evidence

The examination of the epigraphical evidence needs to start with a clarification about the identity of the man named Ἀλέξανδρος in the two inscriptions. His identification will allow us to determine the chronology of the two documents:

a) The decree of Philippoi displays the name *Alexandros* three times (A. 3, B. 5, ll. 11-12), *Philippos* twice (A. 9, B. 10), and *Philotas* and *Leonnatos* once (A. 7).[3] Since Alexander's father, Philip II, founded the Macedonian colony of Philippoi in 356 BC,[4]

---

[1] Museum of Philippoi, inventory num. Λ 37; *SEG* XXXIV 664; Hatzopoulos 1996 II nº. 6.

[2] Archaeological Museum of Thessaloniki, inventory nº. 9229; Vokotopoulou 1986: 87-114; Hatzopoulos 1996 II nº. 62.

[3] Cf. *SEG* XXXIV 664.

[4] App. *BC*. IV. 105.

and Philotas[5] and Leonnatus[6] are well attested among Alexander's Companions, it is safe to identify the *Alexandros* of this inscription with the great conqueror.

b) After the destruction of Olynthus and, consequently, the dissolution of the Chalcidian league by Philip II in 348 BC, Kalindoia became part of the Macedonian kingdom as βασιλικὴ γῆ (royal land).[7] Thus, Alexander III was entitled to establish a Macedonian colony and to dispose of the land around it, as suggested in the dedication of Agathanor. Moreover, Vokotopoulou has pointed out that the calligraphy suits the period *ca.* 330-300 BC.[8]

Both documents show Alexander III making decisions about royal land[9] and its utilization by people living in Macedonian territories; in the first, he also receives an embassy. Were his actions in line with the Argead royal policy? How can we define the boundaries of the Argead king's power?

Modern scholarship has not reached an agreement about the nature of Macedonian kingship and, *grosso modo*, it is possible to differentiate between two main viewpoints: a) the so-called *constitutional interpretation* and b) the *autocratic/absolutist interpretation*.[10] The first underlines the constitutional character of the Macedonian monarchy, since the Argead king ruled aided by a council of Companions, called ἑταῖροι (*hetairoi*),[11] and his power was limited by the army in assembly, variously described as οἱ Μακεδόνες, τὸ κοινὸν τῶν Μακεδόνων, or ἡ ἐκκλησία τῶν Μακεδόνων. The assembly was normally convened by the king or—if the king was a minor or abroad—by one of his representatives, and it ratified the succession to the Argead throne.[12] Its members were granted freedom of speech (παρρησία), decided about matters of war, and adjudicated trials for high treason.[13]

---

[5] Berve 1926 II: 393-397, nº. 802; Heckel 2006: 147-151, nº. 2.

[6] Berve 1926 II: 232-235, nº. 466; Heckel 2006: 216-219, nº. 4.

[7] Errington, *Brill's NP* II (2003: 957), s.v. 'Calindoea (Καλίνδοια; Kalindoia)'; Hatzopoulos / Loukopoulou 1992: 71-74.

[8] Vokotopoulou 1986: 93-95.

[9] Cf. Plu. *Alex.* 15.2-3 about the allotment of the crown property. See Hamilton 1969: 37.

[10] For the scholarly discussion, see, *inter alia*, Lindsay Adams 1986: 43-45; Borza 1990: 232-235; Greenwalt 2010: 151-163; Roisman 2012b: 144; Carney 2015: 265-266.

[11] Companions (ἑταῖροι) were also called φίλοι, or πρῶτοι; cf. Hamilton 1969: 37. All these terms applied to the Macedonian court elite «carry distinct connotations of proximity to, familiarity with, and dependence from the king» (P. Paschides, paper read at the 8th International Symposium on Ancient Macedon entitled *Η Μακεδονία από τον θάνατο του Φιλίππου Β' έως την άνοδο του Αυγύστου στην εξουσία*, Thessaloniki, November 21-24, 2017). Engels 2010: 92: «[the] feudal character and strong personal relationship between the Macedonian kings and their aristocracy was also a social custom and institution which distinguished Macedonian identity from most southern Greek cities».

[12] Hatzopoulos 1986: 291. For a discussion about the role of the Macedonian Assembly under the Temenids, see Hatzopoulos 1996 I: 261-298.

[13] For the constitutional interpretation, see Droysen 1880: 4, 221-225; Paribeni 1947: 24; Kanatsoules 1964: 79-81; 1976: 15-19; Hammond 1989: 54-65; 2000: 142.

The absolutist viewpoint sees the Argead state as a reflection of the king, interpreted as a dominant ruling figure, an autocrat with unlimited powers. The king was the high priest, the military chief-commander and the supreme judge.[14] There are two main arguments in favour of this interpretation: i) there is no evidence of a regular assembly since the sources attest decisions taken by the Μακεδόνες only on very extraordinary occasions—as during the trial of Philotas or the meeting in Babylon following Alexander's death;[15] ii) foreign policy was totally controlled by the king, for he received the embassies and personally took decisions about treaties and alliances, without involving representatives of the Macedonians in the process.[16]

The interpretation of the nature of Macedonian kingship has divided scholarship for decades because the evidence is lacunose. However, I argue that the literary and epigraphical sources leave room for a '*situational* constitutional kinship'.[17] In fact, as Hammond has underlined, even if the evidence does not suffice to show whether a council with constitutional powers and an assembly in Macedon were *formal or regular* or not, it is undeniable that Macedon had a council and an assembly *sui generis*,[18] which took the lead in *certain circumstances*. Surely, the king had complete control of the Companions, since he was able to choose them, to bestow upon them, or deprive them of, powers; nevertheless, in many respects, he associated with the Companions as *primus inter pares*,[19] and they were his important advisers and loyal commanders.[20] To put it in Plutarch's words, the Macedonians were *philobasileis*, fond of their king;[21] this suggests that, although hierarchy and benefits in the Argead court depended upon the king, the *hetairoi* and the Macedonians in army felt that they could influence and actively contribute to their leader's decisions.[22]

---

[14] Errington 1986: 196-199: absolute monarchy centered on the king. See also Errington 1974: 37; Anson 1985: 303-305.

[15] Anson 1985: 305.

[16] Anson 1985: 304.

[17] See, e.g., D.S. XVII.16.1-4 (autumn 335): Μετὰ δὲ ταῦτα ὁ μὲν βασιλεὺς ἐπανελθὼν μετὰ τῆς δυνάμεως εἰς τὴν Μακεδονίαν συνήγαγε τοὺς ἡγεμόνας τῶν στρατιωτῶν καὶ τοὺς ἀξιολογωτάτους τῶν φίλων καὶ προέθηκε βουλὴν περὶ τῆς εἰς τὴν Ἀσίαν διαβάσεως. Furthermore, the Council's decisions from Alexander the Great's reign onwards are described in constitutional terminology (cf: δοκεῖ, κελεύω in Arr. *An.* I.25.5; II.6) even by hostile sources (e.g. *decerno, placeo* in Curt. VI.8.15, 11.10). Cf. Edson 1970: 32: «The kingdom of the Macedonians was most definitively not despotism but a semi-constitutional monarchy based on traditional usage, custom and established precedent»; *contra* Errington 1983: 101: there is no legalised ancient set of customs for the Macedonian state; legalised systems are a product of the modern era.

[18] Hammond 2000: 141.

[19] Alexander is perceived as a Homeric type of leader in second century AD literature: Plu. *Mor.* 331c, 343b.

[20] Hammond 1989: 57.

[21] Plu. *Alex.* 47.5: Κρατερὸν φιλοβασιλέα; Plu. *Aem.* 24.1: ἀεὶ μὲν οὖν λέγονται φιλοβασιλεῖς οἱ Μακεδόνες.

[22] Lindsay Adams 1986: 45.

Furthermore, in foreign policy, it seems that the Argead king dealt with embassies, treaties and alliances *as the representative of the Macedonians*. For example, after the capture of Tyre, Alexander received Darius III's second letter, which offered him the lands up to the river Halys. As Alexander wanted to reject it, he lied about the content of the letter to his Companions, meaning that he was *not completely* free to decide about war and foreign policy, but was subject to his Companions' approval.[23]

The Decree of Philippoi

Found in 1936 during French excavations in the area,[24] the decree for the lands around Philippoi was engraved in two columns on a marble orthostate.[25] Unfortunately, the first lines of both of the columns were lost in World War II and today we possess only five fragments of the decree.[26]

Picture 1: Philippoi

[23] D.S. XVII. 39.2: ὁ δ'Ἀλέξανδρος συναγαγὼν τοὺς φίλους καὶ τὴν μὲν ἀληθινὴν ἐπιστολὴν ἀποκρυψάμενος, ἑτέραν δὲ γράψας ῥέπουσαν πρὸς τὸ ἑαυτῷ συμφέρον προσήνεγκε τοῖς συνέδροις καὶ τοὺς πρέσβεις ἀπράκτους ἐξαπέστειλεν. Cf. Lindsay Adams 1986: 52.

[24] Hatzopoulos 1987: 437, nº. 714.

[25] Orthostates are rectangular stone blocks with little depth that are usually incorporated in a wall.

[26] See Picture 1. Cf. also *SEG* XXXIV 664: 181; Hatzopoulos 1996 II: 25-26, nº. 6.

Col. A:
SEG XXXIV 664: Philippoi 335 BC.

[..........c.27-30....]ρσιδ[...]
[.......c.18.......]ης [.. ἐπ]ρέσβευσαν
[πρὸς βασιλέα Ἀλέ]ξ̣α̣[νδ]ρον καὶ Ἀλέξανδρος
[...c.11....]ν τὴν ἀργὸν ἐργάζεσθαι [....]π
[...c.10...]ιν χώρα καὶ προστελοῦσ[ι ...]
[....c.13..... τ]ὴν ἀργόν· ὁρίσαι δὲ τὴν [χώραν][27]
[...c.12....]ς Φιλώταν καὶ Λεονν[ᾶτον· ....]
[...c.9... ἐπεισβε]βήκασιν τῆς χώ[ρας ..5..]
[..c.7.. ἣν Φιλίπ]ποις ἔδωκεν Φίλ̣[ιππος ...]
[...c.13-14.... κα]ὶ ἐπισκέψα[σθαι ...7...]
[....c.13.....]ασιν τοῦ [....c.13.....]
[....c.12.... ἐ]πεισβεβήκ[ασιν ....c.13.....]
[....c.12....] ἐξελεῖν δ[ὲ ......c.16......]
[....c.12....] πλέθρα δισχ[ίλια ...c.10...]
[....c.12....] Δάτου χώρα [.....c.14.....]
Vacat

Cf. Hatzopoulos 1996 II nº. 6: Philippoi 330 BC

[ὡς ἐπέστειλαν οἱ πρεσβευταὶ ἐκ Πε]ρ̣σ̣ί̣δ̣[ος]
[οἱ ὑπὲρ Φιλίππων καὶ τ]ῆς [γῆς π]ρεσβεύσαν-
[τες ὡς βασιλέα Ἀλέ]ξ̣α̣[νδ]ρον καὶ Ἀλέξανδρος
[περὶ αὐτῶν ἔκρινε]ν̣· τὴν ἀργὸν ἐργάζεσθαι Φιλίπ-[28]
[πους ἣ αὐτοῦ ἐστ]ιν χώρα, καὶ προστελοῦσ[ι φό]-
[ρον εἶναι αὐτοῖς τ]ὴν ἀργόν· ὁρίσαι δὲ τὴν [ἀρ]-
[γὸν χώραν αὐτοῖ]ς Φιλώταν καὶ Λεονν[ᾶτον· ὅσοι]
[δὲ Θραικῶν ἐπεισβε]βήκασιν τῆς χώ[ρας τῆς ἀρ]-
[χαίας ἣν τοῖς Φιλίπ]ποις ἔδωκεν Φί[λιππος, Φιλώ]-
[ταν καὶ Λεοννᾶτον] ἐ̣π̣ι̣σ̣κ̣έ̣ψ̣α̣[σθαι εἰ πρότε]-
[ρον ἐπεισβεβήκ]ασιν τοῦ [διαγράμματος τοῦ Φιλίπ]-
[που ἢ ὕστερον ἐ]πεισβεβήκ̣[ασιν· εἰ δὲ ὕστερον ἐκ]-
[χωρεῖν αὐτούς]· ἐξελεῖν δ̣[ὲ Φιλώταν καὶ Λεοννᾶ]-
[τον ἐκ τῆς ἀργοῦ] π̣λέθρα δισχ[ίλια ...c.12-15....]
[..c.8... τῆς] Δάτου χώρα[ς .....c.16-19......]
Vacat

---

27 Or [ἀργόν]?

28 Now only π is visible, but Hatzopoulos' text is based on Edson's unpublished notes, squeezes and photographs; it is possible that when Edson studied the inscription more letters were visible.

Translation

«... served as ambassadors to the king Alexander and Alexander ... (established that the Philippians) work the untilled land ... the land and they pay tribute ... the untilled land; that Philotas and Leonnatos divide the boundaries ...
(The Thracians) have gone into the land ... which Philip gave to Philippoi ... that they inspect ... (the Thracians) have gone into ... that they set apart ... 2000 *plethra* ... land of Daton».

Col. B:
SEG XXXIV 664

[......c.16...... πρ]οσλα[β]ε[ῖν] ἀπὸ [..c.7..]
μ[...c.11.... στ]αδίους· τ[ὴ]ν μὲν ἄ[λλην]
ν[.....c.15......]ς· ὅσα δὲ τοῖς Θραϊξί[ν ....]
[.......c.18.......]ται καρπίζεσθαι τοὺς Θρ[ά]-
[ϊκας καθάπερ Ἀλέξαν]δρος περὶ αὐτῶν δια-
[τέταχεν· Φιλίππου]ς δὲ ἔχειν τὴν χώραν τὴν
[.....c.14..... ὡ]ς οἱ λόφοι ἑκατέρωθεν ἔχου-
[σιν ...c.9...]η[.c.6..]ρισειραικὴν γῆν καὶ
Δαίνηρον νέμεσθ[αι Φι]λίππους καθάπερ ἔδω-
κε Φίλιππος· τὴν δὲ {γ}ῆν [ὕλην?][29] τὴν ἐν Δυ[....]ι μη-
θένα πωλεῖν τέως ἡ πρεσβεία πα[ρὰ τοῦ Ἀλε]-
ξάνδρου ἐπανέλθηι· τὰ δὲ ἕλη ε[ἶναι τῶν]
Φιλίππων ἕως γεφύρας. vacat
Vacat

Cf. Hatzopoulos 1996 II nº. 6.

[.....c.15...... πρ]ο̣σλαβε̣[ῖν] ἀπὸ [ταύτης]
μ[ετρήσαντας δύο στ]αδίους· τῆ̣ν μὲν ἄ[λλην]
ν[έμεσθαι Φιλίππου]ς, ὅσα δὲ τοῖς Θραιξὶ̣ν [πα]-
[ρὰ τοῦ Φιλίππου δέδο]ται καρπίζεσθαι τοὺς Θ̣ρ[άι]-
[κας καθάπερ καὶ Ἀλέξαν]δ̣ρος περὶ αὐτῶν δια-
[τέθηκεν· Φιλίππου]ς δὲ ἔχειν τὴν χώραν τὴν
[.....c.14..... ὡ]ς οἱ λόφοι ἑκατέρωθεν ἔχου-
[σιν ..c.7.. ὅσ]η [δ' ἔστι πε]ρὶ Σειραϊκὴν γῆν καὶ
Δαίνηρον νέμεσ[θαι Φι]λίππους καθάπερ ἔδω-

[29] Only -ην is visible. *Vidi* in the Museum of Philippoi.

κε Φίλιππος, τὴν δὲ [ὕλ]ην τὴν ἐν Δυ[σώρ]ω̣ι̣ μη-
θένα πωλεῖν τέω[ς] ἡ πρεσβεία {ή}[30] πα[ρὰ τοῦ Ἀλε]-
ξάνδρου ἐπανέλθηι, τὰ δὲ ἕλη ε̣ἶ[ναι τῶν]
Φιλίππων ἕως Γεφύρας. vacat

Translation

«That (the Philippians) receive in addiction from ... stades ... the other (land) ...; to the Thracians as much ... that the Thracians enjoy the fruits (have usufruct), just as Alexander has disposed about them; that the Philippians possess the land that ... where the hills on each side have ... that the Philippians cultivate the land around Seiraike (?) and Daineros just as Philip granted; that nobody sells the land in Dy(soron) until the embassy (sent) by Alexander returns; that the marshes belong to the Philippians until Gephyra».

Commentary

The inscription presents Alexander's decision about the Philippians' right to possess the land of Philippoi and to cultivate the untilled royal land, against payment of tribute. Alexander revises his father's disposition of the estate and grants the Philippians the right to cultivate more land and the Thracians the usufruct of his land.

Col. A

Ll. 1-4: introduction with a mention of the embassy from the city of Philippoi to Alexander III.

L. 1: line probably containing the dating of the documents.[31] Scholars have interpreted this document either as an edict or a royal letter.[32] I consider it an edict, a διάγραμμα,[33] because it contains the king's decision, to be generally imposed both on the Philippians and on the Thracians: cf. col. B. 5-6: δια[τέταχεν (Hatzopoulos: δια[τέθηκεν). By contrast, a letter is usually composed of a preamble (προοίμιον), with the greeting formula x to y χαίρειν, followed by the topic (θέμα), and an epi-

[30] *Emendavi*: Not on the stone.

[31] Hammond 1993b: 386.

[32] Hatzopoulos 1987: 439, nº. 714; Badian 1989: 64 n. 13.

[33] Hatzopoulos 1996 II: 27 (nº. 6) has pointed out that διάγραμμα is the term used in Macedonian inscriptions to describe διατάγματα (royal decrees).

logue (ἐπίλογος), containing a wish of good luck and health.[34] Furthermore, in the document, Alexander does not personally address the Philippians and his actions are described in the third person.

Ll. 3: as Hammond has suggested, I agree that the restoration [πρὸς βασιλέα Ἀλέ] ξ̣α[νδ]ρον is the most likely. The patronymic Φιλίππου and the adjective Μακεδόνα have also been considered as possible integrations for the lacuna before the name Ἀλέξανδρον, but the former normally stands after the name Alexander, and the latter sounds redundant within Macedon.[35]

Ll. 4-15: Alexander's decisions about the territory of Philippoi.

Ll. 4-6: the king authorizes the Philippians to cultivate the untilled land (l. 4, τὴν ἀργὸν ἐργάζεσθαι); however, the Philippians have to pay a tribute (l. 5, προστελοῦσ[ι]).

Ll. 5-6 are too fragmentary either to understand the analogy between the land granted on payment and the rest of the royal land[36] or to assess the φόρος imposed on the Philippians, which was probably a specified amount.

Ll. 6-7: Philotas and Leonnatus are sent by Alexander to Philippoi to divide the land. Philotas, son of the general Parmenion, was the commander of the entire Companions' cavalry in the years 335-330 BC—that is, from the Thracian campaign until his execution in Drangiana for alleged conspiracy against Alexander.[37] Leonnatus was a loyal Companion and a σωματοφύλαξ, a bodyguard of the king.[38] The absence of patronymics—even for a common name like Philotas—shows that the identity of the two individuals was entirely clear to all involved, and that is likely to be because they were prominent members of the king's entourage.[39]

ὁρίσαι (l. 6): Badian (1989: 66-67) claims that the aorist infinitive ὁρίσαι means that Philotas and Leonnatos are not requested to set the boundaries at the time of Alexander's rule, for they had marked the territory under Philip II when he gave the land to the Philippians. However, ὁρίσαι parallels ἐπισκέψα[σθαι in line 10; furthermore, the aorist infinitive does not imply a past event, but a momentary action. Alexander is revising the distribution of the land to the Philippians and the Thracians, and he is making some changes to the previous allotments. Philotas and Leonnatos are

---

[34] See Guarducci 2008: 139, 181. However, Mari 2018: 126 has pointed out that in some of Alexander's interventions in Asia Minor and the Aegean islands the distinction between letters and diagrammata is not as clear cut.

[35] Hammond 1990a: 170. For the title βασιλεύς, see Hammond 1988a: 390; Hatzopoulos 1993: 516-517, nº. 356. See also Arena 2013: 48-75 against the use of the title *basileus* as early as 334 BC, when Alexander's goal was to 'free' Greek cities from the Persian yoke. However, Alexander was free to use the regal title in Macedon; cf. Kholod 2020: 228-241; Mari 2020: 199-217.

[36] Hatzopoulos 1987: 436, nº. 714.

[37] Heckel 2006: 216-219.

[38] Heckel 2006: 147-151.

[39] Hammond 1988a: 383 n. 2.

sent to assign untilled royal land[40] and, therefore, to redefine the boundaries between the *chora* of Philippoi, the royal land, and the Thracians.

Ll. 8-10: the verb ἐπεισβε]βήκασιν (l. 8) implies an encroachment upon the land by the Thracians, who are mentioned in col. B at ll. 3 and 4-5. Philip II founded Philippoi[41] in 356 BC on the site of Krenides-Daton,[42] during his conquest of the region between the rivers Strymon and Nestos; before the Macedonian conquest, this region was inhabited by Thracians, who continued to lay claim to it. Thus, we can assume that at the time of the foundation of the city of Philippoi, not only did the king allot the Philippians a delimited, specific *chora*—having enlarged and populated the territory of Krenides with many settlers—but he also set the boundaries between the Philippians and the Thracians and regulated their respective rights.[43] Alexander is called upon to decide about the Thracians' encroachment[44] and his two Companions, Philotas and Leonnatus, are sent to ἐπισκέψα[σθαι (l. 10), i.e., to inspect and check the territory, and have the duty to re-establish the *status quo* between the Thracians and the Philippians.[45]

Ll. 11-15 are too fragmentary for much sense to be made of them; it can only be said that 2.000 *plethra* (one *plethron* = 10,000 square feet; 2.000 *plethra* = *ca.* 186 hectares) in the territory of Daton have to be spared.

Col. B

Ll. 1-6 present Alexander's decision about the Philippians and the Thracians' exploitation rights on the land around Philippoi. In Col. A, Alexander takes into account his father's arrangements and tries to restore the geographical boundaries between Philippians and Thracians as they were before the encroachment by the Thracians (if any); here, in col. B, he ratifies the use of the untilled land and the legal condition of the two contenders.

The Philippians are entitled to *possess the land* and to *get more* (ll. 1-2); furthermore, they have the right to *cultivate*[46] «the other land» (ll. 2-3), i.e., the βασιλικὴ γῆ. The Thracians obtain only the *usufruct* (l. 4, καρπίζεσθαι) from the Macedonian king and not the ownership of the land.[47]

---

[40] I agree with Hatzopoulos' integration at ll. 6-7: [ἀρ]-[γὸν χώραν αὐτοῖ]ς.

[41] Errington / Eck, *Brill's NP* XI (2007, 23-24), s.v. 'Philippoi'.

[42] Philippson, *RE* IV.2 (1901, 2229-2230), s.v. 'Daton'.

[43] Hammond 1988a: 384.

[44] Collart 1937: 179.

[45] Hatzopoulos 1987: 437, n°. 714.

[46] I accept the restoration ν[έμεσθαι. See *SEG* XXXIV 664: 182.

[47] Hatzopoulos 1987: 437, n°. 714; Hammond 1988a: 384-385.

Ll. 6-13: a summary of the new state of Philippoi's territory after Alexander's intervention:[48] the Philippians shall have their own land (l. 7, ἔχειν τὴν χώραν) and are granted more (stretching as far as Gephyra?); they shall also have the right to cultivate the land around Seiraike and Daineros (ll. 8-9),[49] as Philip II had previously decided. Ll. 10-13 contain two last provisions: a) nobody can sell the «land» (wood?) in Dysoron;[50] b) the marshes belong to the Philippians as far as Gephyra.[51]

L. 10: I agree with Edson (unpublished notes *apud* Hatzopoulos 1996) and Hatzopoulos (1996 II: 28, nº. 6) that one should restore [ὕλ]ην instead of [γ]ην: when in summer 2014 I viewed the inscription in the Museum of Philippoi, I noticed a lacuna wide enough to fit two letters between epsilon (δὲ) and eta (..]ην).

Ll. 11-12 πωλεῖν τέως ἡ πρεσβεία πα[ρὰ τοῦ Ἀλε]-|ξάνδρου ἐπανέλθηι: Alexander wants to take time to reflect about the allotment of the wood in Dysoron[52] and is seeking for more details on the region, which his two men sent to the area will provide him with. After Philotas and Leonnatus' report, Alexander will send to Philippoi detailed instructions about Mount Dysoron. Ll. 11-12 suggest that a) Alexander consulted his men and listened to their opinion on administrative matters (and not only on extreme circumstances, such as trials for high treason) and that b) the king's request for time to reflect is perhaps an implication that it will be some time before he makes his final decision. However, that does not mean that we have to go with a dating that puts him thousands of miles away in SW Iran; rather, it shows the Philippians' eagerness to set on record what has already been decided.[53]

In regards to the chronology of the edict, there is general agreement that November 330 BC is the *terminus ante quem*, for Philotas was executed in that year. The scholarly discussion concentrates around the question whether the ambassadors from Philippoi reached Alexander the Great before[54] or after[55] his departure for the campaign in Asia; the latter hypothesis is based on the restoration of a form of the name Περσίς at the first line in Col. A.

---

[48] *SEG* XXXIV 664: 182.

[49] I agree with the restoration [πε]ρὶ Σειραϊκὴν γῆν at l. 9. Σειραϊκός was maybe a local adjectival form deriving from Σέρραι. Cf. *SEG* XXXIV 664: 182; Hatzopoulos 1987: 437-438, nº. 714; Hammond 1990a: 169 n. 3.

[50] Hdt. V.17; Philippson *RE* V (1905: 1889), s.v. 'Dysoron': mountain range in East-Macedon. For the restoration, see *SEG* XXXIV 664: 181.

[51] γέφυρα (bridge) or Γέφφυρα (toponym attested in Macedon): Hammond (1988a: 384) suggests that ΓΕΦΥΡΑ «was probably a place name [...] in any case, we reach the crossing of a river as the limit of the marshes».

[52] Hatzopoulos 1997: 51.

[53] Cf. Badian 1989: 68.

[54] *SEG* XXXIV 664: 181-182; Hammond 1988a: 383, 1990a: 171-172.

[55] Hatzopoulos 1987: 439, nº. 714, 1990: 530, nº. 495, 1991: 505, nº. 417, 1997: 48-51; Badian 1993: 131, 1994a: 389.

In my opinion, it is most likely that Alexander III received the Philippians during the Balkan campaign (summer 335 BC)[56] when he was in the region. Vatin advanced another plausible hypothesis and suggested that the ambassadors reached Alexander when he was already in Thebes.[57] As Alexander was forced to move swiftly from the Peninsula of Haemus to the South in order to stop the Theban crisis (September 335 BC),[58] he may not have had the time to deal with the land of Philippoi during his northern campaigns.

Either way, the embassy and the decree must have taken place in summer 335 BC, and I reject the possibility of the Philippians going to Persis, where Alexander stayed in Persepolis from January until May 330 BC.[59] In fact, this hypothesis is problematic because it does not explain why the embassy preferred to undertake such a long journey rather than going to Macedon to consult Antipater,[60] the regent appointed by the king. We should consider that:

a) In the period up to 330 BC Antipater was still on good terms with Alexander,[61] and could have easily solved the territorial dispute between the Philippians and the Thracians by reasserting Philip II's decisions;

b) Had Alexander sent Companions back to the Balkan Peninsula during his stay in Persepolis, he would have instructed them to help Antipater face Agis III's threat;

c) After the battle of Gaugamela in October 331 BC, Alexander started to think about the conquest of all Asia. He wished to catch Darius III and be formally recognized the new king of the Persian Empire, so there was no time to send two of the bravest Companions to Philippoi for «such a trivial task as fixing boundaries».[62]

Kalindoia

The second document examined here was inscribed on a white marble stele by the priest Agathanor. This dedicatory stele was found near Kalamoton (Καλαμωτό),

---

[56] For the Balkan campaigns against the Thracians (Getae, Celtae, Triballi and Taulantians), see Worthington 2014: 127-130.

[57] Vatin 1984: 262.

[58] For the events in 335 BC, see Worthington 2014: 131-135.

[59] Hatzopoulos 1987: 439, nº. 714, 1997: 48-50; Badian 1989: 68, 1994a: 389.

[60] Berve 1926 II: 46-51, nº. 94; Heckel 2006: 35-38. See also Badian, *Brill's NP* I (2002: 776), s.v. 'Antipatros'.

[61] E.g., after Philip's murder, it was probably Antipater who hastened to proclaim Alexander king of the Macedonians (Badian, *Brill's NP* I (2002: 469), s.v. 'Alexander the Great'); before crossing the Hellespont, Alexander entrusted half of the standing army to Antipater and appointed him regent (ἐπιμελητὴς τοῦ κράτους); in 330 BC, Alexander also sent large sums of money from Susa to Antipater to help him bring the war against Agis III to an end. Only in 324 BC do Antipater and Alexander seem to have fallen out, and the king dispatched Craterus with the discharged soldiers home to relieve Antipater, now considered too powerful.

[62] Hammond 1990a: 172.

about 12 km south of the lake Bolbe,[63] and its discovery made it possible to identify the site of the ancient city Kalindoia, at the borders between Mygdonia and Bottike.[64] The stone is broken into two pieces; the left top and the right side of the lower part are missing. The inscription is the work of eleven lapicides, whose hands are recognizable from the different shape and height of the letters:[65] the first 19 lines are from the same one; ll. 20-26 are from six different hands (l. 22 was inserted afterwards, like a correction, by the lapicide of l. 23); ll. 27-30 belong to the same hand, ll. 31-32 to two different ones, while ll. 33-34 were engraved by the eleventh lapicide.[66]

Picture 2: Kalindoia

[63] Vokotopoulou 1986: 87; Hatzopoulos 1996 II: 84, nº. 62.

[64] Vokotopoulou 1986: 102-106; Hatzopoulos / Loukopoulou 1992: 71-74; *SEG* XLV 713.

[65] Vokotopoulou 1986: 93; Hatzopoulos 1996 II: 84, nº. 62.

[66] Hatzopoulos 1996 II: 84, nº. 62.

[Ἀγαθά]νωρ Ἀγάθω̣ν̣[ος] | [ἱερατε]ύ̣σας {ας} Ἀσκληπιῶι |[Ἀπόλλ]ωνι ἀνέθηκεν· | [οἵδε] ἱερεῖς ἐγένοντο |5 [ἀφ' ο]ὗ βασιλεὺ̣ς Ἀλέξαν|δρος ἔδωκε Μακεδόσι | Καλίνδοια καὶ τὰ χωρία | τὰ περὶ Καλίνδοια· Θαμίσ|κιαν, Καμακαίαν, Τριπο|10 άτιν : Σιβρας Ἡροδώρου | Τρωΐλος Ἀντιγόνου | Καλλίας Ἀπολλωνίου | Ἰκκότας Γύρτου | Ἡγήσιππος Νικοξέ̣νου |15 Λυκοῦργος Νικάνορος | Ἀγαθάνωρ Ἀγάθωνο[ς] | Μενέλαος Μενάνδ[ρου] | Ἀντίγονος Μενάνδ[ρου] | Ἀντιμένων Μενάν̣δ̣[ρου] |20 Κράτιππος Εὐρυτίο[υ] | Γύλις Εὐ<ρ>υτίου | Κάνουν Ἀσσα̣[—] μι̣κου | Κερτίμμας Κρί̣θωνο[ς] | Φιλώτας Λεω̣ν[ίδου] |25 Πτολέμμας Μ̣[..5..] | Μύας Φιλίσ[κου] | Ἀμερίας Κυδ[ία] | Πάσων Σκύθ[ου] | Φίλαγρος Μενά̣[νδρου] |30 Γυδίας Κρίθω[νος] | Φιλόξενος Ε[— — —] | Περδίκκας Ἀμμα̣[δίσκου] | Νικάνωρ Νίκω[νος][67] | Νικάνωρ Σώ̣σ̣[ο]υ |35 Γά̣δδυς Ἀστί̣ω̣ν̣[ος][68] | Ἀντ̣ιφά̣νης Σώσ[ω]νος | Παρμενίω̣ν̣ Ἀ̣λ[— — —][69] | Γλαυκίας Δαβρ[εία] | Ἅρπαλος Φ̣α̣[— — —]. |40 vacat

TRANSLATION

«Agathanor, son of Agathon, having served as a priest of Asclepius, offered to Apollo (the stele). These became priests since king Alexander gave to the Macedonians Kalindoia and the lands around it, Thamiskia, Kamakaia, Tripoatis. (A list of 30 priests follows)».

COMMENTARY

L. 1: the restoration of the dedicator's name, Agathanor, and of his patronymic, Agathon, is based on the l. 16, in which Agathanor appears as the seventh priest of the list.[70]

Ll. 2-3: *Prima facie* Agathanor is a priest of Asclepius and dedicates to Apollo. The next question is why Agathanor dedicates to Apollo a list of priests of Asclepius. One possible explanation is that such priests functioned as eponymous officials. The argument for this would be a) the failure to indicate the duration of the priesthoods, b) the fact that interpreting them as annual produces a date for the inscription that fits the palaeography of the letterforms, c) Alexander's interest in medicine and in Asclepius. Vokotopoulou, in the *editio princeps* of this inscription, suggests that Agathanor, after

---

[67] According to Votokopoulou 1986, followed by Badian 1989 and Hammond 1990: 169; Hatzopoulos 1996 II: 85, nº. 62: Νικά[νορος].

[68] According to Votokopoulou 1986, followed by Hammond 1990; Hatzopoulos 1996 II: 85, nº. 62: Γαδδῦς.

[69] Hatzopoulos 1996 II: 85, nº. 62: Παρμενίων Ἀ[— — —].

[70] Vokotopoulou 1986: 95.

having been the priest of Asclepius, offered the stele to Apollo, who was Asclepius' father and the most important divinity of Kalindoia.[71] Since Agathanor was the priest of a secondary god of the city, she presumes that he was not the eponymous archon of that year.[72] Conversely, Hatzopoulos thinks that Agathanor was the priest of both of the gods and dedicated a stele containing the list of the eponymous archons of Kalindoia.[73] I agree with Hatzopoulos that the priests of Asclepius could act as eponymous archons, since there are parallels in Macedon, and the priests of Kalindoia were probably granted the right to act as eponymous by Alexander.[74] Moreover, the missing mention of the priesthood's duration suggests that it lasted one year, like the eponymous archonship. However, I consider Agathanor as the priest of Asclepius only: Alexander's interest in medicine increased during the campaign in Asia, and the development of healing practices was particularly tied to the cult of the god Asclepius.[75] Therefore, we can safely state that Asclepius was not a secondary divinity to the king and that the priesthood at the Asclepeion was a title of high importance.

Hatzopoulos' reading of the Greek[76] is also very problematic and this interpretation offers a simpler sentence structure.

L. 4: typical introductive expression in priests' lists.[77]

L. 5-8: chronological element: the list of the priests started in the period following Alexander the Great's donation of the land of Kalindoia and of the territories around it to the Macedonians.[78] Alexander must have granted these territories before leaving for Asia in 334 BC: we know from Plutarch (*Alex.* 15.2) that, before embarking on the Persian campaign, the Macedonian king engaged in allotments of properties and gave «lands, villages, public (of a settlement) income or a harbour» to his Companions.[79] Therefore, we can assume that the reorganization of these territories took place during the winter 335/334 BC, after Alexander's return from Greece.[80]

Agathanor is the seventh on the list and dedicated the stele three years after his priesthood, for ll. 1-19 belong to the same hand; presuming that the first, Sibras, was

---

[71] Vokotopoulou 1986: 96.

[72] Vokotopoulou 1986: 97.

[73] Hatzopoulos 1988: 445, nº. 847.

[74] Voutiras 1993: 260: when Kalindoia became part of the Macedonian domain, the priests of Asclepius were granted with the title of eponymous archons.

[75] Arr. *An.* II.5.8: at Soloi in Cilicia, Alexander sacrificed to Asclepius. Cf. Antela-Bernárdez / Sierra Martín 2016a for Alexander's interest in medicine and the importance of Asclepius; and Antela-Bernárdez / Sierra Martín 2016b for the development of medicine during the Asian campaign, especially in India.

[76] Hatzopoulos 1988: 445, nº. 847: «after having been priest of Asclepius *and* Apollo, he dedicated». Hatzopoulos' interpretation of the Greek text does not explain the missing «καὶ» between the names of the two gods, and such syntax has no parallels in other inscriptions.

[77] Vokotopoulou 1986: 97.

[78] Vokotopoulou 1986: 97; Hammond 1988a: 384; Hatzopoulos 1988: 445, nº. 847.

[79] Plu. *Alex.* 15.2: τὰ τῶν ἑταίρων πράγματα σκεψάμενος ἀπονεῖμαι τῷ μὲν ἀγρόν, τῷ δὲ κώμην, τῷ δὲ συνοικίας πρόσοδον ἢ λιμένος.

[80] Hammond 1988a: 384.

in charge in the year 335/334 BC, the dedication can be dated 326/325 BC and the inscription was gradually engraved for 20 years until 306/305 BC.[81]

L. 6: Μακεδόσι. I agree with Hammond and Hatzopoulos that this δωρεά is not *viritim*, as Vokotopoulou suggests,[82] but to all Macedonians because: a) Μακεδόνες without the article usually stands for τὸ ἔθνος τῶν Μακεδόνων;[83] b) a donation of the city of Kalindoia with the territories under its influence (*chora*) would be too large to be *viritim*. As Anson (2009: 17) has pointed out, a successful Macedonian king ruled through patronage, and the Argeads gave their aristocratic 'cavalry Companions' vast tracts of land—donations which were extended to the heavy infantry when they became the *pezhetairoi* (foot Companions). However, Καλίνδοια καὶ τὰ χωρία (districts)| τὰ περὶ Καλίνδοια seem too big as a donation, and the literary evidence supports this hypothesis: Plutarch's aforementioned passage describes Alexander's *viritim* territorial donation as gifts of smaller scale, such as «lands (ἀγροί), villages (κῶμαι)». Furthermore, in the case of a *viritim* donation, it is unlikely that Kalindoia could have been an independent city with its list of eponymous priests.[84]

Ll. 9-10: Thamiskia, Kamakaia, Tripoatis are juxtaposed without any conjunction: they explain the expression «the territories around Kalindoia».[85] In fact, χωρίον means «land, district, territory»[86] and the endings –ia and –atis characterize regions; thus Thamiskia is the region of Thamiskos, Kamakaia of Kamakai and Tripoatis of Tripoai.[87] While Thamiskos is unattested in other inscriptions, the first mention that we have about Kalindoia, together with Kamakai and Tripoatis, is found in the treaty between Athens and some cities of Bottike, dated 422 BC;[88] later, in *ca*. 360 BC, the city appears in the list of Epidaurus' *Theorodokoi*.[89]

The list of Epidaurus' *Theorodokoi* suggests that in the 5th century BC and in the first half of the 4th century BC the cities of Bottike were independent; in the years 360-350 BC some of them joined the Chalcidian League, which was dissolved by Philip II in 348 BC.[90] From that moment, the region fell into Macedonian hands, and Alexander decided to grant it to the Macedonians. In fact, Kalindoia and the *choria* around it were land conquered by the king, i.e., δορίκτητος βασιλικὴ γῆ (spear won land), and the Argead king was free to manage it as he pleased.

---

[81] See Hatzopoulos 1996 II: 84, nº. 62: 335/4-306/5 BC. It is worth noting that the end of the list coincides with the official extinction of the Temenid dynasty and the usurpation of the royal title by Cassander.

[82] Vokotopoulou 1986: 96-97.

[83] For a list of examples, cf. Hammond 1988a: 386: «it is clear from a number of inscriptions and literary citations that Μακεδόνες without a definite article was used in a political context for the Macedonian people».

[84] Hammond 1988a: 386.

[85] Vokotopoulou 1986: 98; Hammond 1988a: 385.

[86] Cf. Liddell-Scott, s.v. 'χωρίον'.

[87] Vokotopoulou 1986: 98.

[88] *IG* I³, 76.

[89] *IG* IV². I, 94 col. 1b, l. 13.

[90] Vokotopoulou 1986: 102; Hammond 1988a: 385.

Agathanor's inscription indicates that both the king and the Macedonians had the right to possess private properties, which were completely distinct from each other. This induces us to believe that the king was well aware of the important role of the Macedonian subjects in the welfare of his rule, and sought collaboration with them.[91]

Literary / historiographical evidence: the Opis mutiny

All Alexander-historians (Diodorus, Plutarch, Arrian, Curtius, and Justin) agree that, in the aftermath of the soldiers' mutiny[92] at Opis in 324 BC, Alexander gave a speech.[93] On that occasion, the unrest was caused by the king's decision to send back home to Macedon the veterans and the unfit soldiers.

I shall focus on Arrian's version of the events at Opis, as it is the most complete among the extant accounts. At *An.* VII. 8.2, Arrian shows how the Macedonians in Alexander's army felt about the changes that had occurred in his court and, at the same time, what they deemed to be the general impact of the Persian campaign on Macedonian kingship. According to the historian, the Macedonians had been distressed (ἤδη ἐλύπει αὐτοὺς) by three major changes: a) Alexander's adoption of the Persian attire (ἥ τε ἐσθὴς ἡ Περσικὴ ἐς τοῦτο φέρουσα), b) the equipment of the barbarian *Epigonoi* in Macedonian style (τῶν Ἐπιγόνων τῶν βαρβάρων ἡ ἐς τὰ Μακεδονικὰ ἤθη κόσμησις), and c) the introduction of foreign horsemen into the ranks of the Companions (ἀνάμιξις τῶν ἀλλοφύλων ἱππέων ἐς τὰς τῶν ἑταίρων τάξεις).

The situation escalated quickly, as the Macedonians feared that Alexander had been spoiled by Iranian reverence and scoffed at his claims of divine descent. They provocatively invited him to discharge them all from the army, and to campaign himself in company with his father, referring in mockery to Ammon (*An.* VII. 8.3: αὐτὸν δὲ μετὰ τοῦ πατρὸς στρατεύεσθαι, τὸν Ἄμμωνα δὴ τῷ λόγῳ ἐπικερτομοῦντες).

Understandably, the Macedonians grew weary of the extravagances of Alexander's Orientalising policies, but the reasons here outlined are not sufficient to explain such a sudden strong reaction by all the army, especially if we consider that Alexander—as every Macedonian king—was Zeus' offspring via Heracles[94] and that Iranians started joining the Macedonian army before the Indian campaign in 327

---

[91] Hammond 1988a: 389.

[92] For the scholarly discussion over the (inaccurate) term «mutiny», see Olbrycht 2008, 232-251; Howe / Müller 2012: 21-38; Roisman 2012a: 36; Brice 2015: 70-72; Carney 2015: 27-59.

[93] Arr. *An.* VII.7.9-11; D.S. XVI.108.3-109.3; Plu. *Alex.* 71.1-5; Curt. X.2.8-4.2; Iust. XII.11.5-12.10. Cf. Bosworth 1988a: 101: «In this weather of confusion one thing at least is certain: Alexander did make a speech at Opis –or rather several speeches»; cf. Hammond 1999: 249.

[94] Plu. *Alex.* 2.1: Ἀλέξανδρος ὅτι τῷ γένει πρὸς πατρὸς μὲν ἦν Ἡρακλείδης ἀπὸ Καράνου, πρὸς δὲ μητρὸς Αἰακίδης ἀπὸ Νεοπτολέμου, τῶν πάνυ πεπιστευμένων ἐστί.

BC.[95] We can, therefore, conclude that it was not the introduction of Iranian troops, but the release of the Macedonian veterans that deeply offended the Macedonians, as they felt that they were becoming a minority in the army and, most significantly, that their military and political role in the Empire was becoming secondary to that of the Iranians. In fact, Macedonian society was a military one; depriving the Macedonians of their military role meant stripping them of their political power too.[96]

It is worth noticing that the mutiny at Opis represents the opposite of the mutiny at the Hyphasis: in 326 BC Alexander could not proceed with his conquests without the Macedonians; in 324 BC he thought he could proceed without them since with the introduction of the Iranians into the army he had the upper hand. With this card up his sleeve, Alexander's speech at Opis (*An.* VII.9-10) is a rhetorical display of his achievements and good intentions. The monologue is composed of three parts:

a) A catalogue of benefactions and conquests achieved by Philip II (*An.* VII.9. 2-5), who is credited with a civilising role. According to the catalogue, Philip clothed the poor and nomadic Macedonians with the *chlamys* and brought them from the hills to the plain. He made the Macedonians citizens, gave them laws, reorganised them militarily and made them the leaders of the Greeks.

This section displays the classical literary trope of the progression of a community from a primitive to a civilised way of life; surely Arrian added to its rhetoric, but the exaggeration of the Macedonian king's achievements most likely belongs to Alexander himself rather than to Ptolemy or Aristobulus.[97] In fact, Arrian does not draw the reader's attention to his sources and, among the four, Alexander is the person most interested in reasserting Macedonian propaganda on the occasion of the Opis mutiny.

b) After the list of Philip's praiseworthy benefactions, there follows a longer and more significant enumeration of Alexander's achievements (*An.* VII.9. 6-9) and

c) His self-justification as a good king and leader (*An.* VII.9.9-10.4). Alexander points out to the Macedonians his extreme generosity in sharing the empire's wealth and paying off the soldiers' debts; he presents himself as a sober and sparing leader,

---

[95] Olbrycht 2011: 67-82, 2015: 196-210.

[96] Cf. Sisti / Zambrini 2004: 597-598: as Wüst 1953: 419 has pointed out, Arrian's list of complaints does not explain why the Macedonians reacted so loudly; furthermore, Curt. X.2.12 offers another explanation for the Macedonian uproar: for the soldiers, the furlough of part of the Macedonias means that the Asiatic conquest has changed the character of the Argead kingship and that Alexander aims at establishing his rule in Asia rather than returning back to his motherland. Carney 2015: 47: «Hyphasis and Opis caused problems to Alexander not because they were *mutinies* but because they were quarrels that poisoned the relationship between the king and his troops».

[97] Anson 2009: 19: «while the speech has been questioned and certainly is not a *verbatim* transcription, it should be regarded—if not as an accurate reflection of an actual speech—at least as a particularly correct summary of Philip's achievement». *Contra* Würst 1953: 177-188, who dismisses the speech as highly rhetorical. See also Tarn 1948 II: 290-296; Nagle 1996: 151-172.

who eats the same food as, and fights with, his soldiers, and even shows off the wounds everywhere on his body. At last, he gives a reason for his 'Orientalising', presenting it as a consequence of the desertion of his troops, who forced him to turn to the barbarians for protection (a point much stressed by Curt. X.2.19-29).[98]

In the Opis speech, Alexander reworked pieces of Macedonian tradition—such as the pastoral origins of the kingdom, founded by the Temenid Perdiccas led to Aigai by goats[99]—and of Macedonian propaganda: he stresses the fact that he shares food and toils with his soldiers to reassert his Macedonian paternity.

Conclusions

In the first inscription both the Philippians and the Thracians are the recipients of Alexander III's edict, but they are in different positions:[100] the former are allowed to possess their own land and till that of the king against a tribute, while the latter can only enjoy the fruits. Among them there was a difference 'of status':[101] Philippoi, as an autonomous Greek city, sends an embassy to the Macedonian king in order to discuss its position and negotiate, while the Thracians have no voice and are treated as subjects.

In the second inscription, the recipient is the whole ἔθνος τῶν Μακεδόνων (*ethnos* of the Macedonians), which is granted a big δωρεά: the city of Kalindoia and the territories around it. Alexander bestows upon the Macedonians a part of the royal land in order to create a Macedonian city; the Bottiaeans are the subjects while the Macedonians become colonists.

Arrian's Opis speech offers a literary reworking of Macedonian tradition and propaganda, and his account finds parallels in Curtius and Diodorus. Alexander stresses the great progress and achievements of the Macedonians thanks to his father and himself, presenting the changes to the Argead tradition that occurred in his court—such as the Orientalising policy—as either progress or as a necessity forced upon him by his fellow countrymen's misbehaviour.

Summarizing Alexander the Great's policy as it comes across in epigraphical sources from Macedon during the first years of his reign, it can be observed that in the decree of Philippoi he tries to maintain his father's decisions, to restore the situation as it was before the Thracians' encroachment and, for further decisions, he takes time to reflect. Alexander comes across as a grounded and thoughtful person, who acts completely in line with his father's purpose of making Philippoi a political

98 For Alexander's pro-Iranian policies, see Olbrycht 2014: 37-62.

99 Hdt. VIII.137-138. See Hammond / Griffith 1979: 658-661; Hatzopoulos 2011: 47.

100 Hatzopoulos 1987: 437, nº. 714.

101 Cf. Hammond 1988a: 385.

showplace as a free Greek city. In Kalindoia, he settles a new Macedonian city, again following his father's lead; however, in the case of Kalindoia, the Macedonians are called upon to have an active part in the foundation of the colony, since they have been granted the territory. Alexander appears as a generous ruler,[102] whose aim is to please and benefit the Macedonian *ethnos*.

In Macedon, Alexander ruled within an existing institutional frame: city foundations, population transfers, and the creation of a strong, well-trained and loyal army had started with Archelaus (413-399 BC) and reached its peak under Philip II. Even when the nature of his rule had been massively changed by the Persian campaign and we assist at a convergence of the Macedonian and the Achaemenid political systems,[103] Alexander is aware that he is dependent on his Macedonians:[104] at Hyphasis, he has to bend to the army's will to turn back; at Opis, he defends himself for having granted the Persians Macedonian titles, introduced Iranians into the Companion Cavalry, and created the *antitagma* of the *Epigonoi*. With his claim that the Macedonians had abandoned him and left him no other choice than seeking for help elsewhere, not only does Alexander find an excuse for his Orientalisation, but also reasserts his role of *primus inter pares* and presents his actions as those of a Homeric king, in a *constitutional way*. Alexander's claim is, of course, a rhetorical gambit to touch the Macedonians' *ethos*; however, it is worth noting that, even in 324 BC, at a crucial moment of his campaign, he still has Argead policies in mind and he accommodates them to the Iranian cultural and political environment. His father Philip II had already welcomed worthy Macedonians from non-aristocratic families and Greeks among his *hetairoi*,[105] and the *Epigonoi*, trained since their childhood to fight as Macedonians and educated according to Greek standards, were to constitute a group of loyal youth as the Royal *Paides*.[106] The school of the pages was an institution founded by Archelaus and developed by Philip II; it aimed at the constitution of a cadre of able commanders and administrators but also kept as hostages the best sons of the Macedonian aristocracy.[107] Like the Pages in Macedon, the *Epigonoi* would also serve as 'hostages' and allowed the king to keep control of the Iranian aristocracy.

---

[102] Hammond / Walbank 1995: 19.

[103] Weber 2009: 97: There are two phases in Alexander's court: 336-330 and 330-323 BC. The courtly interactions between the king and the aristocracy in the first phase are characterized by Alexander's attempt to accommodate different groups, as he is still greatly dependent on Macedonian tradition. His behaviour towards the inner circle displays both true friendship and intelligent calculation, which grant individuals with influential positions without their own families becoming a threatening factor. During the second phase, and especially towards the end of Alexander's life, Macedonian aristocracy around him is more homogeneous; the Macedonians have to accept a 'strengthening' of the Persian elite. Weber 2009: 98: In fact, a growing merging of Macedonian and Achaemenid traditions in the monarchy is traced back to this period.

[104] Borza 2012²: 317.

[105] Cf. also Archelaus choosing Euripides as a Companion: Gel. XV.20; Ael. *VH*. XIII.4.

[106] Hammond 1989: 56.

[107] Cf. Hammond 1989: 56-57, 1990b: 261-290; Carney 2008: 145-164.

To conclude, the inscriptions show Alexander doing the mundane business of a king to the benefit of a Macedonian-founded Greek city (Philippoi) and making fairly large-scale new territorial arrangements for the benefit of Macedonians (Kalindoia), in line with his father's policies. Opis shows Alexander doing rather different things—this is an issue of political rhetoric, personal charisma, and emotional blackmail in the attempt to apply Argead principles to a new setting. Alexander probably «never thought of his realm as being other than fundamentally Macedonian and Hellenic»,[108] but military training of the Iranians and a partnership in the administration were a *sine qua non* for the stabilization of his vast Empire.[109] Alexander became the hero of the Persian campaign and, no matter his excesses, the Macedonian soldiers needed him to be their king.

However, in his own country, Alexander was no hero: he ruled in Macedon for only two years and abandoned it for Asia; he drained the kingdom of manpower during his campaign; and, with his death, he left the country in chaos: Antipater had to face the Lamian War, which was followed by a dynastic crisis and the end of the Argead royal family.[110]

---

[108] Cf. Brunt 2003: 50.

[109] Hammond 1997: 187.

[110] Bosworth 1986: 1-12, 2002: 1-3; Worthington 2003: 96-98. See also Milns 1999: 769: «In the longer term, however, the Asian campaign of Alexander had a beneficial impact on prices by creating the means whereby an over-populated Greek peninsula could rid itself of a huge number of mouths (via a large scale migration to the conquered lands of Asia) that had to be fed».

La Grecia que dejó atrás Alejandro

Adolfo J. Domínguez Monedero
(Universidad Autónoma de Madrid)

Introducción. Alejandro en Oriente y la situación en Grecia

El inicio de la guerra de liberación, o de venganza (o de ambas), de Alejandro contra el Gran Rey Darío III fue el acontecimiento que elevó a figura histórica incontrovertible al rey macedonio por lo que supone de novedoso en el desarrollo histórico griego, quizá no tanto en el campo de sus objetivos iniciales, pero sí, sin duda, en cuanto a sus logros. La magnitud de esta empresa ocultó, y todavía lo hace, lo que quedó detrás, esto es, la Grecia que, en teoría, acompañaba al hijo de Filipo en su empresa contra el bárbaro. Los escritores que siguen a Alejandro y que escriben de él se centran en su figura y en sus logros, y dejan de lado lo que va quedando atrás. Los distintos territorios que irán siendo conquistados solo son objeto de detalle directo cuando Alejandro interviene en ellos o también cuando, tras su paso, surgen problemas que hay que atender. Solo otros autores que no acompañan a la expedición informan, en ocasiones, de lo que está sucediendo en esas tierras que van quedando atrás aunque, salvo los oradores, casi ninguno de ellos ha llegado mínimamente íntegro hasta nuestros días como, por otro lado, ocurre también con los escritores de Alejandro. Es, pues, tanto más complicado reconstruir qué estaba pasando en la Grecia que dejó atrás Alejandro que lo que ocurría en el centro de atención de la mayor parte de los autores, que era el propio macedonio. No hay, por ende, demasiadas fuentes alternativas que podamos utilizar; la epigrafía es bastante avara a este respecto, al menos para buena parte del periodo, en el que el rey parece más ocupado con la prosecución imparable de su guerra contra territorios cada vez más alejados del Mediterráneo y empieza a aportar algunos datos para el periodo en el que, de regreso a Babilonia, Alejandro empieza a preocuparse de organizar su imperio e, incluso, de planear nuevas acciones militares.

Esa escasez de informaciones no quiere decir que el rey no estuviese atento a lo que ocurría en los distintos territorios que iba conquistando y que no prestase atención a lo que sucedía en Grecia. Aunque había dejado a cargo de la situación en Europa al viejo colaborador de su padre, Antípatro,[1] con el que se comunicaba a través de la correspondencia,[2] este medio también le permitía estar en contacto con una serie de personas de su interés, empezando por su madre, pero sin descartar a otros individuos como su antiguo maestro Aristóteles[3] y Plutarco se admira de que tuviera tiempo libre para escribir a sus amigos tantas cartas.[4] Eso no implica que toda o parte de la correspondencia que se nos ha transmitido entre el rey y todas esas personas pueda ser apócrifa, aunque no todos los autores comparten los criterios para determinarlo.[5] Además de ello, Alejandro debió de recibir embajadas con gran frecuencia, aunque las fuentes solo nos han recordado algunas, en especial las que tuvieron lugar poco antes de su muerte.[6] Por consiguiente, hemos de pensar que estuvo al tanto de lo que sucedía en las diversas partes de su territorio y que, en la medida de sus posibilidades, trató de resolver los problemas que surgían.

Aunque acuciado por tareas que para él serían más urgentes como, en un primer momento, acabar con la resistencia del rey Darío III y, más adelante, vengar su muerte y, por fin, avanzar hacia el Este hasta alcanzar el fin del mundo, los momentos en los que no combatía, sin duda mucho más numerosos que en los que había combates y, por ello mismo, menos tratados por los historiadores, eran una buena ocasión para ir pergeñando el futuro que iba diseñando para Grecia. No obstante, la ocasión que eligió para dar una primera (y significativa) pista, de qué quería hacer con ella fue la embajada de Calístrato de Olinto a los Juegos Olímpicos del año 324 a.C. en donde proclamó el conocido como «Decreto de los Exiliados», prueba evidente de que el esquema que hasta entonces había permanecido vigente iba a sufrir grandes cambios aunque ellos no implicarían la supresión total de la Liga de Corinto pero sí, en la práctica, un vaciamiento de su contenido y su conversión en una herramienta útil para implementar la política del rey.

La política de Filipo y Alejandro hacia Esparta

Sin embargo, no es a este último periodo de las relaciones entre Alejandro y Grecia al que quiero dedicarme en esta ocasión, sino al primero de ellos, que se saldaría con tres acontecimientos que, según Justino, habría conocido Alejandro simultáneamente:

---

[1] Iust. XI.7.1; Curt. IV.1.39; D.S. XVII.118.1; Baynham 1994: 337-338.

[2] Pridik 1893; Hamilton 1961b: 9-20.

[3] Bielawski 1964: 7-34, 1965: 7-12.

[4] Plu. *Alex.* 42.1.

[5] Pridik 1893; Zumetikos 1894; Pearson 1955: 429-455.

[6] Alessandri 1994: 21-36.

> «Entretanto se le entrega una carta de Antípatro procedente de Macedonia, en la que se le daba cuenta de la guerra de Agis, rey de los espartanos, en Grecia; la guerra de Alejandro, rey del Epiro, en Italia; la guerra de Zopirión, su prefecto, en Escitia. Afectado de manera distinta por estos sucesos, sin embargo, se alegró más al conocer la muerte de los dos reyes rivales suyos de lo que le dolió la pérdida del ejército con Zopirión» (Iust. XII.1.4-5; trad. Castro Sánchez).[7]

La entrega de esta carta tendría lugar en Ecbatana, tras la muerte de Darío y en el periodo en el que deposita el tesoro en esta ciudad bajo la custodia de Parmenión, en el verano del 330 a.C., momento que muchos autores aceptan como plausible[8] aun cuando, siguiendo a Arriano, la presencia de Alejandro en Ecbatana, el licenciamiento de los aliados y las disposiciones sobre el tesoro habrían tenido lugar antes de la muerte de Darío, puesto que la capital de Media es el punto de partida para proseguir la misma.[9] Las formas de interpretar estos datos, así como la propia imprecisión de las fuentes, ha suscitado numerosos debates cronológicos que distan de haber sido resueltos por completo y que pueden dividirse en dos bloques: los que aceptan una cronología corta (básicamente primavera y otoño del 331) y los que propugnan una larga (primavera del 331-finales del 331 y primeros meses del 330 a.C.).[10]

La perspectiva que aquí adopta Justino (es decir, Trogo) es de una gran hostilidad hacia Alejandro puesto que equipara, como presuntos rivales suyos, a su tío y cuñado Alejandro el Moloso y al rey espartano Agis III. Mientras que el primero no parece haber dado muestras de desafección hacia Alejandro, más bien lo contrario,[11] el segundo fue un enemigo declarado que movió a una parte importante del Peloponeso a una guerra contra él, lo que hace la comparación arriesgada o, incluso, sospechosa. En esta misma línea Justino llega a asegurar que «cuando se comunicó esto a Alejandro en Partia, fingiendo dolor por su parentesco con Alejandro, ordenó a su ejército tres días de luto» (Iust. XII.3.1).[12]

Como este sincronismo no lo encontramos en otros autores, esta coincidencia debe de haber sido una elaboración de Trogo o de alguna de sus fuentes. Daría, pues, la impresión de que Trogo ha unido la recepción por parte de Alejandro de la noticia del desenlace de estas tres campañas, que se presentan como más o menos contem-

---

[7] *Dum haec aguntur, epistulae Antipatri a Macedonia ei redduntur, quibus bellum Agidis, regis Spartanorum, in Graecia, bellum Alexandri, regis Epiri, in Italia, bellum Zopyrionis praefecti eius in Scythia continebatur. Quibus uarie adfectus plus tamen laetitiae cognitis mortibus duorum aemulorum regum quam doloris amissi cum Zopyrione exercitus cepit.*

[8] Badian 1994b: 291.

[9] Arr. *An.* III.19.7, 20.1.

[10] Cawkwell 1969: 163-180; Borza 1971: 231-235; Lock 1972: 10-27, cuya cronología parece, en general, bastante aceptable.

[11] Domínguez 2014: 203-236.

[12] *Haec cum nuntiata in Parthia Alexandro essent, simulato maerore propter Alexandri cognationem exercitui suo triduo luctum indixit.*

poráneas, para resaltar este contraste entre la alegría por la muerte de sus rivales y la tristeza por la pérdida de su ejército en Escitia. Incluso el lugar de la notificación queda poco claro en Justino puesto que, si en el primer pasaje que comentábamos da la impresión de que recibe la noticia en Ecbatana (capital de Media), en el segundo se menciona de modo explícito Partia. Creemos, pues, posible que la asociación de las tres noticias puede haber tenido un efecto dramático tendente a presentar a Alejandro bajo un aspecto negativo también en esta ocasión. En cualquier caso, tanto Trogo como su epitomador Justino aprovechan esta información para describir las tres campañas aunque, en el caso de Trogo, y como sabemos por los resúmenes de este autor, dedicaba también espacio a narrar la campaña de Arquidamo III en Italia, algo de lo que no queda huella en Justino, estableciendo una clara relación entre la expedición del espartano y la de Alejandro el Moloso en el sentido de que ambos encontraron la muerte con sus ejércitos en Italia.[13] Por lo que se refiere a la campaña de Zopirión, la crítica es unánime en situarla bastante después en el tiempo a partir del testimonio de Curcio.[14]

La opinión que presenta Justino sobre el levantamiento de Agis es también de interés por su tono exagerado:

> «Después de la partida de Alejandro, casi toda Grecia había acudido a las armas ante la oportunidad de recuperar la libertad, siguiendo el ejemplo de los lacedemonios, los únicos que habían despreciado la paz de Filipo y de Alejandro y que habían rechazado sus leyes» (Iust. XII.1.6-7).[15]

Que los sublevados buscasen la libertad no es improbable; sin embargo, parece exagerado decir que se levantó «casi toda Grecia» (*Graecia ferme omnis*). Más adelante volveremos sobre esto, aunque ahora, antes de entrar en esta guerra, conviene hacer alguna observación.

Durante la primera parte de su reinado, Arquidamo III trató de proseguir la tradicional política espartana, a pesar de la alarmante escasez de hombres de su ciudad y de que la situación para Esparta había cambiado radicalmente tras Leuctra y Mantinea. Aprovechando su participación, al final ineficaz, en la Tercera Guerra Sagrada, había atacado a Megalópolis, junto con su hijo Agis, y a Argos (351 a.C.) sin demasiado éxito; tras la derrota focidia, Filipo había maniobrado para reforzar a los tradicionales enemigos de Esparta, como Argos, Mesene y Megalópolis (343 a.C.).[16] Resulta difícil de explicar por qué Arquidamo, en lugar de permanecer en Esparta, se

---

[13] *Dictaeque in excessu res a praefecto eius Antipatro in Graecia gestae, et ab Archidamo, rege Lacedaemoniorum, Molossoque Alexandro in Italia, quorum ibi est uterque cum exercitu deletus.* (Trog. *Prol.* 12).

[14] Curt. X.1.44; Badian 1994b: 275.

[15] *Namque post profectionem Alexandri Graecia ferme omnis in occasionem reciperandae libertatis ad arma concurrerat, auctoritatem Lacedaemoniorum secuta, qui Philippi Alexandrique et pacem soli spreuerant et leges respuerant.*

[16] Hamilton 1982: 61-83; Cartledge / Spawforth 2002: 7-12.

embarca en empresas ultramarinas, tanto en Creta como en Italia, en un momento en el que la situación de la ciudad se va debilitando, sin que tengamos constancia de que el colega del rey, el Agiada Cleómenes II, haya tomado ninguna decisión relevante.

Es posible que la marcha de Arquidamo deba interpretarse como algo más que un intento de labrarse un futuro como comandante de mercenarios, puesto que la ayuda a Tarento pudo venir precedida por la firma de un tratado de alianza (συμμαχία),[17] basado en el parentesco (συγγένεια) que unía a la metrópolis con su colonia[18]. Pero esto no es una causa, sino más bien un pretexto. La presencia de Arquidamo en Esparta podría haber provocado aún más a Filipo, el cual podría haber decidido tomar medidas mucho más drásticas contra la ciudad. Una retirada honrosa a tiempo beneficiaba a Esparta, al tiempo que incrementaba el prestigio del rey en una parte de la Hélade como la Magna Grecia que se veía amenazada por el peligro bárbaro.

La ausencia del rey y la situación general de Esparta hacen que no intervenga en la batalla de Queronea; es más, las fuentes aseguran que la muerte del rey, o la destrucción de su ejército, tuvieron lugar el mismo día que la decisiva batalla que consagró el dominio de Filipo sobre Grecia[19] lo cual, aunque tal vez no es del todo cierto en cuanto a los detalles (el mismo día y la misma hora) sí que apunta a una fecha, al menos, próxima.

La pérdida de buena parte de las fuentes no permite que profundicemos en los detalles de la marcha de Arquidamo, aunque sí sobrevive, recogido en Ateneo (XII.51), un pasaje de Teopompo en el que se asegura que «en el libro 52 dice que Arquidamo el laconio, abandonando el modo de vida patrio, se acostumbró a formas de vida extranjeras y muelles. Por consiguiente, no fue capaz de soportar la vida en casa, sino que estaba ansioso siempre por marcharse a causa de su mal temperamento» (Theopomp. Hist. *FGrH* 115 F 232; mi traducción).[20] Estas causas morales tienen, en nuestra opinión, poco sentido, pero son una excusa fácil para justificar el comportamiento de algunos personajes históricos cuando no se dispone de otras explicaciones más plausibles. Lo cierto es que las posibilidades de Esparta de enfrentarse a Filipo tras el final de la Tercera Guerra Sagrada eran pocas y el propio rey macedonio no estaba dispuesto a darle ni una oportunidad más a Esparta. Si Arquidamo se marcha hacia Tarento hacia el 345 a.C. o poco después, ya en su ausencia (343 a.C.) Filipo entrega dinero a toda una serie de individuos, que enumera Demóstenes y retoma Polibio[21] con el fin de mantener ocupada a Esparta, como muestran los destinatarios de tales ayudas, como las ya mencionadas Argos, Mesene y Megalópolis, entre otras.

---

[17] Theopomp. Hist. *FGrH* 115 F 232; D.S. XVI.63.1.

[18] D.S. XVI.62.4.

[19] D.S. XVI.63.1-2, 88.3-4; Plu. *Cam.* 19.9; Urso 1998: 11-22.

[20] Ἐν δὲ τῆι δευτέραι <καὶ> πεντηκοστῆι φησὶν ὡς Ἀρχίδαμος ὁ Λάκων ἀποστὰς τῆς πατρίου διαίτης συνηθίσθη ξενικῶς καὶ μαλακῶς· διόπερ οὐκ ἠδύνατο τὸν οἴκοι βίον ὑπομένειν, ἀλλ' ἐσπούδαζεν αἰεὶ δι' ἀκρασίαν ἔξω διατρίβειν.

[21] D. 18, 295-296; Plb. 18.14.1-7.

Esta política de aislamiento y debilitamiento de Esparta prosigue, esta vez de forma mucho más violenta, tras Queronea, es decir, tras la muerte de Arquidamo III y reinando ya su hijo Agis III, cuando Filipo invade Laconia y reparte las zonas periféricas de su territorio entre Argos, Tegea, Megalópolis y Mesene[22] llamado por amigos y aliados del Peloponeso (ὀνομαζόμενος ὑπὸ τῶν ἐν Πελοποννήσῳ φίλων καὶ συμμάχων) (Plb. IX.33.9-10). Esto le provocó a Esparta importantísimas pérdidas de territorio,[23] y su destino podría haber sido peor si, al parecer, Asclepio no hubiese protegido a la ciudad;[24] no parece, en todo caso, que Filipo estuviese interesado ahora en que la ciudad se integrase en la Liga de Corinto a la que había renunciado pertenecer[25] la cual, por otro lado, aprobó las nuevas fronteras que había trazado Filipo.[26]

Además, es bastante posible que Filipo maniobrase para impedir que el nuevo rey espartano emprendiese un camino semejante al que había llevado su padre, intentando labrarse una reputación de general en Italia, aunque sobre esto tenemos menos datos. No obstante, la boda entre el rey moloso Alejandro y su sobrina Cleopatra reforzaba la relación entre Macedonia y el Epiro. La muerte de Filipo durante la ceremonia impide conocer los planes del rey, pero lo cierto es que, al año siguiente, cuando Tarento y los italiotas, aún necesitados de ayuda contra distintos pueblos indígenas, vuelven a mirar a Grecia no piensan en Esparta, sino en el tío y cuñado de Alejandro, Alejandro el Moloso. Quienes consideramos que la campaña del epirota se realizó no solo con el consentimiento de Alejandro Magno (y, antes que él, de Filipo) sino que, incluso, formaba parte de un diseño más amplio de lucha contra el bárbaro, de gran importancia en los momentos previos e iniciales de la campaña del rey macedonio, no podemos dejar de considerar que el situar a su tío al frente de una guerra que, hasta hacía unos años había estado dirigida por un rey espartano, era un elemento más de humillación para la ciudad laconia, en una línea parecida a la que había seguido Filipo. Esta humillación podía ser aún mayor si se considera que los motivos aducidos por Arquidamo, entre ellos el parentesco entre Tarento y Esparta, eran ahora dados de lado. Es difícil saber si la posterior enemistad entre Tarento y el Moloso, que se apoyará en otros italiotas frente a ella,[27] tuvo que ver con esta actitud inicial y si la llamada al Moloso partió realmente de Tarento o del conjunto de los italiotas como algunos autores sugieren.[28]

Es curioso que durante todo este periodo no sepamos casi nada del otro rey espartano, Cleómenes II, que a pesar de su reinado de sesenta años y diez meses[29] no pa-

---

[22] Plb. IX.28.6-7.

[23] Roebuck 1948: 84-89, 91-92; Cartledge / Spawforth 2002: 12-13.

[24] Landucci Gattinoni 2013: 273-279.

[25] Iust. IX.5.1-3; Plu. *Mor.* 240a-b.

[26] Plb. IX.33.11-12.

[27] Urso 1998: 23-51.

[28] Chron. Oxy. *FGrH* 255 F 6; Iust. XXIII.1.15; Urso 1998: 24-25.

[29] D.S. XX.29.1.

rece haber realizado nada relevante, más allá de haber ganado la carrera de cuadrigas en los Juegos Píticos del 336 a.C. tras el asesinato de Filipo II; quizá tengan razón Cartledge y Spawforth cuando le definen como «prodigious nonentity».[30]

En esta línea de humillación a Esparta hay que entender la tantas veces comentada dedicatoria que hace Alejandro de los despojos de la batalla del Gránico en la acrópolis de Atenas, con el añadido del epigrama «Alejandro, hijo de Filipo y los griegos, excepto los lacedemonios, de los bárbaros que viven en Asia».[31] En ese momento, justo al inicio de una campaña que nadie pensaba que llegase a ser tan larga y significativa como acabó siendo, Alejandro sigue inmerso en las claves internas de la política macedonia hacia Grecia y, en ella, el aislamiento de Esparta parece haber jugado un papel importante. Reivindicando la victoria sobre los sátrapas como acción común de él y de los griegos, y excluyendo de manera pública, explícita y humillante, a Esparta, asume para sí el ideal panhelénico que tanto peso había tenido durante el siglo IV y que, en algún momento, había encarnado para muchos griegos la propia Esparta en las figuras, entre otros, del abuelo y del padre del propio Agis III, Agesilao II y Arquidamo III. El pensamiento del ateniense Isócrates muestra, a lo largo de sus discursos y cartas de distintas épocas, fluctuaciones en el papel que Esparta podría haber jugado en una eventual campaña contra los persas, pero su papel es considerado, hasta la consolidación de Filipo, como imprescindible para la misma, a pesar de los (graves) defectos que el orador achaca a los lacedemonios.[32] Con esta dedicatoria en Atenas, Alejandro reivindicaba el papel de la ciudad en la lucha contra el bárbaro, y dejaba en evidencia a Esparta por su no participación en la misma. Del mismo modo, castigó de forma severa, encadenando y enviándolos a Macedonia a trabajar a los griegos capturados,[33] de entre los que no pocos eran atenienses; entre los no capturados en esa ocasión también había otros atenienses, incluyendo algunos individuos de buenas familias.[34] Tras una embajada infructuosa que llega hasta Alejandro en Gordio, una segunda, en Tiro, tras su regreso de Egipto, consigue su liberación.[35] Curcio hace coincidir esta decisión de liberar a los prisioneros atenienses con la orden dada a Anfótero de limpiar el mar de piratas,[36] posiblemente tras haber tenido éxito en su campaña previa en Creta, en la que espartanos y persas habían estado actuando contra él;[37] ambas acciones parecen haber formado parte de un mismo diseño y las diferencias de énfasis entre nuestros dos informadores (Arriano y Curcio) pueden deberse a

---

[30] Cartledge / Spawforth 2002: 14-17.
[31] Arr. *An.* I.16.7; Plu. *Alex.* 16.17.
[32] Cloché 1933: 129-145.
[33] Arr. *An.* I.16.6.
[34] Landucci Gattinoni 1994: 59-91.
[35] Arr. *An.* I.29.5-6, 3.6.2; Curt. III.1.9-10, IV.8.12-13.
[36] Curt. IV.8.15; Fernández Nieto 2002: 111-124.
[37] Curt. IV.1.39-40.

que cada una de ellas selecciona de sus entre sus fuentes los aspectos que consideran más sobresalientes.[38]

La política de aislamiento a Esparta, así como el trato dado a los prisioneros griegos capturados en el ejército persa y su rechazo inicial a devolverlos, mostraría que en esos primeros momentos Alejandro sigue actuando como defensor de la lucha de los griegos contra los bárbaros; las primeras medidas que toma en los territorios ya bajo su control en Asia Menor, aunque ya muestran cómo va imponiendo su voluntad,[39] tienen como objetivo recomponer la vida interna de las ciudades después de su liberación de los persas. Como esas ciudades no se integran en la Liga de Corinto, la actuación de Alejandro con respecto a las mismas tiene como precedente la actitud que los reyes macedonios habían mantenido con las ciudades griegas que habían ido siendo integradas en su reino.

Humillación y resentimiento en Esparta: Agis III

No tenemos demasiados datos acerca de cuál ha sido la actitud de Esparta en estos momentos hasta los primeros movimientos de Agis III para buscar un apoyo en los persas ante la actitud de Alejandro que no podía dejar de percibirse en Esparta como el prolegómeno a su próxima ocupación. Sin embargo, la presencia de embajadores espartanos entre los capturados tras la batalla de Iso, entre ellos Euticles[40] y quizá otros, mencionados por Curcio en un pasaje problemático,[41] hizo sugerir a Badian que habían sido enviados por Agis para lograr un acuerdo con el Gran Rey, aunque su captura frustraría este plan.[42] Es posible que la embajada espartana ante el Gran Rey hubiese dado buenos resultados porque es en este momento cuando el propio rey espartano toma la que parece ser la primera acción directa. Según asegura Arriano, se presenta en Sifnos ante Farnábazo y Autofrádates buscando dinero, tropas y naves, porque los sátrapas habrían recibido instrucciones de apoyar las acciones espartanas en Grecia.[43]

Sin embargo, estando allí llega la noticia de la derrota en Iso lo que provoca un inmediato cambio de planes.[44] Farnábazo marcha hacia Quíos con parte de la flota y con tropas para evitar su pérdida y Autofrádates le hace entrega a Agis tan solo de treinta talentos de plata y diez trirremes, que son consignados a su hermano Agesilao, que se hallaba en Ténaro. Con esos recursos el hermano del rey se dirige

---

[38] Bosworth 1988b: 200.

[39] Domínguez 2016a: 76-113.

[40] Arr. *An.* II.15.2.

[41] Curt. III.13.15.

[42] Badian 1967: 174.

[43] Arr. *An.* II.13.4.

[44] Arr. *An.* II.13.5.

hacia Creta[45] donde se inicia una labor de insurgencia para la que la isla ofrecía las mejores condiciones;[46] para contrarrestarla, como habíamos visto, Alejandro envió a Anfótero.

Por lo tanto, da la impresión de que el inicio de la actividad de Agis tiene lugar entre el desenlace de la batalla del Gránico y la batalla de Iso, entre mayo del 334 y noviembre del 333 a.C. En esos meses, que coinciden con el momento de la contraofensiva persa en el Egeo tras la disolución de la flota, debió de producirse la embajada de Euticles ante el Gran Rey que debió de acabar dando resultados si, a pesar de la noticia de la derrota en Iso, Agis recibió apoyo económico y militar, aunque el mismo no habría sido tan importante como el que en un principio esperaba el rey espartano. De haber sido así, cabe preguntarse si Alejandro y, sobre todo, Antípatro no pudieron prever los movimientos espartanos, aunque la respuesta quizá se halle en que ambos pensaban que Esparta era incapaz de cualquier nuevo esfuerzo de guerra.

Las actividades de Agesilao en Creta sin duda tienen que ver, además de con intentar introducir inestabilidad en la isla, con la posibilidad de reclutar allí tropas para llevar a cabo un levantamiento con mayores perspectivas, aunque hay quien prefiere ver esta campaña como un intento de asegurar la isla para que los restos de la flota persa puedan seguir actuando.[47] La intensidad de la acción la deja clara Curcio cuando sitúa las acciones en Creta, en las que Esparta se ve apoyada por 8.000 mercenarios griegos procedentes del ejército persa derrotado en Iso, como la antesala de la guerra que estallará en el Peloponeso: *contractis bellum Antipatro, Macedoniae praefecto* (Curt. VI.1.39-40).[48] De cualquier modo, Curcio considera esa guerra como de poca intensidad (*leviora*), más centrada en el cambio de manos, entre macedonios y espartanos, de guarniciones (*praesidia*), aunque Diodoro parece darle algo más de importancia.[49] Al estallar ese conflicto, poco después de Iso, Alejandro había enviado a Anfótero con el encargo de liberar Creta (*ad liberandam Cretam)* aunque ya en la primavera del 331, cuando estaba en Tiro a punto de dirigirse hacia el Éufrates, le dio al almirante la orden de limpiar el mar de piratas (*ante omnia mare a piraticis classibus vindicare iussus*) (Curt. IV.8.15) lo cual puede sugerir que la situación en Creta estaba en trance de ser controlada y que era más urgente facilitar las comunicaciones por mar, quizá infestado por flotas o flotillas piratas aprovechando la situación de inestabilidad.[50] Como habíamos visto antes, la nueva misión de Anfótero coincide con la devolución a Atenas de sus ciudadanos hechos prisioneros en Gránico. Arriano da una información que puede ser complementaria de la de Curcio cuando asegura, nada más relatar la liberación de estos prisioneros, que

---

45 Arr. *An.* II.13.5-6.

46 Bosworth 1988b: 199.

47 Bosworth 1975: 32-33.

48 D.S. XVII.48.1.

49 Curt. IV.1.40; D.S. XVII.48.2.

50 Fernández Nieto 2002: 111-124.

> «tuvo noticias entonces de que en el Peloponeso se había originado una revuelta, y por ello envió a Anfótero como apoyo a los peloponesios que estuvieron de su parte en la guerra contra los persas y no hicieron caso a los lacedemonios. Encargó además a los fenicios y chipriotas que despacharan cien naves, a más de las que ya había enviado él al Peloponeso bajo el mando de Anfótero» (Arr. *An.* III.6.3).[51]

Algunos autores, sin embargo, cuestionan que ambas informaciones puedan combinarse[52] pero, como hemos visto anteriormente es más razonable pensar que estén relacionadas.

La crítica se ha dividido acerca de si estas acciones hay que considerarlas como el inicio de la guerra (la mayoría) o, por el contrario, como episodios propios de una fase de confusión, pero previa al estallido de la guerra.[53] Bosworth es quien con más intensidad ha defendido que «there is no evidence that Alexander had heard of the war before he sent Menes of Pella to Syrian coast in December 331 with instructions to disburse funds to Antipater»;[54] por lo tanto, en su opinión, Anfótero se habría centrado en Creta (a la que se vincula geográficamente con el Peloponeso según el testimonio de algunas fuentes)[55] antes del estallido de la guerra que este autor sitúa en verano del 331, nada más producirse la partida de Amintas con refuerzos para Alejandro, fecha que se obtiene del dato de que llegó a Babilonia poco antes de que Alejandro reemprendiera la marcha hacia el Este hacia noviembre o inicios de diciembre del 331.[56] Bosworth piensa que, de haberse iniciado las hostilidades con Agis, «it is almost inconceivable that Antipater would have allowed such a substantial proportion of the troops avalaible to him to have left for Asia»,[57] lo cual presupone que el general en Europa (στρατηγὸς ἐπὶ τῆς Εὐρώπης) estaba dispuesto a desatender las órdenes de su rey. Para Badian no hay duda: «Antipater could not keep these men for his own use if the King wanted them»,[58] aunque eso supusiese ralentizar sus planes para poder reclutar un ejército capaz de enfrentarse a Agis. Por otro lado, la liberación de los prisioneros atenienses tenía que ver, sin duda, con la actitud de Atenas, cuya no participación se quería garantizar;[59] no olvidemos que, junto con la retención de estos prisioneros tras Gránico, Alejandro había enviado a Atenas las trescientas panoplias para consagrarlas a Atenea. Del mismo modo, cuando la guerra ya habría

---

[51] Τὰ δὲ ἐν Πελοποννήσῳ ὅτι αὐτῷ νενεωτερίσθαι ἀπήγγελτο, 'Αμφοτερὸν πέμπει βοηθεῖν Πελοποννησίων ὅσοι ἔς τε τὸν Περσικὸν πόλεμον βέβαιοι ἦσαν καὶ Λακεδαιμονίων οὐ κατήκουον. Φοίνιξι δὲ καὶ Κυπρίοις προσετάχθη ἑκατὸν ναῦς ἄλλας πρὸς αἷς ἔχοντα 'Αμφοτερὸν ἔπεμπε στέλλειν ἐπὶ Πελοποννήσου.

[52] Bosworth 1975: 27-43.

[53] Resumen de las posturas en Bosworth 1980a: 279, aunque este autor es partidario de esta segunda opción, es decir, que son actividades que preludian la guerra auténtica: Bosworth 1975: 27-43.

[54] Bosworth 1975: 35.

[55] Ps.-Scyl. 40-48; Str. X.4.1.

[56] D.S. XVII.65.1; Curt. V.1.40-42.

[57] Bosworth 1975: 36.

[58] Badian 1967: 188, 1994b: 268-269.

[59] Badian 1967: 183; Bosworth 1988b: 75.

estallado, y tras conquistar Susa, Alejandro remitió a Atenas las estatuas de los tiranicidas que estaban en la capital persa desde la época de Jerjes,[60] otro indicio de que quería mantener buenas relaciones con los atenienses para evitar que se uniesen a Agis o para mostrar agradecimiento por no haberlo hecho.

Es difícil entender la actitud de Agis desde la partida de Alejandro a Asia sin relación con los preparativos de guerra; asunto diferente es que los objetivos del rey espartano hayan podido ir cambiando a medida que la situación se haya ido transformando en un sentido opuesto a las expectativas que muchos se habían hecho de la campaña de Alejandro. La victoria en Gránico y la rápida marcha que Alejandro llevó a cabo por Anatolia pudo haber sorprendido a muchos que podían esperar que el impulso inicial macedonio pronto quedase detenido ante la compleja situación de Asia Menor; sin embargo, la pérdida del control del mar y el mantenimiento de guarniciones claves como Mileto y Halicarnaso por parte de los persas pudo hacer crecer las esperanzas entre los partidarios del Gran Rey, que esperaban que el ejército que estaba reclutando parase también la ofensiva terrestre de Alejandro. Sería poco después de Gránico y, sobre todo, de la disolución de la flota,[61] cuando Agis debió de iniciar sus conversaciones con los persas para apoyar su esfuerzo de guerra en el Egeo como paso previo para la exportación de la guerra al Peloponeso. La derrota de Darío en Iso no habría acabado de golpe con esos planes, aunque los alteraría radicalmente; Agesilao es enviado a Creta, a donde le acompañará quizá Agis, aunque el rey debió de seguir intrigando en la zona como asegura Arriano (*An.* II.13.6): «Permaneció Agis algún tiempo allí en las islas, y algo más tarde se reunió con Autofrádates en Halicarnaso»[62] y, tal vez, recibió allí más dinero persa.[63] La respuesta de Alejandro ya la hemos mencionado y hay que situarla dentro de toda la estrategia de recuperación de la iniciativa en el mar, encargada a Anfótero y a Hegéloco, y cuya conclusión satisfactoria para los intereses de Alejandro se observa en la llegada de Hegéloco a Egipto, en la época en la que se está procediendo a la fundación de Alejandría, con buenas noticias y abundantes prisioneros rebeldes.[64]

Será el fracaso de la ofensiva naval persa el que precipite los acontecimientos en el Peloponeso. La campaña persa y espartana en Creta formaba parte, sin duda, de un proyecto más ambicioso en el que, según Arriano,[65] se pretendía, incluso, llevar los ataques a la propia Grecia y a Macedonia, algo de lo que Antípatro se había percatado en los primeros momentos y había ordenado a Próteas, hijo de

---

[60] Arr. *An.* III.16.7-8.

[61] Arr. *An.* I.20.1; D.S. XVII.22.5.

[62] Αὐτὸς δὲ τότε μὲν αὐτοῦ ἐν ταῖς νήσοις ὑπέμενεν, ὕστερον δὲ εἰς Ἁλικαρνασσὸν παρ᾽ Αὐτοφραδάτην ἀφίκετο.

[63] Grainger 2019: 57.

[64] Arr. *An.* III.2.3-7.

[65] Arr. *An.* II.1.1.

Andrónico, reclutar naves y tropas en Eubea y el Peloponeso.[66] El problema es que, si seguimos a Arriano, la intervención en Creta se produjo después de la derrota persa de Iso, lo que impide saber si, antes de ese momento, ya habían intentado los enemigos de Alejandro hacerse con el control de la isla. En cualquier caso, la contraofensiva macedonia en el Egeo debió de limitar las posibilidades de éxito de esta intervención, máxime cuando el avance de Alejandro hacia Fenicia acabaría reduciendo y, al final, cortando, el suministro de barcos a los restos de la resistencia persa en el Egeo. El cambio de la misión de Anfótero, que mencionaba Curcio, de liberar a Creta a controlar la piratería y a apoyar a los peloponesios enemigos de Esparta (Arriano) lo hemos interpretado como el final del conflicto en la isla, o su encauzamiento definitivo, por lo que al almirante se le encomendaría una tarea más urgente como era controlar el mar, repleto de naves sin una misión ya clara en una guerra que se está perdiendo y que buscan su propio beneficio practicando la piratería.

Esas nuevas órdenes para Anfótero, que coinciden con la restitución a Atenas de sus prisioneros, son prueba de que Alejandro sabía (o preveía) ya que Agis, aunque privado de la ayuda persa, iba a llevar a cabo el plan que había concebido con su ayuda, que era llevar la guerra al Peloponeso.

Diodoro introduce el relato del inicio de la revuelta de Agis después de mencionar la llegada a Grecia de las noticias sobre la batalla de Gaugamela;[67] a pesar de lo que pueda dar a entender esta sucesión de hechos, debida acaso a la incompetencia de Diodoro al condensar acontecimientos y relacionarlos entre sí, parece claro que las fuentes de Diodoro daban por sentado el origen de la revuelta antes de la derrota de Gaugamela,[68] en especial porque se asegura los griegos «decidieron luchar por su libertad, ahora que todavía se mantenía el poder de los persas» (D.S. XVII.62.1).[69] El argumento que desarrolla Diodoro es que Darío les podría aportar dinero en abundancia para contratar tropas, mientras que Alejandro no podría dividir sus fuerzas.[70] Frente a lo que muchos autores piensan, en el sentido de que esta situación debe de referirse al momento en el que Alejandro se halla ya en camino hacia Mesopotamia,[71] apoyados por una referencia en Esquines a que Alejandro se hallaba más allá del polo norte y de casi toda la tierra habitada (III.165: ἔξω τῆς ἄρκτου καὶ τῆς οἰκουμένης ὀλίγου δεῖν πάσης μεθειστήκει), lo cierto es que este planteamiento de la situación no puede corresponder a un momento distinto a aquel en el que Agis inicia sus con-

---

[66] Arr. *An.* II.2.4.

[67] D.S. XVII.62.1.

[68] Badian 1967: 191; Cawkwell 1969: 172.

[69] Ἕως ἔτι τὰ Περσῶν πράγματα διαμένει, τῆς ἐλευθερίας ἀντέχεσθαι·

[70] D.S. XVII.62.2-3: Βοηθήσειν γὰρ αὐτοῖς Δαρεῖον καὶ χρημάτων τε πλῆθος χορηγήσειν πρὸς τὸ δύνασθαι ξενικὰς μεγάλας δυνάμεις συνίστασθαι καὶ τὸν Ἀλέξανδρον μὴ δυνήσεσθαι διαιρεῖν τὰς δυνάμεις.

[71] Por ejemplo, Cawkwell 1969: 172-173.

tactos con los persas y, en todo caso, antes de la batalla de Iso.[72] Como hemos visto, después de esta batalla se inicia el repliegue persa en el Egeo, aunque era algo que en ese momento quizá no se percibiese y, por ello, Agesilao y Agis intensifican sus acciones en Creta dentro del diseño persa de dominio del Egeo aunque, como hemos visto, el avance de Alejandro hacia Fenicia y la nueva política naval macedonia acabará cerrando ese frente de guerra. Pensar que en vísperas de Gaugamela los persas, cuyo acceso al Mediterráneo había concluido, podían ayudar con dinero a los griegos es absurdo. Hay que pensar, pues, que estos planteamientos encajan bien en la situación existente entre el Gránico e Iso, es decir, en la época en la que se produce la embajada de Euticles y la entrevista de Agis con los generales persas en Sifnos, el único momento, antes de la segunda batalla, en el que las perspectivas para los persas y sus aliados eran halagüeñas.

No obstante, la derrota persa en Iso y la progresiva pérdida del control del Egeo no impide que Agis prosiga sus planes, sobre todo porque los movimientos ya dados no podían dejar de implicar un castigo por parte de Alejandro, posiblemente la propia ocupación de Esparta. Por eso, los prisioneros atenienses son devueltos y se refuerza la acción naval de Anfótero antes de que Alejandro inicie su marcha hacia el interior que, hiperbólicamente, Esquines lleva casi hasta el polo norte. En los Juegos Ístmicos del 332, los «consejeros de los griegos» (οἱ σύνεδροι τῶν Ἑλλήνων) nombraron a quince embajadores para que llevasen una corona de oro como premio para Alejandro y para felicitarle por la victoria de Iso.[73] Curcio da también la noticia pero no pierde la ocasión de decir que esos mismos griegos hasta hacía poco habían estado atentos a lo que ocurría «para seguir a dondequiera que condujese la fortuna a sus espíritus volátiles» (*ut, quocumque pendentes animos tulisset fortuna, sequerentur*) (Curt. IV.5.11). Esta apreciación de Curcio muestra, en todo caso, cómo, sobre todos los indecisos, estaban a la espera de acontecimientos para obrar en consecuencia.

Diodoro menciona también como elemento desencadenante la rebelión de Memnón en Tracia, episodio obscuro al que tiene que hacer frente Antípatro con todas sus fuerzas (πᾶσαν ἀναλαβὼν τὴν δύναμιν) (D.S. XVII.62.5-6); Antípatro tuvo que finalizar esta guerra de la mejor manera que pudo (ὥς ποτ' ἦν δυνατὸν) (D.S. XVII.63.1) para hacer frente a la rebelión de los griegos. Este Memnón parece haber sido rehabilitado y aparece en 326 en el Hidaspes conduciendo 5.000 jinetes tracios como refuerzos para Alejandro (Curt. IX.3.21); en todo caso, los pocos datos que poseemos sobre sus objetivos al rebelarse, cómo Antípatro acabó con su rebelión y, sobre todo, cómo pudo evitar su ejecución siguen siendo puntos obscuros de todo este episodio,[74] aunque no puede descartarse que se haya percibido que la acción de Memnón tenía

---

[72] La importancia que pudo haber tenido esta referencia, así como la que aporta Dinarco (1.34) a la hora de ubicar erróneamente esta guerra ha sido subrayada por Lock 1972: 22-24.

[73] D.S. 17.48.6.

[74] Kanatsoulis 1958-59: 51-55; Badian 1967: 179-180, 183-184; Baynham 1994: 339-340.

que ver con desavenencias con Antípatro y que no era un levantamiento contra Alejandro o, como ha sugerido Grainger, que las acciones (u omisiones) de Memnón hayan provocado la rebelión en Tracia, pero que él no fue quien se sublevó.[75]

Con la rebelión de Memnón en marcha, «los lacedemonios supusieron que había llegado el momento oportuno de hacer los preparativos para la guerra, así que invitaron a los demás griegos a llegar a un común acuerdo en defensa de su libertad» (D.S. XVII.62.6).[76] El envío de embajadas espartanas a las ciudades griegas no pasaría desapercibido a los aliados de los macedonios, pero, con Antípatro en Tracia, poco era lo que directamente podía hacer el general; sin embargo, la respuesta de Alejandro, desde Tiro, fue tanto la ya mencionada liberación de los prisioneros atenienses como el enviar a Anfótero a controlar la piratería y a ayudar a los aliados peloponesios. No sabemos tampoco cómo pudo haber actuado Anfótero aunque quizá el control de las rutas de navegación y de todas esas gentes dispuestas a ser reclutadas podía tratar de evitar que el ejército rebelde creciese demasiado; también su acción podía servir para tratar de mantener a los aliados leales y evitar que la rebelión pudiese extenderse de forma descontrolada haciendo visible, sobre todo en el Peloponeso, una cierta presencia macedonia a falta de otra respuesta que, de momento, no era posible.

La situación en Atenas

Diodoro nos informa con precisión de la respuesta de Atenas a la petición de Agis: «Los atenienses, que recibían un trato de mayor consideración que todos los griegos por parte de Alejandro, no hicieron nada» (D.S. XVII.62.7).[77] Esta observación de Diodoro responde, sin duda, a una realidad, que fue la inactividad de Atenas.[78] Quizá no haya que hacer demasiados esfuerzos para explicar esta actitud; ciertamente, en Atenas, los partidarios de Alejandro podían jactarse de haber recibido la impactante ofrenda de las trescientas panoplias del Gránico y, más recientemente aún, de haber conseguido la liberación de los prisioneros de esa misma batalla. Pero, incluso, los enemigos de Alejandro no habían dado tampoco pasos para aproximarse a los espartanos; Esquines no dejará de reprochárselo a Demóstenes en su discurso *Contra Ctesifonte* (verano del 330) acusándole de inacción frente a Alejandro en tres momentos decisivos: con ocasión del inicio de la campaña asiática, en los momentos previos a Iso y en el inicio de la rebelión de Agis.[79] En este último caso, Esquines le reprocha a

[75] Grainger 2019: 55-56.

[76] Τούτου δὲ περὶ ταῦτ' ὄντος οἱ Λακεδαιμόνιοι καιρὸν ἔχειν ὑπολαβόντες τοῦ παρασκευάσασθαι τὰ πρὸς τὸν πόλεμον παρεκάλουν τοὺς Ἕλληνας συμφρονῆσαι περὶ τῆς ἐλευθερίας.

[77] Ἀθηναῖοι μὲν οὖν, παρὰ πάντας τοὺς ἄλλους Ἕλληνας ὑπ' Ἀλεξάνδρου προτιμώμενοι, τὴν ἡσυχίαν ἦγον·

[78] Antela Bernárdez 2005: 90-97.

[79] Aeschin. III.163-167.

Demóstenes haberse presentado públicamente como muñidor de tal revuelta y haber asegurado a los atenienses que había intentado conseguir la defección de tesalios y perrebos, algo de lo que se burla el orador[80], pero que, de ser cierto, contradice su propio argumento de que Demóstenes permaneció inactivo; es más, Esquines pone estas palabras en primera persona, como si las estuviese pronunciando Demóstenes: «afirmo haber estado detrás de los acontecimientos en Laconia, afirmo haber propiciado la revuelta de tesalios y perrebos».[81] Así, no sería improbable que Demóstenes hubiese estado dando esperanzas a los espartanos en los momentos anteriores al inicio de la guerra, pero que, cuando la misma estalló, optó por no tratar de convencer a sus conciudadanos de unirse a la misma. Eso es lo que le reprocha Esquines y a ello es a lo que no responde Demóstenes.

Aunque, como es sabido, fue Esquines quien acabó perjudicado con esa acción oportunista, saliendo Demóstenes triunfante, eso no impide que aceptemos, con Cawkwell, que «Demosthenes' policy appears to have been to do nothing until Alexander was either checked or defeated by Darius».[82] Quizá Demóstenes podría haber intentado convencer a los atenienses de tomar una postura más activa, pero la experiencia de Tebas estaba aún muy viva en el recuerdo, la derrota del Gránico y la captura de atenienses seguía pesando aún bastante, aunque su liberación pudo calmar muchos ánimos, y quizá las conversaciones con los otros griegos, todos ellos formalmente miembros de la Liga de Corinto, tampoco mostraban un acuerdo amplio para romper con Alejandro. En estas condiciones, en las que incluso el parecer de los atenienses podía estar dividido, opta por no tomar partido directo por Agis, a pesar de que, como aseguraba Esquines, se había implicado en algunas actividades previas en favor de la rebelión.

El enfrentamiento entre ambos rivales oscurece, sin embargo, otras cosas que estaban ocurriendo y que, de no ser por otros autores, desconoceríamos por completo. Se trata de la anécdota que narra Plutarco[83] sobre la actitud de Démades que hay que situar antes del estallido de la guerra en el Peloponeso; los atenienses querían enviar trirremes para ayudar a los que se habían rebelado contra Alejandro (ὡρμημένων γὰρ ἐκπέμπειν τριήρεις βοηθοὺς τοῖς ἀφισταμένοις Ἀλεξάνδρου) y le pidieron a Démades (que estaba al cargo del θεωρικόν) que lo librara; este les dijo que tenía el dinero preparado para hacer entrega de media mina a cada ciudadano durante la fiesta de las Coes, pero que si querían hacer uso del mismo para ese fin, que podían hacerlo. Plutarco concluye diciendo que «los atenienses renunciaron al envío de naves para no quedar privados de la distribución» (*Mor.* 818e).[84] Teniendo en cuenta que las An-

---

80 Aeschin. III.167.

81 Ὁμολογῶ τὰ Λακωνικὰ συστῆσαι, ὁμολογῶ Θετταλοὺς καὶ Περραιβοὺς ἀφιστάναι.

82 Cawkwell 1969: 177.

83 Plu. *Mor.* 818e.

84 Ὅπως μὴ στεροῖντο τῆς διανομῆς, ἀφέντων τὸν ἀπόστολον,

testerias se celebraban hacia el final de nuestro mes de febrero,[85] la petición de ayuda habría llegado algún mes antes de ese momento, pero Plutarco asegura que la ayuda iba destinada a los que se habían rebelado (τοῖς ἀφισταμένοις) que, en ese momento (invierno del 332/331 a.C.), estaban actuando en el sur del Egeo. Por lo tanto, esa petición de ayuda, centrada además en naves, no está en relación directa con la segunda fase de la rebelión, la guerra terrestre, como algunos autores plantean,[86] sino como mucho con la primera fase, en la que Agis, de común acuerdo con los persas, actúa en Creta y en otras islas. Si se quiere vincular este episodio con la guerra de Agis en el Peloponeso habría que situar la petición de ayuda en el invierno del 331, después del rechazo inicial de Atenas a intervenir y quizá como un intento de ampliar el radio de acción de la guerra ante la acumulación de recursos por parte de Macedonia. En todo caso, no parece que podamos precisar más sobre el momento concreto de esa eventual solicitud de ayuda.[87] El filomacedonismo de Démades es bien conocido[88] y, sin duda, actuó en consecuencia diluyendo las aspiraciones bélicas de los enemigos de Macedonia e, incluso, se ha asegurado que en esos momentos este personaje y Demóstenes eran amigos y aliados.[89]

Como algún autor ha subrayado, ese rechazo a participar no tendría que ver, en principio, con la escasez de fuerzas disponibles en Atenas, puesto que la capacidad naval de la misma parece haber sido bastante buena en esos momentos e, incluso, la reorganización de la efebía por Licurgo habría sentado las bases de un renacido ejército ateniense poco después de Queronea;[90] sin embargo, los principales líderes democráticos con experiencia militar se hallaban exiliados y al servicio del Gran Rey,[91] por lo que si la capacidad militar de Atenas no estaba en entredicho, sí faltaba la voluntad entre los círculos dirigentes de iniciar hostilidades contra Macedonia.[92] Si, a pesar de ello, algunos atenienses decidieron participar en esas acciones en Creta, como en algún momento se ha sugerido, es algo que no puede, por el momento, aceptarse o descartarse por completo.[93]

La guerra: la batalla de Megalópolis

Sobre el origen de las hostilidades, a través de Diodoro solo sabemos que se sumaron a Esparta la mayor parte de los peloponesios y algunos otros (D.S. XVII.62.7:

---

[85] Parke 1977: 107-124.
[86] Bosworth 1988b: 202.
[87] Lock 1972: 16-17.
[88] Squillace 1998-2001: 31-46.
[89] Badian 1967: 182-183.
[90] Atkinson 1981: 43; Faraguna 1992: 257-259.
[91] Landucci Gattinoni 1994: 33-61.
[92] Faraguna 1992: 239-243.
[93] Potter 1984: 229-235; Badian 1989: 59-70.

Πελοποννησίων δ'οἱ πλείους καὶ τῶν ἄλλων τινὲς συμφρονήσαντες...). Es un autor contemporáneo, como Esquines, quien nos proporciona más detalles de cómo se sucedieron los acontecimientos. La primera acción de guerra parece haber sido la derrota de un contingente macedonio al mando de Córrago: «Los lacedemonios y el ejército de mercenarios resultaron victoriosos en la batalla y aniquilaron a los soldados de Córrago» (Aeschin. III.165).[94] Poco más se conoce de este episodio, pero la noticia de Esquines nos informa de que, en algún momento previo, seguramente en los meses anteriores, y una vez finalizada la campaña en Creta, ante la llegada de la flota de Anfótero, Agis se retira al Peloponeso con sus mercenarios, los 8.000 supervivientes de Iso, como ya vimos, y quizá otros reclutados después, puesto que Dinarco menciona diez mil.[95] Como Diodoro no nos informa de este episodio, no sabemos si el mismo fue anterior o posterior a la petición de ayuda a los griegos, entre ellos a los atenienses, pero da la impresión de que antes de actuar Agis debió de entrar en negociaciones con diversos estados griegos, incluyendo Atenas donde habría sido acogido favorablemente por Demóstenes si era cierto, como dice Esquines, que se había jactado en público de estar detrás del alzamiento. El ataque a los macedonios debía, pues, ser la señal para iniciar la guerra. Esquines enumera después de narrar esta primera victoria de Agis, los que se unen a su revuelta: «los eleos se pasaron al lado de aquellos, y todos los aqueos con excepción de los peleneos y toda Arcadia con excepción de Megalópolis» (Aeschin. III.165).[96] Dinarco, por su parte, solo menciona a aqueos y eleos.[97] La ausencia de los de Pelene se entiende porque no hacía mucho que los macedonios habían impuesto a un tirano adicto después de acabar con la democracia.[98] Debido a sus trayectorias en los decenios previos, la opción de apoyar a Esparta (o de oponerse a Macedonia) por parte de aqueos y eleos parece perfectamente justificada.[99] El caso de Arcadia, sobre la que las fuentes no son unánimes, es más difícil de explicar, a pesar de los intentos llevados a cabo, aunque en el caso de Tegea sí se han avanzado algunas explicaciones convincentes.[100]

Diodoro nos informa de cómo actuaron los sublevados que, como vimos, según él incluían a la mayoría de los peloponesios y algunos otros: «hicieron que se decretase la guerra, y convocando levas según la importancia de cada ciudad alistaron lo más selecto de su juventud, no menos de veinte mil soldados de infantería y unos dos mil jinetes» (D.S. XVII.62.7).[101]

---

[94] Λακεδαιμόνιοι μὲν καὶ τὸ ξενικὸν ἐπέτυχον μάχῃ, καὶ διέφθειραν τοὺς περὶ Κόρραγον στρατιώτας.

[95] Din. 1.34.

[96] Ἠλεῖοι δ' αὐτοῖς συμμετεβάλοντο καὶ Ἀχαιοὶ πάντες πλὴν Πελληνέων, καὶ Ἀρκαδία πᾶσα πλὴν Μεγάλης πόλεως.

[97] Din. 1.34.

[98] [D.] 17.10; Paus. VII.27.7.

[99] McQueen 1978: 45-49.

[100] McQueen 1978: 49-51.

[101] Ἀπεγράψαντο πρὸς τὸν πόλεμον καὶ κατὰ δύναμιν τῶν πόλεων καταγράφοντες τῶν νέων τοὺς ἀρίστους κατέλεξαν στρατιώτας πεζοὺς μὲν οὐκ ἐλάττους τῶν δισμυρίων, ἱππεῖς δὲ περὶ δισχιλίους.

Sin ninguna duda, el ejército que pudieron reclutar los rebeldes no era demasiado numeroso si los mercenarios de que disponía Agis, y que ascendían a entre 8.000 y 10.000 hombres, seguían figurando entre sus tropas, algo de lo que no hay por qué dudar. La reacción de Alejandro la podemos valorar por dos informaciones. Por una parte, tras haberse resuelto esta guerra, se cuenta que el rey declaró que la misma había sido una «guerra de ratones» (μυομαχία),[102] comparándola con la guerra contra Darío. Sin embargo, cuando el resultado de la guerra era aún indeciso o aún Alejandro no había recibido noticias sobre su final, no parece que se la haya tomado tan a la ligera. Eso lo demostraría el siguiente pasaje de Arriano, relativo a las medidas que toma el rey una vez llegado a Susa (diciembre del 331 a.C.): «Despachó a Menes como gobernador de las costas de Siria, Fenicia y Cilicia, dotándolo de tres mil talentos de plata para que atendiera con ellos las necesidades que Antípatro tuviera con ocasión de su guerra contra los lacedemonios» (Arr. *An.* III.16.10).[103] Es evidente que esa provisión de fondos, de los que ahora disponía Alejandro una vez hecho con el control de algunos de los principales centros del poder aqueménida, muestra que la amenaza no era percibida en esos momentos como pequeña, sobre todo porque a unos meses de haber estallado la rebelión aún no se sabía si otros griegos, además de los inclinados desde el principio a la misma, podrían intentar unirse a ella si no había una respuesta clara y contundente por parte de los macedonios. No es del todo convincente la idea de que en ese momento la guerra había ya acabado pero que Alejandro aún no lo sabía,[104] aunque tampoco puede descartarse por completo dadas las distancias que tenían que cubrir los correos y las informaciones, ya mencionadas, acerca de dónde recibió Alejandro la noticia del final de la guerra (Ecbatana o Partia).

Por lo tanto, Alejandro, que desde Susa se dirigirá hacia Persépolis para proseguir la persecución de Darío, confía en que esa gran suma de dinero bastará para que Antípatro y sus generales se enfrenten a la amenaza. Incidentalmente, diremos que si la reconstrucción que aquí se sigue es aceptable, la noticia de autores como Curcio de que el sofocamiento de la revuelta tuvo lugar antes de la batalla de Gaugamela no parece admisible;[105] la referencia plutarquea a la «guerra de ratones» sugiere que cuando Alejandro recibe la noticia de la derrota de Agis ya se había producido el encuentro definitivo con Darío.

Volviendo a lo que estaba sucediendo en el Peloponeso, no tenemos demasiadas informaciones de cuáles eran los planes de Agis, nombrado *hegemon* de los

---

[102] Plu. *Ages.* 15.5.

[103] Ἐπὶ θάλασσαν δὲ κατέπεμψεν ὕπαρχον Συρίας καὶ Φοινίκης καὶ Κιλικίας Μένητα. καὶ τούτῳ ἔδωκεν ἀργυρίου τάλαντα ἐς τρισχίλια φέρειν ἐπὶ θάλασσαν, καὶ ἀπ' αὐτῶν ἀποστεῖλαι παρ' Ἀντίπατρον ὅσων ἂν δέηται Ἀντίπατρος ἐς τὸν πρὸς Λακεδαιμονίους πόλεμον.

[104] Wirth 1971: 630.

[105] Curt. VI.1.21: *Hic fuit exitus belli, quod repente ortum prius tamen finitum est, quam Dareum Alexander apud Arbela superaret.* Lock 1972: 22; Atkinson 1994: 167; Badian 1994b: 273; cf. Cawkwell 1969: 170-171; Lock 1972: 22.

rebeldes,[106] pero da la impresión, a partir del testimonio contemporáneo de Esquines que su principal acción, tras haber montado su coalición, fue iniciar el sitio de Megalópolis.[107] Parece, incluso, que no hay ninguna otra actividad más allá de esta, puesto que será en el entorno de la ciudad donde se librará la batalla definitiva con Antípatro. Una guerra de sitio podía acabar resultando exitosa, pero sin apoyos internos y sin maquinaria adecuada podía provocar también un parón para cualquier otra iniciativa, a menos que se optase, cosa que no parece haber ocurrido, por dividir el ejército y, mientras que una parte se ocupaba del sitio, la otra podría llevar a cabo otras actividades tendentes a atraerse a otras ciudades a su bando o a evitar que el enemigo pudiese acumular fuerzas. Aunque no tenemos datos precisos, es posible que el sitio de Megalópolis se prolongase durante varios meses acabando con la iniciativa espartana y, tal vez, con los ánimos de sus aliados si tenemos en cuenta, al menos, la gradación de las represalias que impondrá Antípatro a los participantes y sobre las que luego volveremos. Quizá tenga razón Bosworth cuando considera que «the fatal error was undoubtedly the stubborn siege of Megalopolis»,[108] pero, tal y como parece haberlo visto Agis, sin acabar con este poderoso enemigo pocas probabilidades tendría de atraerse más partidarios.

Antípatro, como habíamos visto, resolvió la situación en Tracia, sin que sepamos bien cómo, y se dirigió al Peloponeso con todas sus fuerzas (μετὰ πάσης τῆς δυνάμεως) reuniendo no menos de 40.000 soldados reclutando tropas de entre las ciudades griegas aliadas (προσλαβόμενος δὲ καὶ παρὰ τῶν συμμαχούντων Ἑλλήνων στρατιώτας) (D.S. XVII.63.1). Quizá el reclutamiento de un ejército tan grande no fue fácil, como sugiere Esquines,[109] tal vez por la reticencia de los aliados y porque muchos se mantenían a la expectativa, como indica Curcio cuando habla de «todos aquellos que habían adoptado una actitud de espectadores ante el resultado de la guerra» (Curt. VI.1.16).[110] Sin ninguna duda, «el futuro era incierto» (Aeschin. III.165).[111] Algunos autores, como Badian, piensan sin embargo que una parte importante de ese ejército estaba compuesto por las propias tropas macedonias al mando de Antípatro.[112]

Diodoro no da demasiados datos de la batalla, más allá de indicar que los sublevados perdieron 5.300 hombres y Antípatro, 3.500, y de sugerir que fueron los aliados de los espartanos los que primero cedieron (τῶν δὲ συμμάχων βιασθέντων) lo que acabó provocando que Agis iniciase la retirada. Relata, además, este autor que el rey ordenó a sus soldados que se retiraran mientras que él, solo, revestido con sus armas

---

[106] D.S. XVII.63.1.

[107] Aeschin. III.165.

[108] Bosworth 1988b: 204.

[109] Aeschin. III.165: Ὁ δὲ Ἀντίπατρος πολὺν χρόνον συνῆγε στρατόπεδον.

[110] *Etiam omnis, qui fortunam belli spectaverant.*

[111] Τὸ δ' ἐσόμενον ἄδηλον ἦν.

[112] Badian 1994b: 258-268.

(καθοπλισθεὶς) y apoyado en una rodilla por las heridas que había recibido, guardó su retirada hasta que murió atravesado por una jabalina después de haber matado a algunos.[113]

Curcio nos da una descripción mucho más pormenorizada de la batalla, mostrando sus diversas acciones y, aunque con más detalles, no contradice la visión de Diodoro resaltando, aún más incluso, el propio comportamiento del rey durante la batalla y su acto final, ya herido, de hacer frente al enemigo para favorecer la retirada de sus tropas, idea que también comparte el resumen de Justino.[114] En cuanto a las cifras de los caídos, Curcio coincide con Diodoro en el número de los «lacedemonios» (5.300), pero no en el de los «macedonios» (1.000).[115]

Las consecuencias de la guerra

Derrotados los espartanos y muerto su rey, Curcio, a quien los aspectos morales siempre le interesan, detalla los celos que siente Alejandro por la victoria de Antípatro, aun deseándola, y señala también cómo el viejo general, puesto que conocía bien el carácter al joven rey, «no se atrevió a arbitrar él en persona las condiciones de la victoria sino que sometió a consulta del Consejo de los griegos qué resolución se debía tomar» (Curt. VI.1.19).[116] A pesar del tono de Curcio y de sus motivos, parte de la crítica está dispuesta a aceptar esta tensa relación entre los dos personajes, que se sustanciaría en esa expresión de «guerra de ratones» que conocemos por Plutarco.[117]

De cualquier modo, es cuestionable que la decisión de Antípatro, más allá de si había ya en ese momento celos o no entre el rey y su general, haya tenido que ver con los motivos que aduce Curcio. La guerra había supuesto una violación de la paz común y de los acuerdos que habían suscrito los estados griegos; Antípatro, como representante de Alejandro, había reclutado un ejército de entre los aliados y había acabado con la revuelta. Era, por lo tanto, cometido de la Liga de Corinto resolver los castigos a quienes habían vulnerado los acuerdos.[118] El problema era que Esparta no era miembro de esa alianza y, por lo tanto, la decisión sobre su eventual castigo no estaba en manos de la misma y eso lo demuestra el diferente trato que reciben los participantes; mientras que las responsabilidades de los miembros de la Liga van a ser resueltas dentro de ella, la suerte de los espartanos quedará en manos de Alejandro; no obstante, y antes de esa decisión, Antípatro tomará medidas cautelares. Veamos, pues, en qué consiste ese trato diferente.

---

[113] D.S. XVII.63.2-5.

[114] Curt. VI.1.15; Iust. XII.1.10-11.

[115] Curt. VI.1.16.

[116] *Non est ausus ipse agere arbitria victoriae, sed concilium Graecorum, quid fieri placeret, consuluit.*

[117] Baynham 1994: 341-342.

[118] McQueen 1978: 52-53; Poddighe 2009: 99-120.

Según Curcio, «el Consejo lo único que concedió a los lacedemonios fue el permiso para enviar al rey una embajada y a los tegeatas, a excepción de los instigadores, el perdón por su rebelión; por su parte, los aqueos y eleos fueron obligados a entregar 120 talentos a los megalopolitanos, cuya ciudad había sido sitiada por los aliados de los rebeldes» (Curt. VI.1.20).[119] Puede que nos falten datos o que Curcio haya resumido, pero si comparamos este cuadro con el que daba Esquines de participantes en la rebelión, se mantienen los eleos y los aqueos (aunque Curcio no menciona la excepción, entre estos últimos, de los de Pelene), pero han desaparecido por completo los arcadios, salvo los de Tegea, de los que solo son castigados los instigadores. O no era verdad que toda Arcadia, excepto Megalópolis (Ἀρκαδία πᾶσα πλὴν Μεγάλης πόλεως), se hubiese rebelado o Curcio no nos da toda la información. Recordemos, a este respecto, que Dinarco solo mencionaba a aqueos y eleos.[120] También podemos pensar que, aunque quizá los arcadios hubiesen estado dispuestos a rebelarse y tal vez habían pactado con Agis hacerlo, al final solo los tegeatas, y quizá no de buen grado, se suman a una guerra cuyo principal escenario va a ser Megalópolis. El comportamiento de Tegea no deja de sorprender porque no hay que olvidar que, después de Queronea, Tegea había sido favorecida por Filipo recibiendo parte del territorio desgajado de Esparta. Asimismo, se puede sugerir que el interés de Agis por ocupar Megalópolis podría deberse a que habría servido para atraer a su alianza al conjunto de los arcadios y, tal vez, a otros de esos griegos que seguían siendo espectadores. También puede haber pesado, a la hora de unirse o no en un primer momento, los recelos anti-espartanos que seguían muy vivos en buena parte del Peloponeso, a pesar de que no todos los que no se alinearon con Agis eran pro-macedonios.[121]

Diodoro no se interesa por el castigo a los otros griegos sublevados, sino que centra su atención en Esparta. Tras la derrota, los espartanos envían embajadores a Antípatro que los remite al consejo de la Liga Helénica (τὸ κοινὸν τῶν Ἑλλήνων συνέδριον) que, reunido en Corinto, no toma ninguna decisión y decide remitirle el caso al propio Alejandro. Mientras tanto, y tal vez como decisión propia, Antípatro decide tomar cincuenta rehenes de entre «los más ilustres espartiatas» (τοὺς ἐπιφανεστάτους τῶν Σπαρτιατῶν) mientras que los espartanos envían embajadores a Asia. Según se desprende de Diodoro, esto estaba teniendo lugar en Europa en el periodo que transcurre entre Gaugamela y la muerte de Darío.[122]

Es posible que estos espartanos tomados como rehenes hayan sido jóvenes (Plu. *Mor.* 235b: παῖδας), aunque eso debió de provocar resistencias en Esparta[123] y Esqui-

---

[119] *A quo Lacedaemonii nihil aliud quam ut oratores mittere ad regem liceret precati veniam defectionis praeter auctores impetraverunt. Megalopolitanis, quorum urbs obsessa erat a defectionis sociis, Achaei et Elei centum XX talenta dare iussi sunt.*

[120] Din. I.34.

[121] McQueen 1978: 41-45; Baynham 1994: 339-340.

[122] D.S. XVII.73.5-6.

[123] Plu. *Mor.* 64d, 219b, 235b.

nes, en el momento de escribir su *Contra Ctesifonte*, alude a que esos rehenes habrán de ser enviados a Alejandro para que él decida sobre su destino.[124] Sobre cuándo podrían haber sido remitidos a Alejandro ha habido también debates y algunos autores piensan que no habrían partido hasta, al menos, el 329 a.C;[125] un problema viene del hecho, señalado por McQueen, de que se han solido mezclar los rehenes tomados por Antípatro con los embajadores espartanos que tendrían que haber cruzado Asia para negociar con Alejandro y que habrían sido distintos; si los rehenes fueron remitidos a Alejandro, como parece sugerir (dramáticamente) Esquines, es algo que no puede asegurarse.[126] En un momento no precisado, pero seguramente después del final de la guerra, el embajador espartano ante el Gran Rey, Euticles, fue liberado.[127]

Esparta debió de quedar tan maltrecha, incluso a ojos de los propios espartanos, que no se aplicó la ley que castigaba con la pérdida de derechos (ἀτιμία) a los supervivientes de la batalla, algo a lo que se opondrá Acrótato, el hijo del otro rey, Cleómenes II, lo que le costaría importantes enemistades dentro de la ciudad.[128] Es probable que el hermano y sucesor de Agis, Eudámidas, en apariencia contrario a la guerra[129], haya estado a favor de esta medida.

Un indicio de que Alejandro sabía que la guerra había terminado vendría del licenciamiento de los aliados griegos en Ecbatana en el verano del 330 a.C.,[130] antes incluso de la muerte de Darío.

Las consecuencias de la Guerra no parecen haber sido demasiado duras, a pesar de la importante amenaza que había supuesto y de la magnitud de efectivos empleados. A pesar de la tradición que hace a Alejandro minimizar ese combate en comparación con los que él estaba llevando a cabo, el que unos 70.000 hoplitas y miles de jinetes se enfrenten en una batalla no es un episodio menor. Sin embargo, el castigo no es elevado; de los arcadios, solo los más manifiestamente antimacedonios son represaliados, mientras que el resto de los arcadios, que aparecen mencionados por Esquines, desaparecen del resto de las fuentes. Los eleos y los aqueos son condenados a una multa y no se nos dice nada acerca de otros cambios políticos ni de recepción de guarniciones. A partir de algunas de las anécdotas recogidas por Plutarco, da la impresión de que muchos espartanos esperaban que su ciudad fuese atacada por Antípatro, ante lo cual estaban dispuestos a la muerte; pero la propia Esparta, que había dado motivos evidentes para ser castigada con severidad, recibe el derecho de apelar ante el propio Alejandro, aun cuando Antípatro retenga a cincuenta jóvenes escogidos. Pocas dudas pueden caber de que estas medidas tomadas por la Liga de Corinto

[124] Aeschin. III.133.
[125] Badian 1994b: 277.
[126] McQueen 1978: 54-56.
[127] Arr. *An.* II.15.5.
[128] D.S. XIX.70.5; McQueen 1978: 59.
[129] Plu. *Mor.* 220f.
[130] Arr. *An.* III.19.5. Lock (1972: 26) lo cree así y Badian (1994b: 274) lo acepta.

contaban con la aprobación, cuando no con las propias sugerencias o instrucciones, de Antípatro que parece haber propiciado una política conciliadora; el eco de la destrucción de Tebas estaba aún muy próximo y acaso el general pensaba que otro escarmiento de ese tipo podía ser más contraproducente que el espanto inicial que provocaría; además, algún autor ha sugerido que todo ello, y algunos otros episodios solo relacionados de manera indirecta, podían formar parte de un plan diseñado por Antípatro para crearse una posición propia en Grecia.[131]

Quizá por ello habría que preguntarse si todo el mundo en Macedonia veía las cosas de la misma manera y hay algún indicio de que no era así. Quizá una de las más partidarias de una política de dureza era la propia madre de Alejandro, Olimpíade. Es sabida la larga hostilidad que mantuvieron Olimpíade y Antípatro,[132] exacerbada por las acusaciones que, años después, la reina realizó contra el general y su familia de haber urdido el complot que, según ella y sus partidarios, había acabado con la vida de Alejandro, tema en el que ahora no entraré.[133] Que Olimpíade escribía numerosas cartas a su hijo quejándose de muchos de sus amigos lo asegura Plutarco[134] y que en alguna ocasión Antípatro escribió también al rey una extensa carta (μακρὰ ἐπιστολή) quejándose de su madre lo dice el mismo autor;[135] la autenticidad de estas cartas sigue siendo disputada.[136]

En un momento determinado, y en parte a causa de esa enemistad, Olimpíade se retira al Epiro, donde su hija Cleopatra, ejercía la regencia mientras su marido Alejandro, hermano de Olimpíade, se hallaba en Italia. Aunque seguramente Plutarco exagera, este autor dice que «a la sazón Olimpíade y Cleopatra se habían rebelado contra Antípatro y se repartieron el poder. Olimpíade se hizo cargo del Epiro y Cleopatra se quedó en Macedonia» (Plu. *Alex.* 68.4).[137] Plutarco está mezclando acontecimientos porque, en un primer momento, Cleopatra permanece en el Epiro reuniéndose luego su madre con ella para, en un segundo momento, quedarse ella en el Epiro mientras su hija se traslada a Macedonia. Diodoro asegura que Olimpíade se había visto obligada a refugiarse en el Epiro para sustraerse al odio de Antípatro[138] pero no parece que desde allí haya dejado de intrigar contra Antípatro y Arriano recoge la idea de que, al final, vencido por las calumnias (διαβολαί) que vertía su madre contra el general, Alejandro había decidido, poco antes de su muerte, alejar a Antípatro de Macedonia.[139]

---

131 Mendels 1984: 129-149.

132 D.S. XVII.118.1.

133 Domínguez 2016b: 13-33.

134 Plu. *Alex.* 39.7-8.

135 Plu. *Alex.* 39.13.

136 Hamilton 1969: 104-105.

137 Ὅπου καὶ πρὸς Ἀντίπατρον Ὀλυμπιὰς καὶ Κλεοπάτρα στασιάσασαι, διείλοντο τὴν ἀρχήν, Ὀλυμπιὰς μὲν Ἤπειρον, Κλεοπάτρα δὲ Μακεδονίαν παραλαβοῦσα.

138 D.S. XVIII.49.4: ἡ δ' Ὀλυμπιὰς ἐν τοῖς ἐπάνω χρόνοις ἐτύγχανεν εἰς Ἤπειρον πεφευγυῖα διὰ τὴν πρὸς Ἀντίπατρον ἀλλοτριότητα.

139 Arr. *An.* VII.12.5-7.

No se sabe con certeza cuándo se produce el traslado de Olimpíade al Epiro; en el discurso de Esquines contra Ctesifonte se dice que este último había sido elegido hacía poco (πρώην) embajador ante Cleopatra para expresar ante ella la condolencia de los atenienses por la muerte del rey Alejandro el Moloso,[140] pero cuando sus restos son devueltos al Epiro son ya tanto Olimpíade como Cleopatra quienes los reciben;[141] es posible, como ha sugerido Carney,[142] que madre e hija actuasen de común acuerdo, aunque la posición oficial dentro del reino moloso la ostentaba Cleopatra, como esposa del rey fallecido y madre del futuro rey Neoptólemo, aunque otros autores habían mantenido una postura distinta, creyendo que el traslado de Olimpíade al Epiro habría tenido lugar bastante tiempo después (hacia el 324 a.C.),[143] lo que parece poco probable.

Es por estos años, sin que se pueda precisar con demasiado detalle, cuando conocemos un hecho, a partir de un discurso de Hipérides, que puede tener que ver con la situación que se crea bien durante el periodo de la guerra con Agis o quizá poco después. Es un hecho sabido que la relación de Atenas con el oráculo de Dodona es bastante fluida durante buena parte del siglo IV,[144] fuese cierta o no la idea que mantenía Demóstenes de que Delfos «filipizaba».[145] En sintonía con ello, tanto Olimpíade como los atenienses hacen ofrendas en los santuarios situados en sus territorios respectivos. Así, Olimpíade había realizado la ofrenda de una fiale en Atenas a Higieia en favor de su hijo,[146] y los atenienses, en cumplimiento de un oráculo, habían restaurado la estatua de Dione con gran esmero y enviado una embajada pública y un costoso sacrificio.[147] Sin embargo, la contestación de Olimpíade por carta no deja de sorprender a los atenienses: «Que ella es la dueña de la tierra de los molosos, en la que se encuentra el templo; en consecuencia, no debíamos nosotros mover ni una sola cosa de allí» (Hyp. *Eux.* 25).[148] Como argumenta el orador, esta actitud de la reina, que es considerada algo teatral (τὰς τραγῳδίας αὐτῆς) sorprende porque hasta entonces parece haber habido algún tipo de reciprocidad, al menos en el terreno religioso, entre Molosia y Atenas.[149]

Aunque con dudas, la fecha del discurso parece poder situarse en torno al 330 a.C. y, en todo caso, sorprende la virulencia de la reacción de Olimpíade hacia Atenas, lo que hace pensar que la misma no estaba motivada solo por cuestiones estrictamente religiosas, sino que sería una prueba del malestar que mostraba la reina

---

140 Aeschin. III.242.
141 Liv. VIII.24.17.
142 Carney 2000a: 87, 89.
143 Hammond 1989: 33-34.
144 Palagia 2002: 171-180; Eleftheratou 2016: 191-192.
145 Aeschin. III.130.
146 Hyp. *Eux.* 19.
147 Hyp. *Eux.* 24-25.
148 Ἡ χώρα εἴη ἡ Μολοττία αὐτῆς, ἐν ᾗ τὸ ἱερόν ἐστιν· οὔκουν προσῆκεν ἡμᾶς τῶν ἐκεῖ οὐδὲ ἓν κινεῖν.
149 Hyp. *Eux.* 26.

hacia la actitud de Atenas. Como recordábamos antes, cuando fallece Alejandro el Moloso, los atenienses envían una delegación oficial a mostrar sus condolencias a la viuda, lo que sugiere que, desde el punto de vista de Atenas, al menos, no había ningún motivo de enemistad evidente, como lo mostraría también la labor de restauración de la estatua de Dione. Uno de los motivos que pueden explicar la actitud de Olimpíade quizá tenga que ver con el tratamiento que da Antípatro a los sublevados en la reciente guerra contra Agis y, sobre todo, a Atenas.

Es cierto que Atenas no participó en la rebelión, pero, como habíamos visto antes, sí había recibido peticiones para hacerlo en algún momento y, en todo caso, parece haber sido vista por algunos como una de las ciudades que se mantuvieron a la expectativa y no colaboraron de forma decisiva al esfuerzo de guerra macedonio a pesar de sus evidentes capacidades militares y navales aunque, como ya vimos, una parte importante del pueblo estaba dispuesta a ayudar a Agis, algo que evitaron políticos como Démades, Licurgo y el propio Demóstenes. Quizá por ello, la impresión que muchos tenían, y entre ellos la propia Olimpíade, era que Antípatro había sido demasiado suave, tanto en el castigo de los sublevados, como en no ajustar cuentas con los que no habían apoyado de forma clara a los macedonios en su guerra contra Agis. Y, quizá además de haberse quejado ante su hijo e, incluso, ante el propio Antípatro, un recurso del que ella sí podía disponer era restringir las actividades de los extranjeros en un santuario que, como el de Dodona, estaba bajo su control directo, como deja entender, aun a pesar de que su hija Cleopatra pudiese seguir siendo la regente oficial del reino moloso. Que esta preocupación por los intereses de su hijo y quizá una desconfianza hacia Atenas continuó, lo muestra la solicitud (o la exigencia) (ἐξαιτούμενος) que formulará Olimpíade a los atenienses años después, con ocasión del incidente de Harpalo (324 a.C.) para que se lo entregasen, petición que también hizo Antípatro.[150]

Cuando años después, y tras la muerte de Alejandro, Antípatro, vencedor en la Guerra Lamíaca, imponga sus duras condiciones a Atenas,[151] las mismas van en la dirección de neutralizar la capacidad militar de la ciudad pero, sobre todo, atacar al núcleo del sistema democrático ateniense, como muestra, además de la persecución a los líderes responsables de la guerra, y el acantonamiento de una guarnición en Muniquia, el cambio de sistema político: abolición de la democracia y limitación de la ciudadanía plena solo a quienes tuviesen una renta superior a las 2.000 dracmas que se gobernarían de acuerdo con las leyes de Solón y que sumarían 9.000. Al resto del pueblo se les ofrecieron tierras en Tracia, como consecuencia de lo cual y partieron unos 12.000 (o 22.000).[152] Y Diodoro considera que Antípatro actuó con moderación (φιλανθρώπως) (D.S. XVIII.18.4) porque les permite a los atenienses

---

[150] D.S. XVII.108.7.

[151] Atkinson 1981: 46; Baynham 1994: 349-350; Walsh 2015: 1-27.

[152] D.S. XVIII.18.4-5; Plu. *Phoc.* 27-28.

conservar su ciudad, sus bienes y sus riquezas, consideración, que según Plutarco, les merecen también a casi todos los embajadores atenienses enviados ante Antípatro para recibir sus condiciones.[153] Esta política de colocar guarniciones y abolir regímenes democráticos, aunque Diodoro lo expresa de otro modo (reorganizando el cuerpo cívico y estableciendo normas rectas)[154] fue considerado un comportamiento adecuado (ἐπιεικῶς) (D.S. XVIII.18.8). Ciertamente puede parecerlo si la alternativa era haber actuado como hizo Alejandro contra Tebas; el trato hacia los griegos se vio de un modo menos favorable con el paso del tiempo.[155]

Conclusiones

La política de Filipo y de Alejandro con relación a Esparta y Atenas no pudo ser más opuesta; mientras que, como aseguraba Diodoro, los atenienses eran los que recibían más honores (προτιμώμενοι) (XVII.62.7) de entre todos los griegos por parte de Alejandro, los espartanos eran perjudicados y humillados y, casi, ignorados. Arquidamo III, que se había opuesto, sin demasiado éxito, al avance macedonio, opta por marcharse a Italia quizá como medio para disminuir la tensión que su presencia en Esparta podía provocar; no solo Esparta no participa en la batalla de Queronea, sino que en ese mismo momento, el rey pierde la vida en un oscuro enfrentamiento en la lejana Mesapia, con el castigo adicional de no recibir sepultura. La subida al trono de Agis III viene marcada por la invasión de Filipo que introduce aún más agravios en Esparta, a la que priva de parte de su territorio para entregárselos a sus tradicionales enemigos, Argos, Mesene, Megalópolis y Tegea, y esa decisión es, además, sancionada por la Liga de Corinto, a la que Esparta no pertenece. Y, por si fuera poco, la posibilidad de volver a intervenir en Italia le es cerrada a Esparta en beneficio de Alejandro el Moloso, aliado y familiar de Filipo y luego de Alejandro. La política de hostigamiento y humillación a Esparta no cesa y tras la primera victoria de Alejandro en Gránico, al tiempo que consagra en Atenas trescientas panoplias en nombre propio y de los griegos (número sin duda significativo), resalta la exclusión de Esparta de dicha ofrenda.

Es posible que, con esas actuaciones, Alejandro pensase que había conjurado el peligro espartano para siempre y quizá hubiese sido así de no haber sido por su imprudente decisión de disolver su flota. El contraataque persa y la amenaza inminente sobre Grecia es lo que pudo hacer que Agis empezase a buscar el apoyo del Gran Rey para abrir un nuevo frente en el Peloponeso; la entrevista con los generales en Sifnos, sin embargo, coincide con la derrota de Darío en Iso y, a partir de entonces,

---

[153] Plu. *Phoc.* 27.6.

[154] Τὰ πολιτεύματα συναγαγὼν καὶ καλῶς καταστήσας.

[155] Plb. IX.29.1-4.

el levantamiento está condenado al fracaso, aunque eso aún no se sabía. La campaña en Creta, que quizá no acaba del todo bien para Agis, pudo haberle servido, en todo caso, para tratar de convencer a muchos griegos de que estaba dispuesto a oponerse a Alejandro; sus embajadores recorren el mundo griego, incluyendo Atenas, donde sus propuestas calan favorablemente entre el pueblo, uno de cuyos líderes, Demóstenes, se jactaba de haber intrigado entre tesalios y perrebos e, incluso, haber estado detrás del propio levantamiento espartano. No obstante, otros personajes, entre ellos Démades, calman las expectativas del pueblo ante la aparente pasividad de Demóstenes, mucho más sorprendente si en un primer momento se había mostrado favorable a la rebelión. Pero Alejandro había actuado entretanto y había liberado, al segundo intento, a los prisioneros atenienses capturados en Gránico, no sabemos si como agradecimiento por el rechazo ateniense a secundar a Agis o, quizá más probablemente, como resultado de un acuerdo con Atenas para que se mantuviese al margen.

La posible participación de otros partidarios en la rebelión quizá se resintiese de la negativa ateniense, por lo que era necesario un nuevo golpe de efecto, que se consigue con la derrota del comandante macedonio Córrago y con las noticias que llegan de que Antípatro tiene que sofocar una revuelta en Tracia protagonizada por el general Memnón, que seguramente era independiente de la de Agis y tal vez motivada por rivalidades o desavenencias entre ambos generales macedonios. Ese estado de cosas debió de animar a los más decididos a tomar las armas; al final, y posiblemente a pesar de las promesas, solo intervendrán los eleos y casi todos los aqueos. De los arcadios, que quizá se habían comprometido a participar, todos o al menos parte de ellos, solo parecen haber actuado los tegeatas y, quizá no de buen grado. Aun así, la cifra de soldados reunidos es bastante elevada. La única acción bélica llevada a cabo por Agis parece haber sido el sitio de Megalópolis, algo que puede parecer poco efectivo ante la reacción de Antípatro que, con dificultades o no, pero con los fondos, actuales o potenciales, que pudo poner a su disposición Alejandro, acabó reclutando más de 40.000 soldados. Agis seguramente pensaba que si caía Megalópolis, los arcadios se unirían a su bando y tal vez los numerosos indecisos hiciesen lo propio. Sin embargo, el sitio se demoró más de lo previsto y Antípatro llegó hasta Megalópolis. A pesar de los cerca de 70.000 soldados implicados y de que las bajas superaron, por los dos bandos, los 10.000 muertos, Alejandro se permitió considerarla una "batalla de ratones", lo que podía ofender tanto a Antípatro como, tal vez sobre todo, a los espartanos.

Las condiciones de paz fueron bastante moderadas; fueron castigados los participantes directos, aqueos, eleos y tegeatas, y a los espartanos se les permitió exponer ante Alejandro sus alegaciones. De los otros griegos que se mantuvieron indecisos no sabemos nada más, aunque es seguro que ellos, junto con los partidarios de Macedonia, aprobaron en el συνέδριον de la Liga de Corinto, las medidas que Antípatro había sugerido. Antípatro fue partidario de la moderación en esta ocasión, quizá consciente de que una actitud más dura podría haber provocado, quizá a corto plazo, una sublevación mayor. Otros no lo veían así y Olimpíade, la madre del rey, quizá desautorizada en sus quejas por su propio hijo, lo más que pudo hacer fue prohibir a los atenienses que volviesen a hacer lo que quisiesen en el santuario de Dodona, aunque se mantuvo vigilante hacia Atenas, de la que seguía sospechando.

Este levantamiento, que como dice Justino fue suprimido en su mismo inicio (*in ipso ortu*) (XII.1.9), mostró que el impacto de Queronea y, sobre todo, de Tebas, pesaba aún demasiado en el recuerdo de los griegos. Alejandro, y su general Antípatro, supieron administrar la fuerza y las concesiones para evitar que la revuelta fuese a más, pero, posiblemente, fue responsabilidad de Alejandro al disolver la flota y no poner trabas a las iniciativas navales persas, el haber dado una salida a una Esparta que, según pensaba Alejandro, había quedado por completo fuera del escenario político griego, aislada y, lo que era peor, humillada.

Hay un consenso bastante generalizado a la hora de pensar que, después del 330, y al tiempo que Alejandro iniciaba su camino hacia el Oriente, dejó de preocuparse de modo directo de la situación de Grecia, aunque siguiese recibiendo informaciones; en cierto modo, y tras la recuperación del control naval en el Egeo, la revuelta de Agis III fue el principal problema de importancia que había surgido en Grecia y la batalla de Megalópolis había acabado conjurándolo. Ahora sí podía dejar atrás a Grecia no volviéndose a ocuparse de forma directa de ella hasta su regreso a Babilonia cinco años después. Las decisiones tomadas en ese momento habrían ido madurando en su mente durante ese tiempo y aprovecharon las lecciones aprendidas en estos primeros años de su estancia en Asia.

The Hungry Years: Athenian Grain Supply and the Impact of Alexander's Conquest of Greece*

Borja Antela-Bernárdez
(Universitat Autònoma de Barcelona)

The history of Athens during the last third of the 4th century BC contains many strong contrasts. The defeats suffered in 338 and 321 BC against Macedonia meant a hard and definitive strike and a turning point in the History of Ancient Greece as a whole, and particularly in the development of Athens. In this respect, the period between Chaeronea and the Lamian War, usually called the Lycurgan age, has often been considered as prosperous for Athens, as a consequence of the management of the city by Lycurgus himself,[1] to such an extent that it was observed by scholars as a kind of Silver Age,[2] succeeding the Golden age of Pericles and the Empire. Never-

---

* This paper had a long life before being published. The first aim was to study in depth what Lindsay Adams wrote in 1996, and I understood his paper as a first step to review Alexander's impact. I began to consider some of these ideas around 2011. Later, I discussed the first stage of the research with some colleagues at an internal workshop organized by Prof. Antoni Ñaco del Hoyo, and I kept working after publishing some preliminary perspectives (Antela-Bernárdez 2016a, 2020a; Verdejo Manchado / Antela-Bernárdez 2021). I owe a great deal to the colleagues and friends who helped me to think and discuss the details and sources, such as the kind Yossi Roisman, my closest colleague Marc Mendoza and my friend Javier Verdejo Manchado. Joseph Roisman shared with me some of his thoughts during a meal at the UAB during the Congress of 2017. My dear colleague Laura Sancho also read every paper before being published, and I also enjoy the brilliant ideas and friendship of Tim Howe, who helped me with some of his papers during the Pandemic confinement of 2020. To everyone involved in this long path of inquiries and discussions, I wish to thank you very much. I wish to remember here all the friends and ties I have made with my colleagues around the world during the last few years. The errors, probably many, on these pages are, however, no one's fault but mine.

[1] Despite his important role in Athens, the bibliography about Lycurgus is quite short. For some basic works, see Durrbach 1890: esp. 1-114; Colin 1928: 189-200; Conomis 1961: 72-152; Renehan 1970; Salamone 1976; Humphreys 1985; Merker 1986; Oikonomides 1986; Mossé 1989; Brun 2005b.

[2] Mitchel 1965.

theless, during the times of Lycurgus, despite its healthy economy, the city suffered from serious and repeated crises caused by the difficulties to obtain stable channels of grain supply, with the subsequent consequences of hunger and shortages.

Nevertheless, although we have 'many' sources for the period, it is difficult to specify a clear and exact chronology for these crises and shortages. In his classic work on the subject, Peter Garnsey[3] defended a series of hypotheses, usually accepted as the absolute reference, although Garnsey seems to offer just a handful of ideas and proposals, but not a certain chronological list of facts. Actually, he does not even show all the evidence to defend his opinions, nor does he analyse in detail a period as complex as the Lycurgan age, when the Greek world suffered from a convulsive process resulting from the submission to Macedonian authority under the rule of Alexander, and the subsequent conquest and expansion to the East, significantly shaking up the whole Greek way of living. Our aim here is to review some of Garnsey's perspectives to try to untangle the relationship between goods, markets and foreign affairs (i.e., the war against Persia) during the age of Lycurgus and Alexander (338-321 BC).

In the light of the evidence, Garnsey points out at least five great crises in grain supply and shortages, which meant hunger, in Greece for our period. The first one is probably the result of Chaeronea, as seems to be shown by the lethal speech of Lycurgus' *Against Leocrates*. In this account, we discover how Leocrates himself had fled from Athens in the city's darkest hour, facing the threat of an imminent siege by Philip of Macedon. Leocrates travelled to Rhodes, where he spread the word that Athens had been captured. As a result of Leocrates' activities, the ships with cargo bound for Athens were seized, retained and even boarded, and the grain that should have travelled to feed the Athenians was redirected to other destinations.[4] Maybe when the truth about the situation in Athens was known, the flux of trade would have recommenced.[5] Nevertheless, one may suspect that this stoppage of trade to Athens probably not only worsened the situation of Athens on confronting Philip, but also represented important pressure on the Athenians to negotiate the terms of surrender with the Macedonian king. Also, the grain forced to return to Rhodes, whose initial destination was Athens, was surely sold in other markets (by the Rhodians themselves or by other merchants), before the news about the real situation in Athens

---

[3] Garnsey 1988: 150-164.

[4] Lycurg. *Leocr*. 18: «He landed and entered Rhodes, where, as if he were bringing good news of great successes for his country, he announced that the main city had been captured when he left it, that the Piraeus was blockaded and that he was the only one who had escaped, feeling no shame at speaking of his country's ruin as the occasion of his own safety. The Rhodians took his news so seriously that they manned triremes and brought in their merchantmen; and the traders and shipowners who had intended to sail to Athens unloaded their corn and other cargoes there, because of Leocrates» (transl. Burt 1962). On this speech and Macedonian Hegemony, see Antela-Bernárdez 2016a, 2019.

[5] Lycurg. *Leocr*. 21.

were known, and therefore probably after that, there was not much grain to be transported to the Athenian markets.

Likewise, although we can consider the trade with Rhodes as one of the main markets for food to Athens since the '30s[6], like most of the 4th century, the main grain dealer for the Athenians was the kingdom of Bosphorus. This lets us consider the shortage crisis in Chaeronea as not actually resulting from the absence of grain, but probably from the serious rise in prices. As in our other cases of study the problematics of our evidence does not allow us to go further than conjectures.

The words of Lycurgus against Leocrates deserve special attention. First, the aim of the speech was not to describe historical events, but to stress certain facts for the audience during a judgement. The author attempts to insult the accused, showing his guilt, although he does not seem, despite Lycurgus' efforts, to have infringed any Athenian law. Perhaps, this is why Lycurgus stresses the faults of Leocrates as a traitor and responsible for the sufferings of the Athenians after Chaeronea.

On the other hand, the speech should possibly be linked with another different context, as it was the time not of Chaeronea but of the prosecution of Leocrates, six or, probably, eight years later, in 331/0 BC, when Athens and the whole of Greece were dealing with a complex context and difficulties concerning the management and delivery of food and grain supply.

The second crisis defended by Garnsey is dated to 335, in connection with the Theban uprising and Alexander's harsh response. In this respect, we know that some people like the merchant Chrysipus tried to help Athens with donations and services.[7] Observing carefully the context in detail, and the Athenian position during the conflict, we know that Athens decided not to take part in the Theban rebellion, like the other Greeks, waiting for the result of the siege. Only when Alexander succeeded, and Thebes was razed to the ground, did the Athenians decide to offer shelter to the Theban refugees, gaining Alexander's full attention. Thus, Alexander asked Athens to deliver some of his political enemies, who were actually prominent Athenian politicians opposed to Macedon.[8] The situation was probably tense, at least for a short period, maybe some weeks, and this probably caused an impact on the markets. The Athenian involvement in the aftermath of the Theban rebellion surely moved most merchants bound for Athens to think twice before landing in the Piraeus. However, this did not last more than a few weeks, which leads us to observe the possible impact of these events on the markets with caution. The situation did represent a rise in prices, probably as a result of speculation by some merchants, as the testimony of

---

[6] Maybe linked with the Egyptian grain trade route, as we can infer from Demosthenes' *Against Dionysodorus*. Another possible origin of this grain captured by the Rhodians could be Sicily: Garnsey 1988: 153-154.

[7] D. XXXIV.38-39.

[8] Landuci Gattinoni 2008.

Chrysippus seems to stress: Chrysippus donated cash and not goods, as would have been the case if the problem was caused by a shortage of grain.

Another factor to bear in mind when dealing with the critical times of 338 and 335 for Athenian grain supply is piracy. In my opinion, defining piracy in the ancient world is a quite complex mission. A good example of the problems with piracy is shown by a reference in Demosthenes, who mentions the inability of Philip to import or export goods from Macedon because of the action of pirates.[9] They seem to have been the same people who were responsible for blocking the Macedonian ports, again in another reference in Demosthenes.[10] Who they are, and mainly, how they confronted the most powerful government in the Greek world of the time, are difficult questions to answer.

Thanks to Demosthenes' words, we can observe, at least, that these pirates may have no relationship with Athens, although at specific moments they shared interests with the Athenians. On the other hand, we can consider as pirates the Rhodian ships which had been involved in the boarding of ships with grain for Athens as a result of Leocrates' account of the consequences of Chaeronea for the Athenians in 338. Unfortunately, an overall picture of this problematic situation is hard to build, although we have some information about it. Of special interest is, for our purpose, the naval campaign led by Diotimus, the son of Diopeithes, whose mission was to fight the pirates.[11] Diotimus received honours and public awards, promoted by Lycurgus himself, during the Archonship of Ctesicles, that is to say, in 334/3,[12] which means that the naval campaign took place before this year, probably in 335.[13] This coincidence allows us to suspect a link between the piracy activities and the crisis resulting from the Theban rebellion. On the other hand, we do not know how this campaign occurred, whether any kind of 'military' activity had to be allowed by the Corinthian League, for the date we consider here. Nevertheless, this campaign shows, first, clear maritime insecurity at the time Alexander's campaign began, and the thrill this represented for Alexander's logistics at the start of his invasion of Asia; and, second, the existence of military actions (at least, this one) outside the Corinthian League, in so far as we can hardly consider Diotimus a probable candidate for a mission related to the Macedonian hegemony because of his clear political position against Macedon. Furthermore, Lycurgus would not have celebrated so much the triumph of a successful pro-Macedonian campaign against the pirates if this had taken place in the framework of the Macedonian mechanisms of domination, such as the Corinthian League. In fact, we have no evidence that linked Diotimus' mission with the League

---

[9] D. XVIII.145.

[10] D. XIX.315.

[11] Plu. *Lycurg.* 52.

[12] *EM* 7177; cf. Schwenk 1985: 134-136, with full references concerning this inscription. A recent new analysis of the data can be found in Verdejo Manchado / Antela-Bernárdez 2021.

[13] IG II[2] 1623.

of Corinth. To sum up, the success of Diotimus would mean the establishment of some security on the seas, warranting the circulation of goods for the sake of Greece.

Returning to the pirates, it seems probable enough to suppose a link between the pirates and the campaign against Macedon driven by Persia as a counterattack against Alexander's victorious advance in Asia. We know of Amphoterus' mission in the Aegean, maybe in relation to the third famine crisis of Garnsey's interpretation, around 330/29 BC. The context of these facts is, again, highly complex. First, we know the activities of Alexander on the coast of Asia Minor in 334/3. The conquest of key locations like Miletus and Halicarnassus led the Persians to organize a counteroffensive in the rearguard of the Macedonian army, under the leadership of Memnon of Rhodes, with the aim of isolating the Macedonians in Asia, and returning control of the seas to Persian hands, in order to promote a focus of rebellion against the Macedonian hegemony throughout Greece. This would be for sure a serious blow for Alexander's plans. This Persian counterstrike has received some attention from scholars,[14] but some questions are still open to discussion. For our aims, the fight for control of the Dardanelles, the Thermaic Gulf, and the islands of Mytilene, Tenedos,[15] Chios and Siphnos, is of great importance, that is to say, the main grain route from the Bosphorus to Athens. Another key point at this time would probably have been Crete.[16] The clash for the sea took place between 334 and 333, while the war of Agis and Sparta against Macedon lasted until 331. In this context, the mission of Amphoterus against the pirates, only recorded by Curtius,[17] makes sense for 332. The possibility of linking these pirates near Crete in Amphoterus' mission with those faced by Diotimus is strong enough to consider it. In this respect, the campaign by Diotimus seems to be a first step in the preparations of Alexander's campaign, while the mission of Amphoterus seems to be directed against some small remnants of the Persian army resulting from the maritime counteroffensive of Memnon. Nevertheless, these details are also related to the shortage of grain defended by Grainger for 330/29, just one year after the end of Agis' war on the Greek mainland. It seems hard to me to believe that this shortage of grain and consequently the famine that resulted from it were as short in time as Garnsey argues, and I am tempted to think that it lasted some time longer. Again, we can go back to Lycurgus' *Against Leocrates*, a trial that probably took place in 331, if not even later, but really close to the time of Agis' war. Thus, the criticism of Leocrates' behaviour, and especially his responsibility in the shortage of grain and famine, appear to us as an obvious warning, clearly linked with the times of crisis and maritime strife (333/2) and land war (332/1) experienced

---

[14] Burn 1952: 81-84; Bosworth 1975: 27-43; Ruzicka 1988: 131-151.

[15] [D.] XVII.20.

[16] Cf. Curt. IV.1.39-40. On the other hand, Rhodes, the main agent for the grain trade in the Mediterranean (as we have seen through *Against Leocrates*), remained initially neutral, but finally decided to take part on Alexander's side, sending him ten triremes. Arr. *An.* II.20; Curt. IV.5.4.

[17] Curt. IV.8.15.

by the Greeks who, undoubtedly, encountered difficulties concerning the grain trade and famines around Greece.

A well-known text, falsely attributed to Demosthenes, seems to indicate, for example, that some needs of war allowed the Macedonians to seize grain,[18] and we must therefore consider that the Persians probably did the same, either to solve army needs or as a measure to ensure or guarantee the loyalty of their allies.

Chrysippus talks about three moments of crisis in which he and his relatives helped the Athenians, and it seems clear that the first of these was related to the Theban rebellion. The other two moments, nevertheless, are chronologically obscure, and we can only offer hypotheses. However, if we consider the date of the speech, 328/7,[19] we can trace the details of a possible chronology: one would probably be that of 330/29, and the other, maybe, can be dated to the same 328/7. However, as far as Chrysippus talks about past crises, it does not seem likely that his assessment can refer to the speech's present time. Likewise, we have defended that what Garnsey dated in 330/29 should in fact be considered from a wider scope within a serious long war crisis, between 334 and 331, which provoked continuous shortages in the delivery of goods, mainly grain. In the light of this, we can consider the last phases of this critical moment as the hardest ones, with a rise in prices[20], shortages[21] and famines, in what we can call a long crisis. Finally, then, the third crisis of Chrysippus' speech may be dated to the year before, in 328.[22] On the other hand, both the maritime activities of Diotimus in 335/4 and the interest of Persia and Macedon to control the Aegean route during the period 333-331, clearly seem to show, instead, that the main route for grain to Athens, as it was throughout the 4th century, was mainly the Bosphorus. Some exceptional measures stress this point. Thus, during the '40s, the relation between the Bosphorus and Athens suffered from some decline.[23] We know the existence of a decree dated around 344/3 in honour of Paerisades,[24] that reflects that at least the desire of Athens was to maintain the friendship with the kingdom of Bosphorus. Nevertheless, this may have changed during the '30s. Aeschines' aggressive assessment against Demosthenes, calling him the descendant of some Bosphoreans,[25] may be proof of the decline of this

[18] [D.] XVII.20: «Now, men of Athens, you have most distinctly seen this done by the Macedonians; for they have grown so arrogant that they forced all our ships coming from the Black Sea to put in at Tenedos, and under one pretence or another refused to release them until you passed a decree to man and launch a hundred war-galleys instantly, and you put Menestheus in command».

[19] Garnsey 1988: 155.

[20] Milns 1999.

[21] D. XXXIV.39.

[22] In D. XXXIV.8, Chrysippus explains that during the same year of the trial, Paerisades had to face a war against the Scythians, usually dated for 327.

[23] Garnsey 1988: 153.

[24] IG II^2 212; cf. Engen 2010: 308.

[25] Aeschin. III.171-172.

friendship between Athens and the Bosphorus.[26] At the same time, the exemption of taxes that Paerisades offered those merchants bringing grain to Athens, dated in 327, shows the renewal of the understanding between the two governments.[27] Nevertheless, these changes in the perception of the relation between Athens and the Bosphorus led the Athenians to look for other dealers and markets to ensure the grain supply, initially during the '30s and most often during the '20s. One of these 'new' suppliers was Egypt.

On the other hand, in the speech *Against Phormio*, we can read a harsh description of a crisis easily datable to 327:

> «And he did this, men of the jury, though he was resident at Athens, and had a wife and children here, and although the laws have prescribed the severest penalties if anyone resident at Athens should transport grain to any other place than to the Athenian market; besides, he did this at a critical time, when those of you who dwelt in the city were having their barley-meal measured out to them in the Odeum, and those who dwelt in Peiraeus were receiving their loaves at an obol each in the dockyard and in the long-porch, having their meal measured out to them a gallon at a time, and being nearly trampled to death» (D. XXXIV.37).[28]

The text clearly shows the intense hardness of this crisis, especially if we remember that this was the time of the law forbidding the transport of grain outside Athens, a fact that led us to consider the possibility that this shortage probably began the year before.[29]

In relation to this crisis of 328 or 327, some evidence could be linked to a better understanding of this context. First, we know that Alexander was then in the East, far from the Aegean. The government of Egypt was in the hands of Cleomenes of Naucratis, an obscure character. Of him, we know that in a year of low harvest that produced

---

[26] Engen 2010: 308-309; *contra* Garnsey 1988: 151.

[27] D. XXXIV.36-37: «Now, men of the jury, if it were toward myself only that Lampis were showing contempt, it would be nothing to cause surprise; but in reality he has acted far more outrageously than Phormio toward you all. For when Paerisades had published a decree in Bosporus that whoever wished to transport grain to Athens for the Athenian market might export it free of duty, Lampis, who was at the time in Bosporus, obtained permission to export grain and the exemption from duty in the name of the state; and having loaded a large vessel with grain, carried it to Acanthus and there disposed of it, –he, who had made himself the partner of Phormio here with our money. And he did this, men of the jury, though he was resident at Athens, and had a wife and children here, and although the laws have prescribed the severest penalties if anyone resident at Athens should transport grain to any other place than to the Athenian market; besides, he did this at a critical time, when those of you who dwelt in the city were having their barley-meal measured out to them in the Odeum,1 and those who dwelt in Peiraeus were receiving their loaves at an obol each in the dockyard and in the long-porch, having their meal measured out to them a gallon at a time, and being nearly trampled to death» (transl. Murray 1939). However, although this could have been a XXXIV, not extended to other years, it is also a clue to question the argued harmony of the relationships between both states.

[28] Transl. DeWitt 1946.

[29] This fact can explain the magnanimous exemption of taxes Paerisades gave to Athens.

hunger, Cleomenes forbade the exports of Egyptian grain, and although later he finally allowed the grain to be exported, he raised the prices with a high tax, gaining a great benefit on selling a small part of the grain.[30] This impressive task of Cleomenes as a speculator has a better clue when he raises the prices to a level of 32 drachmas for each *medimnos*.[31] This measure had a terrible impact on the capacity of Greek cities to ensure their grain supply. Also, a speech of the Demosthenic Corpus, with a dubious date[32] of 322, reveals a kind of trade network managed by Cleomenes:

> «This Dionysodorus, men of Athens, and his partner Parmeniscus came to us last year in the month Metageitnion, and said that they desired to borrow money on their ship on the terms that she should sail to Egypt and from Egypt to Rhodes or Athens, and they agreed to pay the interest for the voyage to either one of these ports. We answered, men of the jury, that we would not lend money for a voyage to any other port than Athens, and so they agreed to return here, and with this understanding they borrowed from us three thousand drachmae on the security of their ship for the voyage out and home; and they entered into a written agreement to these terms. In the contract Pamphilus here was named the lender; but I, although not mentioned, was a sharer in the loan. In accordance with this agreement, men of the jury, Dionysodorus here and his partner Parmeniscus, when they had got the money from us, despatched their ship from Athens to Egypt. Parmeniscus sailed in charge of the ship; Dionysodorus remained at Athens. All these men, I would have you know, men of the jury, were underlings and confederates of Cleomenes, the former ruler of Egypt, who from the time he received the government did no small harm to your state, or rather to the rest of the Greeks as well, by buying up grain for resale and fixing its price, and in this he had these men as his confederates. Some of them would despatch the stuff from Egypt, others would sail in charge of the shipments, while still others would remain here in Athens and dispose of the consignments. Then those who remained here would send letters to those abroad advising them of the prevailing prices, so that if grain were dear in your market, they might bring it here, and if the price should fall, they might put in to some other port. This was the chief rea-

[30] [Arist.] *Oec.* 1352a.

[31] [Arist.] *Oec.* 1352b. We must keep in mind that D. XXXIV.39 mentions the price of 16 drachms at a moment prior to the crisis. The price of 32 drachms by Cleomenes meant he doubled the price.

[32] In my opinion, many pieces of evidence allow us to doubt the date of 322 for this speech. Firstly, the text mentions on two occasions that the prosecutors had been waiting two years for their money (D. LVI.16.34). If the speech was delivered in 322, the facts would then be dated around 324. The period of 324/3 in Athens is very complex due to the conflict between Athens and Macedon after Harpalus' flight. Bearing in mind that Harpalus kept a great amount of money with him, if any kind of price rise took place in Athens, it seems strange that Harpalus was not mentioned in the speech. Also, the kind of words dedicated to Cleomenes, an officer of Alexander's administration, seems strange if we confront them with the silence about Harpalus. The text mentions Cleomenes, but says nothing about Alexander or his death in 323, nor about Ptolemy or his deposition of Cleomenes, all these facts closely linked with what the speech explains. The silence seems, then, very controversial. On Harpalus, cf. Badian 1961; Howe 2020. Also, Antela-Bernárdez 2020a.

> son, men of the jury, why the price of grain advanced; it was due to such letters and conspiracies. Well then, when these men despatched their ship from Athens, they left the price of grain here pretty high, and for this reason they submitted to have the clause written in the agreement binding them to sail to Athens and to no other port. Afterwards, however, men of the jury, when the ships from Sicily had arrived, and the prices of grain here were falling, and their ship had reached Egypt, the defendant straightway sent a man to Rhodes to inform his partner Parmeniscus of the state of things here, well knowing that his ship would be forced to touch at Rhodes. The outcome was that Parmeniscus, the defendant's partner, when he had received the letter sent by him and had learned the price of grain prevailing here, discharged his cargo of grain at Rhodes and sold it there in defiance of the agreement, men of the jury, and of the penalties to which they had of their own will bound themselves, in case they should commit any breach of the agreement, and in contempt also of your laws which ordain that shipowners and supercargoes shall sail to the port to which they have agreed to sail or else be liable to the severest penalties» (D. LVI.5-10).[33]

This evidence reveals a great amount of information. First, it is worth recalling here the details of the text *Against Phormio*, especially on the question of the exemption of taxes offered by Paerisades that some merchants, like Lapis and Phormio, used to buy grain at a low price and after that, they sold it where they wanted. Probably, in the case of Lapis, who sold this grain in Acanthus, he had already gained a good profit in the Athenian market. Likewise, delivering his cargo to Acanthus, Lampis acted illegally, in Athenian terms, as far as the transport of grain to anywhere else was forbidden, due to the constant risks of famine and shortage. We must infer here that the prices in Acanthus were probably higher than those of Athens. Thus, Lapis looked for his best benefit, a kind of behaviour that, as we have seen, seems to be widespread among the merchants during the '20s in Greece, if we compare the information of *Against Phormio* and *Against Dionisodorus*.

Secondly, Egypt seems to have been the main supplier of grain for Greece during the 320s. In the agreement between Dionisodorus and his partners, later his prosecutors, they pointed out that the journey had to be from Athens to Egypt and back,[34] although Dionisodorus' aims had probably been to start a route between Athens, Egypt and Rhodes.[35] Likewise, after his visit to Egypt, Dionisodorus decided to go to Rhodes, where he found better prices than the Athenian ones. Despite the prosecutors' opposition, it seems that the ship of Dionisodorus maintained a continuous route between Egypt and Rhodes, always trading with grain.

---

[33] Transl. DeWitt 1946.

[34] Maybe the ban on importing grain to ports outside Attica for Athenians was not in force at the time, or on the contrary it can be also an element to accuse Dionisodorus by his prosecutors.

[35] D. LVI.5.

Both the speech of Demosthenes *Against Dionisodorus* and the *Economics* of Pseudo-Aristotle share a common view of the responsibility of Cleomenes of Naucratis in shortages and control of grain market prices. We hear for the first time about Cleomenes during Alexander's visit to Egypt in 332. It is quite difficult to know whether the speculative activities of Cleomenes began so early, but the coincidence between the time of his first appearance in 332 and the context of conflict and shortage resulting from the war with Agis is not deniable.

On the other hand, Cleomenes' actions were for sure related to the economic policies ordered by Alexander himself. We know, of course, of the excesses committed by some of Alexander's governors while he was far away, conquering the Far East. Nevertheless, when Alexander came back, he punished all those behaviours, and we know nothing about punishing Cleomenes. Also, the strong network led by Cleomenes on controlling the grain trade in the Eastern Mediterranean seems to imply a great political power rather than a simple governor of a conquered region within Alexander's empire. Furthermore, we know of the aim of Cleomenes to gain Alexander's favour by managing some buildings in Alexandria. After Alexander's death, Cleomenes survived the purge and the first distributions of territories in Babylon between the Diadochi, and therefore he remained at the head of Egypt until the arrival of Ptolemy, who found a sum of 8,000 talents in the Egyptian treasury.[36]

This kind of accumulation of wealth by Cleomenes was not unique among the men Alexander put in charge of economic matters, like for example the famous Harpalus. What is surprising here is that this wealth did not seem to be for Cleomenes' own sake, but for the treasury of the satrapy he managed.[37] Although the criticism the Greeks made of Cleomenes' speculation did not link it with Alexander, I guess Cleomenes, like other similar characters such as Antimenes of Rhodes, was just a field agent applying taxation and measures that had the consent of Alexander himself, a measure that we must be sure came from the King's own administration and economic planning.

To sum up, this paper has shown the close links between some critical moments in the everyday life of the Greeks, mainly the Athenians, during Alexander's campaign, first as a consequence of the war against the Persians, and later of Alexander's own desire to collect taxes and obtain profits to manage his own projects.

---

[36] D.S. XVIII.14.1.

[37] Actually, Alexander appointed Cleomenes as the chief of the Egyptian economy, in charge of the collection of taxes: Arr. *An.* III.5.4. On Cleomenes, see Mendoza 2020. About the other officials of Alexander's economic administration, cf. Antela-Bernárdez 2021b.

The Thessalian Lobby

Marc Mendoza
(Universitat de Lleida)

Thessaly during Philip and Alexander's reigns

According to Hesiod, Makedon and Magnes were brothers, sons of Zeus and Thyia.[1] Macedonia and Thessaly had a relationship full of ups and downs, like any fraternal relationship. The decentralized Thessalian system meant that the relations with the Macedonian kings were often established in a multilateral way by their cities and the big aristocratic clans ruling within each one. The alternation in the regional hegemony among the different Thessalian families was, in part, the main reason behind the changing nature of the relationship between Thessaly and Macedonia. This paper does not aim to reconstruct the complete political interaction between the two regions through the ages,[2] but rather will predominantly focus on Larissa —and the Aleuadae clan— and Pharsalus, the main political Thessalian actors during Philip and Alexander's reigns.

The Macedonian monarchy and the Aleuadae had already been long-time allies when Alexander became the Macedon king, with noteworthy precedents during the reigns of Archelaus,[3] Amyntas III,[4] Alexander

---

[1] Hes. *CW* F 3 *apud* Const. Porphyr. *De Them.* II.48b.

[2] For a complete history of Thessaly, see Westlake 1935; Sordi 1958.

[3] Thrasym. F 2; [Herod. Att.] *Peri Politeias*; Arist. *Pol.* 1311b. Around 400 BCE, the Aleuadae summoned Archelaus to help them against a more moderate faction. After seizing Larissa and restoring the Aleuadae to power, the Larissean family conferred upon him citizenship and a recently-gained territory (possibly Perrhaebia). Archelaus installed a garrison in the city and took Larissean hostages. See Westlake 1935: 51-59; Sordi 1958: 148-151; Hammond / Griffith 1979: 139-141; Borza 1990: 164-165. If not otherwise stated, all the dates in this paper are BCE.

[4] D.S. XIV.92.3. After having been dethroned by the Illyrians, Amyntas III was re-established in 391 thanks to Thessalian intervention. Probably, Medius of Larissa, the mightiest man of the region at the time, was the one who headed the Thessalian aid (D.S. XIV.82.5). This Medius was possibly the grandfather of

II[5] and Philip II.[6] Nevertheless, the relationship between Philip and this family was, by far, more complex.[7] He intervened several times in Thessalian politics during his reign and it is even difficult to assess when he first meddled in his southern neighbours' affairs[8]. Due to his first interventions, in around 357, Philip married two Thessalian women:[9] Nikesipolis of Pherae[10] and Philinna of Larissa, maybe an Aleuadae herself.[11] During the Third Sacred War, the tensions between these women's hometowns escalated and Philip interfered again in Thessaly. Philip was called into the country to counteract the growing influence of Lycophron, tyrant of Pherae. Philip fought and defeated Onomarchus' Phocidians, who, in turn, had been summoned by Lycophron.[12] In the next year, the Macedonian king resumed his fight against Pherae and its Phocidian allies, who were vanquished again.[13] Besides the victory itself, the most relevant fact is that Philip was nominated *archon/tagos* of the Thessalian League. During the following years, the king continued pulling the strings in the region through some agents, like the Aleuadae Eudicus and Simus.[14] Thessaly became another battlefield where Macedon and Athens struggled for the leadership of the

---

Alexander III's Companion (see below). See Westlake 1935: 59-66; Sordi 1958: 151-155; Hammond / Griffith 1979: 172-173; Borza 1990: 182.

[5] D.S. XV.61, 67.3-4; Plu. *Pelop*. 26. The Aleuadae asked Alexander II for help to get rid of the tyrant of Pherae. The Macedonian king took over Larissa and promised to relinquish the conquered Thessalian cities to the Larisseans. However, Alexander quickly changed his mind and kept the cities under his control, installing Macedonian garrisons. Then, the Thessalians turned to Pelopidas, who freed those towns and even reached Macedonia in his advance. After the end of the hostilities, Philip, Alexander's brother and future king, was sent to Thebes as a hostage. See Westlake 1935: 51-59; Sordi 1958: 201-214; Hammond / Griffith 1979: 180-181; Borza 1990: 189-190.

[6] For a brief resume of further cultural, religious and, especially, political and institutional affinities between Thessaly and Macedon, see Hatzopoulos 1994.

[7] To write this summarized account of the relationship between Philip and Thessaly, the information is mainly derived from Westlake 1935: 168-216; Sordi 1958: 230-301, 348-368; Hammond / Griffith 1979: 218-230, 267-281, 285-295, 523-544; Borza 1990: 219-221.

[8] It is possible that Philip's first intervention in Thessaly took place in around 358/7. The chronology of the different episodes concerning Philip's Thessalian policy has been widely discussed: Ehrhardt 1967; Griffith 1970; Hammond / Griffith 1979: 218-230; Martin 1981; 1982. Since it is completely out of this paper's scope to address it, the different events will be presented preferably following a relative chronology.

[9] Satyrus F 21 (Kumaniecki) *apud* Athen. XIII.557b-d; cf. Tronson 1984.

[10] Carney 2000a: 60-61. She was the mother of the famous Thessalonike, 'Thessalian victory'.

[11] Philinna of Larissa was the mother of the future king Philip III Arrhidaeus. Though some sources claim that she was a dancer or a prostitute (Iust. IX.7.8; XIII.2.11; Plu. *Alex*. 77.7), this would be due to later propaganda —probably against his son during the Diadochi period. Given the obvious political utility of arranging matrimonies with both the most preeminent —and rival— cities of Thessaly, it is very likely that she was a high-birth woman, probably a member of the Aleuadae clan. His son was raised in the court and he finally reached the Macedonian throne, something unlikely if his mother had been a mere concubine. See Griffith 1970: 70-71; Tronson 1984: 121-122; Borza 1990: 219-220; Carney 2000a: 61-62.

[12] D.S. XVI.34.5-35.6.

[13] Iust. XI.3.2.

[14] D. XVIII.48.

Hellenic world. When the Third Sacred War finally came to an end, the Thessalians were the main 'promoters' of Philip's inclusion in the Amphictyony. This act was generously rewarded from inside this institution afterwards.[15] Although the Aleuadae had been the ones who opened Thessaly's doors to Philip, the growing and unstoppable interventionism of the king eroded their former privileged status and Philip finally turned his favouritism to Pharsalus. Between 344 and 342,[16] the Macedonian monarch meddled once more in Thessaly with the pretext of putting the tyrants out of power.[17] The Aleuadae, who were immersed in a clan's internal crisis,[18] were the most affected —or, at least, their most hostile faction against Philip.[19] After his last intervention, the Macedonian king engaged an administrative and constitutional reform, through the establishment of decadarchies and, not long after, of tetrarchies. This reorganization aimed to weaken the cities' and dynasties' power by reshaping the Thessalian relations' map. The two known tetrarchs were from Pharsalus.[20] This confirms that Pharsalians then rose to the privileged position that the Aleuadae had held during the first years of Philip's reign.

With this previous oscillating relationship, Alexander came to the Macedonian throne. One of his first objectives was to be nominated Thessalian *archon*, like his father before him.[21] He achieved this with no noteworthy difficulties and it paved the way for his subsequent election as Greek *hegemon* in Corinth.[22] It is very likely that part of the success of his request to the Thessalian *koinon* was due to his reconciliation with the Aleuadae. Even though their relationship with Philip ended badly, this does not imply that Alexander followed in his father's footsteps. Just as his position at the head of the Thessalian League was personal and not hereditary —and thus had to be ratified—, his relations followed the same path. The Aleuadae had been traditional allies of the Macedonian kings and it was worth re-establishing good relations in order to secure his power in the neighbouring region.

---

[15] See Westlake 1935: 188-189.

[16] See Squillace 2000: 84 n. 3.

[17] D.S. XVI.69.8; Schol. Dem. *Olynth.* (II) XIV.66 n. 103a; Isoc. II.20-21; Speus. *Socr.* 28.3; D. VI.21-22, VII.32, IX.12-26, 18.48, XIX.260-262, 320; Theopompus (*FGrH* 115) F 81, 208, 209. On the propagandistic scope of the episode, by both pro- and anti-Macedonian sources, see Squillace 2000.

[18] Arist. *Pol.* 1306a. Sordi 1958: 364-368 postulated that the reason behind the crisis could have been the bloody familiar revenge which had Eurydamas, son of Medius, and Simus as the main protagonists. After Philip's intervention, the latter, who had become the tyrant of Larissa (he even issued coinage: Gardner / Poole 1883: 31 nº. 77-78, pl. 6. 9), was expelled.

[19] Polyaen. IV.2.11.

[20] See Westlake 1935: 202-203.

[21] D.S. XVII.4.1; Iust. XI.3.1; Aeschin. III.161.

[22] There is a glimpse of minor opposition: Polyaen. IV.3.23; cf. Westlake 1935: 217-218; Sordi 1958: 302 n. 2. Real or not, it seems obvious that it did not represent a great obstacle for him.

From this chronology, there is an interesting Larissean issue of Eginetic-weight, silver drachmae.[23] On the obverse, there is a portrait of helmeted Aleuas (eponymous mythical founder of the dynasty), a double-axe (Thessalian *tagos*' sign) [24] and the legend ΑΛΕΥ. On the reverse, a right-facing eagle perched in a lightning bolt can be observed, along with the legends ΛΑΡΙΣΑΙΑ and ΕΛΛΑ. After many previous attempts to discern the date and the issuer of these coins, Sordi made an exacting analysis and convincingly connected them with Alexander.[25] The key clue for reaching that conclusion was the reverse, whose iconography clearly recalls other coins issued by Alexander in Macedonia and subsequently imitated in the Eastern satrapies.[26] The eagle type, in turn, had also formed part of previous Molossian coins and was related with Zeus' shrine in Dodona. This sanctuary also plays a key role to unravel the legend ΕΛΛΑ found on the reverse, because it is related to the ancient denomination of Dodona's surrounding area (Hellas).[27] The combination of these two elements is obviously significant to understand this issue's iconography.

As stated, Aleuas' image dominates the obverse, making his first appearance on Larissa's coinage.[28] The unprecedented choice of Aleuas shows how Alexander wanted to establish close links with the Larissean clan, and not with the Thessalians as a whole. According to some sources,[29] when the young king entered Thessaly, he won its inhabitants' favour asserting their common ancestry as Heraclids and Aeacids.[30] The recipients of this message were the Aleuadae, which, like the Macedonian Argeads, claimed their descent from Heracles.[31] However, the addition of the Aeacid branch could be related to a certain reformulation of the family myths. The relation between Dodona and Thessaly was not new and was already known in the 5th century. The Thessalians were supposed to originally come from Thesprotia, the region to which Dodona belonged.[32] Alexander, being a son of Molossian Olympia and Macedonian Philip, incarnated the union of Aeacid and Heraclid lineages. However, it was not the first time that both families had converged. After returning from the Trojan War, Neoptolemus Pyrrhus arrived at Epirus, Dodona being its main ruling centre. There, he married Lanassa, Heracles' granddaughter, originating the Molossian dynasty. It is possible that this marriage was introduced into the myth at some

---

[23] Gardner / Poole 1883: 29 nº. 52, pl. V.11.

[24] See Sordi 1956 [2002]: 159; Mørkholm 1991: 85.

[25] See Sordi 1956 [2002]. More succinctly in Sordi 1958: 302-304; 1984: 9.

[26] See, e.g., Price 1991: no. 91, 96, 101, 159, 160.

[27] Arist. *Meteor.* 1.352a; Schol. *Il.* 21.194; Hesych., s.v. '"Ελλα'. See Sordi 1956 [2002]: 164.

[28] See Helly 1995: 119-120.

[29] D.S. XVII.4.1; Iust. XI.3.1-2; cf. Arr. *An.* II.5.9.

[30] A third connection can be established from the aforementioned kinship between the mythical Makedon and Magnes (see n. 1).

[31] See Sordi 1956 [2002]: 165, 1958: 320-325; Helly 1995: 102, 106, 112-119; Yardley / Heckel 1997: 90; Strootman 2010-11: 54.

[32] See Sordi 1956 [2002]: 165.

point during the 4th century and it would have come together with a growing preference for the name Pyrrhus to designate Achilles' son. This naming could have been decisive because Pyrrhus was also Aleuas' epithet. This conjunction might allow us to identify both characters as one and the same, and, consequently, to reconcile the different versions of the origin of the Thessalians and their ancestral homeland in Dodona's region. The re-elaboration of the myth left room to claim a closer kinship beyond the wider Heraclid common ancestry.[33]

Tagos' symbol of the double-axe clearly displays the event commemorated by this issue: Alexander's ratification as leader of the Thessalian *koinon*. Moreover, the unequivocal portrait of Aleuas indicated the recovered preeminence of the Aleuadae, after their fall from grace with Philip during the 340s.[34] This reconciliation could also have been illustrated by the close relationship between Alexander and Medius of Larissa (see below). This came together with a relative cooling regarding the Pharsalians, having been replaced in their previous primacy in Thessaly. However, Alexander did not turn his back completely on Pharsalus, but rather tried to reach a more balanced situation. He incorporated members of the Pharsalian elite into his entourage, like Hagnon, and the city squadron was the most important one under Parmenio's orders, though this arrangement turned against them afterwards, as will be noted. The state of affairs that Alexander left remained stable, in spite of Demosthenes' attempts to achieve the defection of the Thessalians from the Macedonian side.

The Thessalian contingent in Alexander's army

The Thessalian cavalry was probably the most renowned among the Greek battalions in Alexander's army. Their presence in different missions is widely attested and they were the only Greeks that fought —and played crucial roles— in the three great battles of the campaign.[35] In fact, they were the largest Greek contingent and,

---

[33] See Sordi 1956 [2002]: 166-168. This Aeacid bond could have been commemorated again in Ilion. According to Philostratus (*Her.* 53), Thessalian riders participated in a rite held at Achilles' tomb at the behest of Alexander. There, they supposedly staged a fake cavalry combat. Afterwards, they prayed and made sacrifices to earn the hero's favour for the forthcoming campaign against the Persians. Probably, this act was restricted to the Thessalian elite and, bearing in mind the aforementioned relations, the Aleuadae would have been indispensable participants; cf. Radet 1925: 10-13; Tarn 1948 II: 57; Fredricksmeyer 1958: 148 n. 36.

[34] See Sordi 1958: 304; Helly 1995: 119-120; Squillace 2000: 93 n. 64.

[35] At the Hellespont: D.S. XVII.17.4 (1,800 Thessalian riders; the contingent was reinforced with 200 more men at Gordium: Arr. *An.* I.29.4; on these figures, see Westlake 1935: 222; Helly 1995: 262-263; Strootman 2010-11: 57-60). At Granicus: Arr. *An.* I.14.1-3. At the taking of Dascylium: Arr. *An.* I.17.8. At Sardis: Arr. *An.* I.24.3, 29.3. At the path between Cilicia and Syria: Arr. *An.* II.5.1. At Issus: Arr. *An.* II.8.9; Curt. III.11.3; D.S. XVII.33.2. At Gaugamela: Arr. *An.* III.11.10; D.S. XVII.57.4, 60.8; Curt. IV.13.29. For an overall study of their participation in the campaign, see Strootman 2010-11: 62-66.

unlike the rest of the Greeks, their presence was not exclusively linked to their possible use as political hostages,[36] and they were not part of the so-called 'allies' from the League of Corinth. Their brave actions led them to receive special esteem from Alexander. For example, after the battle of Issus, he commended them, capturing the Persian baggage train and the royal treasure in Damascus in order to lavishly reward them.[37]

The moment and circumstances of their discharge are very telling too. After capturing and setting fire to Persepolis, the Panhellenic campaign of revenge might have symbolically come to an end, although Darius III had not yet been captured. This fact, along with the news arriving from Europe about Antipater's victory over Agis, made the presence of the Greek contingents almost unnecessary.[38] Therefore, Alexander decreed the return of the allied troops to Greece. However, there are two different traditions about the exact time and place of their discharge. Arrian places it at Ecbatana before Darius' death.[39] On the other hand, Plutarch and the *Vulgata* writers set it sometime later. Plutarch writes that Alexander sent them back home after receiving the news about the taking of the Persian king,[40] whereas Curtius and Diodorus state that he did it after his death.[41] However, they coincide that it took place in Parthia, not far from Hecatompylus.[42] In Curtius and Diodorus, in addition, the episode appears closely related with a Macedonian mutiny attempt, placated by Alexander's oratory. There is a minor variation on the causality in the accounts,[43] but it is clear that Macedonian discontent and Greek discharge were closely related.[44]

---

[36] Strootman 2010-11: 51-52. This researcher also states that they could have represented a counterweight to the Macedonian aristocracy. Certainly, their military organization seems to reflect, both in number and distribution, that of the Companions: Hammond / Griffith 1979: 437-438; Strootman 2010-11: 60-62. On the other hand, given their role during the Persian Wars —almost analogous to the Macedonian one—, the Thessalians could have regarded the campaign as a chance to rule out their former faults once and for all: Bernard 1997: 174.

[37] Plu. *Alex.* 24.1. Holt 2016: 120-127 illustratively shows how the Thessalians were profusely rewarded throughout the campaign, comparing their enrichment with the meagre profit of any Macedonian common soldier.

[38] See Badian 1985: 447; Hamilton 1969 [2002]: 112.

[39] Arr. *An.* III.19.5-7.

[40] Plu. *Alex.* 42.5. Moreover, Plutarch singles out the Thessalian discharge, with no word about the Greek allies.

[41] Curt. VI.2.15-17; D.S. XVII.74.3-4.

[42] Justin XII.1.1 is vaguer and only points out the distributed talents.

[43] Curtius explains that, after the allies' dismissal, a rumour spread in the Macedonian camp about their own demobilization too. This rumour almost provoked a stampede that forced Alexander's intervention. On the other hand, Diodorus writes that there was already some previous tension in the air and the discharge of the Hellenic troops was a way to calm down the situation.

[44] Due to Arrian's silence on Macedonian unease and the urgency for Darius' chase, Bosworth (1976: 132-136, 1980a: 335-338; also accepted by Sisti 2001: 523) defended that Alexander did not even enter Ecbatana and, consequently, Arrian's version might be wrong. Arrian would have misunderstood one of his sources (i.e., Ptolemy or Aristobulus), who would have dealt with these issues in an anticipatory digression to avoid showing the Macedonian soldiers' discomfort later in his text. On the other hand, the allied troops

In any case,[45] Alexander seized the chance to generously reward the Thessalian riders' great contribution during the campaign once more. The cavalrymen's wages were ostensibly higher than those of the foot soldiers.[46] Bearing in mind that the Thessalians were the largest cavalry contingent, we can consider it a further display of gratitude towards them.[47] Nevertheless, Alexander left the door open to anyone who wanted to re-enlist.[48]

The Parmenio Connection and the second demobilization

Before continuing to trace the Thessalian riders' career after their re-enlistment, it is necessary to examine their relationship with Parmenio. On several instances, the sources present Thessalian combatants under this Macedonian general's command,[49] who earned a great reputation among them.[50] The organization of the Thessalian squadron seems to reflect that of the *hetairoi*, divided into *ilai*, maybe on a territorial or tribal basis.[51] Among the Macedonian units, there was a special battalion (*ilē basilikē*), a kind of royal guard, not constituted following the aforementioned parameters. Pharsalians would have played this role in the Thessalian wing, being Parmenio's personal guard in the battlefield —in Gaugamela, at least.[52] There is no need to link this military order with their own relationship with Alexander, who would have given preference to the

---

would actually have been discharged in Ecbatana, but without Alexander. However, there is no need to deny Alexander's presence at Ecbatana and the different versions are not mutually exclusive; see Badian 1985: 447; Atkinson 1994: 173-174; Olbrycht 2011: 74. For his part, Goukowsky (1976: 224-225) considers that Diodorus mixed the events, pairing up the discharge with the mutiny. Curtius, in turn, might be recalling the demobilization retrospectively. Goukowsky notes that perhaps this retrospective was already found in Cleitarchus, which could explain Diodorus' confusion. Yardley / Heckel (1997: 181-182) reach similar conclusions. Hammond (1983: 191 nn. 34, 35) points out some weaknesses of this explanation.

[45] The homecoming is also attested in Paros' inscription: B. 5 (106).

[46] Justin (XII.1.1) presents a total amount of 13,000 talents. Arrian (*An.* III.19.5) says that they received the agreed pay and 2,000 extra talents, the same figure stated by Plutarch (*Alex.* 42.5). Curtius (VI.2.17) and Diodorus (XVII.74.3-5) detail that Alexander paid one talent/6,000 *denarii* to the cavalrymen and 1,000 *denarii*/10 *minae* to the infantrymen, as well as their salaries. Diodorus moreover calculates a total amount of 13,000 talents, the same figure found in Justin. In spite of the different ways of displaying the numbers, it seems that the sources converge to a similar total amount; see Bosworth 1980a: 336; Prandi 2013: 122; Holt 2016: 120-121.

[47] Westlake 1935: 227 even considered that they received a higher pay than the rest of the allied cavalry.

[48] According to Diodorus (XVII.74.4), Alexander paid three talents to those who decided to remain. In Robinson's opinion (1949: 193, 1957: 332-333), it was the first evidence of his will to create an imperial army after the end of the Panhellenic crusade.

[49] At Granicus: Arr. *An.* I.14.1-3. At Sardis: Arr. *An.* I.24.3, 29.3. At the path between Cilicia and Syria: Arr. *An.* II.5.1. At Issus: Arr. *An.* II.8.9; Curt. III.11.3; D.S. XVII.33.2. At Gaugamela: Arr. *An.* III.11.10; D.S. XVII.57.4, 60.8; Curt. IV.13.29.

[50] Arr. *An.* III.26.4; cf. Bosworth 1980a: 363.

[51] See Strootman 2010-11: 60-62.

[52] Arr. *An.* III.11.10. The *ilē basilikē* would have been formed by 300 riders. Therefore, maybe we should consider a similar number for Parmenio's guard. See Strootman 2010-11: 60 n. 21.

Larisseans. Given that during Philip's last years Pharsalus had held the primacy, this arrangement might have been preserved for merely logistic reasons.

Thessalians had already fought within Macedonian armies during Philip's reign. In around 341, they had participated in Philip's campaign in Thrace[53] and it is not unlikely that some of them also took part in the battle of Chaeronea.[54] However, given our current focus, a previous instance of Pharsalian collaboration with Parmenio is more significant. In 346, Philip helped Pharsalus to recover Halus —allied with Athens— and Parmenio was the officer in charge of the siege, the capture and the destruction of this Thessalian town.[55] Thus, Parmenio would have had first-hand knowledge of Pharsalian soldiers' skills. We are not aware whether they collaborated in further instances, but we can postulate that the precedent in Halus could have helped him to opt for a Pharsalian personal guard.

The relationship between Parmenio and the Thessalians is relevant to properly assess the fate of those Thessalians who re-enlisted. According to Arrian,[56] they were handed over to Parmenio, who was in charge of escorting the royal treasure to Ecbatana's citadel, and then was supposed tomarch to Hyrcania, bordering the Cadusians. Nevertheless, this latter mission never came to be, and therefore the Thessalians were confined in the garrison of Ecbatana.[57] Media was not, however, their final destination. Not long after, Thessalian volunteers coming from Media joined Alexander's troops in Aria, on their way to Bactria. They were led by their former hipparch Philip, son of Menelaus,[58] and they came together with mercenary riders and Andromachus' mercenaries according to Arrian.[59] For his part, Curtius[60] details that Philip's Thessalians were a group of 130 men and the rest of the party was composed of fresh reinforcements from Greece, Lydia and Illyria. Philip's Thessalians clearly look out of place because they were the only 'unfresh' troops there. Curtius later describes another arrival of troops in Arachosia[61] and pinpoints in this passage that they were from Media, from the detachment left behind with Parmenio. This group was formed by 6,000 Macedonians,[62] 200 nobles,[63] 5,000 Greeks, including 600

---

[53] D. VIII.14; *AP*. IX.743.

[54] See Westlake 1935: 212.

[55] D. XIX.163.

[56] Arr. *An*. III.19.7.

[57] On the possible reasons behind this change of plans, see Robinson 1949: 198, 1957: 333-334; Brunt 1976: 529; Bosworth 1980a: 337-338; Badian 1985: 448; Sisti 2001: 525.

[58] See Heckel 2006: 212, s.v. 'Philip [4]'.

[59] Arr. *An*. III.25.4.

[60] Curt. VI.6.35.

[61] Curt. 7.3.4.

[62] This number coincides with the Macedonians who were entrusted to Harpalus to escort the movement of the treasure (Arr. *An*. III.19.7-8; Brunt 1976: lxxvi-vii, 528-529. Cleitus the Black was ordered to guide these men to Parthia and join the main army.

[63] Brunt (1976: 529) and Bosworth (1980a: 338) considered that they were Companions left behind in the rearguard. Olbrycht (2011: 72-73) defends that they were Iranian noblemen.

cavalrymen, whom Curtius refers to as «the flower of all the king's forces (*haud dubie robur omnium uirium regis:* transl. Rolfe 1962)». Even though they are not explicitly mentioned, it is very likely that Thessalians formed part of the 600 Greek riders. Regarding the two previous instances, the most important difference, in this case, is that these soldiers arrived after Philotas' trial and Parmenio's murder.

The reinstatement of these troops was short-lived. Alexander sent the remaining Thessalians in Bactria back home again, before the crossing of the Oxus, alongside the oldest of the Macedonians.[64] Arrian does not explain the reason behind this decision in this passage, but later, in Coenus' speech on the banks of the Hyphasis, we can read «[t]he Thessalians you sent straight home from Bactria, observing that they had little heart left for further exertions, and you were right» (Arr. *An.* V.27.5; transl. Brunt 1983). Given that the Thessalians had been praised for their bravery so far, this statement sounds especially surprising. This alleged lack of morale might be connected with Parmenio's recent death.[65] However, it was not the discouragement that Alexander was actually afraid of, but the potential risk of mutiny and the spread of their discontent across the rest of the army.[66] Certainly, if most or all of them had been closely attached to Parmenio, the potential risk was larger than a limited squadron of 130 Thessalians.[67] Perhaps, Arrian's Thessalians in Aria were only the advance party of those who later came among the main group from Media in Arachosia. In any case, it is obvious that a contingent formed by over 11,000 men entailed a greater menace. Perhaps the 6,000 Macedonians should be identified with the old Macedonians later discharged at the Oxus. However, Alexander could not do away with such a great amount of soldiers and Curtius states that he only discharged 900 men.[68] Curtius pinpoints that the king selected the ones who were going to be sent back home, and therefore it is likely that the chosen ones were the most unruly or those more closely attached to Parmenio. Alexander was always very reluctant to dismiss Macedonian troops; therefore, there should have been a good reason behind this noteworthy exception.[69]

It was not the first time that Alexander showed a certain fear of Thessalian troops, well aware of their strength. In the winter of 334/3,[70] he discovered an alleged con-

---

[64] Arr. *An.* III.29.5.

[65] See Bosworth 1980a: 374

[66] See Robinson 1949: 194, 1957: 334-335, 341. Robinson also considered Aristander's bad omens before crossing the Jaxartes (Arr. *An.* IV.4.3) as a sign of widespread discontent among the different ranks of the army. Bosworth (1995: 353) thinks that it is wrong to equate demoralization with mutiny. Arrian's remark could either come from the original source or just be Arrian's own inference.

[67] Atkinson (1994: 173) thinks that Philip's 130 riders did not come from Media.

[68] Curt. VII.5.27. The cavalrymen received two talents and the foot soldiers 3,000 *denarii*. The pay is significantly higher than the one for those who left in the first discharge (see n. 46).

[69] See Bosworth 1980a: 374. On Alexander's management of Macedonian contingents, see Bosworth 1986.

[70] Arr. *An.* I.25.

spiracy by Alexander the Lyncestian, who was the commander of the Thessalian cavalry at that time. After consulting his Companions, the king ordered Parmenio to capture the Lyncestian without delay, but in a veiled way to avoid any previous suspicion that could complicate the detention. Arrian describes the concern of Alexander and his Companions and the reason for the urgency of his order in this way:

> «The Companions held that he had originally acted unwisely in committing the best of the cavalry to an untrustworthy officer, and that he should now get rid of him as soon as possible, before he came more popular with the Thessalians and secured their help for a revolution» (Arr. *An.* I.25.5; transl. Brunt 1976).

This passage again stresses the importance of the Thessalian battalion and its perception as a potential threat by its Macedonian counterpart.[71] In the same way, this contingent was always under a Macedonian nobleman's command.[72] Thus, Alexander's generous gifts and rewards during the campaign maybe were not only to recognize their feats but also to gain the loyalty of those men for himself, before any other ambitious officer could obtain it. Therefore, the words that Arrian attributed to Coenus in his speech were not far-fetched and they correspond perfectly well with a reality that can be traced back to the early stages of the campaign. Just as the king had feared Alexander the Lyncestian gaining Thessalian loyalty, he was also almost sure that Parmenio had achieved it and, therefore, keeping them in the army was a risk rather than an advantage, especially after the incorporation of the mighty Iranian cavalry.[73]

When looking at the Thessalian volunteers who remained after the first discharge, there is no indication about their hometown. However, it seems that most of the Phereans would have returned.[74] If, as has been suggested, the second dismissal was related with potential mutiny risk by Parmenio's sympathizers, Alexander would have happily sent back home the members of the Pharsalian *ilē*, which formed Parmenio's personal guard.[75]

Nevertheless, there were some Thessalians —including Pharsalians— who remained in the army and the king's entourage after the second discharge.[76] Their pres-

---

[71] As stated above (see n. 36), Strootman suggests that they could act as a counterweight for the Macedonian aristocracy. The concern which rose within this latter group would back up this suggestion.

[72] See Strootman 2010-11: 62. The three known hipparchs were Calas, son of Harpalus (Arr. *An.* I.14.3; D.S. XVII.17.4); Alexander the Lyncestian (Arr. *An.* I.25.3) and Philip, son of Menelaus (Arr. *An.* 3.25.4, D.S. XVII.57.4; Curt. IV.13.29).

[73] See Olbrycht 2011.

[74] See Helly / Te Riele / van Rossum 1979. They consider that the number of volunteers would have been «négligeable» (227).

[75] This would be corroborated if a certain Cyrsilus from a Delphic inscription is the same as the historian who participated in Alexander's campaign (see n. 108).

[76] In addition, some Thessalians could have remained in eastern satrapies either as settlers or as a garrison force. I gave a presentation about the Thessalian (and Thracian) presence in Central Asia at the Third

ence could suggest that they had not been attached to Parmenio or that they had eventually been disassociated from him.[77] Consequently, they would have held a different position with respect to the rest of their fellow countrymen, and therefore their dismissal at the Oxus was not necessary. Therefore, it would be useful to make a brief prosopography of these individuals and try to assess what role they played in the army and in Alexander's court.

Thessalian prosopography

The most prominent Thessalian in the sources is Medius of Larissa. Son of Oxythemis,[78] it is very likely that he was an Aleuadae of Larissa. This nobleman would have taken part in the expedition from the early stages, even though his first post is attested in 326, as trierarch during the descent of the Indus.[79] After Alexander's death, his military career continued mainly under Antigonus and Demetrius' orders, although he initially backed Perdiccas.[80] However, Medius' notoriety is not the fruit of his military career, but rather comes from his role during Alexander's last banquet. Our man was the one who invited the king to the party in which he fell deathly ill. During Alexander's last days, Medius was frequently at the king's side.[81] This crucial presence during Alexander's last days was eventually perceived as suspicious and his name appeared as one of the plotters in the rumours about an alleged poisoning of the king.[82]

Hellenistic Central Asia Research Network Conference, held in Prague. A written version will appear in the proceedings of this conference. In Aï Khanoum, a heroon dedicated to a certain Kineas was discovered. For many years, after a paper by Robert (1968: 432-438), it was considered that there was a strong presence of Northern Greeks in the region. Kineas was supposed to be a good Thessalian name. However, Robert's hypothesis, mostly based on onomastics, must be questioned. The alleged Northern Greek hegemony is no longer sustained by new and larger onomastics databases. Even though it cannot be rejected outright, Kineas cannot be a trustworthy example to prove the presence of Thessalians in the region. The only certain evidence is the presence of two Aenianians in the second settler revolt in Bactria (D.S. XVIII.7).

[77] For example, they could have been Greek mercenaries who had fought in Darius' army and were incorporated into the Macedonian ranks afterwards (see, e.g., Curt. VI.5.10; D.S. XVII.76.2; Arr. *An.* III.23.8-9, 24.4-5). The presence of Thessalians among these mercenary troops is well-attested (Plu. *Mor.* 181b; cf. Westlake 1935: 225-226), including noteworthy officers, such as Aristomedes of Pherae (Heckel 2006: 47-48).

[78] Arr. *Ind.* 18.7.

[79] Arr. *Ind.* 18.7. Billows (1990: 400-401) suggests that he would have been a Thessalian cavalry officer before that.

[80] See Heckel 1988: 37-38. This brief period in Perdiccas' side is a key piece of information for determining the date and authorship of Alexander's last days' pamphlet.

[81] Arr. *An.* VII.24.4-25.4; Plu. *Alex.* 75.4-76.2, *Mor.* 124c; D.S. XVII.117.1; Iust. 12.13.7-10; Nicobule (*FGrH* 127) F 1 *apud* Athen. X.434c. The growing closeness between Medius and Alexander would have come about after Hephaestion's decease, see Bernard 1997: 134.

[82] Arr. *An.* VII.27.2; Iust. XII.14; Ps.-Callisth. III.31; *Liber de Morte* 97. Medius appears as a necessary collaborator of the alleged poisoner, Iolaus, Antipater's son. Arrian even says that some writers suggested that

Beyond his actual guilt or innocence, the rumours quickly spread. Consequently, it seems plausible that Medius wrote a book that would have had among its objectives to disprove any implication in the king's death. Perhaps an extremely apologetic tone triggered Plutarch's remark about him as «leader and skilled master of the choir of flatterers» (*Mor.* 65c; transl. Babbit 1927); however, it cannot be ruled out that it was not a reference to his book, but to his behaviour in the royal court.[83] The only extant fragment of his work focuses on Media and Armenia, mentioning Parmenio and implicating him in the alleged destruction of some shrines dedicated to the Thessalian hero Jason.[84] It seems logical that, if Medius wanted to refute those veiled accusations against him, he would subscribe the 'official' doctrine, which repudiated Parmenio;[85] especially taking into account that, among the reasons to point to Antipater's involvement in Alexander's killing, there was his grief caused by the deaths of some outstanding Macedonians, like Parmenio, Alexander the Lyncestian or Philotas.[86]

Unfortunately, this sole fragment does not allow us to infer the general tone and scope of his work from it. Besides, only if an exculpatory motivation for his book is accepted would a hostile bias towards Parmenio become necessary in order to prove his unflinching loyalty to the king. Bearzot posited that Medius was the original pro-Parmenio source reflected in Curtius' text.[87] For such an assumption, the key clue would be his allegedly close relationship with Iolaus, whatever its actual nature. Even if those murder accusations were mere gossip, they should have had a certain foundation in real life to be successful. Therefore, Medius and Iolaus could have been friends. However, in 321/0, Medius was the leader of 800 mercenaries who formed part of a wider force commanded by Aristonus and sent by Perdiccas to Cyprus.[88] Back then, Perdiccas and Antipater were already enemies after the former had broken the arranged marriage with the latter's daughter, Nicaea, to marry Cleopatra,

---

they were lovers. Sisti / Zambrini (2004: 658) point out the parallelism with the tyrannicides, Harmodius and Aristogeiton. According to Pseudo-Callisthenes, Medius and Iolaus would have been offended by the king. Justin and the *Liber* also suggest his participation, but they do not detail any particular motivation. Diodorus (XVII.117.5-118.2), Plutarch (*Alex.* 77.1-5) and Curtius (X.10.14-19) also present the rumours about Antipater and his sons' conspiracy, but they do not say a word about Medius' implication. Cf. D.S. XIX.11.8; Plu. *Mor.* 849f; Hamilton 1969 [2002]: 213-215; Bosworth 1971; 2000b; Brunt 1983: 295 n. 1; Yardley / Heckel 1997: 285-288; Sisti / Zambrini 2004: 656-658; Atkinson / Yardley 2009: 234-242; Prandi 2013: 202-207.

[83] Plu. *Mor.* 472d. On Plutarch's opinion, see Bernard 1997: 134-135 n. 6.

[84] *FGrH* 129 F 1 *apud* Str. XI.14.12; cf. Iust. ILII.3.5; Pearson 1960: 68-70; Hamilton 1969 [2002]: 208; Auberger 2001: 116-117; Mendoza 2019a: 160-170. The link between Armenia and Thessaly was not new in Medius' time. On this relationship, see Hecataeus (*FGrH* 1) F 286; Hdt. VII.62.1; D.S. IV.56.1; 10.27; Str. XI.4.8, 13.10; Apoll. 1.9.28; Iust. XLII.3.6; Paus. II.3.8; cf. Markwart 1928; Bernard 1997; De Siena 2001.

[85] See Robinson 1945; Badian 1960; Bearzot 1987; Chaplin 2011.

[86] D.S. XVII.118.1; Iust. XII.14.1

[87] Bearzot 1987: 103-104. She also recognizes the flawlessness of her suggestion given the topic and uniqueness of the extant fragment.

[88] Arr. *Succ.* 10.6.

Alexander's sister.[89] Precisely, Iolaus together with Archias had been in charge of bringing Nicaea to Perdiccas in 322. Thus, it seems that Medius and Iolaus' friendship was not as close as some insinuated or, at least, it worsened very quickly.[90] That was, however, the last known instance of Iolaus' career.[91] In 317/6, he was certainly dead because Olympias desecrated his tomb in revenge for his alleged participation in her son's poisoning.[92] However, there is no indication of the date of his death. Consequently, it cannot be dismissed that Iolaus had already passed away when Medius served on Perdiccas' side. Thus, even if it cannot be simply rejected outright, the relationship between Medius and Iolaus is not conclusive or relevant in relation to a possible bias in Medius' book on Parmenio.

On the other hand, we have to address the personal relationship between Parmenio and Medius himself. He was a Thessalian, and therefore he could have fought in Parmenio's wing several times. If Billows' proposal about Medius being a cavalry officer is accepted,[93] then he would not only have fought under Parmenio's orders, but he could also have been one of his close collaborators. Nevertheless, he was still in the army in 326 and his close friendship with Alexander casts some doubts on any close relationship with Parmenio.

Medius clearly followed a distinguishable career in respect of most Thessalian soldiers. Arrian designates him a *hetairos* in his account of Alexander's last banquet,[94] but we are unaware for how long he had been one. Billows considered that it was in 326, together with his nomination as trierarch, when he entered Alexander's inner circle as a Companion.[95] However, Heckel dissents and thinks that he would have been part of the *hetairoi* from the beginning, given his noble descent.[96] Other non-Macedonian Companions, like Hagnon and Eumenes,[97] were *hetairoi* before their post as trierarchs of the Indus' fleet. Therefore, there is no need to link both

---

[89] D.S. XVIII.23; Arr. *Succ.* 9.20-26.

[90] Another possibility is that this estrangement was due to Antipater's confrontation with the Greeks —Thessalians included— during the Lamian War.

[91] See Heckel 2006: 143, s.v. 'Iolaus [1]'.

[92] D.S. XIX.11.8.

[93] See n. 79.

[94] Arr. *An.* VII.24.4. There is no conflict about the existence of non-Macedonian Companions: Theopompus (*FGrH* 115) F 224 *apud* Athen. IV.167a-b; Hammond / Griffith 1979: 409-410. There is wide evidence of their existence during Alexander's reign: Eumenes of Cardia, Critobulus of Cos, Thoas and Maeander from Magnesia on the Maeander, Andron/Hagnon of Teos, the Cypriots Stasanor of Soloi and Nithaphon of Salamis, Demaratus of Corinth and the more dubious cases of Demetrius 'Pheidon', Eugnostus, Philip of Acarnania and Hecataeus. There were also the Greeks 'naturalized' Macedonians from Amphipolis. See Berve 1926 I: 31; Hammond / Griffith 1979: 352-353; Badian 1982: 39; Borza 1991: 24-25; Anson 2004: 42, 218-220, 245.

[95] See Billows 1990: 400-401.

[96] See Heckel 2006: 158, 317 n. 409.

[97] Eumenes, after arriving at Philip's court, was quickly incorporated into the Companions' ranks, a position that he kept under Alexander. He was from a ruling family in Cardia, no matter what Duris claimed: Plu. *Eum.* 1; Nep. *Eum.* 1.

promotions as Billows defends.[98] On the other hand, and excluding the exceptional case of Stasanor of Soloi and an isolated mission of Eumenes in Sangala,[99] there is no direct evidence about the participation of non-Macedonian companions in any military action. However, it is obvious that the sources could not make an exhaustive collection of all the activities of every more or less renowned man. The only known intervention of a non-Macedonian Companion is that of Demaratus of Corinth at Granicus, when he handed over a spear to Alexander after the king had broken his.[100] Despite this scarcity, this passage could suggest that the Greek *hetairoi* fought close to the king.

These non-Macedonian companions seem to have been born in prominent families from their respective homelands.[101] Even though they cannot be regarded as actual hostages, the purpose behind their presence would not have been far from it. They would have been a clear visual sign and ratification of the alliance between Alexander and those territories, securing the continuity of the union. At the same time, the local families would have seized the chance to give public repercussion to that personal bond, as proof of their closeness with the hegemonic power of their time. The most efficient way to take advantage of this measure was to integrate them as members of the Companions and not to relegate them to minor posts. Therefore, the relationship with the king played a key role and, in any case, any personal link would have been directly established with Alexander, not with an intermediate commander.

Consequently, it seems likely that Medius did not battle alongside the rest of the Thessalians under Parmenio's orders. Stasanor's meteoric career clearly shows that the integration of the *hetairoi* would have been almost immediate. In the case of Medius, moreover, Alexander aimed to establish a close relationship with the Larissean Aleuadae, as the coinage with the eponymous hero's portrait and the recognition of their common mythical roots clearly prove. Besides, the incorporation of a few Greek *hetairoi* would have not implied any great tactical modification of the Companions' squadron.[102] Thus, keeping in mind all the above, Medius would have been by Alexander's side early on. Even if Medius ever fought with Parmenio, it would probably have been for a very short time and he would have

---

[98] See n. 95. Stasanor, though he was not nominated trierarch like the rest, given his duties in other regions, was also a *hetairos* before that date, showing that a long time in service was not necessary to hold that position: Str. XIV.6.3; Arr. *An.* III.29.5.

[99] Arr. *An.* V.24.6-7; Plu. *Eum.* 1.5; Curt. IX.1.19.

[100] Arr. *An.* I.15.6.

[101] We have already highlighted this aspect in Eumenes and Medius' cases. Stasanor would have been a member of the royal house of Soloi (Mendoza 2017: 47 n. 24). The evidence about Hagnon is vaguer, but his role as mediator between Craterus and Miletus in 320 was commemorated in an inscription and in a monetary issue, which could suggest that he was from a prominent family in Teos; see Billows 1990: 386-388.

[102] On the possible Macedonian sensitivity towards the Greeks, see Badian 1982; Borza 1991; Anson 2004: 191-258. The tiny percentage that they represented along with the minor importance of their posts could have eased their integration.

hardly established a relationship as close as he had with Alexander outside the battlefield.[103] Therefore, it is plausible that Medius' book did not necessarily contain a positive bias towards Parmenio, given that he would aim to assert his personal relations with Alexander, which were far more preferable than any dubious link with Parmenio. This would have put the Aleuadae above the rest of the Thessalian clans, which would have been more attached to Parmenio, like the Pharsalians. Perhaps, Medius' text also had as an additional objective to belittle the rival Thessalian groups due to his connection with the treacherous Parmenio instead of the all-powerful Alexander.

The second 'entry' of our prosopography is a man from Larissa who also wrote a book, like Medius. Polyclitus (*FGrH* 128) was the author of a long *History* — at least, eight books long—,[104] full of sensational episodes and curiosities.[105] It is very likely that he participated in Alexander's expedition and his fragments suggest that he could be a member of the escort in charge of moving the royal treasures to Ecbatana.[106] It is possible that he remained in the army after the Oxus' discharge, given that a couple of his fragments are about Indian wildlife.[107] Perhaps, being a Larissean, he could have accompanied Medius when he was nominated trierarch. Nevertheless, the first of his fragments is about the opulent king's bed, his musical entourage in the camp and the famous drunkenness of Alexander. None of these details suggests a close relationship with the king, because he is just echoing some commonplaces about him. Maybe the detail about the entourage in the camp suggests that he was only a common soldier. In any case, the description of Alexander's long drinking sessions puts him closer to hostile writers like Ephippus or Nicobule than the possibly flattering Medius. Therefore, even sharing some characteristics at first sight, they were two completely different men.

Another Thessalian writer was Cyrsilus of Pharsalus. His book might present some similarities with that of Medius because both are quoted in the aforementioned

---

[103] Even considering that Medius spent more time under Parmenio's command, it is not unlikely to regard him changing sides after Parmenio's fall into disgrace. Precisely, regarding Parmenio, there are two examples in his family-in-law. Coenus, his son-in-law, was one of the main advisers in the accusation against Philotas. Cleander, Coenus' son, was among those who murdered Parmenio in Media: Arr. *An.* III.26.4. See Badian 1960: 329, 363.

[104] F 1 *apud* Athen. XII.539a.

[105] See Pearson 1960: 70-77. For example, he is one of the writers cited by Plutarch (*Alex.* 46.1) among those who described the meeting between Alexander and the Amazons.

[106] Cf. F 3 *apud* Str. XV.3.21; Poll. II.150-151; F 5 *apud* Athen. V.206d-e.

[107] F 9 *apud* Ael. *NA.* XVI.41; F 10 *apud Paradoxographus Vaticanus* Rohd. 10. It is also possible to consider a later visit or that he based these fragments on indirect information. In the tenth fragment, he deals with the turtles in the Ganges, a river that Alexander never reached. His information fits in with the traditional descriptions of Indian marvels. The information about the great turtles' shells resembles two passages found in Aelian (*NA.* XII.41, XVI.14), who used Polyclitus' data as F 9 proves, although Megasthenes could also be the primary source. On lizards' skins and turtles' shells during Alexander's expedition, there is a parallel in Curtius: Curt. IX.8.2. See Karttunen 1997: 212-214.

passage on Media and Armenia. However, no other data are known about him beyond his name in this passage.[108]

The second individual from Pharsalus is Ariston, who also attended Medius' ill-fated symposium.[109] There is, though, no further information about him beyond his appearance in the pamphlet about Alexander's last days.[110] However, this single mention would put him in Alexander's inner circle, and therefore his position within the court would be similar to Medius'—although with the difference of the closeness of their respective friendships with the king.

The last known Thessalian is a minor character that appears in Curtius' account about the days following Alexander's death. His name was Pasas[111] and he was sent by Meleagrus as an intermediary alongside Amisus of Megalopolis and Perilaus.[112] We do not know anything else about him, and it thus seems unlikely that he had a close relationship with the king.[113]

Beyond literary sources,[114] there is a further possible case coming from the archaeological records.[115] In 1978, a sublime bronze krater containing the ashes of a man and a woman was found in Macedonia. This piece, known as the Derveni krater, bears the inscription Ἀστιούνειος Ἀναξαγοραίοι ἐς Λαρίσας («Astion, son of Anaxagoras, of Larissa»). It has mostly been dated in the years between 330 and 320, although Barr-Sharrarr suggested a higher chronology.[116] Even so, Astion has been considered a participant in Alexander's expedition and then he would not have gone home, but rather to Macedonia. The richness of this piece suggests that the commemorated man belonged to a wealthy family. Being a Larissean, the Aleuadae stand out as the most likely option, especially when keeping in mind the close bonds

---

108 Auberger (2001: 123 n. 76) suggests some possibilities, such as him being Medius' secretary or editor, or a later writer who quoted Medius. Obviously, nothing can ratify or reject these possibilities. Westlake (1935: 229) pointed out that he could have been a Thessalian *hieromnemones* in 328/7 (Bourguet 1932: 61, IIA, l. 14). The extant text is Θετταλῶν Κυρσίλου Φερ[α]ίου. If he really was our writer, it only adds a scarce piece of information about him: he was sent back home when Alexander dismissed the Thessalian cavalry, unlike Medius, see above.

109 Ps.-Callisth. III.31.

110 See Heckel 1988: 43-44, 2006: 48, s.v. 'Ariston [2]'. Heckel also suggests that he could be the same man that handed over Craterus' mortal remains to his wife (D.S. XIX.59.3).

111 Atkinson / Yardley (2009: 199) consider that his real name could have been Paseas or Pasias.

112 Curt. X.8.15. Amisus is only mentioned in this passage, like Pasas. Perilaus could have been a Greek Companion; see Heckel 2006: 202-203, s.v. 'Perilaus [1]'. Therefore, it cannot be completely ruled out that Pasas was also a *hetairos*.

113 Atkinson / Yardley (2009: 199) maintain that the choice of these three men might respond to an expected neutrality in the conflict because they were Greek. Also, they suggest that Pasas and Amisus could have been members of Eumenes' chancellery and not mercenaries.

114 See the possible case of Polydamas in the Appendix.

115 I thank Dr Palagia for the information about the krater and Astion.

116 See Barr-Sharrarr 2008: 44-45. Palagia (2009) dismisses the new dating and reasserts the traditional lower one.

between this clan and the Macedonian court. Maybe, unlike Medius, Astion did not remain in the army and returned after either of two known discharges. In any case, so long as Astion was really an Aleuadae, this would again prove the recovered close relationship between them and the Argeads.

Conclusions

Thessalians, both as a whole and individually, played important roles throughout Alexander's career:

1) In the early stages of Alexander's reign, Thessaly became the spearhead for the ratification of Macedonian hegemony in Greece. Due to his geographical and cultural closeness, with an intense common past, the young king regarded the Thessalian *tagia* as the first necessary step for his dominion over the rest of the Greek states of the League. The Aleuadae would have played a key role in Alexander's consolidation in Thessaly. In turn, the Macedonian king returned them the federal primacy that Philip had bestowed on the Pharsalians. Nevertheless, Alexander did not completely turn his back on Pharsalus and also established bonds with its aristocracy and its men actively participated in the campaign. The Macedonian monarch tried to settle a balanced arrangement and he likewise incorporated Larissean (Medius) and Pharsalian (Ariston) nobles into his inner circle. However, he could not prevent some Thessalians from battling on the Persian side, like Aristomedes of Pherae.

2) The Thessalian contingent participated and played a relevant role in the great battles of the campaign. The Thessalian cavalry was probably a counterweight and a counterpart of the Companions' battalion. As part of the army's left wing, they battled under the orders of Parmenio and a Macedonian officer was always their commander. Alexander treated the Thessalian riders with special care and recognized their deeds, giving them lavish rewards —on occasions, greater than those received by the Macedonians themselves. Their status within the army clearly distinguished them from the rest of the Greek allies. They always formed a separate squadron, reflecting his particular relationship with the Macedonian king, who was also the *tagos* of the Thessalian League. Inside the battalion, the most prominent combatants seem to be the Pharsalians, who constituted Parmenio's personal guard, maybe due to old links going back to Philip's times.

3) Although Alexander showed clear signs of admiration towards these men's courage, that feeling was combined with a certain concern for them. The first sign of this was the evident urgency to isolate Alexander the Lyncestian before he could assure for himself the loyalty of the mighty Thessalian contingent. Also, the Oxus' discharge can be interpreted in the same way, with Parmenio's death as the possible source of discontent and potential trigger of further problems in the camp. Alexander

decided to manage without their services at the Oxus, along with some of the oldest Macedonians related with Parmenio. It is possible that those whom Alexander was most interested in repatriating were the Pharsalians, given their closeness with the fallen general.

4) Some members of the Thessalian aristocratic families formed part of Alexander's inner circle. Among them, the most well-known was Medius of Larissa, who was one of his *hetairoi* and played a key role during the king's last days as the host of his last banquet and because of his constant presence at Alexander's bedside. Possibly, he rose to Companion status not long after he joined Alexander's ranks. Therefore, it is plausible that he did not fight under Parmenio's orders, although he did fight in the Companions' squadron. It is therefore likely that his book did not necessarily contain a positive bias towards the Macedonian general as has been suggested, but maybe quite the opposite, defending Alexander's standpoint. The differentiation of certain Thessalians is also illustrated by Ariston, who, although a Pharsalian, remained in the court after demobilization, suggesting that he did not establish any bond with Parmenio either.

5) Though not formally constituted, it is possible to metaphorically speak about a Thessalian lobby. On some occasions, it played a noteworthy role in Alexander's decision-making, due as much to his military strength as to his closeness with the king. Ignoring the Thessalian element means disregarding a key factor of the campaign.

Appendix: Polydamas, Thessalian or Macedonian?

Polydamas, one of Alexander's Companions,[117] is scarcely attested in the sources —only in three episodes: Gaugamela, the death of Parmenio, and the discharge at Opis. Berve considered him Macedonian, whereas Heckel regarded him as Thessalian. Even though it could seem irrelevant, a different origin could suggest opposite interpretations about some key episodes of Alexander's career —like Parmenio's murder—, policies and attitudes —especially in relation with the Macedonian old guard.

There is a possible further trace of Polydamas on a Delphic inscription.[118] This is a *proxeny* granted to a certain Polydamas of Arethusa, son of Antheus,[119] which some scholars have identified as our man, being the main argument for Berve considering him a Macedonian.[120] The dating of the document is not clear because the archon's

---

[117] Arr. *An.* III.26.3.

[118] *FdD* III, 1, 186, p. 105 n. 1 = *Syll.*^{3} 269 K.

[119] The reconstruction of the patronymic is hypothetical.

[120] See Hoffman 1906: 200; Berve 1926 II: 322-323 no. 648; Hatzopoulos 1996 I: 192; Tataki 1998: 70; Mari 2002: 300.

name is uncertain.[121] A late 4th to early 3rd century date has been suggested,[122] but the only thing that we can be sure of is that it post-dated Philip's annexation of the Chalcidian Arethusa.[123] His ethnic identity is explicitly described as 'Macedonian'. However, the lack of chronological precision means we cannot be totally sure that they were the same man.

Nevertheless, Heckel considers a Thessalian (Pharsalian) rather than a Macedonian background to be more likely, basically deduced from his closeness to Parmenio.[124] Curtius' description of Polydamas says that «[h]e was by far the dearest of Parmenio's friends, accustomed to stand by his side in battle» (Curt. VII.2.11; transl. Rolfe 1962). As stated above, in Gaugamela, the Pharsalian cavalrymen served as Parmenio's personal guard.[125] Curtius, in his account of the battle,[126] explains that Parmenio sent Polydamas to warn Alexander of the difficulties that his wing was suffering.[127] However, it is important not to fall into hasty interpretations. It is true that we cannot deny the possibility of a Pharsalian origin from this information, but neither can one be confidently asserted. The left wing in Gaugamela was not only formed by Thessalian riders, but also by the allied cavalry, under Erygius' command.[128] Due to the chaotic situation of that flank, we cannot be completely sure that Parmenio sent a man from his personal squadron. He could therefore be either Thessalian (whether or not Pharsalian) or from the allies, depending on who was within reach at that moment. On the other hand, even if we accept that it is more likely that Polydamas formed part of his personal unit, he would not necessarily have to be Pharsalian. As it was his personal regiment, it is plausible that Parmenio added other trustworthy men, whatever their origin. If we accept the statement in the cited passage by Curtius, Polydamas would fit the description perfectly.

In addition, Heckel brings up his possible association with the Thessalian Polydamas from the second quarter of the 4th century.[129] Although this idea is suggestive, this kinship cannot be taken for granted. Polydamas was not an exclusively Thes-

---

[121] Eudochus has been suggested, which would move the date to 272/1 —unviable for our man. However, this reconstruction is highly hypothetical because only the last two letters of the name are extant.

[122] Cf. *Syll.*^{3} 478; see Tataki 1998: 70; Mari 2002: 300.

[123] Cf. *FdD* III, 1, 396; see Hammond / Griffith 1979: 193-194, 358-361, 367 n. 2; Hatzopoulos 1996 I: 190-192; Tataki 1998: 69.

[124] See Heckel 1992: 328-329, 2006: 225-226.

[125] Arr. *An.* 3.11.10.

[126] Curt. IV.15.6-7.

[127] Atkinson (1980: 439), in view of the silence from Arrian about the message, expresses his doubts about the historicity of this detail and proposes that it could be a dramatic addition by Curtius, anticipating the role of Polydamas at the death of Parmenio. Heckel (1992: 328-329), despite accepting the possibility of a dramatic embellishment, finds no good reason to doubt the veracity of Polydamas' intervention. The other Vulgate writers present a very concise version of the history and we cannot rule out the idea that Curtius' source (Cleitarchus?) already gave his name.

[128] Arr. *An.* III.11.10.

[129] Heckel 2006: 334 n. 612.

salian anthroponym,[130] and therefore the evidence is merely circumstantial. Even though the lack of chronologic precision means a reliable identification is impossible, the suggestive Delphic inscription confirms that the anthroponym Polydamas was not epichoric to Thessaly and was also used in Macedonia, invalidating the argument about the possible homonymous ancestor.

Besides his almost incidental role in Gaugamela, Polydamas is mostly remembered in relation to the execution of Parmenio. Polydamas was sent by Alexander on a whirlwind trip through the desert to Cleander, and the other officials in Media, with the order to kill the old Macedonian general.[131] Curtius says that Alexander took his youthful brothers as hostages. Polydamas already seems to be a man of a certain age and this passage is problematic in relation with the age of his brothers. Some solutions have been suggested, mostly based on hypothetical emendations of the text, correcting the actual kinship between Polydamas and these hostages or addressing the actual implications of the terminology employed.[132] The youth of his brothers could be another indication of a Macedonian origin. The Thessalian contingent did not receive any reinforcements after Gordion,[133] and therefore it is unlikely they formed part of the contingent if they really were that young. Besides, they cannot be regarded as hostages of a noteworthy Thessalian family because Curtius also states that Alexander did not know them beforehand. This youth fits in better with a Macedonian background. Very young Macedonians are attested among the Royal Pages,[134] and it is not unlikely that they belonged to them, whatever his actual kinship with Polydamas. In this case, the issue of Polydamas' ethnicity is not trivial. A Thessalian origin could reveal Alexander's distrust of the Macedonian old guard. Sending a foreigner to execute that mission would have undermined Alexander's detente policies attested after the crisis arising following Philotas' affair.[135]

Besides, it is noteworthy that he was the only one of those involved in Parmenio's murder who survived. Cleander, Agathon, Sitalkes and Heracon were executed after Alexander's return from India.[136] Although some kind of connection between these executions and Parmenio's murder has been suggested,[137] it is clear from the sources that they were formally sentenced, accused of wrongdoing against the local popula-

---

[130] A search on *LGPN* database shows 25 results, distributed throughout the Hellenic geography.

[131] Arr. *An.* III.26.3; Curt. VII.2.11-33 (without mentioning his name: D.S. XVII.80.3; Str. XV.2.10).

[132] For different solutions, see Berve 1926 II: 322-323 no. 648 (sons, not brothers); Atkinson 1994: 257 (*iuvenis* included men up to 45 years old); Heckel 1992: 328-329 (nephews, not brothers). Nevertheless, we have some other examples of significant age differences among (half-) siblings. Kynnane, Philip's first daughter, was over 20 years older than Europa, his last daughter.

[133] Arr. *An.* I.29.4.

[134] On the Royal Pages, see Hammond / Griffith 1979: 401-402; Hammond 1990b: 261-290; Strootman 2007: 181-185; Carney 2008; Sawada 2010: 405-406.

[135] See Badian 1960: 334-338.

[136] Arr. *An.* 6.27.4-6; Curt. 10.1.1-9.

[137] See Atkinson / Yardley 2009: 78.

tion. It is very likely that Polydamas did not remain in Ecbatana once the assignment was fulfilled, but rather returned to announce to Alexander the success of the mission —and as long as Curtius' account is to be believed, carrying Parmenio's head. After all, Alexander still had Polydamas' brothers in his hands. Consequently, he could not be blamed for the same crimes, real or made-up, and die like the rest of those involved.

After this episode, we do not meet Polydamas again until Opis, when he was sent back home along with other veterans escorted by Craterus.[138] A scrutiny of the list of other men discharged at Opis reveals that they were all Macedonians —Polyperchon, Cleitus the White, Gorgias, and Antigenes.[139] His presence at such an advanced stage as Opis also suggests that he would be another of these long-term Macedonian officials. Had he been Pharsalian, he would most probably have been dismissed at the Oxus, given the apparent lack of a close personal relationship with Alexander. The close friendship with Parmenio and his age fit better with a Macedonian Polydamas. Certainly, they could have established their good relationship from the siege of Halus,[140] and the presence of this old friend could have been decisive when choosing the Pharsalians as his personal guard in combat, but in this case it would have been such an intimate friendship as suggested by Curtius. Therefore, the continuity of Polydamas suggests that his position was not exclusively dependent on his friendship with Parmenio, but confirms that the most probable solution is that he was one of the senior Macedonian officers from the former generation, like the rest of his companions on the return to Europe.

The only remaining option to support Heckel's theory is to imagine that Polydamas became a 'naturalized Makedon' after being granted estates in Macedonian territory by the king.[141] However, in this case, it would be difficult to consider him a proper Thessalian, for he would be a Macedonian for practical purposes.[142]

Therefore, after critically examining all the extant information and the arguments raised by Heckel, we must conclude that the scales are tipping towards a Macedonian rather than a Thessalian origin:

1) The two basic arguments put forward by Heckel (proximity during Gaugamela, and his Thessalian homonym) are completely circumstantial and cannot support a Thessalian origin with any certainty.

---

[138] Iust. XII.12.8.

[139] On these individuals, see Heckel 2006, 30, 87-88, 127, 226-231, s.v. 'Antigenes [1a]', 'Cleitus [3]', 'Gorgias [1]'. On the alleged Amadas, see Yardley / Heckel 1997: 277.

[140] See n. 55.

[141] See n. 94.

[142] For example, note that Arrian (*Ind.* 18.3-8; cf. Brunt 1983: 358-359 n. 4), when giving the list of trierarchs, considers Nearchus of Crete, Larichus, brother of Erigyius, and Androsthenes of Thasos to have all been established in Amphipolis, as Macedonians. If the man in the inscription is our Polydamas, this would be a further confirmation of this hypothetical 'naturalization'.

2) Such a close relationship with Parmenio is better explained by a Macedonian background rather than an association resulting from a possible meeting in Halus.

3) The youth of his brothers and his presence in the army cannot be satisfactorily explained by a Thessalian background, but they could have been Macedonian Royal Pages.

4) Appointing a foreigner to a very important commission like Parmenio's murder would have sent a wrong message to the Macedonian staff in those delicate moments. A Macedonian man would have reinstated the 'lawfulness' and 'transparency' of this execution in their eyes.

5) His non-dismissal at the Oxus, when Alexander did away with the Thessalians and the oldest Macedonian soldiers, shows that his post was independent of his relations with Parmenio. The absence of personal, intimate bonds with the king discards the comparison between his situation and that of Medius and Ariston.

6) His discharge at the Opis, along with other veteran Macedonian officials, clearly suggests that he was himself one of them and not an 'intruder' in that list.

7) If we identify him with the man mentioned in the Delphic inscription, this would place his origin in Arethusa, a Chalcidian city annexed to the Macedonian kingdom.

Therefore, when the diverse circumstantial pieces of evidence are combined, it seems more likely that Polydamas was a veteran Macedonian officer from the generation that had already fought under the orders of Philip and that was later inherited by Alexander. He was a loyal man of the old guard who Alexander could rely on when undertaking the delicate decision of Parmenio's elimination in spite of their previous friendship.

The tides of War

Fortunate of Being Conquered: Asians Who Profited from Macedonian Imperialism in 331–323 BC*

Jaakkojuhani Peltonen
(Tampere University)

Many modern politicians, soldiers and civilians agree that in war there are no victors, only losers. However, it can be argued that the mechanism of war is based on the view that war profits especially those who succeed as victors. But what about those locals representing the losing side, are they to be considered merely as helpless victims of war? In this paper, I study the impact of Macedonian conquest (331–323 BC) on the conquered local aristocratic men and women. I examine whether the members of Asian, Bactrian, and Indian high-classes profited from the invasion by foreign intruders and what this reveals from the mechanism of imperialism. Instead of portraying ancient Asians as passive victims who merely suffered from Alexander's conquest, I approach them as actors who aimed to profit from the invasion and who were willing to cooperate with the attacker. It is to be argued that the local aristocrats had their own strategies and aims as the new ruler of Asia invaded their lands.

Macedonian conquest of Persia should be regarded in the context of other wars of aggression. The cooperation between conquerors and conquered has been a dominant factor of the mechanism of imperialism in the history of warfare. Prior to the Macedonians, Assyrians and Persians evidently intended to find suitable collaborators among the conquered people. Similarly, after Alexander, Roman Emperors, crusaders in the Middle Ages, conquistadors in Mexico, British imperialists in India, Nazis in France during World War II, Soviets in Eastern Europe, US troops in modern Iraq or Afghanistan have collaborated with locals who, in turn, benefited from

---

* I want to express my gratitude to Doctor Kenneth Moore for checking the language and giving me several good comments and suggestions.

the invasion. Sometimes these locals were regarded as 'traitors' by their kinsmen. Hernán Cortés had allies, with the ethnic group of Tlaxcalan, whom some Mexicans have considered as 'traitors' since they helped Spanish in the invasion of Tenochtitlan, capital of the Aztec empire.[1] Similar sentiments were shared towards Marshal Philippe Pétain, who presided over the Vichy government, which collaborated with the Nazis during World War II.[2] It could be argued that finding suitable collaborators have made the conquest possible in many historical contexts. On the other hand, among the conquered population there have been those who have benefited from the arrival of foreign conquerors. Thus, for them, the invader may have been greeted as a welcomed 'liberator'.

I examine the conquered 'barbarians' cooperating with Alexander and profiting from Macedonian invasion. The previous scholarship has been interested in the power-relations between the invading Macedonians and the Asian ruling classes. For example, there are studies on the Iranians' position under Alexander's rule. Also, the fact that Alexander used the administration of Persian regime in the conquered Asian territories has been discussed by the scholars.[3] The discussion whether Alexander's conquest benefited or made havoc for the peoples of Asia began already in Antiquity and continued in Europe throughout the Enlightenment.[4] However, during the recent years, Alexander scholars have paid much attention to the sufferings, destruction, and death the Macedonian conquest brought to the people of Asia.[5] This critical view of Alexander's imperialism was probably a counter-reaction to the previous heroic presentations of Alexander's reign and conquest expressed in certain studies pub-

---

[1] Cf. Mills 1998: 90-92. Bosworth 2000: 47 sees similarities on the way Alexander and Cortés allied with the locals.

[2] Cf. Webster 2001.

[3] Badian 1965 and Bosworth 1988: 229-245 give a chronological presentation of Alexander's satrapal government and his appointments. Bosworth 1980 discusses Alexander's policy of fusion. A probably the most famous and heated scholarly debate was about so-called Alexander's policy of fusion which was presented by Tarn (1948 II: 399-451). The view was especially based on Alexander's famous prayer of reconciliation after the Opis mutiny in summer 324. Cf. Arr. *An.* VII.11.8-9. Badian 1958b, and Bosworth 1980: 14 attacked against Tarn's views. Alexander's adoption of eastern ways and court protocols have been discussed more recently. For example, Fredricksmeyer 2000; Romm 2010: 380-387.

[4] For an extremely positive view of the impact of Alexander's conquest to locals, see Plu. *Mor.* 329a-d. For an extremely critical view, see Oros. III.17-20. Cf. Peltonen 2019: 52-54, 199-202. Briant 2017 offers extensive scholarly discussion on the opposite views of Alexander's conquest that existed in Europe during the Enlightenment.

[5] Bosworth 1988, 1996; Worthington 1999; Heckel 2015; Holt 2016. Evidently, Macedonian invasion brought destruction and sufferings to the peoples of Asia. However, the amount of suffering depended on time and place. When the Macedonian invader launched sieges and succeeded to capture the city by force, habitants were robbed, some of them raped, sold to slavery, or they were killed in the hands of the invading armies. For example, we know that the inhabitants of Thebes, Tyre, Persepolis and several cities in India faced severe human sufferings. Unfortunately, I have not been able to include in my analysis research published after early 2020. Therefore, I was not able to include to this study the scholarly discussion that can be found from Heckel 2020.

lished in 20th century.[6] Yet, a balanced view of the Macedonian conquest requires that we also give attention to individuals and local groups among the conquered people who somehow profited from the invasion.

Admitted, a scholar has to be careful when deciding whether some group or an individual should be named as a traitor, opportunist or flatterer. Also, it is somewhat challenging to measure the quantity and quality of success: who were the actual benefiters of the conquest; does the immediate rise of the status or the increase of material wealth define the actual benefactors among the conquered people? For example, someone could argue whether it really benefited Bactrian Rhoxane to become Alexander's wife since in the end she was killed for being the mother of Alexander's child. On the other hand, if some Persian noble did not lose his or her title, should we automatically include him or her as a collaborator?

The surviving histories of Alexander, which include Diodorus, Curtius, Plutarch, Arrian, and Justin, provide the main information of the groups and individuals who profited from the Macedonian invasion.[7] However, these accounts are not contemporary texts but were written some 300–400 years later, in the Roman world.[8] Therefore, we must take into consideration the fact that they were written in a different cultural context. For example, the Roman perspective evidently influenced on the way these authors presented the concept of imperialism. It is important to remember the gender aspect too. Our sources were composed by Greco-Roman upper-class *men* whose values reflect patriarchal system and male dominance. However, we should also take into account the context of the lost, first-hand contemporary texts that the Roman-time authors later used when arranging their second-hand narratives. The first-hand authors like Callisthenes, Ptolemy, Aristobulus, and Nearchus, observed the war of aggression from the side of the victors.[9] Often these contemporary accounts were intended to glorify and idealize the Macedonian war in Asia, Bactria, and India, and make it appear as a 'justified' operation. Unsurprisingly, these sources written by the Macedonians and Greeks are more interested in their fellow-countrymen than in the lives of the barbarians. Also, these passages are often short and scrappy and, therefore, they represent only a small portion of the lives of men and women who gained favor in the eyes of the Macedonian king. Unfortunately, the lives of the ordinary people are rarely visible

---

[6] Tarn 1948 and Hammond 1981 being the most famous representatives. Especially, Tarn's view of Alexander as supporter of brotherhood and unity among the people of Asia, allegedly motivated the critique expressed by Badian and Bosworth.

[7] Heckel 2006 is an excellent guide to all minor characters in the story of Alexander and the Macedonian conquest. In this paper, I have benefited enormously on the collected information by Heckel on the Asians who somehow appear in the sources. When it comes to the Persian names, I follow nomenclature given by Heckel.

[8] Bowden (2014: 5) reminds us that despite decades of research, we still have no reliable method for determining which accounts can be trusted.

[9] For a short survey of these contemporary writers in the early Hellenistic period, see Zambrini 2007.

to us in the sources. When the ancient historians wrote about the conquered, they mostly paid attention to the aristocratic and royal locals.

Instead of a chronological approach, I deal with the topic thematically. Firstly, as one interesting group of locals, I discuss those being neglected by the previous regime but whom Alexander enthroned or appointed as new satraps. Secondly, I analyze cases where locals initiated the cooperation with the Macedonian conquerors and changed sides when searching for their own benefit. Thirdly, I pay attention to the religious agents that profited from the conquest as well as individuals who allegedly used their beauty and charisma to make an impression to the king. In all these cases, I scrutinize how Alexander's regime benefited from the cooperation with the locals and how the king rewarded those starting to cooperate with him.

Looking for mutual benefit and cooperation

To begin with, it should be mentioned that the ongoing war marked a new division of power to the members of the Asian, Bactrian, and Indian high-class. As a general rule, Alexander retained the structure of Persian imperial rule and maintained the system of taxation. However, the administrative appointments when establishing the Macedonian rule in the conquered area was another question: whether to let the satrap appointed by the Persians to continue in power or to replace him by a Macedonian or an Asian one.[10]

When analyzing the conquered people's relationship with Alexander, we can start by categorizing them in two different groups: those who gained personal favor from of Alexander and those who found themselves in his disfavor. Among the first category, there were those who 1) were previously neglected by the Persian regime, and 2) the satraps and local monarchs who retained their former status and even gained more authority from the Macedonian conquerors. Some of the local aristocrats instantly submitted to Alexander while others initially fought against the Macedonians but later succeeded in winning king's favor.

In 334 BC, Alexander intruded with his armies in Asia. As we know, the first part of the campaign was addressed to the panhellenist motivation of war: to revenge the Persians and give freedom to Greek city states.[11] Our sources give the impression that freedom and independence were given to Greek cities of Anatolia, especially if they were willing to submit to the Macedonian rule.[12] It could be argued that for the

---

[10] For example, Macedonian Kalas was appointed as a new satrap and he replaced Persian Arsites. Arr. *An.* I.17.1 (see below).

[11] For recent studies of Alexander's panhellenistic war-propaganda, see Flower 2000; Faraguna 2003; Squillace 2010; Kremmydas 2013.

[12] D.S. XVII.24.1. Arr. *An.* I.17.11, 18.2. This given freedom was conditional, cf. what happened to the city of Aspendus (Arr. *An.* I.27.3-4).

local Greeks the invasion signified improvement in some level.[13] At least the propaganda of war demanded that the Macedonian conqueror treated well the Greeks of Anatolia as they were their liberators.

When Asian cities surrendered to Alexander, voluntarily or after a siege, one of the first tasks was to re-arrange the local administration. While entering the conquered city or territory, the invader personally met the satraps and other members of local upper class, nominated by Darius. When Alexander and his Macedonian staff met them, they searched for potential collaborators who would swear allegiance to them and start to cooperate with the new establishment. Those who decided to voluntarily submit to Alexander were used in Macedonian propaganda. This is seen in the letter Alexander allegedly wrote to Darius. In the letter he writes: «I am also responsible for all the men who fought on your side, survived the battle, and fled to me, and who remain with me not unwillingly, but have joined my camp voluntarily».[14]

Finding suitable collaborators was also a necessary task since the Macedonian army was to penetrate further into the Persian Empire. Without cooperation with the local members of the high class, the conquest would have been impossible to succeed. Even though Alexander nominated locals as satraps or let local monarchs continue to rule, Macedonian garrisons were often established in the conquered area. Also, Macedonian officers (*strategoi* or *episkopoi)* were nominated to preside over the local satrapy as representatives of the Macedonian king and his army.[15] This stresses the fact that the military side of government was laid in the hands of Macedonians while the civil administration was delegated to the natives.[16] This however, does not change the fact that the local members of Iranian, Bactrian, and Indian upper classes were recruited to high posts in the administration. In addition, a satrap was still technically a commander in his province as he had been under the Persian regime. Interestingly, the sources mention Persian commanders serving in Alexander's army stressing the fact that even Asians could serve in the army and fight alongside the Macedonians if they subordinated themselves to Alexander.[17]

The crucial decision a member of a local ruling-class had to make was to decide whether to remain loyal to the previous regime or support the Macedonian invader.

---

[13] The alleged profit that Alexander's conquest brought for the Greeks in Anatolia is not scope within this study. Briant (2010: 35-36) is critical on the actual profit but sees that Greeks did not regard Alexander as liberator; cf. Faraguna 2003: 113. Nawotka 2003 is an important contribution because it pays attention to the epigraphic evidence.

[14] Arr. *An.* II.14.7: ὅσοι τῶν μετὰ σοῦ παραταξαμένων μὴ ἐν τῇ μάχῃ ἀπέθανον, ἀλλὰ παρ' ἐμὲ κατέφυγον, τούτων ἐπιμέλομαι καὶ οὐκ ἄκοντες παρ' ἐμοί εἰσιν, ἀλλὰ αὐτοὶ ἑκόντες ξυστρατεύονται μετ' ἐμοῦ. (Transl. Pamela Mensch)

[15] Arr. *An.* I.17.7-8. (Sardis); Arr. *An.* I.23.6 (Caria); Curt. IV.5.9 (Tyre); Arr. *An.* III.1.3 (Pelusium); Arr. *An.* III.16.4, VII.18.1 (Babylon); Arr. *An.* III.16.9, Curt. V.2.16-17 (Susa); Arr. *An.* III.29.1 (Aornus); Arr. *An.* IV.5.2 (Maracanda); Arr. *An.* IV.17.3. Curt. VIII.2.14 (Bactria); Arr. *An.* V.8.3 (Taxila).

[16] Bosworth (1988: 229-245) frequently reminds by this aspect in Alexander's policy in Asia.

[17] Badian 1965: 174; Bosworth 1988: 236-237.

In some cases, those who remained loyal to the Persian regime lost their status and sometimes their lives. We know that the cities of Tyre and Gaza chose to fight against Alexander and their leaders and inhabitants suffered in the subsequent sieges.[18] If Curtius Rufus is to be believed, Batis, the satrap of Gaza, suffered painful death in the hands of the conqueror.[19] In contrast, Persian commanders of Sardis and Damascus did not remain loyal to Darius (see below).[20] Again, Gerastratus at Aradus and Enylus at Byblos both could retain their position as kings, but they had to help Alexander's siege against Tyre.[21] Evidently, also the Jews faced a similar dilemma when the king asked supplies from the Jewish high-priest during the siege of Tyre.[22] It could be argued that for the members of local aristocracy cooperation with the Macedonian invader was an option with hope of favor in return.

For those neglected by the previous regime, the Macedonian War of Aggression may have been seen as an opportunity to improve their status. As far as we know, one of the first locals who won the favor of the Macedonian conqueror and decided to cooperate with him was Queen Ada of Caria. Alexander replaced the Persian satrap Orontopates with Ada in winter 334-333 BC. Alexander allegedly encountered Ada, who appealed to the king in order to recover the position of her ancestors. As a result, Alexander made Ada the ruler of the whole country of Caria and accepted the title of her son.[23] Ada's relationship with Alexander was described as warm and maternal.[24] It could be asserted that Ada herself arranged this meeting and won the favor of the conqueror not only by her personal charisma but because it was compatible with the plans of the conqueror.[25]

Another aristocrat neglected by the Persian regime was Sidonian Abdalonymus, perhaps the most famous individual for whom Alexander's war meant a notable rise in status. When Alexander arrived at Sidon in 332 BC, he regarded the previous king of Sidon, Straton II, as a loyal supporter of Darius and empowered Hephaestion to nominate a new king. Hephaestion found Abdalonymus and chose him as the new king. Abdalonymus belonged to the Sidonian royal house but, according to the clas-

---

[18] For the siege of Tyre, see Curt. IV.4.12-17, Arr. *An.* II.24.4-5. For the siege of Gaza, see Curt. IV.6.30, Arr. *An.* II.27.7.

[19] Curt. IV.6.29.

[20] Cf. Curt. III.13.3-4, V.1.44; D.S. XVII.21.7, 64.5.

[21] Arr. *An.* II.20.1, 3.

[22] J. *AJ.* XI.317. According to Josephus, Jews managed to achieve king's favor in the end (see below).

[23] Arr. *An.* I.23.7-8; D.S. XVII.24.2; Plu. *Alex.* 22.4-5.

[24] Plu. *Alex.* 22.4-5. In Plutarch, Ada, whom Alexander called his mother, sent to the king yummies and even bakers and cooks.

[25] The former satrap of the area, Orontopates, was faithful to Darius since he led the resistance in the city of Halicarnassus and, after escaping the city, he fought at Gaugamela. In Caria, Alexander established a small Macedonian garrison: Arr. *An.* I.23.

sical tradition, he had been living as a gardener on the outside of political life.[26] The historicity of the story of Abdalonymus as a gardener seems to be a side-issue here, but more important is the way that the Macedonian invasion impacted on Abdalonymus' status and position. Besides the literary tradition, there exists epigraphical evidence that Abdalonymus really did become the king of Sidon.[27]

The encounter between Abdalonymus and Alexander portrayed in the literary tradition is idealized. In Curtius, it was Abdalonymus' physical and noble character which made impression on Alexander.[28] Diodorus portrays Abdalonymus as a man suitable to govern: wise and good in all respects who had been living in poverty. For Diodorus, it was an indication of the power of *Tyche* (chance/guiding goddess), which makes kings out of gardeners.[29] Above else, this 'from rags to riches' story of Abdalonymus served the Macedonian propaganda well. It was to give an impression that the Macedonian regime worked for the common good by selecting the 'right men to rule' and liberate the Sidonians from unsuitable rulers. The Sidonians in fact had rebelled against the Persian regime some decades before, and therefore the Macedonian invasion may have been seen positively by the locals.[30]

It is generally thought that Abdalonymus was buried in the *Alexander sarcophagus* that was found in modern Lebanon.[31] The reliefs of the sarcophagus portraying Abdalonymus with Alexander may proclaim his sincere gratitude to Alexander and Hephaestion for making him the king of Sidon. It is possible that the relief was on display while Abdalonymus lived, to serve as propagandistic self-promotion.[32] Later, Abdalonymus even received Persian spoils and an adjoining city as an additional territory from Alexander.[33] Evidently, Abdalonymus profited from the Macedonian invasion and became a supporter of Macedonian regime.

About a year later, in 331 BC, as Alexander's campaign proceeded, he continued his policy to appoint locals in the high administrative posts. For example, the Egyptians Petisis and Doloaspis were appointed as «Nomarchs of Egypt».[34] It is suggested that Alexander divided Egypt into two satrapies and, therefore, Petisis and Doloaspis

---

[26] Curt. IV.1.15-23; D.S. XVII.47.1-6; Iust. XI.10.8-9; Plu. *Mor.* 340d. Bosworth (2003: 182-183) and Burstein (2007: 143-149) consider 'the gardener story' as a motif adapted from Late Near Eastern sources.

[27] For the bilingual Greco-Phoenician text that mentions Abdalonymus as the king of Sidon, see Kantzia 1980; Sznycer 1980.

[28] Curt. IV.1.25-26.

[29] D.S. XVII.47.6.

[30] For the Sidonian revolt against the Persians, see Wiesehöwer 2016. According to Arrian, the people of Sidon hated Darius and invited Alexander to enter the town, see Arr. *An.* II.15.6.

[31] For Abdalonymus as the occupant, see Stewart 1994: 294-306.

[32] Stewart 1994: 298.

[33] Curt. IV.1.26. Diodorus says Abdalonymus became Alexander's friend (*filos*) while Plutarch writes that Abdalonymus became one of Alexander's Companions (*hetairoi*). See D.S. XVII.47.6; Plu. *Mor.* 340d.

[34] Arr. *An.* III.5.2.

were responsible for judicial and administrative matters in them.[35] We lack information of their previous status, but it is probable that the Macedonian invasion did mean enhancement in Petisis' and Doloaspis' status and authority.[36]

Among the local Persian elite there were those who had ended up in disgrace by Darius and, therefore, were seen as potential collaborators by the Macedonian invader. This becomes evident in the way that the Persian Oxydates was elevated to power in 330 BC. Curtius writes: «Oxydates, a Persian nobleman kept in shackles because he had been condemned to execution by Darius, was freed and given the satrapy of Media by Alexander».[37] A parallel description comes from Arrian: «He [Alexander] appointed Oxydates satrap of Media, a Persian who had been arrested by Darius and imprisoned at Susa; this made Alexander trust him».[38] At this stage of the campaign, Darius was still alive and the Macedonian king did not want to face Persian revolts at Susa. By appointing Oxydates, Alexander wanted to protect his rear. It was about placing Oxydates under a debt of gratitude. He probably calculated that for Oxydates there was no reason to support Darius, who had just sentenced him to death.[39]

Alexander nominated Persians as his satraps, but in some cases these local aristocrats did not remain in power for too long. For example, three different Asian nobles were nominated as satraps of Parapamisadae. In 330/29 BC, the Persian Proexes was nominated as the satrap of Parapamisadae with the Macedonian commander Niloxenus as his overseer.[40] However, two years later, in 327 BC, Proexes was replaced for unknown reasons by the Persian Tyriespis, who is said to have put down a revolt.[41] In 325 BC, Tyriespis was in turn removed and executed because of the charges made by the locals and because of his greed and arrogance.[42] He was replaced by Oxyartes, father of Rhoxane, who enjoyed the king's favor.[43] In a similar way, the satrap of Susiana, the Persian Abulites, surrendered the city of Susa and was allowed to retain his satrapy. However, later Alexander executed him along with his son since Abulites

---

[35] Burstein (2008: 189-191) refers to demotic ostracon dated to the reign of Alexander. This text mentions Alexander and Pediese (referring to Petisis) as the satrap. Burstein argues convincingly that 'nomarch' in Arrian refers to old Persian title satrap.

[36] We know Doloaspis was later in sole charge of administration of Egypt. At the time of Alexander's death, Cleomenes of Naucratis was appointed as the satrap of Egypt. For a scholarly discussion on Cleomenes' possible usurpation as the new satrap, see Burstein 2008: 186-189.

[37] Curt. VI.2.11: *Oxydates erat nobilis Perses, qui a Dareo capitali supplicio destinatus cohibebatur in vinculis; huic liberato satrapeam Mediae attribuit.* Transl. John Yardley.

[38] Arr. *An.* III.20.3: τὸν στρατὸν Μηδίας μὲν σατράπην ἀπέδειξεν Ὀξυδάτην Πέρσην ἄνδρα, ὃς ἐτύγχανε πρὸς Δαρείου ξυνειλημμένος καὶ ἐν Σούσοις εἰργόμενος·τοῦτο αὐτῷ ἐς πίστιν ἦν πρὸς Ἀλέξανδρον. Transl. P. E. Brunt.

[39] Oxydates did not succeed to remain in king's favor and was later displaced, see Arr. *An.* IV.18.3.

[40] Arr. *An.* III.28.4. For reasons behind Alexander's policy to nominate Proexes, see Howe 2016: 169.

[41] Arr. *An.* IV.22.5.

[42] Curt. IX.8.9; Arr. *An.* VI.15.3.

[43] Arr. *An.* VI.15.3. Curtius writes that Alexander had tie affection with him. Cf. Curt. IX.8.10.

had not sent supplies to the king when ordered to do so.[44] The high-ranking Persians could win first Alexander's favor but afterwards fall into disgrace with the king.

As indicated, when analyzing our sources, we have to take into account the fact that they were written from the Macedonian perspective, portraying the nominated Persians violating their duties and thus deserving to be removed from their former posts. Alexander had a clear strategy to reorganise power among the locals and win the favor of the ruling-class in the area. Even though our sources may sometimes idealize the extent of the cooperation on the part of the collaborators, we can conclude that the invader searched primarily for their own benefit: to control the conquered areas by the help of the locals who were willing to cooperate with the invader.

Barbarians changing sides and searching for allies

In the following section, my aim is to explore how the Asians themselves took the initiative in trying to reach a settlement with the Macedonian conquerors. The members of the Asian elite classes played an active role in seeking the favor of Alexander. Instead of being passive victims of conquest, our literary sources present them as actors who tried to maximize the profit by changing sides. In the very early stages of the war, some notable Persians willingly welcomed the Macedonian invader in their cities. The Persian Mithrenes surrendered the city of Sardis to Alexander without resistance.[45] In return, Alexander gave him Armenia.[46] Curtius calls him a traitor (*prōditor*) who had betrayed Sardis. [47] Additionally, we know of the anonymous military governor of Damascus who handed allegedly all Darius' treasures in the city along with his money to Alexander.[48]

After Darius suffered losses in the major battle of Gaugamela –and after Bessus' usurpation– the cooperation of the Iranian aristocracy with Alexander became intense.[49] We know several notable Persians who turned to support Alexander's re-

---

[44] Arr. *An.* VII.4.1. Plutarch writes that Alexander did not kill Abulites but throw him to the prison: Plu. *Alex.* 68.7.

[45] D.S. XVII.21.7.

[46] Curt. V.1.44. Cf. D.S. XVII.64.5. In contrast, Arr. *An.* I.17.4. Arrian does not mention that Alexander gave Armenia to Mithrenes but writes that the citizens of Sardis and other Lydians were permitted to keep their ancient customs and they were granted freedom.

[47] Curt. V.1.44. Briant (2015: 157-161) sees that Curtius sometimes takes Darius' side against Alexander most likely because he used a Persophile source, and because Curtius intended to stress the importance of monarchial loyalty.

[48] Curt. III.13.3-4. The military governor (whom Curtius calls as a traitor [*prōditor*]) sent letter to Alexander but in the end, he was killed by his own men.

[49] For the scholarly discussion whether Bessus' war against Alexander should be regarded as rebellion at all, see Howe 2016: 170.

gime. For example, the Persian Mazaeus had fought against the Macedonian troops at Gaugamela but later surrendered Babylon to Alexander. As a result, he was appointed as the satrap of Babylon and, quite possibly, Mazaeus was even granted the right to mint silver coins.[50] Later, when Mazaeus died, Alexander appointed the Iranian Stamenes as the new satrap of Babylonia.[51] Also Artabazus, characterized often as 'Darius' most loyal supporter', found favor in Alexander's eyes and served later in the Macedonian army. Artabazus was not able to stop Bessus from arresting king Darius but he fled from Bessus' camp alongside with his followers and surrended to Alexander in Hyrcania.[52] Our sources portray the encounter between Alexander and the elderly Artabazus filled with dignity and mutual respect. The old man offered Alexander his right hand and praised Alexander while the young king brought horses for Artabazus but himself walked along him. Interestingly, Artabazus is told to have been in exile at the court of King Philip in Macedonia in 352-349/8 BC. Also, he was the father of Barsine, Alexander's mistress.[53] This background information adds an interesting aspect to his active cooperation with Alexander. After his encounter with Alexander, Artabazus was sent alongside the Macedonian commanders to fight against the rebel Satibarzanes.[54] Additionally, Alexander appointed him as the satrap of Bactria.[55] Another turncoat was the Indian Sisicottus, who had been fighting along with Bessus but, after Alexander conquered Bactria, he decided to join Alexander's forces. According to Arrian, Sisicottus had «shown himself especially trustworthy» and the Macedonian king nominated him as ruler of the Assacenians after the conquest of Aornus.[56]

Darius' mother Sisygambis is perhaps the most prominent example of a person who 'changed sides' and made cooperation with the invader. Being depicted as a second mother to Alexander, it is suggested that there was a strong bond between her and Alexander.[57] In Susa, the queen mother and her daughters were provided with tutors in order to learn Greek.[58] Interestingly, there is an occasion where Sisygambis used her authority over Alexander.[59] During Alexander's campaign against the Uxians, the Uxians sent a plea for Sisygambis to beg for mercy. The

---

[50] Arr. *An.* III.16.4; Curt. V.1.44; D.S. XVII.64.5-6. Badian (1965: 173 n. 4, 175) argues that Mazaeus had strong Babylonian connections, possible a Babylonian wife, and therefore he wanted to save Babylon from destruction. Cf. Bosworth 1988: 235-236.

[51] Arr. *An.* IV.18.3; Curt. VIII.3.17 calls him Ditamenes.

[52] Curt. V.12.18, VI.5.2-6; Arr. *An.* III.21.4; D.S. XVII.23.7.

[53] D.S. XVI.52.3-4; Curt. V.9.1, VI.5.2.

[54] Curt. VII.3.2; Arr. *An.* III.28.2.

[55] Arr. *An.* III.29.1. A year later, Artabazus insisted to step down from the post because of his old age: Curt. VIII.1.19; Arr. *An.* IV.17.3.

[56] Arr. *An.* IV.30.5; Curt. VIII.11.25.

[57] Curt. III.12.17, V.2.22; Iust. XIII.1.5.

[58] D.S. XVII.67.1.

[59] Curt. V.3.12-15.

satrap of the Uxians, Medates was married to the daughter of Sisygambis' sister. After hesitating, Sisygambis wrote a letter to Alexander to pardon her relatives. In response the king pardoned all the prisoners and left the city intact. According to the literary tradition, Sisygambis is said to have mourned fatally after hearing that Alexander had died.[60]

Local elites taking the initiative for making an alliance with the Macedonian conquerors had most likely opportunistic motives. Besides escaping the possible military conflict with the invader, one possible motive for their initiative was an assumption that the Macedonian army would attack their old enemies. This was evident both in the early stages of the campaign as well as later when Alexander's armies penetrated the river Oxus and the borders of India. In winter 334/3 BC, the Pisidians from Selge approached Alexander by envoys. Alexander had just fought against their old enemies, the Termessians. Thus, wanting to achieve king's favor and support in their rivalry against the Termessians, the Pisidians from Selge sought a treaty with Alexander.[61] Six years later in the spring of 328 BC, the Scythian ruler Pharasmenes, King of the Chorasmians who lived in lower Oxus, decided to meet Alexander. Pharasmenes had decided not to join in the war against Alexander by Spitamenes. Instead, he offered Alexander his support in warfare against his neighbors the Amazons and Colchians, and promised to act as a guide.[62] Alexander formed friendship and alliance with Pharasmenes, whom he sent back to his home. The king promised that he would call for Pharasmenes' services after subduing all Asia. It can be argued that the Scythian Pharasmenes intended to profit from the state of war by making Alexander his ally and in this way achieved greater dominance over the region.

In the spring of 326 BC, Taxiles (the ruler of Taxila), whose personal name was Omphis, wanted to encounter Alexander personally and make a formal submission to him.[63] Most likely, Omphis wanted to have Alexander's support in war against his enemies, Abisares and Porus.[64] The vast Persian Empire was heterogeneous, and different entities and peoples had to strife with each other when the foreign invader penetrated their parts of the Empire. Evidently, these local struggles benefited Alexander. When he and Taxiles met, they greeted each other with lavish gifts.[65] According to Arrian, Alexander annexed large quantities of the

---

[60] Curt. X.5.19-25; D.S. XVII.118.3; Iust. XIII.1.5. Curtius regards the grief of the queen mother as a proof that the king had treated her gentle. Curtius stresses that Sisygambis had found 'protector' in Alexander who guarded her family's interests. But after achieving news of Alexander's death, the queen mother decided to expire.

[61] Arr. *An.* I.28.1-8.

[62] Arr. *An.* IV.15.4-6.

[63] For the account of Omphis/Taxiles' encounter and his submission to Alexander, see Curt. VIII.12.4-16; D.S. XVII.86.3-7.

[64] Cf. Curt. VIII.12.12-14; D.S. XVII.86.5-6. Cf. Arr. *An.* V.18.7.

[65] Curt. VIII.12.12-14. Cf. Str. XV.1.28. In the literary tradition also, Phegeus who ruled area near the Hyphasis acted similarly as Taxiles by encountering Alexander and giving gifts to the Macedonian conqueror.

neighboring territories to Taxiles' realm as he had requested.[66] Taxiles sent supplies for the Macedonian army but also received from Alexander thirty elephants taken from Barsaentes. Diodorus calls him Alexander's friend (*philos*) and ally (*symmachos*).[67] Instead of brutal conquest we can see traces of a genuine cooperation between the conqueror and the conquered.[68]

Porus (a ruler of Paurava) was another Indian rajah who eventually profited from the Macedonian invasion, and started to cooperate with the Macedonian regime. The Battle of the Hydaspes River was fought in 326 BC. Before the battle, Porus had rejected the demand to pay tribute to Alexander.[69] The most powerful ruler of the Punjab area clearly believed in his chances to defeat the Macedonian army in open battle. In the fierce fighting that followed, both armies had severe casualties. However, surprisingly, Alexander did not annihilate the defeated Porus but regarded him as a worthy opponent and made him his ally. Alexander retained Porus' kingdom and gave him a territory larger than he had formerly held.[70] In addition, Alexander succeeded in making an alliance between Porus and Taxiles; also Alexander added to Porus' territory those nations he later subdued. Yet, the conqueror, expected favor in return: we know that Porus and Taxiles gave Alexander a fleet after the Macedonians turned back to the west and remained as important allies.[71]

After Darius' and Bessus' had lost the war against Alexander, for many Asians there was no reason to fight back but rather to search ways to retain their position under the new regime. One could argue that there have been possible fabrications in ancient data when they portray that a defeated enemy received even greater lands and possessions after being subjugated. Admittedly, in the sources, the Macedonian invaders are represented as a better regime compared to the Persian one. However, the picture of the Asians taking the initiative in collaborating with the new monarch and searching for his favor is a plausible one. Yet, the historicity of this cooperation and strategy of giving rewards for the possible collaborators should not be rejected. Alexander needed help from the locals in the administration of the vast areas. This is especially the case in the guarding of his rear for campaigns in the remote eastern places like Bactria and India, where he needed cooperation with the locals.

Phegeus was also ready to start the cooperation and give information to Alexander on the kingdoms in the east, see D.S. XVII.93.1-2; Curt. IX.1.36.

66 Arr. *An.* V.8.2

67 D.S. XVII.86.7.

68 Taxiles took 5,000 of his soldiers and accompanied Alexander's army to fight against Porus at Hydaspes river. After the battle ended, Taxiles is said to have presented the terms to Porus who evaded him: Arr. *An.* V.8.5, 18.6-7.

69 Curt. VIII.13.2.

70 Arr. *An.* V.19.3; Curt. VIII.14.45; Plu. *Alex.* 60.8.

71 Cf. Curt IX.3.22; Arr. *An.* V.19.3; Curt. VIII.14.45; Plu. *Alex.* 60.7-8. Cf. *Itin. Alex.* 111.

Conquest benefiting local priesthoods

Most likely, Alexander's religiosity was a prominent part of his personality.[72] As a monarch of Macedonia and conqueror of Asia, Alexander paid a lot of attention in arranging religious ceremonies and sacrifices to several gods.[73] Before making any important decisions and after successful operations the king would ensure the favor of the gods. Against this background it is hardly surprising that religious groups of the conquered people profited from the way the foreign conqueror venerated local gods.

Among the local religious agents, the oracle of Ammon benefited enormously from the king's religious policy, which is stressed in Alexander's visit at Siwah in 331 BC. As far as we know, the king was ready to travel several hundreds of miles on a journey that took six weeks.[74] At the oracular site, Alexander listened to the oracle's response and when leaving the oracle, he gave rich gifts to the priests.[75] We could assert that the priests of Ammon were aware of the king's arrival and ready to cooperate with the new ruler of Egypt. The content of the oracular consultation between Alexander and the priests was enigmatic already in Antiquity. There were various traditions on what the king asked for the oracle and what the priests replied to him. However, evidently the oracular answers pleased the young monarch.[76] In Curtius, the high-priest is willing to flatter the king by giving desirable answers.[77] The oracle of Ammon clearly made cooperation with the invaders giving them sense of divine acceptance and help.[78] This cooperation continued, some seven years later, when Alexander sent envoys in order to consult the oracle after Hephaestion's death.[79] It is not exaggerated to state that the oracle of Ammon clearly profited from the invasion.[80]

During his stay in Egypt, Alexander sacrificed at Memphis to the Egyptian god Apis. Alexander paying homage to Apis was probably a conscious response

---

[72] For discussions on Alexander's religiosity, see Edmunds 1971; Fredricksmeyer 2003; Dreyer 2009; Bowden 2017. For example, the historical reconstruction of Alexander's visit to the oracle of Ammon/Zeus in Siwah and its relationship between his divinity has received enormous interest and scholarly discussion in the previous scholarship. Cf. Tarn 1948 II: 347-359; Brunt 1976: 467-480; Bosworth 1977: 51-75; Badian 1981: 27-71; Fredricksmeyer 2003; 270-273; Cartledge 2004: 221-222, 266-270. Bowden 2017 recently represents different approach by exploring the attitudes of the Alexander historians concerning divination.

[73] Holt 2016: 107-110.

[74] Fredricksmeyer 2003: 270; D.S. XVII.49.2-51.3; Curt. IV.7.5-32.

[75] Curt. IV.7.28; D.S. XVII.51.4; Plu. *Alex.* 27.4.

[76] Arr. *An.* III.4.5.

[77] Curt. IV.7.26.

[78] Justin (XI.11.6) writes that Alexander even sent men ahead to bribe the priests.

[79] Arr. *An.* VII.14.7, 23.6.

[80] Even though, famous Greeks had visited oracle of Ammon before Alexander, the site became even more famous after Alexander's invasion and tourists today want to visit the site because Alexander made the journey to Siwah.

to the crimes carried by Cambyses II, who had defiled the temple some 200 years before.[81] This action may be seen as a public manifestation on behalf of the local god and its priesthood. In addition, Arrian writes that Alexander was planning to build a temple of Isis in Alexandria side by side with the Greek temples.[82] Also, the Greek *Alexander Romance* especially praises Alexander's religious policy in Egypt. This may reflect to the king's tolerant religious policy towards Egyptian priesthoods as well as the Egyptian origins of the *Romance*. Also, an Egyptian inscription announces that Alexander had renovated the chapel of Tuthmosis III. In the inscription, Alexander's is called with full pharaonic title, which stresses his policy of religious inclusiveness and the way the Macedonian conqueror was perceived in Egypt.[83]

Alexander's policy seems to have profited other local religious agents too. In Babylonia, Alexander rebuilt temples of Bel and encountered the Chaldean priests. Arrian writes that Alexander did everything the Babylonian priests, advised and even sacrificed to Bel in a manner they prescribed.[84] It seems that the new king of Babylon maintained the status of the Chaldean priests, who accompanied the king later in the campaign.[85] Babylonian astronomical diaries show that the Babylonian scholar-priests continued their practice of observing the heavens during the reign of Alexander, just like they had done during the reigns of previous Babylonian kings. Based on the fragments of the diary, it could be argued that the Chaldean priests treated Alexander with the same sense of loyalty as they had treated their previous Babylonian and Persian kings.

Josephus' narrative of Alexander's visit in Jerusalem has been regarded usually as non-historical fiction and religious propaganda.[86] Admittedly, the narrative goes too far when proclaiming the might of God and Jewish culture and nation; however the king's positive reaction to the local priesthood would match with his religious policy in Egypt and Babylonia.[87] In the Jewish tradition, the high priest Jaddua welcomed Alexander as a figure who enjoyed divine blessing and was willing to cooperate with the conqueror.[88] In return Alexander allowed the Jews to retain their rights. The decision of the Jewish priests to cooperate with Alexander and the king's alleged decision to favor them would explain the existence of the positive literary tradition

---

[81] Arr. *An.* III.1.4. Cf. Hdt. III.27-29.

[82] Arr. *An.* III.1.5.

[83] Bowden 2014: 65-67.

[84] Arr. *An.* III.16.5, VII.17.1-4.

[85] Cf. Bowden 2014: 94-95.

[86] J. *AJ.* XI.306-345. Many scholars have assessed the story as a totally unhistorical episode. Marcus (1937: 512-532), Momigliano (1979), and Cohen (1982: 68) consider it unhistorical, while Nawotka (2010: 195-196) argues for the veracity of the visit.

[87] Cf. J. *AJ.* XI.331-338.

[88] In Josephus' account the Jewish high-priest was first unwilling to cooperate with Alexander since he had sworn his allegiance to Darius: J. *AJ.* XI.318.

around his visit to Jerusalem itself, and the position Jews enjoyed during the reigns of Alexander and his Ptolemaic successors.[89]

In summary, the king respected the religious authority of the local priesthoods and let them be as guardians of divine power and knowledge. This may have derived not only from the pragmatic political reasons but also from Alexander's own religiosity. The positive treatment of the local religious priesthood can be seen in relation with the way the king treated the cities and its people generally.[90] Sometimes the local religious elites received funding from the king to rebuild their shrines. On the other hand, the conquered priests had to be willing to flatter the king and present him as a foreign invader enjoying divine favor. In a similar way, the oracle of Ammon, priests of Marduk in Babylon, and the Jewish high-priests proclaimed that the Macedonian invasion was foreseen by God's prophet and/or was expected to be successful. At the same time, these religious leaders and intermediaries of god had to be willing to proclaim that their current ruler Darius had lost this 'divine' blessing, and thus changed sides in the ongoing war between Alexander and Darius.

Winners in Aphrodite-Contest: Gaining king's favor by Sexual services

Not only bold but also beautiful individuals won Alexander's favor. At least that is the impression our ancient sources give when portraying extraordinary beauty and sexual services as a way of gaining personal favor of the king.[91] In contrast to ancient historians, modern scholars have sometimes viewed Alexander as a pragmatic statesman who 'never sacrificed policy to emotion'. Or, if he did, it was because of his angry temper, use of alcohol and psychological consequences of combat injury.[92] The King's possible emotional and sexual motives have been mostly disregarded when analyzing his policy making.[93]

One of the figures who is said to have made personal impact on king by his physical attractiveness is a 'good looking' eunuch, Bagoas (already favourite of Darius III). Aside from the short passages of Plutarch and Athenaeus, Curtius is the

---

89 Cf. Ps.-Callisth. II.24. Tropper (2013: 136-156) sees the Rabbinic tale on the visit in Jerusalem as developed from Josephus' narrative.

90 In contrast to benign treatment of local religious agents, in India some of the brahmans who resisted the Macedonians and encouraged locals to rebel were killed: Arr. *An.* VI.7.4, 16.5.

91 Here we are referring to members of high-class. Evidently, there were women who suffered as 'prices of war' in the hands of the Macedonian. For a discussion on the fate of women, see Heckel 2015: 253-258.

92 Cf. Badian 1958a: 146. For the possible role of alcohol in Alexander's reign, see O'Brien 1992. For physical injures and psychological consequences of combat injury, see Heckel 2015: 261-264.

93 Chugg 2012 seems to be in this respective exception by paying attention to Alexander's love life. Cf. Chugg, 2012: 66. However, in Chugg the emphasis is laid on the way Alexander's alleged lovers might reveal of the king's personality.

only ancient author writing about Bagoas.[94] Even though Tarn famously rejected the historicity of Bagoas, in the more modern research, scholars regard Bagoas as historical figure.[95] Alexander allegedly encountered Bagoas in 330 BC just after the king Darius had died. The eunuch succeeded to win Alexander's personal favor. However, according to Curtius, his impact on Alexander was harmful, since –under the influence of Bagoas– he made some 'bad' decisions.[96] Curtius stresses that as Bagoas gave his body to Alexander, he was able to control the king. For example, Nabarzanes, the Persian commander at battle of Issus, who together with Bessus had plotted against Darius, was pardoned because Bagoas' influence on Alexander.[97] Secondly, by his alleged authority over Alexander, Bagoas was able to ruin his personal enemy, Persian Orsines. According to Curtius, Orsines was an innocent man who was killed because of the plot of the wretched eunuch.[98] We do not know how long Bagoas succeeded to remain in king's favor or what happened to him after Alexander died.

Accounts of royal women enjoying Alexander's favor have been already stressed in the cases of queen Ada and the royal mother Sisygambis. Yet, in our sources their relationship between Alexander is portrayed as maternal, as they adopted the king as their son. When it comes to women using their sexual charisma over the king, the Indian Queen Cleophis is said to have successfully used her sexual attractiveness to gain influence over the king. Cleophis, queen of the Assacenians, managed to remain as a queen in spite of her warfare against the Macedonians in Massaga. Curtius mentions that the queen came to meet Alexander with a group of ladies of noble birth, and because of her beauty, she gained not only a pardon but also restitution of her former status.[99] Justin stresses the queen's sexual power over Alexander: «[Cleophis] regained her throne, which she ransomed by sleeping with him, attaining by sexual favors what she could not by force of arms…Having thus degraded herself Queen Cleophis was called the 'royal whore' by the Indians.»[100] It has been suggested that

---

[94] Plu. *Alex.* 67.3; Ath. XIII.603b. Cf. Ael. *VH.* III.23.

[95] Tarn (1948 II: 319-322) regarded Bagoas as an invented figure and the stories related to him as a way of attacking Alexander by the peripatetic school. Cf. Badian 1958a. Ogden (2009: 213-217, 2011: 167-170) does not explicitly deny the historicity of Bagoas. Also, Chugg (2012: 152-164) sees Bagoas as a historical figure who was entrusted also governmental and diplomatic duties. On Bagoas in the ancient sources and his modern reception, see Baynham 2018. Baynham (2018: 616-618) does neither regard Bagoas as an invented figure.

[96] Cf. Curt. X.1.25-27.

[97] Curt. VI.5.23.

[98] Curt. X.22-38, 42.

[99] Curt. VIII.10.34-35.

[100] Iust. XII.7.9-11: *Quae cum se dedidisset ei, concubitu redemptum regnum ab Alexandro recepit, inlecebris consecuta, quod armis non poterat…Cleophis regina propter prostratam pudicitiam scortum regium ab Indis exinde appellata est.* (Transl. J. C. Yardley). Orosius whose account often follows Justin states similarly: «The queen…bought her kingdom back by sleeping with him [Alexander]». (Oros. III.19.1; transl. A. T. Fears).

when mentioning Cleophis, the Latin authors were referring to Cleopatra, whose relationships with Caesar and Antony were notorious in the Roman world, and who was also called as 'whore-queen'.[101] Moralizing portrayals of Bagoas and Cleophis reflect Roman gender-system and ideals of manliness. The king is presented as a warning example of wrong conduct for the contemporary audience. For Roman authors, the head of the state should not let his passions to influence on his political decisions. This view reflects the Greco-Roman high-class culture, where manliness implied an ability to govern one's passions and ability to make political decisions free from inferior motives.

Naturally, it is difficult to get access to king's bedroom and these narratives above seem to have reflected court rumors that may have spread among the army and the locals. However, we should not assert that the historical Alexander was immune to sexual attractions as we do not expect it from modern rulers and presidents, whose sex-lives have provoked public scandals. Even if we may doubt the historicity of the king following his sexual instincts, the source material reveals how the authors saw mechanisms of imperialism in the Greco-Roman world. According to their world-view, sexual attractiveness was used as a tool to appeal to the representative of ultimate power. The sexual appetite of the monarch could make a major difference and alter his political decision.

In this context, it is worth mentioning two aristocratic women, Rhodian Barsine and Bactrian Rhoxane, who became the wives of Alexander. Both bore Alexander a son and they both were later murdered because of their affiliation with the king. However, Barsine was probably only a concubine, thus his child with her was not considered a viable heir. Ancient historians tend to stress that Alexander was above else impressed by their beauty.[102] The Sogdian or Bactrian warlord Oxyartes prepared magnificent banquets where his daughter Rhoxane danced with 29 maidens. Evidently, Oxyartes aimed to strengthen his relations with the Macedonian king.[103] However, in the literary tradition, Alexander was charmed by Rhoxane's beauty and decided to marry her.[104] Arrian remarks that contemporary authors accompanying Alexander (most likely referring to Ptolemy and Aristobulos) eulogized the beauty of Rhoxane, equal only to the beauty of King Darius' wife.[105] Moreover, Arrian and Plutarch praise Alexander for not raping the maiden but treating her respectfully by marrying her.[106] However, modern-day scholars have underlined the political reasons behind Alexander's behavior. According to them, he was merely seeking collaborators among the Bactrian nobles. The marriage with Bactrian princess was to be seen

---

[101] Cf. Ogden 2011: 150-151. Cf. Plin. *NH.* IX.119.

[102] For Alexander being impressed by Barsine's beauty, see Iust. XI.10.2-3; Plu. *Alex.* 21.4-5.

[103] Cf. Curt. VIII.4.22, 27. Cf. Plu. *Alex.* 47.4.

[104] Plu. *Mor.* 332e; cf. 338d; Curt. VIII.4.

[105] Arr. *An.* IV.19; Plu. *Mor.* 332e. Cf. Curt. VIII.4.23-24.

[106] Arr. *An.* IV.19.5-6; Plu. *Alex.* 47.4. Cf. Str. XI.11.4,

as a symbol of reconciliation.[107] Yet, we should not ignore such possible motives Rhoxane, and the aristocratic class of Bactrians, may have had when intending to influence on Alexander.[108] The Image of the wedding of Alexander and Rhoxane was presented in Aetion's contemporary painting and the same motif is believed to be depicted in one of the frescoes in Pompeii.[109] Evidently, this marriage became a talking point throughout the empire. We can assert that the historical Rhoxane followed her father's will when becoming Alexander's wife. She continued to seek her family's interests when possibly influenced Alexander's decision to give Oxyartes the satrapy of the Parapamisadae.[110] In addition, we know that Rhoxane's brother became a member of royal troops (*agema*) in 324 BC.[111] As a wife of Alexander, she achieved prestige greater than she had had before.

The Asian aristocrats intended to win the king's favor not only by their sexual charm but also by their royal appearance and dignity. In the literary tradition, for example Porus' height, beauty and valor made impact on Alexander.[112] Furthermore, the Indian king Sophytes, who voluntarily surrendered to the king, and who retained his kingdom, arranged an impressive encounter with Alexander. He is said to have dressed in gold and purple with pearls hanging from his ears when handing a theatrically golden scepter to Alexander. Sophytes, who came to meet Alexander with his two grown-up sons, is portrayed as surpassing all other barbarians in physical attractiveness.[113] It could be stated that during the Macedonian invasion, Iranian, Bactrian or Indian conquered nobles intended to appeal to the king by ways they thought to be effective. Local nobles knew well that in monarchies the head of the state had enormous authority to lift up or relegate their new subjects. The fact that many of the conquered locals found Alexander's favor doubtlessly irritated the Macedonian upper-class. It is said to have been one of the reasons for mutinies and conspiracies characteristic to Alexander's reign, especially as the idea of Panhellenistic crusade lost its head of steam.

---

[107] Usually scholars do not deny the possibility that Alexander had passion and love for the Bactrian princess; cf. Holt 2006: 90.

[108] Holt (2006: 88-89) gives an opposite interpretation of historical Rhoxane, presenting her as a mere object, a prize of war, who resembled more modern Afghan girl Sharbat Gula pictured on the cover of *National Geographic* than a woman having her own will. However, the status of Rhoxane belonging to a local high-class was evidently better than a girl who had witnessed Taliban reign. In addition, we could assume that the position of the women was slightly different in ancient Bactria 2,300 years ago than it was under the reign of Islamic fundamentalist Taliban.

[109] Cf. Lucian. *Herod.* 4-6. For a discussion of Aetion's painting and the fresco in Pompeii, see Stewart 1994: 181-190.

[110] Arr. *An.* VI.15.3; Curt. IX.8.9-10.

[111] Arr. *An.* VII.6.5.

[112] Arr. *An.* V.19.1-2.

[113] Curt. IX.1.28-30; D.S. XVII.91.7.

Conclusions

Whether the members of Asian high-class should be view as traitors or opportunists depends on the way we see the mechanism of war. The Macedonian imperialism changed the existing power relations and forced the local aristocrats to decide whether to be loyal to king Darius or surrender to Alexander with hope of gaining notable position in the administrative networks of the new regime. It can be stated that in this new situation that the members of the Asian, Bactrian, and Indian upper classes were not passive victims but actors who tried to profit from the war. Their adaptive strategies entailed following the course of the conquest and allying with the conqueror at the opportune right time if possible. From the Persian perspective, possibly, those who had served previously Darius but decided to serve Alexander were turncoats.

The idea of cooperation and interaction between Asian nobles and their Macedonian conquerors can be clearly identified in the source material. In many occasions, the conqueror chose to reward a certain group of the conquered locals. The Macedonians allowed them to retain their former status, providing them wealth and a promise that the invading armies would not harm them. On the other hand, the conqueror expected something in return. The conqueror demanded allegiance and supplies, and if the local satrap failed to respond to king's demands they were in danger of losing their position.

Obviously, Alexander's, or his representative's, goal was to find suitable collaborators and supporters. The locals were aware that gaining the personal favor of Alexander was a key-factor in order to retain or improve their status. This upper-class used a variety of methods when trying to gain Alexander's favor. They tried to appeal to Alexander's martial values, personal admiration, generosity, religious beliefs, and sexual desires. Their methods may have derived from their own value system which they assumed Alexander shared with them. After achieving the king's favor, they tried to use their authority over Alexander (cf. Bagoas, Sisygambis, Taxiles) in order to protect their friends or revenge their enemies.

According to my analysis, the available sources (Diodorus, Curtius, Arrian, Plutarch and Justin) support the idea that the Macedonian conquest did not automatically worsen the position of the Asian elite but sometimes even enhanced it. None of these texts support the Senecan or Orosian view that the Macedonian conquest meant merely havoc and destruction for the peoples of Asia. We can assume that the Macedonian invaders had to find locals who would start to cooperate willingly with them to enable the Macedonian army to continue their titanic conquest. Instead of being mistreated, those willing to change sides were pardoned and even rewarded. When making appraisals on Alexander's war of aggression, we must remember that the conquest did not mean suffering for all the Asians.

The source material also reveals how the authors saw the mechanisms of imperialism in the Greco-Roman world. For the Romans, Alexander's campaign was an example of organizing the expansion of an Empire. Evidently, Roman emperors and generals as well as later conquerors, like Hernán Cortés, Peter the Great, or Charles XII of Sweden read these texts and applied Macedonian strategies and lessons when waging wars of aggression against foreign territories.

A Lasting Impact? Alexander the Great and the Ruin/Creation of Persepolis

Eran Almagor

The Empire that Alexander built soon crumbled after his death. The world he has created immediately changed with his departure, so that few of the things he established actually survived him. Still, several events during his Asiatic campaign left a long-term impression. One notable case is Alexander's sacking of the palace complex in Persepolis in the spring (April/May?) of 330 BCE,[1] which altered the significance of the place. By this act of violence, Alexander's imperialist misconduct left an imprint on both history and historiography. Let us examine these outcomes. First, the effect of Alexander's deeds on giving the name «Persepolis» to the site.

What's in a name? Prior to Alexander, all over the Hellenic world, the name «Persepolis» meant something completely different. Literally, the epic word «Persepolis» or rather «Perseptolis» signified «sacker (or destroyer) of cities», from the verb πέρθω (fut./aor. πέρσ-).[2] The city par excellence to be destroyed was, of course, Ilion. The epithet «destroyer of cities», became a typical one of Odysseus, most famously in the second line of the *Odyssey*, where the two components of the compound word appear side by side: Τροίης ἱερὸν πτολίεθρον ἔπερσε.[3] It is probably

---

[1] See Hamilton 1969: 98; Borza 1972: 241; Lane Fox 1973: 267; Sancisi-Weerdenburg 1993: 177; Briant 2002: 851. Green 1991: 317: «early June» appears too late.

[2] Cf. Theognostus, *Canones sive De orthographia* 569: πέρσω, περσεπόλις; *Scholia in Aristophanem, Scholia in Nubes (scholia anonyma recentiora)*, 967d: περσέπτολιν] πολιορκητικήν, τὴν πορθοῦσαν τὰς πόλεις. See Wackernagel 1925: 36.

[3] Cf. H. *Il.* I.164, II.133, 13.380, XVII.407, XXI.433. See *Il.* XVIII.342 (πέρθοντε πόλεις). The epithet Πτολίπορθος also appears: *Il.* II.278, X.363 (Ὀδυσσεὺς), etc. Cf. Hld. III.2.4; cf. *AG* IX.485: περσέπολιν Τρώων («destroyer-of-[the]-city of the Trojans»). Curiously, Heckel 2007: 82 compares the animating force of the meeting of Alexander with the Greek unfortunates before the sacking of Pesepolis (D.S. XVII.69.2-9; Curt. V.5.5-24; Iust. XI.14.11-12) to the story of Odysseus itself: «Like the wretched Odysseus, who slaughters the suitors of

through some conflation with the similarly sounding name of the son of Nestor, Perseus (Hom. *Od.* III.412-4; cf. Ps.-Apollod. I.9.9) and this appellation of Odysseus, that the name was applied to a joint offspring of the families of Odysseus and Nestor, as can be seen in a fragment attributed to Hesiod (West / Merkelbach Fragment 221 = Eustathius, *In Hom. Od.* XVI.118 p. 1796.39 Stallbaum): «well-girded Polycaste, the youngest daughter of Nestor, was joined in love with Telemachus thanks to golden Aphrodite and gave birth to Persepolis» (Τηλεμάχωι δ' ἄρ' ἔτικτεν ἐύζωνος Πολυκάστη | Νέστορος ὁπλοτάτη κούρη Νηληϊάδαο | Περσέπολιν μιχθεῖσα διὰ χρυσῆν Ἀφροδίτην; transl. Evelyn-White, slightly amended).[4] According to another version, Persep(t)olis was the son of Telemachus and Nausica.[5] As is known, Alexander is reported to have emphasized his links with the heroic world of the Trojan War,[6] even competing with Achilles for glory.[7] He is also said to be a descendent of Perseus (Arr. *An.* III.3.2), through his connection with Heracles.[8] Thus, the word and its epic meaning were not strange to Alexander; the epithet was even used to depict one of his mythic relatives.

We should note that there was no particular Persian connotation in the name Persepolis within the passages mentioned. This is also evident when the name Persepolis was transferred from a mortal to a god, in particular Athena, in the fifth century BCE, designating her as «Pallas Persepolis»; this was done by either Stesichorus or, as suggested by Eratosthenes, by the poet Lamprocles.[9] It is preserved in two versions, the parodic rewriting of its *incipit* by Aristophanes in in the *Clouds* (967: Παλλάδα περσέπολιν δεινάν, «Pallas, destroyer of cities, the terrible [goddess]»)

Penelope after suffering further abuse in the guise of a beggar, they give a sense of purpose and immediacy to the capture of Persepolis and the torching of its palace».

[4] Cf. Steph. Byz. *Eth.* s.v. 'Περσέπολις' IV.120 Billerbeck: πόλις Περσίδος [...] ἔστι δὲ καὶ ὄνομα κύριον υἱοῦ Τηλεμάχου («City in Persia; [...] proper name of the son of Telemachus»).

[5] Cf. Eustathius *In Hom Od.* XVI.118 p. 1796.41 Stallbaum, citing Arisotle and Hellanicus (Ἀριστοτέλης δὲ ἐν Ἰθακησίων πολιτείᾳ [F 506 Rose] καὶ Ἑλλάνικος [*FGrH* 4 F 156] δὲ Τηλέμαχόν φασι Ναυσικάαν γῆμαι τὴν Ἀλκινόου καὶ γεννῆσαι τὸν Περσέπτολιν. Cf. Dictys (*FGrH* 49 F 10).

[6] Alexander descended from Achilles on his mother's side (Plu. *Alex.* 2.1, *Pyrrh.* 1.2, *Mor.* 332a-b; Curt. IV.6.29). Cf. D.S. XVII.1.5, 97.3; Arr. *An.* I.12.1-5; Plu. *Alex.* 8.2, 15.8-9, cf. *Mor.* 343ab; Curt. VIII.4.25-6. See O'Brien 1992: 13, 20-1, 56, 59, 87, 109, 161, 166; Maitland 2015; Heckel 2015a: 21-25, 30-32. The parallels were presumably stressed after Alexander's premature death (cf. Hom. *Il.* 19.409). Alexander is said to have visited Achilles' tomb at Troy (Arr. *An.* I.12.1-2). Ameling 1988 asserts the historicity of Alexander's imitation of Achilles.

[7] Cf. Arr. *An.* VII.14.4. Achilles himself always strove to be the best over the others : Hom. *Il.* VI.208, XI.783-4 with O'Brien 1992: 9. For Alexander Myth and the heroes of old, see Bosworth 1996: 98-132; cf. Stoneman 2019: 84.

[8] On his father's side (D.S. XVII.1.5; Plu. *Alex.* 2.1; Arr. *An.* II.6.4, cf. IV.10.7, 11.6, V.26.5, VI.3.2). See O'Brien 1992: 22, 87, 163. See the examples listed in Heckel 2015a: 25-30.

[9] Cf. *Scholia in Aelium Aristidem (scholia vetera)* Dindorf, *Or.* XLVI.162,7-8; *P. Oxy.* XIII.1611. See *Scholia in Aristophanem, Commentarium in Nubes (scholia recentiora Tzetzae)*, Holwerda 966a-967b; Joannes Tzetzes, *Schol. in Aristoph. Nub.* 967a, *Chiliades*. I.25.686. Cf. Suda, s.v. Τηλέπορον, τ 490 Adler. Cf. Dover 1968a: 215.

and previously in a lost comedy by the playwright Phrynichus.[10] There is no Persian context for this poem, and there are no Persian allusions –not even a tongue-in-cheek insinuation in Aristophanes. The most remarkable thing is the continuation of this literary epithet, so that in the post-Alexander period, when Callimachus (*In lavacrum Palladis* = hymn. 5, 43: ἔξιθ', Ἀθαναία περσέπτολι, χρυσεοπήληξ...), uses «Athena Persepolis», no connection with Persia is discernible.

Yet, it is undeniable that an implicit Persian allusion of the epithet was also used in Greek literature, once in a tragedy and once in a comedy. In the play *Persians* (65-66), Aeschylus calls the very Persian army «Persepolis» (Perseptolis), i.e., destroyer of cities: πεπέρακεν μὲν ὁ περσέπτολις ἤδη | βασίλειος στρατὸς εἰς ἀντίπορον γείτονα χώραν («The royal army, dealing destruction to cities, has passed to the neighboring land upon the facing shore»; transl. Smyth). That this is to be seen as a play on words is obvious from the context and the mention of the flower of Persia immediately before (τοιόνδ' ἄνθος Περσίδος αἴας).[11] The second play on the similar sound of Persepolis and Persians comes in a lost work of the comic playwright Eupolis, two generations later. In what is essentially a parody of Aeschylus, Eupolis mocks an Athenian politician by giving him a Persian sounding name - Marikas: πεπέρακεν μὲν ὁ περσέπτολις ἤδη Μαρικᾶς («Marikas dealing destruction to cities, has passed»).[12] These two clever references which play with the similarity of sounding names do not necessarily mean that a specific location as «the city of the Persians» is alluded to.[13] In fact, it is important to notice that the jest only works if there was not a specific city designated as «the city of the Persians» at the time. As Christopher Tuplin (1996: 140 n. 17) very elegantly put it: the «[...] presumed Athenian ignorance of the place means that they failed to see the irony of *Pallas Persepolis*... or *Marikas persepolis*». Of course, there is nothing ironic in itself with mentioning Pallas Persepolis, but it does show that Athenians or Greeks did not call any place by the name of Persepolis in the fifth century. There is correspondingly no mention of Persepolis as a name of a place (nor as an epithet) in the texts of Herodotus, Thucydides, Xenophon and other fourth century authors, in both fragmentary or extant works.

This is part of the cultural and literary background of the soldiers engaged during and after the destruction of palace complex in Persia. In fact, the destruction

---

[10] Παλλάδα περσέπολιν κλῄζω πολεμαδόκον ἁγνάν | παῖδα Διὸς μεγάλου δαμάσιππον («Pallas, the destroyer of cities I summon, war-sustaining, pure, daughter of great Zeus, horse-taming»). Alternatively, there may have been two hymns to the goddess. See Benuzzi 2019: 139 n. 49.

[11] The irony is misrepresented by Mousavi 2012: 9-10: «the destiny of the Persians was to wage wars and sack cities». By contrast, the word refers to the calamity about to hit the Persians themselves.

[12] Cf. *Scholia in Persas (scholia recentiora)* Dindorf, *ad.* 65: κωμῳδεῖται ταῦτα. Εὔπολις ἐν Μαρικᾷ. See Cassio 1985.

[13] The play also appears in the later Dio Chrysostom, where Pallas Persepolis (*Or*. XIII.19) appears before the mention of the Persians in XIII.23-25.

and ransacking may have actually given rise to the site's name. The designation «Persepolis» was perhaps never meant to reflect the place as «city of the Persian» or «city of Persae» in a straightforward and uncomplicated manner.[14] If it were that case, it is most likely that the compound word would have had a different linking vowel between the compound constituents.[15] The compound «Persepolis» is also not constructed exactly in the manner of places ending in a vowel.[16] Even if the palace complex in the plain of Marvdašt was known to the Greeks before Alexander as uniquely identical with the name of region/people, namely, Πέρσαι (and that is somewhat doubtful),[17] corresponding to its Old Persian and Elamite equivalents for the region, people and the site (respectively, Pârsâ, Ba-ir-ša),[18] the form Περσαίπολις (Πέρσαι + πολις) is meagerly attested and does not appear where we would expect to find it;[19] the latter form strikes one as a hypercorrection rather than an original form in use.[20] It is more probable that the compound name was formed with a verbal stem in its first constituent (the verb πέρθω/ πέρσ-), as indeed typical of use of the /e/ vowel.[21] We have on the one hand a site sacked or destroyed and on the other the name of the site probably coming from the root «destroy» or «sack». This is too

---

[14] Cf. Wackernagel 1925: 37-39.

[15] Either the long /a/ of the first declension stem as befits the nouns Πέρσης or Πέρσαι (e.g., Νεάπολις; cf. Kakarikos 2015: 254-255; -η is rare: cf. Smyth, 1920: 247, §871a) or, preferably, the thematic /o/ connecting the compound constituents, and serving the role of a compound marker: see Nöldeke 1887: 140; Herzfeld 1935: 45. The vowel /o/ substitutes -α of the stem by analogy to o-stems: Smyth 1920: 247, §871b. Cf. Ralli 2008, claiming it is a semantically empty linking element between the first and the second constituents. Kakarikos 2015: 256. The /o/ vowel was typical in the Hellenistic period (e.g., Σκυθόπολις for example in Josephus - if this compound has indeed anything to do with Σκύθης; yet cf. 2 Macc. 12:29-30).

[16] E.g., Βεργέπολις, based on the Thracian city of Βέργη (Βέργη + πολις); Steph. Byz. *Eth.* II.69-70 Billerbeck.

[17] For instance, Herodotus III.30 («sent away to Persia»; ἀπέπεμψε ἐς Πέρσας; cf. VIII.98: ἔπεμπε ἐς Πέρσας) could mean the region at large and not specifically the palace complex. Cf. also Xen. *Cyr.* VIII.5.20 (εἰς Πέρσας ἐπορεύετο). See further examples in Wackernagel 1925: 40-1. Similarly inconclusive are texts which may not reliably reflect the original pre-Alexander text, like the rendition of Ctesias *FGrH* 688 F 36 (= Antigon. *Hist. mir.* 15): «Ctesias maintains that something similar to this happens in Ecbatana and Persia [...]», καὶ ἐν Ἐκβατάνοις δὲ καὶ ἐν Πέρσαις Κτησίας ἱστορεῖ παραπλήσιόν τι τούτοις [...]. Cf. F. XIII.32 (Xerxes arrived in Persia: εἰς Πέρσας παραγίνονται); F XV.48: back to Persia; εἰς Πέρσας, where the royal graves in Persia may be those of Naqsh-e Rostam. See Herzfeld 1935: 45. Also in Berossos *ap.* Clem. Alex. *Protr.* V.65.3: [...] Ἐκβατάνοις <καὶ> Πέρσαις καὶ Βάκτροις [...]. Other examples may be paraphrases: e.g., Plu. *Art.* 7.3 (Artaxerxes hiding in Persia, ἐνδύεσθαι τῇ Περσίδι) and 22.1 (Antalcidas coming up to Persia; Ἀνταλκίδαν [...] εἰς Πέρσας ἀναβάντα), *pace* Radt (2008: 636), who also mentions Plu. *Alex.* 69.1 –both of which are inconclusive examples. Cf. Arr. *An.* III.18.10 for an admittedly later tradition.

[18] See Xpa.14 (inscription, Gate of All Nations: «...much else that is beautiful was built in this Pârsâ, which I built and my father built»; transl. Kent). See PF 2-8, 30-33, 54, 95-97, 326, 430, 701, 722, 739, 835-837, 1224, cat. Q etc., PT 37-47 etc.

[19] Only as v.l. to Str. XV.3.6 and Ael. *NA* I.59.

[20] *Pace* LSJ s.v. Περσέπολις: «Shd. perh. be written Πέρσαι πόλις (cf. A. «Πέρσης» 1.1 b)» and Wackernagel 1925: 40-43.

[21] Cf. Smyth 1920: 249, §881; cf. 159, §485.

much of a coincidence to be ignored or explained away. Furthermore, in Greek texts, the indisputable first event associated with the site, whose name probably has to do with «destruction» is one of destruction. This too is far from being coincidental.

As Scott (1938: 65) mentioned years ago, «[t]he name appears to be a grim pun connected with its destruction by Alexander». The pun at the expense of the Persians was an ironic reminder of the previous might of the Empire, formerly the «sacker of cities» itself,[22] whose symbol of power now lay in ruins. This name was perhaps also given in some measure in retribution to the sack of Athens, as our sources repeatedly claim for the deed itself (e.g., D.S. XVII.72.6; Str. XV.3.6; cf. Arr. *An.* III.18.12). The name was bestowed either during the very day the palaces were damaged or immediately afterwards, when the horror was still fresh, for the irony to be punchier.[23] The people who dubbed the place with this tongue-in-cheek epithet knew their Aeschylus or their Aristophanes; this designation could even have been born at a symposium, by drunken revelers of the type which appears in some of the versions of the stories of destruction, pending on the truth of these portrayals (below).

If all this is true, then the site of 'Persepolis' was created in the Greek-speaking mind *on the very day* the site was destroyed and on the very day it lost its political significance. The site, with its ruins of artistic architecture and iconography, immediately became a symbol signifying not the weakness of the current Persian Empire, but, turning the page to a new era, the power of what the Empire *was*.[24] It was not despite the destruction that the site gained its importance and appreciation later on, but *because* of it.[25] It has become a place associated with devastation, which was later continuously disfigured and looted.[26] Yet, the site proved to have an impressive long-lasting endur-

---

[22] Cf. Hdt. VII.220.4.

[23] It does not have to be Callisthenes who came up with the name; see, however, Radet 1931: 198.

[24] Cf. Already Droysen 1877 [1833]: 362-363. See Razmjou 2005: 315: «After the fall of Persepolis, the political and administrative center in Pars was transferred to the nearby city of Estakhr. For the inhabitants of Estakhr, Persepolis served as a memory and reminder of a past era of magnificence and glory». Cf. n. 83 below.

[25] *Pace* Harrison 2008: 56, both attitudes of identification with and disdain towards/disregard of the Achaemenid site displayed in modern-era (or even Sasanian era, for that matter) Iran are not that far apart in that the emphasis in all these approaches is on awareness of the *break* with the imperial past. This is evidenced by the continuous policy to leave the palace complex in its current physical desolate state (and even by inadvertently causing it damage: see Mousavi 2012: 71 on the asphalt road constructed near the site for the 2500th anniversary). Contrary to Harrison 2008: 55, the appreciation expressed by outsiders at the sight of the ruined palace complex was not merely because of comparison to modern neglect or modern corrupt Persia («[t]he 'desolation' of Persepolis and Pasargadae is only representative of Persia's more general decline from ancient greatness»), but their appreciation was generated *because* of the physical remains. The assertion Harrison brings (and misquotes) from Lord George Curzon 1892: 1.10, namely, that «[t]he Persia of Herodotus and Xenophon - was immeasurably superior to mediaeval Persia in its attributes and is even now more respectable in its ruin» actually compares the physical remains to the textual Greek representations, making the ruined site a better testimony to the former greatness of Achaemenid Persia.

[26] Cf. Mousavi 2012: 70.

ance among the places Alexander has 'created', despite the fact that it is a place of ruin, a desolate place.[27] As a ghost-town of sorts 'Persepolis' persists to this very day,[28] re-identified by western travellers to the site from the seventeenth century onward.[29]

In the words of Olmstead (1948: 522-523), who draws a comparison between these remains and those of the Macedonian sites:

> «The Macedonia of Alexander has disappeared, almost without a trace. Its older capital Aegae is a malaria-ridden site and nothing more [...] The tombs of the the Macedonian rulers, where Alexander had thought to be gathered to his fathers, have never been found; his own capital, Pella, is a mass of shapeless ruins [...] Nothing has been preserved of the original Alexandria [...] But Persepolis stands to this day, preserved by its very burning. The palaces of Darius and Xerxes still tower above the plain, a marvel to the passing wayfarer».[30]

Once destroyed, the ruins were intended to be left as a reminder of the Achaemenids' former glory, establishing Persia's Disgrace, as it were.[31] It was to be the living wreckage of an empire, quite apart from the nearby royal tombs in the mountain behind Persepolis (Kuh-i Rahmat, «Mountain of Mercy»)[32] or in Naqš-e Rostam.[33] This second point of impact, the image of the site, may have been Alexander's intention in the ransacking of the place. After the Macedonians took control of the city and the palace complex, it is hard to imagine that the site was looted contrary to Alexander's wishes. Even our sources are almost unanimous in asserting that it was not (as opposed to what they say about the burning of the complex; see below): Persepolis' treasures were carefully transported elsewhere. The inevitable ensuing damage to the site, one may infer, served Alexander in two ways. Since it was still unclear whether

---

[27] This is partially because the lower parts of several buildings have been hidden from sight for centuries, buried under debris of crumbled walls and decomposed mud bricks.

[28] Cf. Milns 1968: 139: «Persepolis never recovered from its violation and became a ghost-town». At some point, however, in the post-Achaemenid era, the terrace was occupied by travellers; Roaf 1983: 159. Cf. Herzfeld 1934: 44, 46-7; Mousavi 2012: 74, 76.

[29] See Mousavi 2012: 96-154. By the locals the place was also thought (from the Sasanian era) to be the centre of the mythic hero-king Jamshīd, and aptly called *Takht-e Jamshīd* («Throne of Jamshīd»). See Shahbazi 1977; Omidsalar 2008; Mousavi 2012: 83-94.

[30] Cf. Milns 1968: 139: «The fire in the palaces preserved the magnificent stone reliefs, among the finest examples of Persian art [...] There remain too the impressive ruins of the palace-area –the staircases, the friezes and the imposing columns».

[31] Cf. The anecdote on Alexander and Xerxes' fallen statue (Plu. *Alex*. 37.5). Alexander could have ordered the reconstruction of the site, even upon his return in 324 BCE, but never did: see Fredricksmeyer 2000: 163-4. Thus, Green 1991: 321 is not strictly accurate in saying «[w]hen Alexander left these smoking ruins behind him, he could hardly know that his act of incendiarism had immortalized Persepolis for all time».

[32] See Schmidt 1970: 99-107.

[33] Alexander is said by Arrian (*An*. III.22.1) to have arranged for the body of Darius III to be sent «to Persia and be buried there», but it cannot be in either of the two aforementioned places. Cf. D.S. XVII.73.3; Plu. *Alex*. 43.7, *Mor*. 343b; Iust. XI.15.14; Plin. *NH*. XXXVI.28.132. See Bosworth 1980a: 345.

the Macedonians and Darius' army would meet again for another military encounter, the looting and sacking of this religious and ceremonial centre[34] were meant to damage the morale of the Persians[35] while uplifting the spirits of the soldiers, who did part of the pillaging.[36] Yet, there was probably another reason: to display (to both parties) the irreversibility of the political situation, and instill the idea of a *translatio imperii* through a damaged Achaemenid centre, which lost its prominence.[37] Alexander could not afford to destroy the well-known cities of Babylon or Susa, for otherwise it would have raised serious doubts among the Greeks and Macedonians on his ability to rule the newly acquired areas (cf. the fictional debate in Arr. *An.* III.18.11). Instead, he chose to convey this message through a site that was beyond the horizon of Greek imagination up to that point, in that it was less known, or little recognized by the Greek speaking world,[38] so that the demolished place could be re-invented

---

[34] On this trait of the place, see Pope 1957; Lane Fox 1973: 255, 258; Root 1979: 153-161. Cf. Fredricksmeyer 2000: 149.

[35] See Andreotti 1950: 590; Badian 1967: 189; Nawotka 2010: 254; Jamzadeh 2012: 64. Cf. Borza 1972: 243-245, at 245, who maintains that «If Persepolis itself was as important a symbol as we have made it out to be, it is at least possible that its obliteration served to thwart Darius' opportunity to revive [...] the end of Persepolis may have discouraged those who would, under other circumstances, have rallied to the Achaemenid's side». Cf. Olbrycht 2014: 89: «Alexander's aim was thus to break the spirit of resistance among Persians and to destroy the original centers of Achaemenid power». According to Fuller 1960: 228, it was more than that: by seizing the treasure at Susa and Persepolis, Alexander deprived Darius of the means to recruit another army. For Darius' threat, cf. Grainger 2007: 79.

[36] Cf. Bosworth 1988b: 92: «the promise of plunder had probably been a potent stimulus over the past months [...] and the looting had the pious justification of revenge». Cf. Morrison 2001. See Anson 2013: 158: «The pillaging of Persepolis [...] was then also a part of a new campaign to win his troops over by means of largesse». Cf. Grote 1856: 236; Green 1991: 316; cf. Green 1991: 408 on looting in India: «[w]hen his veterans' loyalty hung in the balance, to lose local goodwill was a cheap sacrifice». One has to bear in mind that Alexander and his army waited for a long time in Persepolis: four months (Plu. *Alex*. 37.6; but cf. Wirth 1971: 621); see Badian 1967: 189. Briant 2010: 110 opposes this. Heckel 2009: 40 exaggerates when he claims: «Greek allies, mindful of the League's propaganda, demanded the destruction of the city in the hope of sating their hunger for revenge and booty». Yet, as long as Greek soldiers were in Alexander's army, he could never really cease to be attentive to their reaction. Although he dismissed the soldiers of the League of Corinth following the changes in the strategic situation and the character of the ensuing warfare (when Ecbatana was secured and Darius fled to the east, cf. Borza 1972: 242), Alexander still employed any of them who would serve him for pay (Arr. *An.* III.19.6; D.S. XVII.74.3-4; Curt. VI.2.17; cf. Plu. *Alex*. 42.5).

[37] See Nöldeke 1887: 83-4. Briant 2002: 852 believes this act was directed at the Persians: Alexander «demonstrated to the recalcitrant Persians that the age of imperial grandeur was over, unless they turned to him *en masse*». Cf. Briant 2010: 111. Also Nawotka 2003a: 75. See Brosius 2003: 182: «The destruction of the centre of the Achaemenid kings not only marks the end of Persian power, it also manifests Alexander's position as conqueror». Yet, cf. Mederer 1936: 75-80; Wiesehöfer 2001: 106. It is quite the contrary of what Bloedow 1995: 38 asserts, «such an alleged symbolic gesture would have little weight so long as Dareius was still alive and had control over a substantial portion of the empire» and *pace* Mousavi 2012: 70: «Whether during his stay in Persia Alexander sought to win over the Persian population or to receive the legitimacy of an Achaemenid king –I believe– had no effect on the destiny of Persepolis».

[38] See Herzfeld 1935: 45; Pope 1957: 129; Olmstead 1948: 520; Fredricksmeyer 2000: 148; cf. Nawotka 2003a: 71; 2010: 61. Yet, cf. Lewis 1977: 74; Wiesehöfer 2001: 25.

as a marker of a dramatic historical change.[39] In the words of Herzfeld (1935: 44), focusing of the burning of the palaces:

> «Persepolis ended in flames and these flames were a symbol. Perhaps they were intended to be, at any rate they have been, a sign to the world of the beginning of a new epoch [...] The Ancient East was dead, the conflagration of Persepolis its funeral pyre».

Alexander perhaps envisioned the looting and ransacking as a visual testimony to stamp the notion of a beginning of a new epoch in the entire region, in which the Macedonians not only free the Greeks of Asia Minor,[40] but the Argeads also succeed the Achaemenids as rulers of Asia.[41] The site could serve no other purpose from that moment on, and indeed Alexander would not tolerate another –Macedonian or Persian - using the place as a power base.[42]

If so, we may see the impact of the event in the sentiments of some of his contemporaries. For instance, one may suspect that it was after this event, more than the victory at the Battle of Gaugamela, that the court historian Callisthenes of Olynthus in his «Exploits of Alexander» (Ἀλεξάνδρου πράξεις; Str. XVII.1.43),[43] depicted Alexander in an appropriate manner as a great conqueror of Asia. Among the scenes, which he related and are now found scattered in extant literature, were perhaps Alexander's act of thrusting a spear in the ground of the Troad, signifying that Alexander would receive Asia from the gods as a spear-won prize;[44] similarly, Callisthenes may have emphasized the famous story of Alexander in Gordium, Phrygia, where according to a local tradition, the rule of all Asia would be granted to whoever would be able to unfasten the complex knot that bound the yoke of the wagon of Gordius, the founder of the Phrygian dynasty, to the wagon's beam –a feat which Alexander somehow accomplished;[45] likewise, with the same intention, Callisthenes may have elaborated Alexander's journey to the oracle at Siwah, evoking that taken by Sem-

---

[39] Cf. Droysen 1877 [1833]: 360-363; Briant 2002: 851.

[40] See the inscriptions marking a new age mentioned by Dreyer 2009: 222 n. 27.

[41] See Plu. *Alex.* 34.1. This is different from being a Persian ruler or the King of Kings. See Plu. *Demetr.* 25.6. Cf. Hammond 1986; Fredricksmeyer 2000: 149.

[42] According to Sancisi-Weerdenburg 1993: 185, the plunder (with destruction) was to ensure that items could not be used to propagate political power by the men left behind. Cf. Green 1991: 320: «once Alexander moved on eastward it would form an obvious rallying-point, both religious and political, for any nationalist resistance movement». The same consideration may underlie the fact that when Alexander did return to the region from the east (325/4 BCE), he executed Orxines, satrap of Persis, ironically (given what Alexander's men did) for plunder of the shrines and royal tombs and for killing many unjustly (Arr. *An.* VI.30.2; cf. Curt. X.1.22-38); see Lane Fox 1973: 409; Brosius 2003: 189.

[43] Pearson 1960: 33: «an encomiastic biography rather than a history».

[44] D.S. XVII.17.2; cf. Iust. XI.5.10.

[45] Cf. Plu. *Alex.* 18.1-4; Arr. *An.* II.3; Curt. III.1.14-18; Iust. XI.7.3-16. See Pearson 1960: 38; Schachermeyr 1973: 161-162.

iramis (D.S. II.14.3, perhaps told by Ctesias).[46] Callisthenes may have published his work in Greece in instalments,[47] and it may be that parts of his work were disseminated in Greece. It may have also been the ruin of Persepolis which led Aeschines to echo this Macedonian propaganda in a well-known passage of his *Against Ctesiphon* (III.132):

> «Is not the king of the Persians [...] who demanded earth and water of the Greeks, he who dared to write in his letters that he was lord of all men from the rising of the sun unto its setting - is he not struggling now, no longer for lordship over others, but already for his life?» (transl. Adams).[48]

Alexander's actions in Persepolis therefore seem to be a deliberate attempt to influence the mindset of contemporaries. The image would last for years to come. Demetrius of Phaleron, in the beginning of his lost work *On Fortune* (Περὶ τύχης), as reported by Polybius (XXIX.21.1-7 = *FGrH* 228 F 39) summed up this sentiment. Writing presumably in 306 BCE (most likely after his ten-year rule in Athens ended: D.S. XX.45.5) and looking back at the last fifty years,[49] Demetrius recounts the vicissitudes of fate, in that the rise of Macedonia was necessarily entwined with the demise of Persia:[50]

> «For if you consider not countless years or many generations, but merely these last fifty years, you will read in them the cruelty of Fortune. do you think that fifty years ago either the Persians and the Persian king or the Macedonians and the king of Macedon, if some god had foretold the future to them, would ever have believed that at the time when we live, the very name of the Persians would have perished

---

[46] Arr. *An.* III.3.3-4.5; D.S. XVII.49.2-51.4; Curt. IV.7.5-28; Iust. XI.11.2-12; Plu. *Alex.* 26.11-27.11; Str. XVII.1.43. On a certain comparison between Alexander and Semiramis, perhaps influenced by Callisthenes' appropriation of the story, see Curt. VII.6.20.

[47] Cf. Pearson 1960: 23. Yet, cf. Lane Fox 1973: 95; Anson 2013: 6: «the actual provenance of the work is unknown».

[48] Οὐχ ὁ μὲν τῶν Περσῶν βασιλεύς [...] ὁ γῆν καὶ ὕδωρ τοὺς Ἕλληνας αἰτῶν, ὁ τολμῶν ἐν ταῖς ἐπιστολαῖς γράφειν ὅτι δεσπότης ἐστὶν ἁπάντων ἀνθρώπων ἀφ' ἡλίου ἀνιόντος μέχρι δυομένου, νῦν οὐ περὶ τοῦ κύριος ἑτέρων εἶναι διαγωνίζεται, ἀλλ' ἤδη περὶ τῆς τοῦ σώματος σωτηρίας; Indeed, if it were not because of the failure of Agis' war, it may have been the ruin of Persepolis which made Aeschines choose (and miscalculate) to resume in court the case relevant to an old event (from 337/6 BCE) specifically in late summer 330 (cf. Hansen 1974: cat. 30, nn. 16-17), and not, for instance, immediately after Gaugamela (late 331); yet cf. Cawkwell 1969: 170-3. Cf. Bosworth 1975: 38-9. In any case, the speech as we have it is the circulated published version, which was revised; see Dover 1968b: 167-9.

[49] Cf. Walbank 1979: 393-395. Demetrius wrote a book on «Artaxerxes» (D. L. V.81), presumably Artaxerxes II (d. 359/8 BCE) which exemplified the zenith of the Persian Empire according to him. Demetrius' «fifty years» is a rhetoric hyperbole and does not have to be taken literally (cf. Overtoom, 2013: 587), although Polybius, by adding three years in his own version of contemporary upheavals (fifty-three years in 1.1.5) does seem to be aiming at precision. D.S. 31.10 appears to insinuate that Demetrius composed the work in 318 BCE.

[50] Cf. Tuplin 2014 for the Greek sentiment.

> utterly —the Persians who were masters of almost the whole world— and that the Macedonians, whose name was formerly almost unknown, would now be the lords of it all?» (Plb. XXXIX.21).[51]

While it is true that none of these authors explicitly mentions Persepolis, there was surely an event that signaled to all the irretrievable change, and the likeliest candidate for such an occurrence is the sacking of the Achaemenid ceremonial centre.[52] Besides his effect on the history of the site, Alexander thus also heavily influenced the historiographic depiction of Persepolis. First, through the attitude of contemporaries. Notoriously, historians always face the problem of periodization. It is the difficulty of setting divisions on what is obviously indivisible - namely, the great causal chain of being or the great temporal chain. This obstacle of imposing time-frames on what was not admitted to be thus categorized by contemporaries appears to be avoided with the dramatic event in Persepolis. In this case, the modern view[53] seems to be corroborated by the ancients themselves.

Furthermore, the well-known event of the impairment of the Achaemenid royal residence soon took a life of its own. It appears in several variants in our admittedly very scanty historiographic evidence. Diodorus (XVII.70-72) and Curtius Rufus (V.6.1-9, 7.1-10) have the fullest accounts, but it may be the case that the two scenes they describe basically refer to the *same* reality of devastation of the palace complex –once in a version highlighting pillage, and once exaggerating the conflagration. If these are two versions of the same event, then the two pictures may ultimately come from two different sources. The two scenes follow the same sequence in both authors, and are similarly separated, but by different interim portrayals:[54]

(1) According to Diodorus (LXX.1-71.3a), Alexander incited his soldiers to plunder the city, describing it as the most hateful in Asia. The Macedonians raced into it, slaughtering all the men whom they met and looting the

---

[51] εἰ γὰρ λάβοι τις μὴ χρόνον ἄπειρον μηδὲ γενεὰς πολλὰς ἀλλὰ πεντήκοντα μόνον ἔτη ταυτὶ <τὰ> πρὸ ἡμῶν, γνοίητ᾽ ἂν ὡς τὸ τῆς Τύχης χαλεπὸν ἐνταῦθα. πεντηκοστὸν γὰρ ἔτος οἴεσθ᾽ ἂν ἢ Πέρσας ἢ βασιλέας τῶν Περσῶν ἢ Μακεδόνας ἢ βασιλέας τῶν Μακεδόνων, εἴ τις θεῶν αὐτοῖς προὔλεγε τὸ μέλλον, πιστεῦσαί ποτ᾽ ἂν ὡς εἰς τοῦτον τὸν καιρὸν Περσῶν οὐδ᾽ ὄνομα λειφθήσεται τὸ παράπαν, οἳ πάσης τῆς οἰκουμένης ἐδέσποζον, Μακεδόνες δὲ πάσης κρατοῦσιν, ὧν οὐδ᾽ ὄνομα πρότερον ἦν. Cf. The theme of transcence of fortune in Lucr. III.1029-33.

[52] As Borza 1972: 243 claims for Alexander: «It may be only our own *post factum* judgments that see the battle at Gaugamela as decisive because it was in fact decisive. Alexander may not have felt so certain»; presumably, neither was anyone else. Yet, Persepolis probably marked a watershed, at least for Callisthenes and Aeschines, and in hindsight for Demetrius as well.

[53] Cf. Wheeler 1968: 63: «Persepolis in 330 BC saw the end of an era. But by the same token it also saw the beginning of another». Cf. Schachermeyr (1973: 290).

[54] Cf. Briant 2010: 108. *Pace* Sancisi-Weerdenburg 1993: 180: «literary analysis of the narrative structures cannot bring us any nearer to a solution of the problem why Alexander destroyed the Achaemenid palaces». Bloedow 1995: 29 at first mistakenly writes that «Diodorus relates only the latter», i.e., the fire scene, but soon (39) corrects himself by referring to Diodorus' first scene.

residences. Diodorus claims that the famed palaces «fell victim to violence and utter destruction» (πρὸς ὕβριν καὶ παντελῆ φθορὰν ἀπεδέδεικτο; transl. Welles). Diodorus even maintains that the Macedonians fought with each other over the plunder and concludes that the city exceeded all others in misery. Alexander himself took possession of the treasure, which he transported elsewhere as he intended to destroy Persepolis completely (εἰς τέλος ἔσπευδε καταφθεῖραι). This corresponds to Curtius' version (V.6.1-9), which is embellished in the part of Alexander's speech to the Macedonians, and includes a slightly different account of the looters' greed and cruelty, together with a mention of the Persians' self-immolation.[55] Both authors (D.S. XVII.71.2; Curt. V.6.9) maintain that beasts of burden were used to transfer the treasure (120,000 talents) elsewhere.[56]

(2) In both authors an interlude appears.[57] Diodorus (XVII.71.3-8) has a description of the city, royal tombs and the palaces. Curtius (V.6.11-16) incorporates first a unique depiction of an expedition conducted by Alexander in Persia, after leaving Nicarchides (as commander of the citadel), Parmenion and Craterus (as commanders of the army and baggage) and Tiridates (as treasurer) in charge of the place. Curtius (V.6.17-20) immediately continues with Alexander's campaign against the Mardi (of Hyrcania). Interestingly, a break also appears in Plutarch's sequence (*Alex*. 37.5-7), separating his mention of the plunder (*Alex*. 37.3-4) and his account of the burning of the palace (*Alex*. 38). In this break, Plutarch relates two anecdotes on Alexander and the statue of Xerxes and on the royal throne of Darius. Arrian (*An*. III.18.11) similarly separates the two items, by mentioning the appointment of Phrasaortes the son or Rheomithres as satrap of Persepolis.

(3) The story of the incineration scene is narrated by Diodorus (XVII.72.1-6) as an outcome of Alexander's feasting and drinking with his comrades in celebration of his victories (which are not specified). An inebriated Alexander was persuaded by an intoxicated Thais, the Athenian courtesan, into spontaneously setting fire to the palaces in revenge for the destruction of the

---

[55] One interesting difference is that in Diodorus (XVII.70.5) the looters would even cut the hands (τὰς τῶν ἐπιβαλλόντων τοῖς ἀμφισβητουμένοις χεῖρας ἀπέκοπτον) of others contending for plunder, while Curtius (V.6.5) has them tearing and carrying the limbs (*membra*) of statues. One may suspect that both authors embroidered the imagery of a shared source. This picture is ironic given the (probably fictioal) story of mutilated Greeks meeting Alexander just prior to [or during] the capture of Persepolis (D.S. XVII.69.2-4; Curt. V.5.3-7; Iust. XI.14).

[56] Cf. Plu. *Alex*. 37.3. In an aside, Curtius (V.6.10) mentions that the loot taken from Pasargadae was added to this sum of money. A similar aside appears in Arrian (*An*. III.18.10). Cf. Str. XV.3.9 for different figures.

[57] *Pace* Hammond 1992a: 360: «Curtius, without any digression».

Greek temples.[58] Curtius (V.7.2-7) as well as Plutarch (*Alex.* 38.1-8) tell a largely similar narrative. Arrian briefly mentions the burning (III.18.11-12), and disregards many details, adding a cautionary warning from Parmenion not to do so, together with Alexander's reply (both probably apocryphal).

It would appear that all our extant accounts of the devastation of Persepolis ultimately derive from the same text, in which the scenes of the plunder and the burning appeared in this sequence. Plutarch abbreviates the first scene[59] –only mentioning a «great slaughter of prisoners» (Φόνον [...] πολὺν τῶν ἁλισκομένων) and butchering of inhabitants, and maintains that he read Alexander's own order to that effect (ἐκέλευεν ἀποσφάττεσθαι τοὺς ἀνθρώπους).[60] Arrian downplays both scenes.[61] It is important to note that Arrian's abbreviated account (or even that of Strabo), i.e., the suppression of the banquet and Thais, or the addition of a (fictional) debate between Alexander and Parmenion, is not an independent, separate 'version' or 'tradition', and certainly not an 'official' one, but rather an adaptation (or an epitome) of the same story of a great conflagration.[62] The dividing line cuts rather between the two scenes; it is there where the real variance lies.

Given the fact that all four accounts display different connections between the two scenes, it would appear highly likely that there was no narrative link between them in their assumed common source.[63] And yet the two are separated in all four texts. This would lead to the conclusion that somehow, they were differentiated in the original source, presumably as different items in a list, and perhaps partially thin on details, bearing in mind the different ways our extant accounts embellish an original phrasing. The two scenes (the pillage/the burning) may have been sequentially presented in some sort of a collection of anecdotes related to Alexander, assembled

---

58 Cartledge 2004: 9 describes the fire in this version as «almost an afterthought».

59 *Pace* Briant 2010: 108 n. 16: «omitted by [...] Plutarch».

60 Plutarch perhaps found it in the so-called *Ephemerides* (royal journals or diary of the daily records), presumably a forgery. See Pearson 1955: 437, 455; cf. Hamilton 1969: 97. This fake diary probably included various letters and most likely made use of colourful descriptions found in other works. The counter arguments of Hammond 1988b are not convincing.

61 Cf. Baynham 2003: 22. This is true regardless of the probable attempt of Arrian's main source, Ptolemy, to ignore (Lane Fox 1973: 263) the role of Thais, the mother of three of his children (Athen. 13.576e), in the deed (but cf. Borza 1972: 235 n. 12). See Baynham 2003: 11: «Arrian's version is not only very brief, but loaded with his own opinion, and he seems uncomfortable with the whole affair».

62 It is contrary to the prevailing view among scholars. See Hamilton 1973: 88; Hammond 1992a: 360; O'Brien 1992: 103; Bloedow 1995: 29; Flower 2000: 113-4; Brosius 2003: 182 n. 23; Briant 2010: 109; Nawotka 2012: 254; Mousavi 2012: 64, 69; Anson 2013: 154. Borza 1972: 234 is close to acknowledge this truth, but then (235) asserts that «It is more likely that the Thais story did not appear in [Arrian's] source». See Bosworth 1980a: 329-31 for the conciseness of Arrian's and Strabo's depictions. As Bloedow (1995: 37) rightly points out, in both these 'versions', Alexander is said to regret the deed later (in Arr. *An.* VI.30.1, six years later). This fact indicates that the two 'versions' are not that dissimilar.

63 Unconvincingly, Tarn 1948: 2.116-22 claims that Curtius used Diodorus' work. See Pearson 1960: 217 n. 23.

from different sources.[64] If this supposition is true, then nothing precludes us from postulating the two scenes as two competing accounts of the sack of Persepolis. The authors tried to accommodate the two in various ways; for instance, in the portrayal of the Diodorus, the plunder allegedly excluded the palaces and occurred only in the city (D.S. XVII.70.1; cf. Curt. V.7.10). Diodorus, however, also mentions that the world famous palaces fell victim to destruction (XVII.70.3) during the plunder,[65] and Curtius (V.6.9) rightly mentions the two scenes as belonging to the same place (which he sees as the «city», *urbs*).[66]

Evidence for the interchangeability of the stories may be seen in the following facts. Curtius mentions flames already in the *first* story: the Persians set their own houses on fire, which the enemy seemed about to do a little later in any case (*quod paulo post facturus hostis videbatur*: V.6.7), so that they would be burned alive with their families. Curtius also places Alexander's campaign against the Mardi after the plunder of Persepolis (V.6.17-19), while Arrian puts this episode after the burning of the palaces (*An.* III.24).[67] Curtius mentions the campaign in Persis after the first scene, while Diodorus (XVII.73.1) places it after the second.[68] Irrational Bacchic frenzy, associated with the second story (e.g., XVII.72.1), is also alluded to in Diodorus' account of the plunder: the participants were carried away by their emotions (συνεκφερόμενοι τοῖς θυμοῖς: XVII.70.5).[69] There may have been thus some duplication involved in the scenes.

It is difficult to know which was the earliest to be recorded, but we know that the second story comes from Cleitarchus (Athenaeus XIII.576de),[70] that is, mid to late

---

[64] Cf. Jacoby 1921: 631 for the idea that Curtius did not use Cleitarchus' work directly.

[65] Cf. Hammond 1992a: 361: «an expression which can only mean the Apadana».

[66] Unfortunately, the presentation of a separation between the two scenes of plunder in the city and the burning of the palace is followed by modern scholars. See, for example, Grote 1856: 237-240; Olmstead 1948: 520-521; Borza 1972: 242; Lane Fox 1973: 259; Bosworth 1988b: 92-93; Green 1991: 315-316; O'Brien 1992: 101; Flower 2000: 113; Briant 2010: 108; Brosius 2003: 183; Heckel 2007: 83; Nawotka 2010: 250; Mousavi 2012: 57; Anson 2013: 154. It is clear that the vast sums of money, including gold and silver bullion, plundered on this occassion and trasported elsewhere, were those hoarded in the treasury on the terrace (as almost all scholars agree: e.g., Borza 1972: 242-243, Bosworth, 1988b: 92; Mousavi, 2012: 69). If this is the same place where the army did the looting (as Curtius implies), then the latter was the palace complex as well. Therefore, Goukowsky 1976: 100 n. 2 is right in claiming that the army plundered the terrace; cf. Sancisi-Weerdenburg 1993: 183; Hammond 1997: 115.

[67] In both cases the section is apparently not in its proper context. Cf. Hammond 1992a: 360 n. 22: «The Mardi [...] were a different tribe from the Mardi of Hyrcania». Yet, Briant 2002: 851 accepts Curtius' account.

[68] Cf. Arr. *An.* III.19.2. See Hammond 1992a: 360 n. 22.

[69] Note that Wirth 1971: 624-5 casts doubt over the reality of the masacre and plunder and assumes a confusion with the military clash before the taking of the city. Cf. Olmstead 1948: 520.

[70] ὁ δὲ μέγας Ἀλέξανδρος οὐ Θαίδα εἶχε μεθ' ἑαυτοῦ τὴν Ἀττικὴν ἑταίραν; περὶ ἧς φησι Κλείταρχος ὡς αἰτίας γενομένης τοῦ ἐμπρησθῆναι τὰ ἐν Περσεπόλει βασίλεια («And did not the great Alexander keep Thais about him, who was an Athenian courtesan? And Cleitarchus speaks of her as having been the cause that the palace of Persepolis was burnt down»; transl. Yonge). See Wilcken 1932: 145; Goukowsky 1976: 98 n. 3; Bosworth 1988b: 93. Yet, cf. Borza 1972: 234. There is no evidence that the first story of plunder was told by Cleitarchus as well (*pace* Hammond 1992a: 363).

third century BCE.[71] Cleitarchus did not enjoy a good reputation as a historian,[72] and his focus on the burning of the site underemphasizes the element of plunder. After all, it would appear that Alexander's aim in reaching Persepolis was presumably first and foremost to ransack its treasures.[73] In fact, the first story (of the plunder) is broader than the second. There are two elements in the story of plunder: one is planned (the thorough removal of Achaemenid treasure from the terrace), the other is unintentional and unpredictable (the extent of killing and the fires).[74] Moreover, there is archaeological evidence for both the plunder[75] and for the fires,[76] which usually accompany a looting of such proportions, in a manner that may correspond to the first story. The evidence points out to a hasty pillage,[77] and the reason for the haste may lie in the scale of the fires which erupted during the looting and their quick spread. The evidence also indicates partial burning of the site.[78] One cannot assume that this is because specific buildings were especifically targeted, nor that some ideology was

---

[71] See Pearson 1960: 215, 218-9. Cleitarchus' *Histories* recounted the reign and the campaign of Alexander the Great to his death in least twelve books; cf. D. L. I.6. See Pearson 1960: 213: 14/15 books in all. The prevailing view favours a 'high' dating, in other words, that he lived at the end of the fourth century or the beginning of the third century BCE: see Jacoby 1921: 625-626; Hamilton 1961a; Badian 1965a; Baynham 2003: 10-11; Zambrini 2007: 20; Prandi 1996: 69-71 and 77-79. Yet, other scholars, perhaps more convincingly, propose a date later than the 280s BCE: Tarn 1948: 2.5-29; Pearson 1960: 226-242; Hazzard 1992: 52-56; Ravazzolo 1998: 31-44.

[72] In antiquity, Cleitarchus' work was obviously widely read, especially in late republican and early imperial times (Plin. *NH* 10.70.136), but it was not valued. Quintilian *Inst*. X.1.74 approves Cleitarchus' talent, but not his accuracy. Cicero *Brutus*, 42-3 accuses the historian of false details concerning the death of Themistocles. Cf. Str. XI.5.4; Curt. IX.5.21. See Pearson 1960: 212; Cartledge 2004: 255. See Bosworth 2000a: 14 on the historical and historiographic problems with Cleitarchus' account of Persepolis.

[73] See Olmstaed 1948: 519; Schachermeyr 1973: 286; Hamilton 1973: 87-88. Cf. Alexander's haste once he received the letter from Tiridates concerning the danger of pillage from the local population (Curt. V.5.2; cf. D.S. XVII.69.1-2).

[74] If the first scene also occurred on the terrace, as our sources seem to imply, Bloedow 1995: 38 is patently wrong in claiming «there was only *material* destruction in connection with the torching of the palace –no loss of life, or destruction of personal property». His following assertion «[t]here was, however, plenty of the latter [...] in respect of the *city*» should aply to the palace complex as well.

[75] See Schmidt 1953: 75, 122, 131, 159, 179-80, 183, 185-189, 191-192, 206; Hammond 1992a: 359, 364. Cf. Mousavi 2012: 63.

[76] Cf. Schmidt 1953: 73-75, 78-79, 131-132, 157, 170, 173-174, 177, 181, 184-185, 239; Sancisi-Weerdenburg 1993: 181; Mousavi 2012: 61-63. Especially in the Apadana, the Throne Hall and also the Treasury.

[77] Cf. Schmidt 1953: 75: «pieces of gold foil and gold tacks were scattered all over the floor». See Hammond 1992a: 359: «There is only one explanation for the failure of the pillagers to return and make a clean sweep of residue. The pillaging itself was done not only at speed, as the excavators noted, but also during a short time, so that the pillagers were able to collect and remove only what was most valuable and easily carried off».

[78] Cf. Schmidt 1953: 122, 189, 191, 197-198, 262-263 on buildings which show no effect of fire: (263): «At any rate, it appears that there was no general conflagration», but rather «separate fires», which, he goes on to conjecture, were methodically put to the combustible contents of the main rooms. Cf. Sancisi-Weerdenburg 1993: 181-185.

behind such partial incineration.[79] It is more likely that some of fires started by accident and spread to several buildings by chance.[80] In any case, the archaeological evidence does not support a full-scale conflagration of the sort that Cleitarchus mentioned and the subsequent total obliteration as envisaged by Curtius.[81] We propose that the focus on the burning of the site (exaggerated and embroidered in any case)[82] in Cleitarchus' version appears to be secondary and derivative to that of the plunder (which obviously involved a fire of some sort) and therefore should be taken as the chronologically latest of the two.

Following this supposition, we can observe another important impact of Alexander on historiography with regard to Persepolis. The association of the site with its being a symbol of destruction probably led to the imaginary elaboration of what really happened. If Cleitarchus' portrayal was chronologically the more recent of the two variants, he created the burning scene of Persepolis based on the awareness that the complex was a ruined and ransacked place. Furthermore, Persepolis became a location, which would have a symbolic meaning in the ensuing power struggles. For instance, in organizing a magnificent banquet and ceremony to the allied forces (that is, of the coalition supporting the kings –Alexander's young son and misfit brother– against Antigonus: D.S. XIX.21.2, 22.1) in Persepolis (317 BCE), Peucestas, the satrap of Persis, surely hoped to obtain an honour which would help him

---

[79] It cannot be assumed, for instance, that only buildings associated especially with Xerxes were targeted, as proposed, for instance, by Luschey 1968: 28; and cf. Tarn 1948: 1.54; Schmidt 1953: 239; Sancisi-Weerdenburg 1993: 182-3, 185; Wiesehöfer 2001: 106. It is untenable because all the buildings were associated with Xerxes (cf. Mousavi 2012: 68) and the fire was uncontainable. This also has nothing to do with any alleged image of Alexander as following Cyrus II rather than Darius or Xerxes (Müller 2011: 113-117, Olbrycht 2014: 53, based on Str. XI.11.4, cf. XV.3.7-8; Arr. *An.* VI.29.4-11; Curt. X.1.22; 30; cf. O'Brien 1992: 187, Nawotka 2010: 268, 341-342; Briant 2010: 111), if he indeed tried to project such a self portrayal (and at that point in time rather than in 324 BCE) – this would have been irrlevant in any case to the Greek/Macedonian soldiers ransacking the place and to the local/Persian population, insulted by the pillage itself.

[80] Cf. Seibert 2004/2005: 88-90. The fact that «the damage to the construction was [...] a consequence of the demolition of the contents» (Sancisi-Weerdenburg 1993: 183) does not neccesarily mean that all the fires have been lit on purpose to destroy the contents (cf. 184-185). Some may have been an accidental outcome of the looting, which Sancisi-Weerdenburg admits was still going on at the time.

[81] Cf. Curzon 1892: 180: «[...] none of the earlier travellers found in any of the edifices on the platform the least traces of destruction by fire, and were therefore puzzled how to reconcile with the visible ruins the story, attested by a consensus of ancient historians, of the conflagration of one or more of the Persepolitan palaces by Alexander [...]». Yet, he goes on to mention that the ashes of cedar wood in the Hall of a Hundred Columns (the Throne Hall) do provide such evidence (cf. Schmidt 1953: 132). Curzon probably referred to comments like that of Fergusson (1851: 199): «there is no evidence of fire at Persepolis, nor any sign of its having been so completely ruined as Quintus Curtius and other authors would lead us to suppose». Cf. Wiesehöfer 2001: 25.

[82] Cf. Jamzadeh 2012: 66: «in the stories and memories of Alexander's devastating act, the conflagration had been so massive that it had been remembered as having consumed the entire city, not leaving any traces behind».

gain the supreme command of the troops instead of Eumenes.[83] Similarly, it was important for Antigonus to have Persepolis (in 316 BCE) as the location, where he would redistribute the satrapies of his new administration (D.S. XIX.46.6, 48.1).[84] In both these scenes, Persepolis was depicted (by Hieorynus of Cardia?) as the capital/ imperial seat (τὸ βασίλειον). Later on, in a description in 2 Maccabees (9:2), which only underscores the fact that the site's inclusion in imperial campaigns has become a literary convention,[85] Antiochus IV Epiphanes enters the place called Persepolis (εἰς τὴν λεγομένην Περσέπολιν), and unsuccessfully attempts to rob its temples and control the city (the mention of Persepolis as a form of an *imitatio Alexandri*?).

Another way in which Alexander altered the meaning of Persepolis is the manner in which its importance was posthumously enhanced in an exaggerated way. For instance, it became «the most prosperous place» (πλουσιωτάτης δ' οὔσης τῶν ὑπὸ τὸν ἥλιον) to use Diodorus' phrases.[86] This led to a certain rewriting of previous texts. The most striking example is an elaboration of the account of Xenophon in the *Cyropaedia* (VIII.6.22) on the seasonal travelling of the Persian kings. Xenophon mentions only a winter stay in Babylon, a spring sojourn in Susa and a summer respite in Ecbatana.[87] Yet, Athenaues (XII.513f), probably from Aristobulus and Chares, rough contemporaries of Alexander, tells us that the Persian kings spend their winters at Susa and their summers at Ecbatana, their autumns in Persepolis; and the rest of the year in Babylon.[88] This appears like an attempt to correct and expand Xenophon's depiction, in light of the new importance of Persepolis: one may note that both accounts begin in the winter. While it makes perfect sense in Xenophon, who emphasizes Babylon, to speak of a season that essentially corresponds to the beginning of the Spartan year, it is not understandable why the other description begins with the winter. Both accounts have Susa and Ecbatana in the same sequence, but while in Xenophon the seasons follow in natural order, this is not the case in the account of Athenaeus. In the latter's passage, Babylon is inexplicably relegated to «the rest of

---

[83] Bosworth 2002: 121-122. According to Herzfeld 1935: 45, however, it is not the royal terrace which is meant but rather the nearby town, later known as Istakhr (from Stakhra, i.e., 'stronghold', of Fars).

[84] Cf. Bosworth 2002: 162.

[85] Cf. Schwartz 2008: 353. Cf. 2 Macc. 1: 13. It was in fact in Elam: Plb. XXXI.9.1; 1 Macc. 6: 1-4; J. *AJ*. XII.354-8; App. *Syr*. 66.

[86] Cf. Str. XV.3.6 on Persepolis as «the most beautifully built city», and «the largest», next to Susa, with a remarkable palace and extravagant treasures (ἦν δὲ ἡ Περσέπολις μετὰ Σοῦσα κάλλιστα κατεσκευασμένη μεγίστη πόλις, ἔχουσα βασίλεια ἐκπρεπῆ, καὶ μάλιστα τῇ πολυτελείᾳ τῶν κειμένων).

[87] αὐτὸς δ' ἐν μέσῳ τούτων τὴν δίαιταν ποιησάμενος, τὸν μὲν ἀμφὶ τὸν χειμῶνα χρόνον διῆγεν ἐν Βαβυλῶνι ἑπτὰ μῆνας: αὕτη γὰρ ἀλεεινὴ ἡ χώρα: τὸν δὲ ἀμφὶ τὸ ἔαρ τρεῖς μῆνας ἐν Σούσοις: τὴν δὲ ἀκμὴν τοῦ θέρους δύο μῆνας ἐν Ἐκβατάνοις: οὕτω δὴ ποιοῦντ' αὐτὸν λέγουσιν ἐν ἐαρινῷ θάλπει καὶ ψύχει διάγειν ἀεί. See Tuplin (1998).

[88] καὶ οἱ βασιλεῖς ἐχείμαζον μὲν ἐν Σούσοις, ἐθέριζον δὲ ἐν Ἐκβατάνοις. κληθῆναι δὲ τὰ Σοῦσά φησιν Ἀριστόβουλος καὶ Χάρης διὰ τὴν ὡραιότητα τοῦ τόπου... ἐν Περσεπόλει δὲ διατρίβουσι <τὸ> φθινόπωρον καὶ ἐν Βαβυλῶνι τὸ λεῖπον τοῦ ἐνιαυτοῦ μέρος.

the year», without any concrete season. All this does indeed seem superficial, in an attempt to allot a place to Persepolis, which is added in a forced way to the original three items list.

Lastly, there were also some inadvertent outcomes to the sacking of Persepolis. The first is the impact of this event on the eventual image of Alexander himself. From antiquity to the modern era, the burning of the palace complex was associated with failure and shame, so that Alexander allegedly soon regretted it[89] or that it was blamed on others (Thais).[90] It signalled a visible change in his character as a ruler corrupted by power.[91] It portrayed him as a tyrant, disregarding the wise advice of his 'Tragic Warner'.[92] It did not change the attitudes of his Macedonian and Greek soldiers about the nature of the campaign or win their support for the possibility of establishing his kingdom of Asia.[93] It has caused him to lose any legitimate claim to rule in the east,[94] or in the words of Heckel (1997: 207), «[i]n the long term, the act was detrimental to the cause of Hellenic rule in Asia». In popular local culture, reflected in Firdowsi's tenth century CE *Shāhnāma*, Alexander was associated with a dramatic destructive act (of the *Avesta*).[95] This fiasco has only increased the image of Alexander as a failed leader and statesman, which some scholars find hard to accept.[96]

The second unplanned result has impacted the image of Persia. It may be that by the destruction, the upper floors of the northern fortification wall collapsed, by which

---

[89] Curt. V.7.10-11; Plu. *Alex.* 38.8; cf. Arr. *An.* VI.30.1.

[90] The manner in which Alexander is tainted by the deed can be seen in the ironic presentation (Plu. *Eum.* 2.3) as if the Macedonian kind ordered to burn Eumenes' tent to reveal whether he embazzeled money –an act Alexander soon regretted (!).

[91] The so-caled Peripatetic view. See Wardman 1955: 96, 101 on Plutarch's depiction. Fire thus became a trait of Alexander's troubled personality; see Almagor 2011: 15. Cf. Lane Fox 1973: 267. See, however, Green 1991: 443.

[92] In this case, Parmenion (Arr. *An.* III.18.11); cf. Hdt. I.88. See Carney 2000b: 272; Cf. Sancisi-Weerdenburg 1993: 177-178, 180.

[93] See Anson 2013: 158-159.

[94] See Badian 1958c: 497, 1967: 187-90, 2000: 264. Cf. Eddy 1961: 37, 58-61; Balcer 1978; Green 1991: 319; Heckel 2009: 40. See Gabriel 2015: 104: «The destruction of Persepolis, the religious capital of the country, only created popular support for the insurgency».

[95] See Jamzadeh 2012: 66, cf. 173. Cf. *Greater Bundahishn* 33.14: the ruler Alexander came to Iranshahr and burned the *Avesta*.

[96] Failure: Cf. Badian 1965b: 177: «his sole serious error of judgement»; Bloedow 1995: 40: «that great *blunder* in the history of Alexander». Even proverbially so: cf. Carney 1996: 571: «[Alexander's h]aving a sexual relationship with the wife of Darius would seem to be the sexual equivalent of Alexander's burning of Persepolis (and surprising for the same reasons, in as much as it too jeopardized with the Persians his themes of legitimacy and continuity)». See, however, Borza 1972: 245: «for Alexander himself the Persepolis outcome need not necessarily be regarded as a failure». Puzzle: Badian 1967: 189; Lane Fox 1973: 261; see Cartledge 2004: 100: «the burning of the palace at Persepolis remains a bit of a conundrum [...] and regrettably [we] have to leave as such». There may be a tinge of irony, not lost on ancient authors, in that Calanus, the Brahman who accompanied Alexander from India killed himself in Persepolis by self-immolation, a symbolic gesture. Cf. Arr. *An.*VII.3.1-6; D.S. XVII.107.1-6; Str. XV.1.68; Plu. *Alex.* 69.6-8. Cf. Chares *apud* Ath. X.437a.

some 30,000 (mostly Elamite) clay tablets, the *Persepolis Fortification Texts*, were preserved.[97] The tablets were discovered in the archaeological excavations of the Oriental Institute of Chicago University expedition to Persepolis (headed first by E. Herzfeld, 1933-4).[98] By these texts (relating particularly to administrative transfers of food commodities in the years 509-494 BCE), scholars were able to see just how well-organized Achaemenid rule in Persia was, a fact that is only highlighted against the chaos and partial disorder caused to the region by the Macedonian troops and brought about by Alexander. It was in this manner that portions of Achaemenid history were able to escape the hellenocentric grip of classical texts.

In this brief chapter we saw the impact of Alexander's destruction of the palace complex in Persepolis on history and historiography. The former Persian site was given a new name and a new meaning by its Greek speaking pillagers at a decisive moment which spelled the transfer of power between them. Ironically, from that alarming moment onward, the ruins of the Persian past endured through the very act of destruction, shedding light on both the period of Achaemenid glory and the character of its conquerors. Thus, eventually the remains of Persepolis silently tell us the failure not of the Achaemenid Empire but of its vanquisher. In this way, while Alexander has purposely forever spoiled the memory of the palace complex, he unintentionally let Persepolis eternally taint the accomplishment of its *perseptolis*.

---

[97] Cf. Milns 1968: 139: «The fire in the palaces [...] baked hard palace documents inscribed in clay that otherwise would have crumbled away». See Olmstead 1948: 523.

[98] See Hallock 1969: 1; *Dusinberre* 2005: 150-1; Henkelman 2008: 176.

Comunicación y conquista: La información como elemento estratégico en la campaña asiática

Mario Agudo Villanueva
(Karanos – *Editorial Board)*

La Historia de la Comunicación es una disciplina joven, en la que se trabaja desde hace poco tiempo en comparación con otros estudios humanísticos. Sin embargo, el papel que ha desempeñado su objeto de investigación a lo largo de la evolución de las sociedades humanas se remonta a nuestros albores como especie y adquiere, en muchas ocasiones, un determinante cariz estratégico. El interés por el estudio de la historia de la comunicación fue despertando a lo largo del siglo XX. Inicialmente, se centró de forma exclusiva en la práctica periodística. A la sombra del positivismo que dominó la segunda mitad del siglo XIX, comenzaron a gestarse los pioneros trabajos de Hatin (1853-1859), Cucheval-Clarigny (1857), Andrews (1859), Winckle (1875), Piccardi (1881) y, ya en el siglo pasado, George Weill. Este enfoque restrictivo se amplía de forma progresiva a medida que algunos investigadores subrayan el papel esencial de la comunicación en toda sociedad organizada y, por tanto, la sitúan como protagonista de una función estructural que nos la presenta como un sistema paralelo a otros, como el socioeconómico o sociopolítico.[1] En esta línea, el profesor Pizarroso ha destacado que la Historia de la Comunicación Social «cobra verdaderamente la dimensión de una disciplina histórica científica, capaz de revelar nuevos aspectos a historiadores que se ocupan de otras parcelas y no sólo de "ilustrar" más o menos una fuente de mayor o menor importancia».[2]

Pese a estos esfuerzos, la disciplina no escapa a la fragmentación y dispersión que caracteriza al mundo de la comunicación en general. García Galindo ha puesto de

[1] Timoteo Álvarez 1978: 403-405.

[2] Pizarroso 1996: 90.

manifiesto la importancia de avanzar en la superación de la Historia de los Medios por una Historia de la Comunicación Social, considerada de forma global y procurando de forma simultánea «la convergencia explicativa de la comunicación social con los avances de la historiografía general, que permita contextualizar la historia de la comunicación como parte del proceso histórico general».[3] Este es el enfoque de extensas y meritorias obras, como la de César Aguilera en el panorama español,[4] que surgen con el propósito de revisar el papel desempeñado por la comunicación y la gestión de la información a lo largo de la historia de la Humanidad. No es nuestro propósito profundizar en el estado de la cuestión en relación con los estudios de historia y comunicación, el lector puede acudir para ello a los muchos análisis que se han realizado sobre la materia.[5] Solo pretendemos identificar el marco científico en el que tiene cabida un estudio como el que queremos presentar a continuación: el del papel de la información como elemento estratégico durante la campaña asiática de Alejandro Magno.

Para completar este planteamiento preliminar, centrándonos ya en nuestro objeto de estudio, debemos considerar que el ejército macedonio estuvo sometido a lo largo de su periplo asiático a un entorno geográfico, social, cultural, bélico y político cambiante y, a medida que progresaba hacia el interior del continente, desconocido; al mismo tiempo que se iban operando importantes transformaciones en su propio seno, pues a su núcleo tradicional se fueron adhiriendo contingentes de otras nacionalidades gracias a la conquista de nuevos territorios. Los retos que se presentan durante este período de tiempo otorgan un papel determinante a la información, entendida como el conjunto ordenado de datos elaborados que construyen un mensaje que modifica el estado original de su receptor, otorgándole, de alguna manera, una posición de mayor ventaja o disposición para afrontar una determinada situación (informar). En este sentido, la información se convierte en un elemento estratégico de primer orden, en la medida en que supone el instrumento básico para la toma de decisiones en el campo de las operaciones, tanto a nivel externo como interno, y permite, por tanto, garantizar la correcta adaptación de la organización al medio en el que se desarrolla.[6]

Aunque es posible obtener información por vía no comunicativa, como veremos, el cauce habitual para disponer de un buen sistema de recopilación de datos es la comunicación.[7] En este sentido, nos apoyaremos de forma parcial en otra disciplina

---

[3] García Galindo 1996: 37.

[4] Aguilera *et al.* 1998

[5] Ruiz Acosta 1997: 185-202; Amaya Trujillo 2010: 149-171.

[6] Aunque se aleja del objeto de este trabajo, es interesante en este punto el concepto de estrategia formulado como el patrón de los objetivos, propósitos o metas y las políticas y planes esenciales para conseguir dichas metas, establecidas de tal manera que definan en qué clase de negocio la organización está o quiere estar y qué clase de organización es o quiere ser (Andrews 1971: 18).

[7] Martín Serrano 1982: 80.

de reciente creación: la teoría de la comunicación en las organizaciones. Si bien estamos ante un ámbito de análisis que surge en el contexto de la lógica democrática liberal, pues tiene una clara orientación institucional y empresarial, también lo es que la comunicación en las organizaciones, como en cualquier relación humana, es un elemento decisivo, básico y fundacional, que tiene varias dimensiones, unas *ad intra* y otras *ad extra*.[8] Si acudimos a la teoría de los sistemas sociales, las organizaciones pueden definirse como sistemas abiertos compuestos de subsistemas interdependientes que para sobrevivir precisan encontrarse en equilibrio con el gran sistema social, el entorno. Este equilibrio se consigue mediante la adaptación a las condiciones del medio o su control total. Como la organización tiene dependencias externas e internas, los canales de comunicación que se desarrollen tienen que mirar tanto hacia el exterior como hacia el interior. En este sentido, la comunicación organizacional es el instrumento que permite a la entidad establecer y mantener sus relaciones con el entorno y entre sus subsistemas.[9]

Centrándonos ya en la materia que nos ocupa, un análisis detallado del relato de Flavio Arriano desde esta perspectiva revela un total de 233 referencias, complementadas por 44 en el texto de Quinto Curcio Rufo, 18 en el de Diodoro y 16 en el de Plutarco.[10] A lo largo de este trabajo desgranaremos el tipo de información recogida por Alejandro Magno, cuáles son las fuentes y los instrumentos de los que se sirve para ello y qué resultado le proporciona a la hora de conseguir sus objetivos. Para ello dividiremos el análisis en dos grandes bloques: comunicación externa y comunicación interna. Entendemos la primera como cualquier interacción del ejército macedonio con su entorno para recopilar datos de interés y la segunda, como es fácilmente deducible, por las interacciones que tienen lugar en su propio seno.

Información e inteligencia: la comunicación externa

En el proceso de recopilación de datos del entorno durante una campaña militar de conquista y control del territorio como la emprendida por Alejandro Magno, la gestión de la información está, en la mayoría de los casos, dentro de lo que generalmente se conoce como inteligencia militar. Como han señalado algunos autores, la precisión de este sistema durante el periplo asiático del monarca macedonio resultó fundamental para el éxito de su proyecto.[11] No son muchos los investigadores que se

---

[8] Galdón 2004: 27.

[9] Sotelo Enríquez 2004: 48.

[10] El número de referencias es superior al mencionado en Curcio, Diodoro y Plutarco, pero solo añadimos como complementarias aquellas que ofrecen un matiz diferente a las anteriores o bien no son mencionadas por los otros historiadores. No hemos acudido al testimonio de Justino porque no había referencias que aportaran aspectos nuevos al objeto de la investigación.

[11] Green 1974: 405; Borza 1977.

han prodigado en el estudio de esta materia, pero tenemos un interesante artículo de Donald Engels en el que analiza el sistema de inteligencia militar macedonio desde el punto de vista estratégico –conocimiento requerido para afrontar objetivos generales– y desde el punto de vista táctico –conocimiento necesario para acometer las misiones que tienen el fin último de lograr el objetivo general.[12]

A pesar de la sensación de imprevisión que se deriva de las famosas palabras de Badian («When Alexander invaded Asia, he almost certainly had no idea how far he would go or what the end would be»),[13] parece que todos los riesgos que Alejandro asume en territorio asiático han sido estudiados convenientemente de acuerdo con la información que obra en su poder en cada momento. No se inician nuevas etapas sin haber asegurado la retaguardia y sin haber obtenido información del panorama que su ejército tiene que afrontar en el futuro.[14] En este pasaje de Arriano tenemos un claro ejemplo de esta inquietud:

> «Comparecieron también unos embajadores de los escitas europeos, que son el pueblo más populoso de cuantos en Europa habitan. Alejandro dispuso que algunos Compañeros les acompañaran a su regreso, so pretexto de pactar un acuerdo amistoso, aunque la verdadera intención de esta expedición era espiar la naturaleza de la región escita, el número de sus habitantes, sus costumbres y las armas que emplean cuando van a la guerra» (Arr. *An.* IV.1.1-2; Guzmán Guerra 1982, trad.).

Más interesante, si cabe, resulta este otro fragmento, situado ya en territorio indio, en el que el abanico de informaciones recogidas por Alejandro se amplía, incluso, al ámbito social y político:

> «Le habían llegado noticias a Alejandro de que el territorio de la otra orilla del Hífasis era una tierra próspera, de hombres laboriosos, nobles en la guerra, y que regían sus asuntos privados en buen orden. La mayoría de ellos vivían bajo regímenes aristocráticos, sin plantear sus gobernantes exigencias más allá de lo razonable. Estos pueblos tenían gran cantidad de elefantes, más incluso que los demás indios, mayores en tamaño y más valerosos. Estas noticias no hicieron sino aumentar en Alejandro los deseos de proseguir sus conquistas» (Arr. *An.* V.25.1-2).

Sin embargo, si tenemos que destacar algún episodio en relación con el carácter estratégico de la información, quizás tendríamos que quedarnos con este extenso texto relacionado con las costas del Golfo Pérsico:

> «Le incitaba no menos a esta empresa la prosperidad del país, del que había oído que en sus oasis crece la casia, y de sus árboles se extrae la mirra, el incienso, que

[12] Engels 1980: 327-329.

[13] Badian 1965b: 166.

[14] Briant 2012: 34. Sobre esta cuestión se puede consultar también Engels: 1980; Borza 1995: 223-224; cf. Badian 1965b, 1994: 285-289.

de sus matorrales se corta cinamomo y que en sus praderas crecen espontáneamente los nardos. Por otra parte, estaba la extensión del país, cuya costa era, según sus noticias, no menor que la de la India, y que a lo largo de ella se hallaban gran número de islas y puertos repartidos por todas las playas del país, capaces de cobijar a su flota y proporcionar asentamiento a las más prósperas ciudades del futuro [...] Todas estas informaciones le fueron facilitadas a Alejandro por Arquias, que había partido con un triacóntoro para inspeccionar la costa en dirección a Arabia y había llegado hasta esta isla de Tilo, sin atreverse a proseguir su viaje más allá. Andróstenes, sin embargo, que partió en otro triacóntoro, navegó costeando la mayor parte de la península arábiga. Con todo, el que más lejos llegó fue el timonel Hierón, natural de Solos, a bordo también de otro triacóntoro facilitado por Alejandro [...] Fue Nearco quien dijo oponerse a ello, ya que una vez que hubiera terminado de costear el golfo pérsico podía informar a Alejandro de todo aquello por lo que se había originado esta expedición; a él no le había mandado nadie a costear el Gran Mar, sino inspeccionar la zona próxima a la costa, qué hombres la habitaban, los fondeaderos que en ella hubiera, puntos de agua, costumbres de sus moradoers, y si alguna parte de la región produce buenos frutos, y cuál es estéril. Precisamente esta había sido la causa de que el ejército de Alejandro se hubiera salvado, cosa que no habría acaecido si ellos se hubieran adentrado más allá de los desiertos de Arabia» (Arr. *An.* VII.20.2-10).

Este fragmento muestra de forma nítida la preocupación de Alejandro por la exploración y catalogación de las fortunas locales, así como también por la investigación de las capacidades productivas de los terrenos que se van a conquistar, lo que denota una clara intención de planificación y explotación de sus recursos naturales, tal y como han señalado autores como Briant.[15]

Si descendemos al nivel táctico, que está en el plano operativo, nos encontramos con algunas referencias de interés que permiten conocer el tipo de información que se recopilaba antes de misiones concretas. Aunque no corresponde a la campaña asiática, hemos considerado oportuno citar este fragmento de la campaña del Danubio:

> «Se le presentaron unos mensajeros con la noticia de que Clito, hijo de Bardileo, se había sublevado y que se le había añadido Glaucias, rey de los taulancios. Le dijeron también que los autariatas le atacarían a su paso, y que por ello convenía que se alejara a toda prisa. El rey de los agrianes, Lángaro, se había mostrado aun en vida de Filipo bien dispuesto para con Alejandro, incluso había acudido ante él al frente de una legación; en esta ocasión se presentó ante él con los más apuestos y mejor armados componentes de su guardia personal. Enterado de que Alejandro indagaba acerca de los autariatas, sobre quiénes y cuántos serían, le dijo que no debía preocuparse por los autariatas, ya que eran los menos belicosos de estas tierras» (Arr. *An.* I.5.1).

---

[15] Briant 2012: 87.

En este pasaje encontramos varios datos interesantes. En primer lugar, que los datos más relevantes antes del combate son quiénes y cuántos eran los autariatas. Gracias a la aclaración de Lángaro, interpretamos que el quiénes hace referencia a su beligerancia. De los mensajeros que portan la noticia inicial no sabemos nada, aunque dado el conocimiento que tenían de las intenciones del enemigo, bien podrían ser habitantes de aquellas tierras –conocedores del valor que para su futuro podría tener una información útil para un enemigo superior– o, incluso, por su exhortación a la huida, cabría la posibilidad de que fueran enviados de los mismos enemigos.

El desconocimiento práctico del terreno conduce al ejército macedonio a recopilar información de todo tipo, tal y como muestra este otro pasaje:[16]

> «Se informó, empero, Alejandro de que la mejor época para emprender la navegación era la que va del principio del invierno, justo en el momento del ocaso de las Pléyades, hasta el solsticio de invierno, pues en esta época soplan por tierra (como cuando esta queda regada por abundantes lluvias) unas suaves brisas, muy adecuadas para la navegación de cabotaje, tanto si se hace a remo como a vela» (Arr. *An.* VI.21.2).

En esta línea se sitúa también este fragmento, en el que las pesquisas sobre el entorno continúan:

> «Alejandro reparó las averías lo mejor que pudo en las actuales circunstancias y ordenó que algunos se adelantaran en dos bajeles río abajo para inspeccionar la isla en la que, según decían los indígenas, podían anclar la flota en esta travesía hasta el mar. El nombre de la isla era Ciluta. Este destacamento informó a Alejandro que en la isla había buenos fondeaderos, así como que se trataba de una isla de gran tamaño y de agua abundante» (Arr. *An.* VI.19.3).

La necesidad de información abarca todas las facetas de la vida cotidiana del ejército, tal y como podemos observar en una anécdota que nos relata Diodoro y que explica cómo los macedonios tuvieron que colgar sus hamacas de los árboles para evitar la mordedura de unas serpientes cuyo veneno resultaba mortal. Gracias a los indígenas, dieron con la raíz de una planta que servía como antídoto.[17]

La ausencia de información, o la imprecisión de determinados datos, genera incertidumbre, en especial en los momentos previos a los enfrentamientos bélicos, donde cualquier indicio sobre posición, número o armamento del individuo resulta crucial para el diseño de la estrategia de combate. Quinto Curcio Rufo nos presenta

---

[16] Los griegos tenían un importante conocimiento acumulado sobre el Imperio persa, transmitido a través de diferentes vías, como el comercio, los enfrentamientos bélicos, los períodos de ocupación militar de las colonias griegas, la actuación de los griegos como mercenarios o, incluso, de la literatura (Engels 1980: 328); sin embargo, una vez sobre el terreno, cualquier dato puede resultar clave.

[17] D.S. XVII.90.7.

a un Alejandro dubitativo en algunos estadios de la campaña, como es el caso de los prolegómenos de Gaugamela:

> «Los que evaluaban el número de tropas de Darío (en la medida en que podía ser conjeturado desde lejos) con dificultad pudieron hacer creer a Alejandro que, después de haber perdido tantos miles de soldados, aquel había logrado poner en pie un ejército con mayores efectivos todavía» (Curt. IV.9.11; Pejenaute Rubio 2008, trad.).

> «Había comenzado a avanzar por esta ruta cuando he aquí que los oteadores, que habían sido enviados por delante, trajeron al amanecer la noticia de que Darío estaba al llegar. Alejandro iba al frente de su ejército con sus tropas dispuestas y la formación cerrada. Pero en realidad se trataba de persas rezagados, alrededor de 1000, que habían dado la impresión de un gran ejército: y es que cuando no puede descubrirse la verdad, el miedo agranda lo falso» (Curt. IV.10.10).

Por todo ello, nos dice Curcio (IV.12.21) que en la víspera de Gaugamela: «Alejandro se mostraba indeciso, y en una tardía evaluación pasaba revista bien a su propio plan, bien al de Parmenión». Algo que no ocurre en otras ocasiones, como en la previa de la batalla del Hidaspes, cuando dispone de una información más precisa: «Al tener Alejandro un conocimiento exacto del contingente de tropas enemigas, cayó sobre estos con la caballería que les acompañaba» (Arr. *An.* V.15.2).

En otras ocasiones, el retraso en la recepción de noticias sobre un determinado acontecimiento provoca que se inviertan esfuerzos en balde. Es el caso de la muerte de Memnón, que no había llegado a oídos de Alejandro a su debido momento, lo que provocó que el macedonio diseñara todo un operativo para proteger su retaguardia:

> «Con el fin de no tener que temer ningún contratiempo en la retaguardia, puso al frente de la escuadra, anclada en el Helesponto, a Anfótero y de las tropas de tierra a Hegéloco, con la orden de desmantelar las guarniciones enemigas de Lesbos, Quíos y Cos. A estos generales les fueron asignados, para gastos de guerra, 500 talentos; a Antípatro y a los que protegían las ciudades griegas, les fueron remitidos 600 y, de acuerdo con las cláusulas del tratado, a los aliados les fueron exigidas naves con las que velar por la defensa del Helesponto. Y es que todavía Alejandro no se había enterado de la muerte de Memnón, en relación con el cual tomaba aquellas precauciones» (Curt. III.1.19-21).

Aunque quizás, el caso más grave de fracaso derivado de la imposibilidad de obtener suficiente información lo tenemos durante la travesía por el desierto de Gedrosia, tal y como ha señalado Engels:

> «To plan and prepare a successful march through the Gedrosian Desert, extensive knowledge of the region's climate, rainfall, distances, topography, and agricultural resources had to be collected first. Alexander was able to obtain part of this intelligence, but not all. For example, from information concerning the resources and extent of the region, he correctly calculated that the army would need to carry a four-month supply of food to cross the desert successfully. As was mentioned

earlier, the army could only remain self-sufficient in food for about ten days in a desert such as the Gedrosian»[18].

Pese a estas lagunas, el sistema de captación de información de Alejandro le permite, en la mayoría de los casos, obtener una ventaja competitiva sobre sus adversarios. Así lo vemos en multitud de pasajes de la campaña asiática, a veces sin dejar a sus enemigos margen de respuesta. Es el caso de la llegada a Tarso:

> «Le llegaron noticias por entonces de que Arsames, que antes planeaba conservar la ciudad de Tarso para los persas, pensó ahora abandonarla al haberse enterado de que Alejandro ya había sobrepasado las Puertas, por lo cual los habitantes de Tarso temían que Arsames se entregara al saqueo de la ciudad antes de abandonarla. Enterado de esto Alejandro, llevó a la carrera hacia Tarso a la caballería y las tropas más ligeras, para que Arsames, al percatarse de lo inmediato de su ataque, abandonara Tarso y se reuniera con el rey Darío sin dejarle expoliar la ciudad» (Arr. *An.* II.4.5-6).

En el asedio de la roca de Aornos, se produce otro episodio que revela la habilidad del ejército macedonio para interceptar mensajes del enemigo o hacerse con información clave en los momentos más oportunos:

> «Enviaron una embajada a Alejandro entregándole la roca a cambio de negociar por sí mismos su salvación. Sin embargo, habían urdido la siguiente estratagema: iban a ocupar todo el día en estas negociaciones, con objeto de cuando llegara la noche, poder escapar furtivamente cada cual a su pueblo. Informado Alejandro de sus intenciones, les concedió un poco de tiempo para que se retiraran y destruyeran el cerco que fortificaba la Roca por todas partes, aguardando hasta que los bárbaros empezaron a retirarse» (Arr. *An.* IV.30.2-3).

La enorme maniobrabilidad y la rapidez de acción que caracterizan a los macedonios en combate, alabada por las mismas fuentes históricas[19], puede explicarse, en gran medida, por los recursos destinados a la captación de información. Un hecho que se contrapone a los rudimentarios sistemas de algunos de los pueblos sometidos, que son sorprendidos en multitud de ocasiones, lo que deja en entredicho sus capacidades en este sentido. Es el caso de los mardos, por poner un ejemplo:

> «Nunca creyeron que Alejandro llegara a atacarles, especialmente porque ya se había alejado considerablemente de ellos, razón por la cual fueron sorprendidos con la guardia baja. Muchos de ellos se refugiaron en los montes de su región, que son extremadamente altos y cortados a pico, en la idea de que Alejandro no se llegaría hasta allí. Pero al hacer acto de presencia Alejandro, los mardos enviaron una embajada aceptando su rendición» (Arr. *An.* III.24.3).

---

[18] Engels 1980: 338-339.

[19] Cabe recordar este pasaje: «Yo ninguna cualidad alabaría con más justicia en Alejandro que su rapidez» (Curt. V.5.3).

En una circunstancia semejante se encontró Musícano, que gobernaba el país más feliz de la India, según noticias llegadas a Alejandro, pero que no había enviado embajadores para ofrecer la paz ni ponerse al servicio de los macedonios. El monarca teménida viajó tan rápidamente a sus dominios que, antes de que se hubiera enterado de que se había puesto en marcha hacia allí, ya se encontraba ante él, arruinando cualquier posible organización defensiva[20].

Por el contrario, el ejército macedonio es sorprendido cuando baja la guardia. Nos cuenta Arriano que Darío atravesó el paso Amánico, en dirección a Iso, hasta ponerse a espaldas de Alejandro sin que este se apercibiera de ello. Este movimiento sorprendió tanto al monarca macedonio, tan seguro de sus sistemas de información, que al tener noticias de ello, envió en un triacóntoro a algunos de sus hombres para confirmar si eran reales o no aquellas noticias[21].

Para concluir con este bloque, cabría hablar de cierto tipo de informaciones filtradas con fines desestabilizadores, en lo que podríamos considerar claros exponentes de desinformación[22]. Durante la vertiginosa persecución de Darío tras la batalla de Gaugamela, Arriano nos cuenta que a Alejandro:

> «Le llegaron noticias, mientras proseguía en su avance, de que Darío había tomado la decisión de salirle al encuentro y hacerle frente de nuevo tras haber recibido refuerzos de los escitas y los cadusios. Ante ello dispuso Alejandro que se preparara el ejército para el combate, y que le acompañaran los animales de carga con sus cuidados y el resto de la impedimenta, y al cabo de doce días alcanzó la región de Media. Una vez allí, tuvo información de que la fuerza con que Darío contaba no era considerable, por no habérsele añadido ningún contingente cadusio ni escita; antes bien, supo que la determinación de Darío era continuar la huida» (Arr. *An.* III.15.3-4).

No se puede asegurar con rotundidad que estemos ante un ejercicio de desinformación, pero dos noticias tan seguidas y contradictorias en tan escaso lapso de tiempo hacen pensar que quizás se trate de informaciones filtradas por Darío para obtener una cierta ventaja en su estrategia de retirada hacia las tierras del interior. De la misma manera, tenemos noticia de otras filtraciones intencionadas en las líneas macedonias. Es el caso de la información que nos aporta Curcio Rufo en este otro pasaje: «Darío había dado orden de que se corriera la voz de que daría 1.000 talentos a quien asesinara a Alejandro» (Curt. III.5.16). Una nota que fue interceptada por Parmenión y acabó por salpicar a Filipo, médico que finalmente sanó al rey macedonio de unas severas fiebres al inicio de la campaña.[23]

---

[20] Arr. *An.* VI.15.5-6.

[21] Arr. *An.* II.7.1-2.

[22] Según el diccionario de la RAE: «Dar información intencionadamente manipulada al servicio de otros fines» (Consultado en www.rae.es; fecha de consulta: 04/05/2018).

[23] Curt. III.6.4-16.

Fuentes de información para la reconstrucción del entorno

En alguno de los pasajes reproducidos anteriormente hemos podido comprobar cómo la información llega hasta Alejandro de mano de diferentes tipos de fuentes. En algunos casos son integrantes de su propio ejército, pero en otros son poblaciones indígenas, prisioneros, desertores o embajadores. Conocemos por los textos históricos que Alejandro mantenía siempre un cuerpo de vigías destacado en la vanguardia de su ejército, que recibía el nombre de *pródromos*, al menos hasta la muerte de Darío—según ha señalado Bosworth—,[24] como comprobamos en este pasaje:

> «Dejando atrás la ciudad de Colonas, se presentó al poco en Hermoto. Envió por delante del ejército unos vigías a los que comandaba Amintas, hijo de Arrabeo, a los que acompañaban también los hombres del escuadrón de los Compañeros, a cuyo frente iba Sócrates el hijo de Satón, recién llegados de Apolonia. Finalmente, también se añadirían cuatro escuadrones de los denominados *pródromos*» (Arr. *An.* I.12.7).

La función de este contingente queda más clara en el siguiente fragmento, que narra el cruce del río Tigris:

> «Al cuarto día de haberlo cruzado, los *pródromos* le anunciaron que habían divisado jinetes enemigos por la llanura, aunque no habían podido conjeturar de qué número se trataba [...] A continuación comparecieron otros *pródromos* diciendo que habían podido distinguir con mayor precisión los jinetes enemigos, y que serían, a su parecer, unos mil» (Arr. *An.* III.7.7).

Estas avanzadillas también servían para evitar ataques sorpresa, como nos cuenta Curcio Rufo (III.4.13) con motivo de la llegada de los macedonios a Tarso: «Alejandro había dado orden de que un destacamento de tracios, equipados con armamento ligero, le precediera y reconociera los senderos a fin de evitar, de parte del enemigo, un ataque por sorpresa contra los que avanzaban por el desfiladero».

Sin embargo, estos destacamentos del ejército no constituyen la única manera de captar información. En muchas ocasiones los informadores son enemigos capturados, como Sisines, un persa que había sido enviado para entrevistarse con otro Alejandro, el hijo de Aérope, para ofrecerle una recompensa por matar al rey. El emisario persa fue interceptado por Parmenión, quien obtuvo de él toda la información necesaria.[25] Con ocasión de la batalla de las Puertas Persas, otro prisionero, un pastor bilingüe, según la tradición de la *Vulgata*, es el que aparece como guía.[26]

En la medida en que disponían de información útil de carácter operativo, los rastreadores del enemigo eran también una presa jugosa a la hora de obtener datos

[24] Bosworth 2005: 315.

[25] Arr. *An.* I.25.3; Curt. III.7.11-15.

[26] Curt. V.5.4; D.S. XVII.68.5; Plu. *Alex.* 37.2.

para diseñar la estrategia de combate, como se desprende de este episodio del periplo macedonio por Mesopotamia:

> «Capturó Alejandro por el camino algunos rastreadores del ejército de Darío y por ellos se informó de que Darío (que, a su vez, los había desperdigado para obtener informaciones) estaba asentado a las orillas del río Tigris, decidido a impedir el paso de Alejandro en caso de que este lo intentara. Le informaron igualmente que en esta ocasión el ejército de Darío era más numeroso que el que le había hecho frente en Cilicia» (Arr. *An.* III.7.4-5).

En ocasiones, la obsesión de ambos bandos por conseguir información desencadena escaramuzas como la descrita en este pasaje previo a Gaugamela:

> «Alejandro se puso al frente del escuadrón real, de uno de la caballería de los Compañeros y de los pródromos peonios, y haciéndolos avanzar a toda prisa ordenó que el resto del ejército le siguiera en orden de marcha. Cuando los jinetes persas vieron acercarse a toda prisa a los hombres destacados por Alejandro, emprendieron veloz huida. Alejandro los persiguió con insistencia, y aunque la mayoría de ellos consiguieron escapar, otros perecieron al quedar sus caballos agotados por la carrera, y aun otros fueron capturados vivos en sus monturas. Alejandro se informó por ellos de que Darío no estaba lejos con un numeroso ejército» (Arr. *An.* III.8.1-2).

La tensión previa a la batalla obliga a los contendientes a apurar al máximo esta tarea, ya que cualquier duda puede pagarse con la derrota en el campo de batalla. Hasta instantes antes del enfrentamiento de Gaugamela, el monarca macedonio dispone de importantes novedades: «Informado Alejandro de estos preparativos por unos vigías persas cogidos prisioneros, se detuvo allí mismo por espacio de cuatro días» (Arr. *An.* II.9.1).

Una categoría semejante a la de los prisioneros es la de los desertores, para quienes la información supone un salvoconducto que puede librarles de un destino poco edificante. Este matiz lo observamos en la siguiente referencia de Curcio: «Allí fue capturado Melón, el intérprete de Darío: enfermo, no había podido seguir la marcha del ejército y, al ser sorprendido por la rapidez de Alejandro, se hacía pasar por desertor» (Curt. V.13.7).

Nos encontramos con varias referencias a desertores a lo largo de la campaña, pero esta es especialmente ilustrativa por lo que supone de interés operativo para el ejército macedonio:

> «Aún no habían llegado a un tiro de flecha cuando un desertor, de nombre Bión, corriendo todo lo que daba de sí, llegó al rey anunciándole que Darío había enterrado "abrojos" allí por donde creía que el enemigo haría avanzar su caballería y que había marcado el lugar con una señal a fin de que sus propias tropas sortearan la trampa. Alejandro dio orden de vigilar al desertor, convocó a sus generales y, tras exponerles lo que le había sido anunciado, les advirtió que se desviaran de la zona indicada e informaran a la caballería del peligro» (Curt. IV.13.36-38).

Algunos desertores adquirían una buena consideración dentro del ejército, ya que su conocimiento del terreno y, en general, del entorno, podía ser muy útil, como vemos en este otro fragmento:

> «Alejandro mandó llamar a un indio desertor, hombre en quien podía además confiar y buen conocedor del territorio, para mandarlo a Tolomeo durante la noche con una carta en la que decía a Tolomeo que atacara a los bárbaros desde lo alto del monte cuando viera que Alejandro se había acercado a la Roca» (Arr. *An.* IV.29.4).

Las poblaciones indígenas constituyen también una fuente muy rica de información. Hemos visto líneas arriba el episodio de las serpientes venenosas, pero hay otros más, por ejemplo, esta referencia de Arriano (*An.* III.21.7): «Llegó a sus oídos la noticia de que los bárbaros habían decidido continuar su marcha por la noche, por lo que preguntó a los indígenas si tenían conocimiento de que existiera algún camino que les condujera más rápidamente a los fugitivos». O esta de Curcio (IX.9.5): «Hizo desembarcar, sin embargo, en una chalupa a unos pocos en la orilla a fin de que tomaran contacto con los campesinos, que estaban desperdigados por un lado y por otro, esperando que estos le podrían ofrecer información más precisa».

Las embajadas son otra fuente destacable. En el relato de Arriano hemos registrado un total de 48 referencias a legaciones de los más diversos orígenes, desde los más remotos, como el famoso pasaje de las embajadas de Babilonia[27] hasta las de los pueblos que van siendo sometidos a su paso. En este sentido, resulta de interés este fragmento de Diodoro, en el que nos da cuenta del orden de visita que Alejandro fijó cuando le presentaron una lista de embajadores, ya que nos permite aproximarnos a los asuntos sobre los que solía despacharse:

> «Los primeros de los que se ocupó fue de los que se presentaban en defensa de los santuarios; en segundo lugar, de los que llevaban regalos; seguidamente, de los que tenían conflictos con sus vecinos; en cuarto lugar, de los que tenían problemas particulares, y en quinto, de los que deseaban presentar argumentos en contra del regreso de los exiliados» (D.S. XVII.113.3; Torres Esbarranch / Guzmán Hermida 2012, trad.).

Da la impresión de que no todas las embajadas eran voluntarias. A juzgar por algunos pasajes del periplo de Alejandro como los dos siguientes, acaecidos en la India:

> «Continuó hasta el río Cofén, enviando por delante un heraldo a Taxiles y a los indios vecinos de este lado del río, ordenándoles que le salieran a su encuentro según se fuera aproximando a cada uno de sus pueblos. Así lo hicieron Taxiles y los otros gobernadores, que le presentaron los dones de mayor aprecio entre los indios, y con la promesa de poner a su disposición los veinticinco elefantes que ellos tenían» (Arr. *An.* IV.22.6).

---

[27] Arr. *An.* VII.15.4.

En caso de no presentarse, el destino podría ser el que esperaba a Musícano, dado que no «había comparecido ofreciéndose a sí mismo y su país a Alejandro, ni había enviado embajadores para tratar de paz. Es más, ni siquiera le habían enviado presente alguno» (Arr. *An.* VI.15.5).

Alejandro como emisor de mensajes: Control territorial, coacción y propaganda

En el continuo ejercicio de interacción con su entorno, el ejército macedonio es también una importante fuente de mensajes. Buena parte de ellos van dirigidos hacia los gobernantes o hacia las poblaciones de los territorios que han sido o van a ser conquistados, como vemos a continuación:

> «Nombró Alejandro sátrapa de la región en que gobernaba Arsites a Calas, ordenando a sus súbditos que le aportaran los mismos tributos que antes traían a Darío. A todos los bárbaros que voluntariamente descendieron los montes y se le entregaron les permitió regresar a su patria» (Arr. *An.* I.17.1).

La presencia de las huestes macedonias solía provocar el terror en ciertas poblaciones indígenas, que huían antes de que la llegada de los conquistadores. Este es el motivo por el que Alejandro trata de evitar estas fugas mediante el envío de jinetes o heraldos:

> «Mientras él llevaba a cabo estas acciones con su infantería, despachó a los jinetes a otras dos ciudades vecinas, con el encargo de que vigilaran a sus habitantes a fin de evitar que estos, informados de la captura de las otras ciudades cercanas y de la proximidad del avance de Alejandro, se dieran a la fuga y resultara difícil su persecución. Los hechos ocurrieron tal como él había supuesto, de modo que el envío de la caballería se produjo en el momento más oportuno» (Arr. *An.* IV.2.5-6).

En otras ocasiones, Alejandro enviaba heraldos para conminar a sus enemigos a la rendición, como cuando envió a Oxiartes para convencer de ello a Corienes,[28] o cuando despachó a Eumenes, su secretario, a dos ciudades que se habían alzado junto a Sangala, para informar a sus habitantes de que si se entregaban serían tratados amistosamente.[29] No en todos los casos el tono era amistoso, como podemos descubrir en esta referencia: «Alejandro dio a conocer un pregón anunciando que pasaría a cuchillo a todos los uxios del a región si no le devolvían su caballo. Proclamar el pregón y presentarse uno con el caballo fue todo una» (Arr. *An.* V.19.6).

En otra categoría diferente deberíamos situar este tipo de comunicados, que nos trasladan al ámbito de la propaganda:

---

[28] Arr. *An.* IV.21.6-7.

[29] Arr. *An.* V.24.6-7.

«Alejandro, proclamado rey de Asia, ofrecía solemnes sacrificios a los dioses, y premiaba a sus amigos con riquezas, casas y cargos de gobierno. Intentando ganarse el favor de los griegos, escribió a los gobernantes que todas las tiranías estaban abolidas, y que se gobernaban según sus propias leyes» (Plu. *Alex*. 34.1-2; Guzmán Guerra 1986, trad.).

La propaganda constituye una de las ramas de estudio más interesantes de la Historia de la Comunicación Social[30]. Al afrontar su análisis en el mundo antiguo corremos el riesgo de considerar todo fenómeno que implique algún tipo de comunicación a la sociedad como un acto de propaganda, aunque sea de manera implícita. Por tanto, conviene antes hacer una precisión terminológica. Entendemos por propaganda, siguiendo a Edwards, la expresión de una opinión o una acción por individuos o grupos, deliberadamente orientada a influir opiniones o acciones de otros individuos o grupos para unos fines determinados.[31] Por tanto, como ha matizado Pizarroso, la propaganda es un proceso de comunicación que disemina, difunde, da a conocer o promociona ideas. En consecuencia, su finalidad es la influencia y tiene, en efecto, una intención persuasiva.[32]

La propaganda puede difundirse a través de la palabra hablada, de la imagen (representaciones artísticas, construcciones arquitectónicas, monedas y otras creaciones), de los espectáculos públicos, de acciones o hechos ejemplarizantes, de la palabra escrita y de la censura, entendida como inhibición de la información[33]. Como el lector puede imaginar, la cantidad de hechos propagandísticos que salpican la vida de Alejandro Magno, igual que la de su padre Filipo, es lo bastante amplia como para dedicarle una monografía. Dado el carácter general de este trabajo, solo apuntaremos que a lo largo de la campaña asiática se observan tres constantes propagandísticas, que podemos definir en función del público destinatario de las acciones y de los efectos pretendidos por ellas.

En primer lugar, podemos hablar de una fase que se prolonga desde el inicio de la campaña hasta la batalla de Gaugamela y la casi simultánea derrota de Agis III de Esparta en territorio heleno, ambos acontecimientos acaecidos en el año 331 a.C. Durante este período, predominan acciones propagandísticas en línea con el panhelenismo[34] que impulsa la "guerra de represalias" contra un enemigo al que los mecanismos de propaganda macedonia acaban por hacer responsable, incluso, de la muerte de Filipo y del que generan una incesante cantidad de informaciones peyorativas, entre ellas la de la cobardía de Darío.[35] En este contexto podemos entender este episodio descrito por Plutarco tras la victoria en el río Gránico:

---

[30] Se pueden destacar dos estudios interesantes sobre la propaganda durante la campaña asiática: Muccioli 2004; Kholod 2011.

[31] Edwards 1938: 40.

[32] Pizarroso 1993: 26-28.

[33] Pizarroso 1993: 30-31.

[34] Sobre la utilización del panhelenismo por Filipo II y Alejandro es interesante Antela 2007.

[35] Sobre el incendio de Persépolis es interesante Borza 1972.

> «Dio noticias de su victoria a los griegos, y en particular mandó a los atenienses trescientos escudos cogidos a los prisioneros, e hizo inscribir sobre el resto de los despojos esta ambiciosa inscripción: "Alejandro, hijo de Filipo, y los griegos –excepto los lacedemonios– de los bárbaros que habitan Asia"» (Plu. *Alex.* 16.17).

En la arenga previa a la batalla Isos, Arriano (*An.* II.7.4-7) pone en boca de Alejandro frases que tratan de ensalzar de forma propagandista las virtudes del panhelenismo frente a la barbarie: «hombres libres contra esclavos», «los de Darío combaten por una soldada (y tampoco es que sea muy espléndida), los de nuestro bando lo hacen libremente, en defensa de Grecia» o «el bien común de los griegos».

En una línea semejante podemos inscribir otras acciones propagandísticas de Alejandro, como la devolución de las estatuas de bronce de los tiranicidas, Harmodio y Aristogitón, que habían sido robadas por Jerjes en la campaña del 480 a.C.,[36] o la carta dirigida a los gobernantes griegos que mencionábamos con anterioridad. Sin embargo, la acción propagandística más importante de este período, que pone fin a la llamada "guerra de represalias", es, a nuestro juicio, la quema de Persépolis. Si bien algunos autores no parecen defender esta tesis,[37] este testimonio de Arriano (*An.* III.12.1) podría dejar clara la intención de Alejandro: «Alejandro contraargumentó que él quería hacer pagar a los persas lo que estos habían hecho al atacar Atenas, derribar e incendiar los templos de la Acrópolis, y vengar así cuantas maldades habían cometido contra Grecia».[38]

Una vez disipados los problemas en territorio heleno, sofocada la revuelta espartana, y tras penetrar en el corazón de Persia, Alejandro tiene que afrontar otro reto: ganarse a los súbditos de Darío mediante la sumisión de sus elites. Se inicia así una segunda fase de acciones propagandísticas en la que los gestos van a tener un papel fundamental. En este contexto cabe entender estas palabras que Quinto Curcio Rufo pone en boca del monarca macedonio:

> «Si queremos conservar Asia, no sólo atravesarla, debemos repartir con sus habitantes nuestra clemencia: su lealtad hará nuestro imperio estable y eterno [...] En efecto, veo en muchos pueblos costumbres que no deberíamos avergonzarnos de imitar y un imperio tan grande no puede gobernarse más que por este procedimiento: enseñándoles algo nosotros y aprendiendo algo nosotros de ellos» (Curt. VII.8.12-14).[39]

En efecto, a partir de Gaugamela, Alejandro comienza a realizar gestos propagandísticos que tienen como público objetivo a la nobleza persa, cuya confianza

---

[36] Arr. *An.* III.16.7-8.

[37] Briant 2012: 102-106.

[38] Sobre el origen del tema propagandístico de la venganza helena, puede consultarse Hatzopoulos 1997.

[39] Un pasaje semejante lo encontramos en Plu. *Alex.* 47.5.

y apoyo pretende ganarse.[40] Así hay que entender, por ejemplo, la presentación de la captura de Bessos como un acto de implacable venganza por la afrenta sufrida por Darío. Por otro lado, una serie de decisiones simbólicas apuntan en esta dirección. En Babilonia, nombra por primera vez un sátrapa iranio, Maceo,[41] medida que se repetirá posteriormente en más ciudades y que también podría interpretarse en clave pragmática.[42] Sin embargo, se producen otros gestos de mayor impacto, sobre todo la adopción de la ceremonia de la *proskynesis* y otras costumbres persas, como el modo de vestir. Como es bien sabido, estos gestos hacia la población local, no fueron bien acogidos en el seno del ejército macedonio, ya que, según Plutarco: «este espectáculo resultaba odioso a los macedonios (Plu. *Alex.* 45.4). La tensión alcanza su punto más álgido con la muerte de Clito[43] y la condena de Calístenes,[44] que las fuentes nos narran como resultado de la abierta oposición de ambos a esta deriva orientalizante.

Es precisamente este creciente descontento y el interés de Alejandro por continuar la campaña hasta los confines del mundo conocido lo que desencadena la tercera fase de acciones propagandísticas, que podríamos extender hasta la vuelta a Babilonia, y en la que el público principal de las acciones pasa a ser su propio ejército, en especial, el núcleo de veteranos macedonios que, en cierto momento de la campaña, se sienten dolidos como nunca antes lo habían estado por la adopción de la vestimenta persa y la inclusión de bárbaros en los batallones de Compañeros.[45] Consciente de esta situación, vemos a Alejandro recurriendo al uso del mito de Dioniso como fundador de Nisa, del que Flavio Arriano (*An.* V.2.1) nos cuenta que el rey «estaba seguro de que los macedonios continuarían de muy buen grado, aun a costa de penosos esfuerzos, con tal de emular y superar las hazañas de Dioniso».[46] Uno de los episodios de mayor carga propagandística, es el discurso de Alejandro ante el motín del Hífasis, cuando trata de atraer a los soldados macedonios a su causa con palabras dirigidas directamente a generar una respuesta emocional, al menos tal y como nos lo traslada Arriano.[47] Podríamos dedicar todo un artículo a los elementos

---

[40] Sobre Alejandro y los persas puede consultarse Bosworth 1980 y la obra más general de Briant 1996.

[41] Arr. *An.* III.16.4.

[42] Parece lógico pensar que si no hay motivos para la sospecha, lo más razonable es mantener en el poder al sátrapa local si la intención es la de ganarse a las poblaciones conquistadas. En todo caso, como acreditan las fuentes, Alejandro siempre deja una guarnición macedonia y a macedonios al frente de responsabilidades clave. Cf. Briant 2012: 107-110.

[43] Arr. *An.* IV.8; Curt. VIII.1.22-52; Plu. *Alex.* 50-51.

[44] Arr. *An.* IV.10-11; Curt. VIII.5-6; Plu. *Alex.* 52-55.

[45] Arr. *An.* VII.8.1-3.

[46] Otro episodio semejante nos lo presenta Curcio cuando explica que, al llegar al río Oxo, se excavaron varios pozos para encontrar agua, pero no aparecía. Finalmente, de uno de ellos brotó el líquido elemento, cerca de la tienda del rey. Hicieron correr la noticia de que había surgido súbitamente y el mismo Alejandro quiso que la tropa creyera que había sido un regalo de los dioses (Curt. VII.10.14).

[47] Arr. *An.* V.25.3-7.

retóricos de este pasaje, pero dejaremos el apunte para proseguir con la segunda parte de este capítulo, dedicado a la comunicación interna.

Comunicación interna: De la coordinación operativa a la cohesión

En el ámbito de la comunicación interna debemos distinguir cuatro planos. Uno puramente operativo, que tiene el objetivo de coordinar las acciones de combate; otro, en un nivel más estratégico, que permite disponer de información suficiente para gestionar los territorios conquistados; otro motivacional, que busca mantener cohesionado y concentrado al ejército en su objetivo; y un último que podríamos llamar coercitivo, que garantiza el sometimiento de cualquier conducta sediciosa.

La coordinación en combate es el nivel más primario de comunicación interna. Dice Curcio que el ejército macedonio estaba siempre dispuesto a detenerse y a avanzar, ligero de tropa y bagaje, atento no solo a la señal de su comandante sino también al menor ademán.[48] Prácticamente todos los especialistas han coincidido en señalar que el ejército de Alejandro estaba muy bien entrenado y, por los resultados, no cabe duda de que la excelencia en el combate era una de sus mejores armas. Se sobreentiende, por tanto, que los macedonios estaban bien coordinados en combate y que manejaban una serie de códigos comunicativos que les permitía conocer qué acción debían desarrollar en cada momento. Desde el toque de corneta o trompeta, que anuncia el inicio del ataque o la retirada,[49] hasta operaciones de mayor complejidad, como la que nos narra Arriano (*An.* V.11.2) en los momentos previos a la batalla del Hidaspes: «Alejandro había apostado centinelas a lo largo de toda la ribera a una distancia adecuada para poder verse mutuamente y transmitirse las órdenes que se les pudieran comunicar, y así fueron pasando mensajes orales y señales de fuego durante varias noches».

Esto implica la existencia de un código específico, que permita emitir señales que rápidamente puedan ser interpretadas en uno u otro sentido a lo largo de una cadena de transmisión de información en la que prima la rapidez y la eficacia. Estos sistemas de comunicación implican, necesariamente, un minucioso trabajo previo de estudio y coordinación. Las señales son convenidas y ejecutadas de acuerdo con un plan, tal y como podemos comprobar en dos referencias, la primera en relación con la batalla de las Puertas Persas y la segunda, en la toma de Masaga:

> «Justo en el momento en que Alejandro atacaba la empalizada, las trompetas, haciendo oír su voz, avisaron a Crátero y sus hombres para que iniciaran el ataque al muro» (Arr. *An.* III.18.8).

---

[48] Curt. III.3.27.

[49] Arr. *An.* VI.3.2; D.S. XVII.33.4, 45.7.

> «Pero cuando ya los disparos enemigos alcanzaban a sus tropas, Alejandro hizo girar rápidamente y a una señal convenida su falange, lanzándola al contraataque y a la carrera contra ellos» (Arr. *An.* IV.27.3-4).

Estas acciones adquieren una importancia mucho mayor a medida que el ejército macedonio se adentra en Asia Central, momento en el que, tal y como señalara Hammond, Alejandro divide a su ejército en contingentes más pequeños y móviles, a modo de comandos[50]. Podemos confirmar esta tendencia en momentos como el sometimiento de los uxios,[51] uno de los primeros episodios de este tipo de acciones en suelo asiático, o en las maniobras para la toma de la Roca de Aornos, donde Ptolomeo realiza señales de fuego según la contraseña convenida para indicar que ha terminado su misión con éxito.[52]

El modo en el que se transmitían este tipo de códigos bien podría ser el indicado por Arriano (*An.* III.9.6-7) antes de Gaugamela: «Creía conveniente que cada jefe exhortara a sus propios hombres, los capitanes a sus soldados, el jefe de escuadrón a sus subordinados, y los taxiarcos a los hombres bajo sus órdenes, e igualmente los jefes de infantería a sus soldados».

Toda una cadena de mando bien engrasada que, sin embargo, también podía fallar, fruto de la precipitación o las ganas de destacar sobre el resto. Un episodio de este tipo se manifiesta durante la toma y destrucción de Tebas:

> «Perdicas se lanzó contra la empalizada enemiga sin aguardar la señal de combate a dar por Alejandro, y tras romper aquella, arremetió contra los primeros vigilantes tebanos. Amintas, el hijo de Andrómeno, que estaba en formación junto a Perdicas, marchó tras él, conduciendo su propio batallón al ver que Perdicas se adentraba en la empalizada. Percatado Alejandro de todo esto, y para evitar que al estar solos fueran a ser interceptados por los tebanos y verse en apuros, puso en movimiento al resto del ejército» (Arr. *An.* I.8.1-2).

Un caso que se repite más tarde, cuando Cárano, comandante de caballería, intentó atravesar el río Politimeto, a fin de poner a buen recaudo a sus hombres, sin informar de ello a Andrómaco. Acto seguido, fueron tras ellos los hombres de infantería, sin autorización de nadie, produciéndose un desordenado y peligroso descenso hacia el cauce por sus escarpadas riberas. Los bárbaros se percataron del error de los macedonios, por lo que se lanzaron contra ellos, lo que supuso un serio revés para el ejército de Alejandro.[53]

Nos encontramos también con otra forma de comunicación: el envío de mensajeros en pleno fragor de la contienda, un recurso extremo, pero realmente eficaz, como

---

[50] Hammond 1992b: 250.

[51] Arr. *An.* III.17.2-6.

[52] Arr. *An.* IV.29.2.

[53] Arr. *An.* IV.5.7-8.

en el transcurso de la batalla de Gaugamela, cuando Parmenión envía un mensaje de socorro a Alejandro,[54] o cuando el propio monarca macedonio, en pleno enfrentamiento en el Hidaspes, manda como mensajero a Taxiles para que se entreviste con Poro.[55] No es descabellado pensar que existiera un rol específico en el seno del ejército cuya función fuera, precisamente, la de actuar como heraldo en caso de necesidad. Con ocasión del asedio de Tiro, hay un momento que nos habla de la dificultad de comunicarse en plena batalla. Se trata del pasaje en el que los tirios tratan de contactar con los compañeros embarcados al ver la maniobra envolvente de los macedonios, pero no les oyen por las voces y el caos de la refriega.[56]

La comunicación interna, si es rápida y fiable, es una herramienta básica de control del territorio, pues permite intervenir de una forma rápida en caso de corrupción, sedición o altercados. A lo largo de la campaña asiática se producen diferentes episodios en los que Alejandro tiene que frenar su avance para controlar movimientos de resistencia. La insurrección de Satibarzanes, que había matado a Anaxipo y estaba armando a los arios para dirigirse a la ciudad de Artacoana para unirse a Bessos, fue sofocada por Alejandro con una vertiginosa campaña que sorprendió a los rebeldes sin que estos pudieran imaginar que llegaría con tal celeridad.[57]. Otro ejemplo es la revuelta de Espitámenes, a la que Alejandro puede responder también gracias a la agilidad de sus sistemas de comunicación.[58] Sin embargo, el caso más paradigmático se produce antes del inicio de la campaña asiática, con la contundente respuesta contra Tebas, que pone de manifiesto que tan importante como el rápido avance de las tropas macedonias era que su capacidad de reacción estaba asegurada por la agilidad de sus sistemas de información.[59]

Llegamos así al papel de la comunicación interna como elemento motivador y cohesionador. La dimensión emocional de la organización es uno de los aspectos más importantes para asegurar la consecución de sus objetivos. El ejército macedonio experimenta importantes transformaciones en su seno, derivadas de la integración de contingentes que antes habían formado parte del enemigo. Un ejército como el persa que, en palabras de Curcio Rufo, carecía de «unidad» y no estaba «aplicado a seguir las órdenes de un solo jefe» y en el que reinaba la «confusión general».[60] Pero Alejandro no solo se encuentra con el reto de integrar estos nuevos efectivos tras derrotar a Darío, algo que resulta problemático, como hemos visto, sino también hacer que griegos y macedonios lucharan en pos de un objetivo común, lo que a veces parecía una quimera, tal y como pone de manifiesto el episodio del enfrentamiento

---

[54] Arr. *An.* III.15.1.
[55] Arr. *An.* V.18.6-7.
[56] Arr. *An.* II.22.4.
[57] Arr. *An.* III.25.5-7.
[58] Arr. *An.* IV.3.7, 5.3.
[59] Arr. *An.* I.7.4.
[60] Curt. III.8.26.

entre el griego Dioxipo y el macedonio Corago, que acabó, según Diodoro, con un profunda división entre ambos bandos.[61]

En este contexto, Alejandro demuestra tener varios registros comunicativos. En algunos pasajes vemos a un rey cercano, que sabe dirigirse de una manera empática a sus soldados, como es el caso de este fragmento:

> «En su discurso fúnebre hizo el elogio de cuantos habían llevado a cabo alguna acción destacada en el combate, bien que se hubiera enterado de ello él personalmente, bien que le hubiera llegado la información a base de otros, honrando así a cada uno de sus hombres, y añadiendo una compensación en dinero según el propio merecimiento de cada cual» (Arr. *An.* II.12.1).

Un pasaje semejante sobre la manera que tenía el rey de dirigirse a sus hombres es este que testimonia Curcio Rufo: «Conforme iba recorriendo a caballo la formación, se dirigía a sus soldados con palabras distintas según conveniera a la índole de cada uno» (Curt. II.10.4).

Ambos episodios no solo ponen de manifiesto que Alejandro disponía de una gran inteligencia emocional, tal y como se definiría hoy en día, sino también que manejaba un importante conocimiento de su tropa, proporcionado, como es lógico, por un buen sistema de recopilación de información. De la misma manera que este instrumento servía para motivar y cohesionar, también servía para vigilar. Es algo que vemos claramente en el caso de Filotas:

> «Alejandro tuvo noticias de la conspiración de Filotas, el hijo de Parmenión. Ptolomeo y Aristóbulo dicen que ya Alejandro había tenido información de ella en Egipto, pero que entones no le dio credibilidad por la antigua amistad que es unía, por el honor que Parmenión, padre de Filotas, con todo mérito, había recibido de Alejandro, y la propia confianza a que se había hecho acreedor Filotas» (Arr. *An.* III.26.1-2).

La acusación que se lanza sobre Filotas es, precisamente, que habiendo llegado hasta él información sobre una posible conspiración contra Alejandro, no hubiera informado de ella.[62] Incluso Plutarco va más lejos y comenta que sobre Filotas se había establecido un sistema de vigilancia para el que habían destinado a una mujer, Antígona.[63] Más allá del proceso contra Filotas, interesante por cuanto que pone de manifiesto el engranaje de este sistema, tenemos constancia de su existencia por otras referencias, como esta, en la que incluso se habla de informes que llegaban al rey por el malestar de la tropa ante la suerte corrida por Parmenión y su hijo:

---

[61] D.S. XVII.101.3.

[62] Arr. *An.* III.26.2-3.

[63] Plu. *Alex.* 49.1.

> «El ejército pensaba todas estas cosas y hasta el rey llegaban informes que hablaban de sedición. Él no se dejó conmover por tales informes sino que, sabiendo muy bien que los vicios originados por el ocio desaparecen con la actividad, dio orden de que todo el mundo se presentara en el vestíbulo de su tienda» (Curt. VII.1.4-5).

Nos cuenta también Arriano que Alejandro, conocedor de las opiniones contrarias que había desatado entre los macedonios el asunto de la *proskynesis*, les autorizó a que se olvidaran de esta ceremonia.[64]

Estos episodios demuestran que en el seno del ejército macedonio existía un importante sistema de recopilación de información orientado a salir al paso de cualquier circunstancia que pudiera afectar a su cohesión y su adhesión a la causa del rey. En este sentido, aparece un enemigo común a todas las organizaciones: el rumor. Un episodio muy interesante se produce con motivo de la muerte de Parmenión. Alejandro es perfectamente consciente del impacto que la noticia puede tener para el núcleo central de su ejército y, por tanto, trata de anticiparse al rumor para dar su propia versión de los acontecimientos en un hábil ejercicio de control informativo. Curcio (VII.2.15) pone en boca de Alejandro estas significativas palabras dirigidas a Polidamante: «Marcha a la Media y entrega a mis prefectos unas cartas escritas de mi puño y letra. Se impone que lo hagas con rapidez a fin de que tomes la delantera a los rumores. Quiero que llegues allí de noche y que, al día siguiente, des cumplimiento a las órdenes escritas».

Alejandro no había dejado nada a la improvisación. Junto a Polidamante envió una carta con la orden de que fuera leída una vez que se descubriera la muerte de Parmenión, consciente de las airadas reacciones que provocaría entre sus hombres. En el comunicado explicaba el complot que se había urdido contra su persona y la necesidad de llevar a cabo la ejecución.[65] Pero no acabaron aquí las acciones destinadas a sofocar las reacciones de sus soldados ante tal proceso. Nos cuenta Curcio una anécdota que no deja lugar a dudas del control total que Alejandro ejercía sobre las comunicaciones de su ejército:

> «Alejandro pensó que debía separar de del resto del ejército a todos aquellos que le constaba que habían lamentado abiertamente la muerte de Parmenión. Formó con ellos una cohorte y puso al frente de ella a Leónidas [...] En efecto, queriendo poner a prueba los ánimos de sus soldados, hizo saber a todos los que habían escrito cartas a Macedonia que podían entregarlas a los encargados de su propio correo personal, que las transportarían con toda lealtad. Todo el mundo contaba a sus allegados, sin doblez alguna, lo que sentían [...] De este modo llegaron a manos del rey las cartas tanto de los que se encontraban a gusto como de los que se quejaban del servicio y los que descubrió que en sus cartas murmuraban de las penalidades fueron agrupados en una cohorte aparte y se les obligó a acampar, como señal de

[64] Arr. *An.* IV.12.1.

[65] Curt. VII.2.28-32; Arr. *An.* III.26.3-4.

> escarnio, separados de sus compañeros, con la idea de echar mano de su valor en el campo de batalla y de mantener alejada de los oídos crédulos la libertad de sus expresiones» (Curt. VII.2.35-38).

Nos hemos permitido la licencia de transcribir prácticamente íntegro este largo pasaje debido a su gran relevancia, en cuanto que pone de manifiesto la preocupación de Alejandro por la opinión de sus soldados, el ejercicio de control autoritario de sus comunicaciones y la política de hechos ejemplarizantes a modo de propaganda interna, de manera que el resto de la tropa no se vea tentada a seguir el camino de los apartados. Por el testimonio de las fuentes no parece que esta estrategia coercitiva fuera aislada. Arriano nos cuenta lo siguiente:

> «Le pareció a Alejandro que era este un momento muy oportuno para liquidar las deudas que algunos de sus hombres tuvieran, para lo cual encargó se hiciera una lista de lo que cada cual debía para proceder a la liquidación. Al principio solo unos pocos se atrevieron a dar sus nombres, por temor a que se tratara de una estrategia de Alejandro a fin de conocer quiénes de sus soldados no tenían bastante con su paga y quienes vivían incluso con derroche» (Arr. *An.* VII.5.1-2).

Quizás este tipo de prácticas está en el temor de la tropa a expresar su opinión de forma abierta, tal y como queda de manifiesto en momentos de especial tensión, como el famoso motín de Opis, a propósito del cual nos dicen Arriano y Curcio que ningún soldado osaba dirigirse directamente al rey, esperando que sus jefes y generales mostraran su descontento por ellos.[66]

Existe otro pasaje que nos muestra otra táctica comunicativa: la censura. Se produce con motivo del desastre de un destacamento del ejército macedonio durante la ofensiva de Espitámenes. Según Curcio (VII.7.39), perecieron dos mil soldados de infantería y trescientos de caballería, por lo que se toma la siguiente decisión: «Esta derrota la mantuvo hábilmente en secreto Alejandro, amenazando con la muerte a los que habían llegado procedentes del campo de batalla, si divulgaban lo sucedido».

Es comprensible esta obsesión de Alejandro por el control de los rumores. El propio Curcio (IX.4.22-23) escribe unas palabras muy reveladoras: «Toda muchedumbre, y más una formada por soldados, se deja llevar por impulsos inestables; por eso, poner fin a una sedición no es más difícil que hacerla brotar». En efecto, a lo largo de la campaña asiática se dan una serie de factores externos e internos que amenazan la cohesión del ejército y la integridad del rey, lo que explica la asunción de ese rol autoritario. Por poner dos ejemplos, las ya mencionadas misivas de Darío para incitar a los soldados griegos a matar a su rey, interceptadas por Parmenión;[67] el episodio de Hárpalo y su fuga con parte del tesoro real,[68] rumores sobre la muerte del

---

[66] Arr. *An.* V.27.1; Curt. IX.3.1.

[67] Curt. IV.10.16-17.

[68] Curt. X.2-3; Plu. *Alex.* 41.8-9.

propio rey tras el asedio a la ciudad de los malios,[69] o el mismo motín del Opis,[70] son muestras de las dificultades que tenía la gestión de la comunicación en el ejército.

La información como elemento estratégico

A lo largo de este trabajo, que por la amplitud, extensión y profundidad de alguna de las referencias no hemos podido tratar con profundidad, se ha puesto de manifiesto la importancia de la obtención de información como elemento estratégico a lo largo de la campaña asiática, tanto en la interacción del ejército con el entorno en el que se desenvuelve, como en su propia cohesión interna. En este contexto, Alejandro Magno, en calidad de rey de los macedonios, es el vértice de todo el entramado comunicativo del ejército, si bien es cierto, como ha señalado Engels, que es la única referencia que nos proporcionan las fuentes, lo que nos impide conocer cómo se organizaba administrativamente esta tarea y cuántos equipos o personas estaban implicados en ella.[71] El monarca es el destinatario final de todas las informaciones y quien decide cómo debe actuarse a partir de los datos obtenidos. En esta tarea se descubre a un Alejandro minucioso, en ocasiones preocupado por disponer de datos sobre los más mínimos detalles, para diseñar así una estrategia de campaña de garantías. A medida que el ejército macedonio progresa en el interior del territorio asiático, las necesidades informativas van en aumento, así como también la complejidad del sistema, no solo por la distancia que se debe recorrer entre los diferentes puntos del imperio, sino también por la imperiosa necesidad de dividir sus contingentes.

En cuanto a la gestión de la información a nivel interno, Alejandro se muestra paternalista en algunos momentos, pero tremendamente autoritario en otros. En efecto, casi la totalidad de noticias que las fuentes históricas nos han dejado sobre este aspecto nos presentan a un rey preocupado por poner freno a los rumores que amenazan la cohesión del ejército y, sobre todo, a los que suponen un menoscabo de su autoridad. Por descontado, se muestra absolutamente intransigente en los casos en los que su vida es amenazada de alguna manera. Se trata de un estilo de dirección autoritario que se desarrolla en situaciones de extraordinaria dificultad para la consecución de ambiciosos objetivos.

Esperamos haber podido poner de manifiesto la importancia que la comunicación y el manejo información tuvieron a lo largo de la campaña asiática. Un peso específico que pocas veces ha sido reconocido en la amplia y variada historiografía consagrada al rey macedonio, pero que gracias a los estudios multidisciplinares, en este caso los de Historia de la Comunicación Social, Teoría de la Comunicación en las Organizaciones e Historia, hemos podido desgranar, aunque solo haya sido ligeramente.

---

[69] Arr. *An.* VI.12.1-3.

[70] Arr. *An.* V.25.2; Curt. IX.2-3.

[71] Engels 1980: 327.

Alexander the Reader: Herodotus and the Royal House of Macedonia

Antonio Ignacio Molina Marín
(Karanos – *Co-Director)*

During the last few years, many scholars have written about the readings of Alexander the Great. Although Plutarch is the only source who mentioned the readings of the Macedonian king,[1] it is a common and accepted opinion among historians that Alexander was a great reader. According to the same author he was *filomathes*, friend of wisdom. Certainly, this opinion of Plutarch comes from Onesicritus of Astipalea,[2] a student of Diogenes who converted Alexander to a philosopher in arms.[3] In this way, Alexander became a philosopher who liked to speak to foreign sages, an explorer who wanted to see the ends of the earth with his own eyes.[4] This is understandable when we bear in mind that he was student of Aristotle, which for historians produces the irresistible temptation to link mentor and student[5]. From this point of view, it is logical to look for other possible readings that fit in with a man such as Alexander.

Following this thought, scholars have added many titles to the list of authors known by Alexander. In fact, if all these theories were to be believed, Alexander would have read almost all of the significant Greek writers. As an example, Alexander has been linked by both ancient and modern historians to Hesiod,[6] Hecataeus,[7]

---

[1] Plu. *Alex*. 8.

[2] Brown 1967: 359-361.

[3] Str. XV.1.64: εν όπλοις φιλοσοφουντα.

[4] Gómez Espelosín 2010: 61: «La *imagen* del explorador de nuevos mundos que se adentraba constantemente hacia lo desconocido ha subyugado poderosamente a antiguos y modernos».

[5] Molina Marín 2017: 295.

[6] D.Chr. II.12. Alexander says that Hesiod beat Homer because he competed against people who were effeminate and hedonist.

[7] Daskalakis 1966: 229.

Scylax,[8] Pindar,[9] Herodotus,[10] Ctesias,[11] Hippocrates,[12] Xenophon,[13] Plato,[14] and Isocrates.[15] If other authors mentioned by the sources are included (Homer, Aeschylus, Sophocles, Euripides, Philistus, Telestes and Philoxenus), it could be said that, certainly, Alexander is worthy of being called the 'Great', given that he read even more Greek writers than most of the classical philologists.

Alexander's interest in ancient Greek culture and literature is not being questioned. Rather, the intention here is to highlight the fact that scholars have exaggerated this passion of the Macedonian. Somehow, Alexander has become a new paradigm of the *uomo universale*. Every period has its own image of the Macedonian conqueror, and the list of readings has changed depending on the requirement of the time. During the Middle Ages, it was said that he learned Hebrew, Latin and Babylonian.[16] To date, this phenomenon is still occurring: scholars have described Alexander as a man of science.[17] He was not just another warrior, he was truly interested in every field of knowledge, and although it was thought that he never wrote anything during his lifetime, some researchers have attributed the creation of theatre plays to Alexander.[18]

From this point of view, the connection of the Macedonian king to one of these authors, Herodotus of Halicarnassus, will be studied in this article. The main purpose of this paper is to propose a new form of analysing the relationship between Alexander and Herodotus. Scholars have always assumed that the Macedonian knew the historian because of the influence of Aristotle; therefore, the intention here is to question this fact, given that Herodotus was a significant author for Macedonian society in addition to the Alexander historians. Thus, this alleged interest could come from the pen of one of our sources. In other words, there are many possibilities that

---

[8] Freeman 2011: 269.

[9] Alexander spared Pindar's house when he destroyed Thebes: Ael. *VH* XII.57; Plu. *Alex*. 11.12; cf. Instinsky 1961.

[10] Snyder 1966: 91; Hamilton 1969: 56; Badian 1982: 34; Bowersock 1989; O'Brien 1992; Bosworth 1996: 149.

[11] Sarton 1952: 330: «we may assume that Aristotle's most famous pupil, *Alexander the Great, read* him too»; Badian 1996: 20: «Ctesias, an author, incidentally, whom Alexander must have read»; Freeman 2011: 269.

[12] Martin 2012: 165.

[13] Stark 1958: 200-210; Lane Fox 1973: 162, 164, 238; Schachermeyr 1973: 86; Green 1974: 283; Manfredi 1984: 15-21; O'Brien 1992; Due 1993: 53-60; McGroarty 2006: 121: «This is nonsense. The idea that Alexander the Great led his forces with a spear in one hand and Greek literature in the other (Xenophon, and, Homer, of course) is simply not tenable»; Burliga 2014: 134-46; Kegerris 2015: 134-161.

[14] *Them*. 9.148 Dind. Cf. Novotny 1977: 273: «that Alexander the Great read Plato and understood him, no doubt through the influence of Aristotle».

[15] Merlan 1954.

[16] Lane Fox 1973: 53.

[17] Bodson 1991: 130; Alvar 2000: 83-84.

[18] Kotlinska 2005: 49-50; Stoneman 2015: 29: «Alexander was a great reader, and perhaps even an author»; Müller 2016: 258.

Alexander never actually read the works of Herodotus. The analysis will be divided into three parts. The first part focuses on the similarities between Herodotus' work and Macedonian Panhellenism. The second studies the influence of Herodotus on the Alexander historians. The final section compares some passages of *Histories* to famous events in Alexander's life.

Herodotus and Macedonia

Herodotus, the so-called «father of history»,[19] played an important role in the history of Macedonia, given that he was in charge of introducing the Old Kingdom to the Greeks. Indeed, nothing is known about ancient Macedonia until the publication of *Histories*. Because of Herodotus, Macedonian foundational myths, that is to say the folktale of Perdiccas and his siblings, are known.[20] He established the name and number of the first seven kings of Macedonia in addition to the geographical and political separation between Upper and Lower Macedonia. Almost everything known about Alexander I of Macedonia comes from Herodotus. Perhaps he stayed in Macedonia during the reign of one of these kings: Amyntas I,[21] Alexander I or Perdiccas II.[22] The reason why Herodotus was buried in the Macedonian Pella can only be understood, according to the *Suda,* in this way. Although this story is probably false, it would not be credible if Herodotus had never been in Macedonia[23]. Moreover, it is Herodotus who defined the Macedonian King as a Greek ruling over Macedonians: «ὡς ἀνὴρ Ἕλλην Μακεδόνων ὕπαρχος» (V.20.4).

The work of Herodotus acquires special importance due to the context of the Panhellenic war in which Alexander's expedition took place. At the same time, thanks to Herodotus, both Philip and Alexander could begin their war of retribution against the Persians, because even though the Macedonians had been allies of Xerxes in the Greco-Persian wars, Herodotus excused the Macedonians of Alexander I, making them look like allies of the Greek cause. Only in one speech by Demosthenes are the Macedonians accused of medizing[24]; therefore, Philip and Alexander's contemporaries should accept Herodotus' account.[25] Also, due to Herodotus, the Macedonians

---

[19] Cic. *Leg.* I.5.

[20] Hdt. VIII.137-138.

[21] Suda s.v. 'Ἑλλάνικος': «...Hellanicus spent time with Herodotus at the court of Amyntas, king of Macedon, during the time of Euripides and Sophocles, and he overlapped with Hecataeus of Miletus, who was born during the time of the Persian Wars, or a little before. Hellanicus lived until the time of Perdiccas, and died in Perperene, on the mainland opposite Lesbos...»

[22] Ogden 2011: 58-62.

[23] Priestly 2014: 34: «It therefore seems highly probable that this tradition developed well after Herodotus' death».

[24] D. VI.11.

[25] Cf. Speus. XXVIII.3-4.

avoided some Greek *poleis* such as Athens waging a Panhellenic war against them, which occurred during the Lamian war.[26] In other words, without Herodotus there would not be a connection between Macedonians and Greeks. He was not only the first page of Macedonian history; he was also the person who defined the identity of the whole people and their kings. Therefore, it is not ridiculous to state that Herodotus was a well-known author in Macedonia before Alexander the Great.

Herodotus and Panhellenism

According to Peter Green, Panhellenism was an ideal policy of unity and collaboration between all Greek states.[27] During the 4th century, the Macedonian kings, specifically Philip II and Alexander III, used this concept to further their own ends and strengthen their hegemony in Greece. In order to do that, the Macedonians presented themselves as avengers of the sacrileges against the Olympian gods. In this context, it should be understood as the war against the Persians. This was the resource used to consolidate control in Greek *poleis*.

During the conquest of Persia, Alexander used the Panhellenism flag as a means to maintain and to justify the unity of his alliance. To do this, Herodotus was a very useful tool in his hands. Most of the Alexander historians borrowed from the Herodotean *Histories* to make their stories interesting and familiar to their readers. In addition, they also connected their narrations to the tradition of Panhellenism. There are indeed many examples of this connection in our sources:

a) The Crossing of the Hellespont

The crossing of the Hellespont was the first similarity of the Macedonian expedition with the Herodotean story of the Persian wars. Like Xerxes, Alexander threw a golden cup into the sea as an offering to the sea gods.

> «Sacrificing a bull to Poseidon and the Nereids in the midst of the Hellespont strain, and pouring into the sea a drink offering from a golden bowl» (Arr. *An.* I.11.6; transl. Brunt 1973).[28]

---

[26] Brosius 2003: 230: «Philip's claim to be champion of the Greek cause to avenge Athens and the destruction of her temples in 480/479. This claim is incompatible with the fact that in the same war the Macedonians had fought on the Persian side against Athens and her allies»; 237: «The reason why Philip wanted a Persian war was to keep Persia out of Greek politics. The enmity towards Persia was created because of Persian involvement in Greek affairs. Philip's real enemy was Greece».

[27] Green 1996: 6.

[28] ἐπειδὴ κατὰ μέσον τὸν πόρον τοῦ Ἑλλησπόντου ἐγένετο, σφάξαντα ταῦρον τῷ Ποσειδῶνι καὶ Νηρηίσι σπένδειν ἐκ χρυσῆς φιάλης ἐς τὸν πόντον.

> «At sunrise Xerxes poured a libation from a golden phial into the sea, praying to the sun that no accident might befall him which would keep him from subduing Europe before he reached its farthest borders. After the prayer, he cast the phial into the Hellespont, and along with it a golden bowl, and a Persian sword which they call 'acinaces'» (Hdt. VII.52.2; transl. Godley 1982).[29]

This act can be understood as an emulation of the Persian king, but in fact, this kind of offering was very common in Greek religion and it was a *leitmotiv* of Alexander to make this sort of sacrifice every time he crossed a strong stream.[30] Most scholars have related the crossing of Alexander's stay in Troy to the visit of Xerxes, but this visit was also very common before the start of the Asian campaign.[31]

b) Phayllus of Crotone

Phayllus was a Pythian champion who took part in the first of the Persian Wars and was therefore honoured by Alexander.

> «All these people who live this side of Thesprotia and the Acheron river took part in the war. The Thesprotians border on the Ampraciots and Leucadians, who were the ones who came from the most distant countries to take part in the war. The only ones living beyond these to help Hellas in its danger were the Crotonians, with one ship. Its captain was Phayllus, three times victor in the Pythian games. The Crotonians are Achaeans by birth» (Hdt. VIII.47; transl. Godley 1982).

> «He sent also to the people of Croton in Italy a portion of the spoils, honouring the zeal and valour of their athlete Phäyllus, who, in the Median wars, when the rest of the Greeks in Italy refused to help their brother Greeks, fitted out a ship at his own cost and sailed with it to Salamis, that he might have some share in the peril there. So considerate was Alexander towards every form of valour, and such a friend and guardian of noble deeds» (Plu. *Alex.* 34.2; transl. Perrin 1919).

We should ask ourselves: could Alexander have definitely known who Phayllus was without having read Herodotus' book? Scholars have seen this passage as evidence of Alexander reading Herodotus.[32] However, the fact that the story is known does not mean that the author has been read. If we take into account the strong orality of these stories, we must conclude that the tale could have come from members of Alexander's staff.

---

[29] ὡς δ᾽ ἐπανέτελλε ὁ ἥλιος, σπένδων ἐκ χρυσέης φιάλης Ξέρξης ἐς τὴν θάλασσαν εὔχετο πρὸς τὸν ἥλιον μηδεμίαν οἱ συντυχίην τοιαύτην γενέσθαι, ἥ μιν παύσει καταστρέψασθαι τὴν Εὐρώπην πρότερον ἢ ἐπὶ τέρμασι τοῖσι ἐκείνης γένηται. εὐξάμενος δὲ ἐσέβαλε τὴν φιάλην ἐς τὸν Ἑλλήσποντον καὶ χρύσεον κρητῆρα καὶ Περσικὸν ξίφος, τὸν ἀκινάκην καλέουσι.

[30] Molina Marín 2016: 57-8.

[31] Borgeaud 2010: 339-353.

[32] Vasunia 2001: 256-258.

c) The Persian Gates

The crossing of the Persian Gates marked another significant moment in the campaign. The story of the Lycian shepherd who guided Alexander there reminds us directly of the Thermopylae. The Lycian is an alter ego of Ephialtes, the celebrated shepherd who led Xerxes and betrayed the Greek cause.[33] The whole episode is an invention that serves to avenge the Greeks.[34]

d) Darius's dream

Even some of the many dreams described by our sources seem to have been rewritten to strengthen the similarities with Herodotus.[35] Darius's dream may have been inspired by the dream of Xerxes. In both cases, someone wears an object that belongs to his enemy; in both cases, the *magoi* give a wrong interpretation even when they know that it is not true.

e) Amyntas, Charidemus and Demaratus

Amyntas and Charidemus are paralleled to Demaratus, the Spartan king who accompanied Xerxes.[36] Both answered truthfully, praising their enemies against the wishes of the Persian kings. In other words, Amyntas and Charidemus are deliberate imitations of Herodotus.[37]

f) Egypt

Occasionally, these similarities clarify the contraposition between Alexander and the Persian kings. Thus, unlike Cambyses, Alexander was a pious king with Egyp-

---

[33] Hdt. VII.215

[34] Burn 1973: 121:«...a Persian Thermopylae, and like Thermopylae it fell»; Renault 1975: 128: «By one of history's revenges the story of Thermopylae was now acted on reverse»; Heckel 1980: 172-173: «like Xerxes, Alexander has reached a critical point: his luck has run out and success appears to depend upon his ability to take the pass... like Xerxes Alexander must extricate himself from this situation, and here the vulgate authors inject the fictitious Lykian herdsman... it scarcely requires imagination to see that this Lykian herdsman has a counterpart in the Herodotean Ephialtes»; Zahrnt 1999: 1384: «Geschehen an den Thermopylen auf, und der lykische Hirte sei das Gegenstück zum herodoteischen Ephialtes, der einst die Sache der Griechen verraten hatte»; Bowden 2014: 39: «The similarities between the accounts of the battles at the Hot Gates and the Persian Gates are too great to be coincidental».

[35] Hdt. VII.19; Plu. *Alex.* 18.6-7; cf. Curt. III.3.2.

[36] Hdt. VII.235, 237.1.

[37] Cf. Blaensdorf 1971: 11-24.

tian beliefs.[38] Cambyses's army and Alexander faced a great many challenges during their journey to Siwah, but contrary to the Persians, Alexander was able to arrive at Siwah with the help of the gods.[39]

g) Eclipse

Superstition is another cause of contraposition among them. Both (Xerxes and Alexander) were afraid because of an eclipse, but significantly, Herodotus and the Alexander historians agreed that the Moon is a symbol for the Persians and the Sun for the Greeks. This association is again borrowed from *Histories*.

> «The army then wintered, and at the beginning of spring was ready and set forth from Sardis to march to Abydos. When they had set forth, the sun left his place in the heaven and was unseen, albeit the sky was without clouds and very clear, and the day was turned into night. When Xerxes saw and took note of that, he was moved to think upon it, and asked the Magians what the vision might signify. They declared to him, that the god was showing to the Greeks the desolation of their cities; *for the sun (they said) was the prophet of the Greeks, as the moon was theirs*. Xerxes rejoiced exceedingly to hear that, and kept on his march» (Hdt. VIII.37; transl. Godley 1982).

> «[...] *but they declared that the sun represented the Greeks and the moon the Persians*, and that whenever the moon suffered eclipse, defeat and slaughter was foretold for those nations and they enumerated ancient examples of Persian kings whom an eclipse of the moon showed to have fought without the favour of the gods» (Curt. IV.10.5-6; transl. Rolfe 1946/1962)

h) Ziggurat of Marduk

The most evident contrast between Alexander and Xerxes was their behaviour with respect to the temple of Marduk in Babylon; whereas the latter wanted to destroy the ziggurat, the Macedonian tried to rebuild it.[40]

i) Harmodius and Aristogeiton

Xerxes took the statue of the Tyrannicides during the Persian Wars. Alexander returned this sculpture to the Athenians at some time during his campaign.[41] However,

---

[38] Hdt. III.29; Arr. *An*. III.1.4. Antela Bernárdez 2016: 243: «Alexander's behaviour is clearly intended to be compared in contrast with the memory of preceding Persian conquerors, placing them in stark contrast to his own ability to accept the religious practices of conquered people».

[39] Cf. Hdt. III.25-26; Plu. *Alex*. 27.1-4.

[40] Kuhrt / Sherwin-White 1987: 69-78.

[41] Arr. *An*. III.16.7, VII.19.2; Plin. *NH*. XXXIV.70.

other sources say that it was Seleucus[42] or Antiochus.[43] Bosworth resolves this contradiction by suggesting that Alexander merely promised to return the statue group.[44] According to Claudia Gafforini, Alexander returned the statue group, but Antiochus III tried to win the favour of the Athenians by claiming this in the name of Seleucus.[45]

j) Persepolis

A new act of Panhellenic propaganda was the burning of Persepolis. Alexander burned the palace of Xerxes. The interpretations for this act are numerous; however, the important point is that the spirit of the Panhellenic crusade motivated it Moreover[46], the parallel between events at Persepolis and the burning of Athens is evident.[47]

k) Branchidae

The slaughter of the Branchidae also reflects knowledge of the work of Herodotus[48] by Alexander and his historians.[49]

*

As shown above, the number of parallels between the *Histories* of Herodotus and the conquest of Asia by the Macedonians is so numerous that they cannot simply be a mere coincidence. This may be partly due to the fact that he was the author who wrote about the Persian Wars, and this new conflict was indeed a continuation of the former. The Panhellenic crusade of the Macedonians was also a reason to use the landmarks of the Greeks against the Persians. Finally, it must be taken into account that the Macedonians themselves formed part of these acts of propaganda. They made a prominent entrance in the story of the Greek people by killing the Persian ambassadors.[50] In other words, the story of Macedonia and its inhabitants was also

---

[42] Val. Max. II.10, ext. 1.

[43] Paus I.8.5.

[44] Bosworth 1980: 317.

[45] Gafforini 1989: 17-23.

[46] Arr. *An*. III.8.12.

[47] Howe 2015: 173.

[48] Hdt. VI.19.

[49] Str. XIV.1.5 (cf. Amm. XIX.1.31; Curt. VII.5.28-35; Plu. *Mor*. 557b; Suda, s.v. 'Βραγχίδαι'); Tarn 1922: 63-66; 1948 II: 272-275; Seibert 1972: 144-145; Parke 1985: 59-68; Prandi 1985: 83-87; 105-109; Bosworth 1988b: 108-109; Holt 1988: 73-75; Briant 1996: 771-772; Hammond 1998: 339-344; Flower 2000: 117-118; Holt 2005: 40; Heckel 2008: 95; Nawotka 2010: 273-274; Freeman 2011: 240-241; Gabriel 2015: 93-94.

[50] Hdt. V.18.

related to these accounts, and Herodotus was the person conveying the information for both Macedonians and Greeks.

Herodotus and the Alexander historians

It is known that Theopompus of Chios made an epitome of the *Histories* of Herodotus: «Theopompus of Chios wrote an Epitome of the *Histories* of Herodotus in two books, a *Philippika* in seventy-two books, and Hellenic» [51]. It has been suggested that the epitome was not really a separate work, but merely formed part of the *Philippika*.[52] In any case, this epitome would have been written during his stay at the court of Philip II in Macedonia, and therefore it could have even been a commission by the king himself. In spite of this, there are a few scholars who argue that Philip II knew and read Herodotus' work.[53] People prefer to think that Alexander's interest in Herodotus comes from Aristotle and not from his Macedonian environment[54]. However, his interest can hardly be attributed to Aristotle, given that he once disparagingly called Herodotus a *mythologos* or *mythologiser*[55]. The same cannot be said of Callisthenes of Olynthus, who was a great follower of Herodotus[56]. Nevertheless, it seems that no historian has

---

[51] *FGrH* 115 T1 FF 1-4. Flower 1997: 161: «The fact that Theopompus made a epitome of Herodotus, which was the first of its kind in Greek literature, regardless of whether it was intended for publication, is of the greatest significance».

[52] Hornblower 2006: 310.

[53] Kienast 1973: 269: «Philipp, der ein gebildeter Mann war, wird neben den Werk Herodots zumindest die Schriften Xenophons gekannt und von ihnen mancherlei Anregungen empfangen haben»; Badian 1996: 369: «Kienast rightly pointed out that, as an educated man in the Greek tradition, Philip would have read at least Herodotus and Xenophon»; Flower 2000: 103: «...their reading of Herodotus may have inspired Philip and Alexander».

[54] O'Brien 1992: 223: «We know that Aristotle instructed Alexander in Homer, and the philosopher is probably also responsible for arousing Alexander's interest in Aeschylus, Sophocles, and Euripides. Beyond these works, and a few others (lost or minor), we may be reasonably certain that the king was familiar with the writings of Pindar, Herodotus, and Xenophon»; Crompton 2003: 20: «Aristotle knew a great deal about geography and the cultural associations of many peoples from around the Mediterranean world; his knowledge in this regard came primarily from the Greek historian Herodotus»; Cawthorne 2004: 6; Gehrke 2015: 90: «The conclusion that Alexander knew the work of Herodotus cannot be avoided».

[55] Arist. *GA*. 756b. Cf. Momigliano 1958: 6: «He calls Herodotus a story-teller».

[56] Murray 1972: 205: «Callisthenes too is known to have followed Herodotus almost word for word on occasions»; Prandi 1985: 82: «La conoscenza dell'opera di Erodoto che Callistene rivela attraverso i frammenti delle Alexandrou Praxeis non è certo motivo di stupore: i logoi dello storico di Alicarnasso costituivano per gli intellettuali del IV secolo, come già per quelli della fine del V, la fonte più organica e ricca di notizie sull'entità geografico-etnica che era politicamente controllata dall'impero persiano; Erodoto era inoltre lo storico del conflitto greco-persiano nella sua fase 'eroica' e il teorizzatore di quella antilogia fra libertà greca e schiavitù barbarica che informò di sé il pensiero greco e che si riproponeva in tutta la sua (propagandistica) attualità in concomitanza di una spedizione antipersiana»; Hornblower 2006: 310: «Callisthenes follow Herodotus closely on at least one complicated geographical point; he even described the Athenian fining of the tragedian Phrynichus for his play about the fall of Miletus without making reference to Herodotus at all, although he is the palpable source»; Schillace 2010: 173: «Callisthenes modeled his narrative after Herodotus»; Howe 2015: 173: «Kallisthenes made extensive use of Herodotos».

argued that Callisthenes was the only one responsible for paralleling the Macedonian expedition with the Persian wars. On the contrary, it is assumed that he wrote according to the wishes of his master, Alexander[57]. If we conclude that Callisthenes personally took the initiative to transform Alexander into a Panhellenic hero, we can accept without any problem that he was the same person who challenged the wishes of Alexander about introducing the *proskýnesis* in his court. However, this would imply that we refuse to view the image of Alexander as an embodiment of good or darkness, or as a turning point in history, which is unthinkable.

In any case, Callisthenes' influence on the rest of the Alexander historians was immense, and through him, most of these authors continued with the same Herodotean topics. Thus, we can see identical motifs in their works: the sources of the Nile,[58] elephants, gold ants, etc. There are also many parallels between Herodotus and Hieronymus of Cardia in their descriptions of Scythians and Nabateans.[59] Therefore, it is not an overstatement to say that because of the Macedonian conquest of Asia, Herodotus' fame extended throughout the Hellenistic age.

Herodotus, Alexander I and Alexander the Great

Much has been said about the mythical models of Alexander, but to a lesser extent than his Macedonian models. Alexander I Philhellene was also a significant paradigm for him:

a) Both shared the same name. It is equally likely that Alexander's father named him in this way in honour of his big brother (Alexander II) or the greatest king in the history of Macedonia, Alexander Philhellene.

b) Both were linked to the Olympic Games. Alexander I took part in the Games (Hdt. V.23) and the young Alexander refused to participate (Plu. *Alex*. 4).

c) Both acted as messengers: Alexander I in the Persian War (Hdt. VIII.136); Alexander III was a messenger in *Alexander Romance*.

d) Both were defenders of women: Alexander I (noble Macedonian women); Alexander III (noble Persian women).

e) Both killed their guests during a banquet: Alexander I (Persian ambassadors), Alexander III (Cleitus the Black).

f) Both showed great respect towards Pindar (D. Chr. II.33; Solin. IX.13).

---

[57] Flower 2000: 105: «He [Callisthenes] seems to have written up Alexander's campaign as a great Panhellenic crusade, surely with his patron's approval».

[58] Hdt. II.22; Arr. *An*. VI.1.2-3; Str. XV.1.17-18, 25.

[59] Bosworth 2002: 169-209.

Nevertheless, the greatest similarity between them is in the words that Alexander said after visiting the family of Darius:

> «Then the Persians, seeing beautiful women before them, spoke to Amyntas and said that there was no sense in what he had done. It would be better if the women had never come at all than that they should come and not sit beside the men, but sit opposite them to torment their eyes (ἀλγηδόνας σφίσι ὀφθαλμῶν)» (Hdt. V.18.4; transl. Godley 1982).

> «But as for the other captive women, seeing that they were surpassingly stately and beautiful, he merely said jestingly that Persian women were torments to the eyes (ἀλγηδόνες ὀμμάτων). And displaying in rivalry with their fair looks the beauty of his own sobriety and self-control, he passed them by as though they were lifeless images for display» (Plu. *Alex.* 21.5; transl. Perrin. 1919).

Thus, ἀλγηδόνες ὀμμάτων «was to be applied as description of women who excited men's passions but denied them sexual gratification».[60] In Alexander's case, this expression is a direct allusion to the words that the Persian ambassadors said during the banquet in which Alexander I killed them.

The phrase must be understood as more than a simple recognition of the beauty of the Persian women by Alexander. Alexander's words refer directly to the behaviour of the Persian ambassadors; in spite of the fact that they do not show any respect for the Macedonian women, Alexander is magnanimous with the family of his enemy. The strong intertextuality of the entire passage offers another reading:

1) Alexander III definitely took revenge for the insult suffered by the noble Macedonian women and his subjects during the Persian occupation.

2) Unlike the Persians, Alexander is a true conqueror because he knows how to behave in a godly way with the vanquished Persian women.

3) The meaning of Alexander's words cannot be understood without reading Herodotus' *Histories* beforehand. This questions whether the Macedonians, who were close to the king, were capable of understanding all its nuances. The speech had a significant meaning for Herodotus' readers and the Macedonians who knew the story. However, given that most Macedonians were illiterate, it is logical to assume that the story was rewritten by a Greek who wrote for a Greek audience, as did all ancient historians. In other words, Callisthenes, and not Alexander, was the maker of this story. This historian had no hesitation in admitting that he turned Alexander into a Greek hero:

> «But I think quite out of place the remark of Callisthenes (if correctly reported), that Alexander and his achievements were all dependent on himself and his history. He himself (he said) hoped for no glory in coming to Alexander, but rather to

[60] Keaveney 1978: 270.

> make Alexander famous in the sight of men; and again, that Alexander's share in divinity did not depend on Olympias' fanciful story of his birth, but upon his own account of Alexander which should be given to the world in his history» (Arr. *An.* IV.10.2; transl. Robson 1929).

Alexander I's banquet must have had a great influence on Macedonian tradition. Many interpretations have been made about it, but it is unquestionable that it is an invention created from the famous banquet between the Lapiths and the Centaurs. The Persians are represented as superb centaurs, who drunk on wine and lust, try to abuse the Macedonian nobles. Murder is a necessary requirement in order to erase the submission of Macedonia to Persia, since in this way the 'earth and water' tokens of submission agreed by Amyntas were never delivered to Darius.[61] The action takes place at a banquet, as this is the best way to reflect the differences between Macedonians and Persians: «ξεῖνε Μακεδών, ἡμῖν νόμος ἐστὶ τοῖσι Πέρσῃσι» (Hdt. V.18.2); «ὦ Πέρσαι, νόμος μὲν ἡμῖν γε ἐστὶ οὐκ οὗτος» (18.3). Similarly, Alexander attributed a misunderstanding with the queen Sisygambis to Macedonian customs: «Therefore Alexander in person came to her and said: Mother, in this clothing which I am wearing you see, not only a gift of my sisters, but also their handiwork. It was our customs that led me astray (*nostri decepere me mores*)» (Curt. V.2.20; transl. Rolfe 1946).

Like the centaurs, the Persian guests demanded women for sexual company from their hosts. The transformation of the ambassadors into mythical monsters mitigates Alexander's crime because he had broken the law of the gods by killing his guests. As a result, Alexander is a king who kills the beasts in order to protect his *oikos*, which is symbolized by the Macedonian women. This is not, however, sufficient reason to explain the strong connection between Persians and Centaurs. Why did the Macedonians choose to describe their enemies and themselves in this way?

The Lapiths were identified with the Perrhaebians, and we can therefore conclude that they were also chosen for being the Greek people closest to the Macedonian border. However, Herodotus included the Perrhaebians among the people who paid tribute to the Persians during the Persian Wars.[62] If the Macedonians were trying to erase their cooperation with the Persians, the association with the Perrhaebians was not the best way.

It must be concluded that the myth was chosen after centauromachy became a symbol of the fight against the Persians,[63] that is to say, sometime between the completion of the western pediment of the temple of Zeus at Olympia (460 BC) and the

---

[61] Hdt. V.18.1.

[62] Hdt VII.132.1.

[63] Anagnostou-Laoutides 2011: 30: «The centaurs were conflated with lawless, oriental tyrants who deserve punishment». Cf. S. *Tr.* 1095-1096: «the savage tribe of beasts, half horse, half man, the lawless, mighty, violent Centaurs».

finishing of the Parthenon (*ca.* 432 BC), when Herodotus was finishing his *Histories* (*ca.* 430 BC). As in the previous case, it is more likely that the historian, Herodotus, and not the king, was the origin of this folktale.

Bucephalus and Alexander

Finally, the banquet of Alexander I is comparable to the well-known history of the taming of Bucephalus. The story has been interpreted in different ways. While some scholars proclaim its veracity[64], most of them maintain that it is a metaphor for Alexander's transformation into an adult.[65] It is likely that the whole story is a fiction created by Onesicritus, whose main purpose would be to show how the young Alexander knew how to control his passions. In fact, there are many similarities between rider and horse; they had the same age and an identical character. In a sense, Alexander was controlling himself when he domesticated Bucephalus.

Nevertheless, there are also resemblances with Alexander I's banquet:

1) Two young (νέος; νεώτερον) princes become adults performing a feat: Alexander I has the courage to oppose the mighty Persians (Hdt. V.19.1: ὑπερδειμαίνων τοὺς Πέρσας); Alexander III tames a savage beast (Plu. *Alex*. 6.2: ἄγριον καὶ ἀκόλαστον).

2) Both have success over their elders (Plu. *Alex*. 6.2: πρεσβυτέροις); while Amyntas and Philip are incapable of doing anything, their sons achieve a significant victory.

3) At the beginning of the story, the fathers appear in the role of rulers; however, towards the end they are substituted by their sons, because they allow their sons to act in their place. It is their own disability that makes them pass on the torch to their

---

[64] Hammond 1997: 1: «On my interpretation we owe this vivid account to an eyewitness, one Marsyas of Macedon, who was an exact contemporary of Alexander». Carolyn Willekes argued in the congress of Utah of 2014 that the young Alexander could have tamed Bucephalus with a Thessalian technique.

[65] Whitmarsh 2002: 180-181: «In accordance with a common collocation in Greek literature, and one that is particularly emphatic in the celebrated chariot metaphor of Plato's *Phaedrus* (246a-57b), the horse is assimilated to the unruly passion of the youth, which must be 'broken' by paideia… and Alexander's education is metaphorically linked with the breaking of horses when Plutarch describes it, by way of a quotation from Sophocles, as 'a job for many bits and rudders'»; Constantinou 2004: 125: «the taming of Bucephalus served as a rite of passage… In Plutarch's biography of Alexander, horsetaming becomes a distinctive metaphor for the rule of Greece. Unlike Philip, who only manages to disturb and change the state of affairs in Greece, Alexander does a Bucephalian move and makes Greece 'tame under his yoke' (*katazeuxai kai tithaseusai:* Plu. *Alex.*11). Then he moves to 'tame barbarian kings' and 'the wild and brutish Asia' (*basileis barbarous ēmerountes; Asian… tēs anēmerou kai thēriōdous hēriōdous: Mor.* 328b-329a)»; Chandezon 2010: 184: «Maîtriser Bucéphale annonçait tout ce qui allait suivre pour Alexandre et le destin exceptionnel qui l'attendait. En parvenant enfin à monter Bucéphale, Alexandre commençait d'une certaine manière le processus de conquête»; Grethlein 2013: 116: «Philip's dictum with which Plutarch closes the scene alerts the reader to Alexander's later conquest: Alexander will subjugate entire countries just as he tamed Bucephalus».

progeny. The weakness of Amyntas serves to increase the value of Alexander I. In the same way, *Philippos* meaning 'lover of horse' makes his failure even greater.

While Philip is just an Olympic champion, Alexander is a true Homeric hero: a tamer of horses (ἱππόδαμος).

1) The fathers emphasize the youth of their sons through their speeches:[66]

> «My son, you are angered, and if I guess your meaning correctly, you are sending me away so that you may do some violent deed» (Hdt. 5.19.2; transl. Godley 1920)[67].

> «My son, seek thee out a kingdom equal to thyself; Macedonia has not room for thee» (Plu. *Alex*. 6.5; transl. Perrin 1919).[68]

Somehow, with this folktale about the Persian ambassadors, Herodotus establishes the way in which a Macedonian prince becomes a good king: by defeating his predecessor.

This Plutarchean tale is, however, also similar to the ascension to the throne of Darius I,[69] who became king because of his horse. Through the horse, their contemporaries recognized the royal charisma of Darius and Alexander. Although Alexander did not become king with the taming of Bucephalus, he demonstrated that he was already prepared to rule Macedonia.

Both Alexander and Ebares used tricks in order to tame the horses. In both texts, the sun plays a significant role. Macedonians and Persians had the sun as their main symbol.[70] Alexander and Darius both have horses related to the sun.[71] The sunlight could symbolize royal charisma, and therefore, it is another Herodotean reference to Perdiccas I and his siblings:

> «They said it was only just that they should have their wages before they departed. When they spoke of wages, the king was moved to foolishness and said, 'That is the wage you merit, and it is that I give you', pointing to the sunlight that shone down the smoke vent into the house. [5] Gauanes and Aeropus, who were the elder, stood astonished when they heard that, but the boy said, 'We accept what you give, O king', and with that he took a knife which he had with him and drew a

---

[66] Ogden 2017: 60-61.

[67] ὦ παῖ, σχεδὸν γάρ σευ ἀνακαιομένου συνίημι τοὺς λόγους, ὅτι ἐθέλεις ἐμὲ ἐκπέμψας ποιέειν τι νεώτερον.

[68] 'ὦ παῖ,' φάναι, 'ζήτει σεαυτῷ βασιλείαν ἴσην Μακεδονία γάρ σε οὐ χωρεῖ'. Cf. Anderson 1930: 17, who sees in this remark the beginning of the prophecy (Ps.-Callisth. I.15, 17) that the rider of Bucephalus would rule the world.

[69] Hdt. III.85.

[70] Curt. IV.14.24.

[71] Greenwalt 2016: 32: «...the Argead house long before Alexander employed solar symbolism in its claims of divine sanction for its rule».

line with it on the floor of the house round the sunlight. When he had done this, he three times gathered up the sunlight into the fold of his garment and went his way with his companions» (Hdt. VIII.137.4-5; transl. Godley 1920).[72]

Conclusions

— Herodotus' work was not only important for the Macedonians from a geographical and ethnogeographical point of view.[73]

— Alexander historians, mainly Callisthenes, used him as a model to write about the crusade against the Persian Empire.

— The influence of Herodotus in Alexander and his historians cannot be explained only by Aristotle, given that Herodotus had too much presence in the history of Macedonia.

— The existence of an epitome of Herodotus in the court of Philip II establishes an interest in his work prior to Alexander's period.

— The mentions of the sun in the eclipse, the taming of Bucephalus and the folktale of Perdiccas and his siblings show that the Macedonians had more symbols in common with Persians than they wanted to admit.

— Alexander's phrase about the beauty of Persian women comes from Herodotus and in the context in which it is said could have come from Callisthenes.

— If Onesicritus is behind Alexander's interest in Xenophon[74], the person responsible for Alexander's interest in Herodotus may have been Callisthenes.

— Given the importance of Herodotus to the Macedonians and the historians of Alexander, it cannot be categorically affirmed that Alexander had read Herodotus, which has always been the traditional belief.

---

[72] οἳ δὲ τὸν μισθὸν ἔφασαν δίκαιοι εἶναι ἀπολαβόντες οὕτω ἐξιέναι. ἐνθαῦτα ὁ βασιλεὺς τοῦ μισθοῦ πέρι ἀκούσας, ἦν γὰρ κατὰ τὴν καπνοδόκην ἐς τὸν οἶκον ἐσέχων ὁ ἥλιος, εἶπε θεοβλαβὴς γενόμενος 'μισθὸν δὲ ὑμῖν ἐγὼ ὑμέων ἄξιον τόνδε ἀποδίδωμι,' δέξας τὸν ἥλιον. [5] ὁ μὲν δὴ Γαυάνης τε καὶ ὁ Ἀέροπος οἱ πρεσβύτεροι ἔστασαν ἐκπεπληγμένοι, ὡς ἤκουσαν ταῦτα: ὁ δὲ παῖς, ἐτύγχανε γὰρ ἔχων μάχαιραν, εἴπας τάδε 'δεκόμεθα ὦ βασιλεῦ τὰ διδοῖς,' περιγράφει τῇ μαχαίρῃ ἐς τὸ ἔδαφος τοῦ οἴκου τὸν ἥλιον, περιγράψας δέ, ἐς τὸν κόλπον τρὶς ἀρυσάμενος τοῦ ἡλίου, ἀπαλλάσσετο αὐτός τε καὶ οἱ μετ᾽ ἐκείνου

[73] Vasunia 2001: 248-288; Taietti 2016.

[74] Due 1993.

DESCRIBING A BRAVE NEW WORLD

El conocimiento de la isla Taprobane en época de la expedición de Alejandro

Manuel Albaladejo Vivero*
(Universidad de Valencia)

Recientemente, se ha publicado un artículo de investigación[1] en el que se plantea la posibilidad de que Onesícrito de Astipalea[2] hubiese viajado en una misión de reconocimiento a Taprobane,[3] isla del océano Índico que debe ser identificada con Sri Lanka.

Onesícrito fue uno de los intelectuales que acompañaron a Alejandro Magno en su expedición y, según varios autores antiguos, se había formado en la "escuela" cínica liderada por Diógenes de Sínope.[4] El relato que escribió Onesícrito acerca de la expedición y del propio Alejandro llevó por título Πῶς Ἀλέξανδρος Ἤχθη. En cuanto a la posible fecha en que fue compuesto, ha habido diversidad de opiniones; así, Jacoby consideró que la fecha de redacción pudo haber estado comprendida entre el 320 y el 310 a.C., es decir, poco tiempo después de la muerte de Alejandro; además, Jacoby dio por hecho que autores como Clitarco y Nearco se valieron de lo escrito por Onesícrito, sobre todo para criticarlo y desmentir sus embustes.[5] Por su parte, Brown consideró que su obra no debió de estar circulando antes de la llegada al trono de Lisímaco en Tracia, es decir, en 304 a. C.[6]

---

* Este trabajo ha sido realizado gracias a la ayuda del proyecto de investigación HAR2016-76098-C2-1-P, *Historiografía y geografía antigua: representación del espacio y transmisión de saberes*, concedido por el Ministerio de Economía, Industria y Competitividad.

[1] Mariotta 2017: 113-120.

[2] Strasburger, *RE* XVIII.1 (1939), s.v. 'Onesikritos' (460-467).

[3] El nombre con el que la conocieron los geógrafos griegos y romanos procede de su antiguo nesónimo, Tambapanni.

[4] *FGrH* 134 T 1 = D.L. VI.84; T 2 = Str. XV.1.65; T 3 = D.L. VI.75-76; T 5a = Plu. *Mor.* 331e.

[5] Jacoby 1930: 469, 471.

[6] Brown 1949: 7.

Los fragmentos que han llegado hasta nosotros acerca de la biografía y del contenido de la obra de Onesícrito básicamente están contextualizados a partir del momento en que la expedición macedónica llegó a la India, donde el escritor fue nombrado timonel (κυβερνήτης) de la nave real una vez que Alejandro se vio obligado a abandonar sus planes de avance hacia el Este y tomó la decisión de construir una flota para descender por el río Hidaspes hasta la desembocadura del Indo.[7]

Posteriormente, Onesícrito participó en la navegación comandada por Nearco de Creta, que zarpó del puerto de Patala (en el delta del río Indo) y concluyó en la cabecera del golfo Pérsico. Al comparar los relatos compuestos por ambos personajes (Nearco y Onesícrito) queda bastante claro que tuvieron grandes diferencias en cuanto a la interpretación de las órdenes recibidas de Alejandro, además de una evidente rivalidad personal. No en vano, Arriano de Nicomedia afirmaba que Onesícrito decía de sí mismo que había sido el almirante de la flota macedónica (navarco), y no el piloto de la nave real.[8]

La falta de credibilidad de lo escrito por el propio Onesícrito ya fue manifestada por otros autores antiguos, como sucede con Estrabón, que afirmó que a Onesícrito se le podría llamar piloto mayor no de Alejandro, sino de maravillas, y que superó a los demás acompañantes del rey a la hora de relatar prodigios.[9] El mismo autor de Amasía también señaló que los mayores falsarios que escribieron sobre la India fueron, por este orden, Deímaco, Megástenes y, luego, Onesícrito y Nearco.[10] Igualmente, Aulo Gelio lo mencionó entre los autores de narraciones increíbles cuyas obras encontró a bajo precio en un puesto de libros en Brindisi.[11]

Los antecedentes que hemos mostrado hasta ahora deben ponernos en alerta ante las noticias que proporcionó Onesícrito acerca de Taprobane. En concreto, fue una vez más Estrabón quien recogió el testimonio de este autor, después de haber descrito las características de la isla; para ello, utilizó el de Amasía el testimonio de Eratóstenes de Cirene,[12] quien había señalado que Taprobane era una isla situada en alta mar, a una distancia de siete días de navegación hacia el sur de la región de los coníacos (es decir, de la costa meridional de la India), además de indicar que Taprobane tenía 8.000 estadios de longitud en dirección a Etiopía (esto es, hacia el Oeste). El último dato acerca de la isla que Estrabón recogió en este pasaje procedente de la obra de Eratóstenes fue el de la existencia de elefantes en ella.[13]

---

[7] *FGrH* 134 T 4 = Arr. *Ind.* 18.9; T 5a = Plu. *Mor.* 331e; T5b = Plu. *Alex.* 66; T 5c = Str. XV.2.4; T 6 = Arr. *An.* VII.5.6.

[8] Arr. *An.* VI.2.3. Sobre las discusiones entre Nearco y Onesícrito, consúltese Bucciantini 2015: 83, 145-147.

[9] *FGrH* 134 T 10 = Str. XV.1.28.

[10] *FGrH* 134 T 11 = Str. II.1.9.

[11] Gell. IX.4.1-3.

[12] Que, desde luego, no había visitado ni la India ni Taprobane, por lo que se basó en lo escrito fundamentalmente por los historiadores que habían acompañado a Alejandro en su expedición; véase Weerakkody 1997: 36-37; Bianchetti 2014: 24-25.

[13] Str. XV.1.14 = III B, 12 Berger: Τὴν δὲ Ταπροβάνην πελαγίαν εἶναί φασι νῆσον ἀπέχουσαν τῶν νοτιωτάτων τῆς Ἰνδικῆς τῶν κατὰ τοὺς Κωνιακοὺς πρὸς μεσημβρίαν ἡμερῶν ἑπτὰ πλοῦν, μῆκος μὲν ὡς

Acto seguido de esta presentación de Taprobane, con sus características geográficas básicas, Estrabón pasó a recoger el testimonio de Onesícrito al respecto. En concreto, el de Astipalea había escrito que la isla tenía un tamaño de 5.000 estadios, sin distinguir entre longitud y anchura[14], y que distaba de tierra firme nada menos que una navegación de veinte días, que además ese periplo era laborioso, ya que había que utilizar unos barcos que apenas tenían velas y carecían de quilla en un lado y otro. A esto añadió Onesícrito que había otras islas[15] entre la India y Taprobane, aunque ésta era la más meridional. Por último, había monstruos anfibios en el mar alrededor de la isla, algunos de ellos eran parecidos a bueyes, otros a caballos y otros animales terrestres.[16]

Por su parte, unas décadas después de la *Geografía* de Estrabón, Plinio compuso su *Historia Natural*, que en su libro sexto dedicó cierto espacio a la descripción de Taprobane y, especialmente, a recoger las noticias de una supuesta embajada que habría llegado a Roma en época de Claudio procedente precisamente de dicha isla. En todo caso, hay que tener en cuenta que Plinio no tuvo un conocimiento directo de la obra de Onesícrito, sino que la citó a través de lo que había leído en Juba II de Mauritania.[17]

De modo que Plinio recogió, en primer lugar, que Taprobane había sido considerada durante mucho como otro mundo y era llamada «el país de los antíctones»,[18] y fue gracias a los logros de Alejandro cuando quedó demostrado que claramente se trataba de una isla. A continuación, el naturalista pasa a recoger el testimonio de Onesícrito, a quien erróneamente definió como *praefectus classis* o almirante de la flota, quien habría escrito que en Taprobane se criaban unos elefantes de mayor tamaño y más belicosos que los de la India.[19]

ὀκτακισχιλίων σταδίων ἐπὶ τὴν Αἰθιοπίαν· ἔχειν δὲ καὶ ἐλέφαντας. Τοιαῦται μὲν αἱ τοῦ Ἐρατοσθένους ἀποφάσεις. Προστεθεῖσαι δὲ καὶ αἱ τῶν ἄλλων, εἴ πού τι προσακριβοῦσιν, εἰδοποιήσουσι τὴν γραφήν. Edición de Leroy 2016: 12. También interesa consultar Str. II.2.2 = II B, 22 Berger. Por su parte, Plinio el Viejo también recogió otra noticia de Eratóstenes acerca de Taprobane en *NH.* VI.81: Eratosthenes *et mensuram prodidit, longitudinis VII stadium, latitudinis V, nec urbes esse, sed vicos DCCL*. Edición de André / Filliozat 1980: 44-45.

[14] Posiblemente se refiriese al perímetro de la isla; véase Weerakkody 1997: 28, quien también comenta que los propios habitantes de la India en época antigua pensaban que Sri Lanka tenía un tamaño desmesurado.

[15] Que Biffi (2005: 164) identificó con el archipiélago Lakshadweep, al sur de la costa malabar.

[16] Str. XV.1.15 = *FGrH* 134 F 12: Οἷον περὶ τῆς Ταπροβάνης Ὀνησίκριτός φησι μέγεθος μὲν εἶναι πεντακισχιλίων σταδίων, οὐ διορίσας μῆκος οὐδὲ πλάτος, διέχειν δὲ τῆς ἠπείρου πλοῦν ἡμερῶν εἴκοσιν· ἀλλὰ κακοπλοεῖν τὰς ναῦς, φαύλως μὲν ἱστιοπεποιημένας, κατεσκευασμένας δὲ ἀμφοτέρωθεν ἐγκοιλίων <καὶ> μητρῶν χωρίς. Εἶναι δὲ καὶ ἄλλας νήσους αὐτῆς μεταξὺ καὶ τῆς Ἰνδικῆς, νοτιωτάτην δ᾽ ἐκείνην. Κήτη δ᾽ ἀμφίβια περὶ αὐτὴν γίνεσθαι, τὰ μὲν βουσί, τὰ δ᾽ ἵπποις, τὰ δ᾽ ἄλλοις χερσαίοις ἐοικότα. Edición de Leroy 2016: 12.

[17] Plin. *NH.* VI.81 = *FGrHist* 134 F 13: *Taprobanen alterum orbem terrarum esse diu existimatum est Antichthonum appellatione. Ut insulam liqueret esse Alexandri Magni aetas resque praestitere. Onesicritus, classis eius praefectus, elephantos ibi maiores bellicosioresque quam in India gigni scripsit*. Edición de André / Filliozat 1980: 44; cf. Desanges 2012: 63-73. Acerca del conocimiento que tuvo Plinio de la obra de Onesícrito a través de Juba, véase Brown 1949: 108; Sallmann 1971: 86 n. 100, 150, 182, 206.

[18] Es decir, de los habitantes del hemisferio sur de la Tierra. También recogió esta denominación Mela III.70.

[19] Eliano (*NA.* XVI.18) recogió una información similar sobre los elefantes de Taprobane, aunque no citó a Onesícrito. Como explicó Weerakkody (1997: 32), las observaciones de nuestro autor son erróneas y proceden de la confusión que había en el mundo antiguo entre el tamaño de los paquidermos africanos y el de los indios.

Bastante tiempo después de la época de Plinio, entre los siglos III y IV, escribió Solino su *Collectanea rerum memorabilium*, donde también hizo referencia a Taprobane.[20] En su texto, Solino vuelve a hacer referencia a la consideración que hemos visto en Plinio acerca de la isla como "otro mundo", habitada por los antíctones. Llama la atención su referencia al hecho de que en la época de la expedición de Alejandro quedó demostrado que Taprobane era efectivamente una isla, una afirmación que en la obra de Plinio aparece bastante velada.[21] Da la impresión de que, en este pasaje concreto, Solino utilizó alguna otra u otras fuentes diferentes de Plinio, quizás Varrón o el propio Juba II,[22] para ir más allá del texto pliniano y afirmar de manera absoluta que Onesícrito viajó a la isla de Taprobane. Como estamos viendo, Solino fue el único autor antiguo que defendió la historicidad de tal hecho.

No cabe duda de que la cuestión central a la hora de analizar estos fragmentos es la de intentar averiguar quiénes fueron los informantes de Onesícrito. Según nuestra opinión, no debería considerarse que hubiese podido navegar hasta una latitud tan meridional, ni tampoco ningún otro miembro de la expedición de Alejandro, pero, además, tenemos la afortunada casualidad de que estamos especialmente informados acerca de la actividad desarrollada por nuestro autor incluso desde antes de mediados de julio del 325 a. C.[23] (llegada del grueso expedicionario macedónico a la Patalene o delta del Indo) y septiembre/octubre del mismo año (comienzo del periplo de Nearco, del que formó parte él mismo). Se ha argumentado que no era del todo imposible realizar una navegación de ida y vuelta a Sri Lanka en el plazo de los dos meses que median entre la llegada a Patalene y la partida del periplo, aunque el propio investigador ha reconocido la complicación de tal viaje debido al fuerte monzón del suroeste.[24] A esto se podría añadir que el propio Onesícrito gozó de un cargo de cierta relevancia en la organización de la navegación comandada por Nearco (aunque no tanto como él se jactaba); lo cierto es que resulta complicado pensar que hubiese estado ausente Onesícrito durante todo el periodo en el que se estaba preparando la flota que emprendería dicho periplo. De modo que únicamente cabría aceptar la hipótesis de que Onesícrito hubiese tenido que obtener información sobre la isla Taprobane mediante los informadores locales del noroeste de la India,[25] a través de uno o posiblemente más intérpretes, con todos los riesgos inherentes a este tipo de operaciones comunicativas (falta de entendimiento en cuanto a los objetivos perseguidos, afán de los interlocutores locales por agradar a los recién llegados, exageraciones típicas de los ambientes marineros, etc.)

---

[20] Sol. 53.1-2: *Taprobanem insulam, antequam temeritas humana exquisito penitus mari fidem panderet, diu orbem alterum putaverunt et quidem quem habitare Antichthones crederentur. Verum Alexandri Magni virtus ignorantiam publici erroris non tulit ulterius permanere, sed in haec usque secreta propagavit nominis sui gloriam. Missus igitur Onesicritus praefectus classis Macedonicae terram istam, quanta esset, quid gigneret, quomodo haberetur, exquisitam notitiae nostrae dedit.*

[21] Según afirma Mariotta 2017: 114.

[22] Brown 1949: 108; Sallmann 1971: 9-20.

[23] Sisti / Zambrini 2004: 546.

[24] Mariotta 2017: 118 n. 25.

[25] Weerakkody 1997: 32-33, donde recoge bibliografía anterior; Marcotte 2016: 41.

Aceptar esta hipótesis ayudaría a explicar, sobre todo, la cifra de veinte días de navegación para alcanzar la isla recogida tanto por Estrabón[26] como por Solino,[27] basándose ambos en lo escrito por Onesícrito. La versión que procede de Eratóstenes[28] (y que también sigue Plinio)[29] la establece en siete jornadas. Pues bien, esos veinte días sería la duración de un periplo comenzado en la Patalene y no la de un periplo iniciado al sur de la India, a pocos kilómetros de distancia del norte de Sri Lanka, confusión que llevó a Herrmann a pensar que Taprobane podía ser identificada con Sumatra, que efectivamente se encuentra a veinte días de navegación del extremo meridional de la India.[30]

Otra cuestión relevante a propósito de estos posibles contactos entre el noroeste de la India y Sri Lanka sería la de intentar dilucidar en la medida de lo posible cuál fue el papel de Taprobane en el terreno del comercio marítimo internacional durante la época de la expedición de Alejandro (rutas de navegación, puertos). Para ello, es imprescindible acudir al registro arqueológico cingalés, que durante las últimas décadas se ha visto favorecido de una forma considerable.

En primer lugar, hay que admitir que la mayor parte de los asentamientos portuarios excavados en Sri Lanka ofrecen una tipología similar a sus paralelos de la India occidental, que hasta la fecha son mejor conocidos. Esa tipología consiste en la existencia de un *emporion* situado en las cercanías de las desembocaduras de los ríos (o incluso, a veces, un poco antes de la propia desembocadura), pero este *emporion* siempre está bajo el control de una capital política que ha permitido su existencia por motivos de control comercial y de percepción de impuestos. De hecho, este es el panorama que podemos deducir de algunos documentos tan relevantes como el *Periplo del mar Eritreo*,[31] el famoso documento que constituye un *unicum*, de carácter subliterario,[32] y que ha sido fechado, según la opinión común, a mediados del siglo I d.C.[33] Este texto consiste en una serie de informaciones acerca de la situación comercial en la región del océano Índico, así como de diversas apreciaciones a propósito de las condiciones de navegación, remarcando los posibles peligros debido a los vientos, las aguas pocos profundas o la actitud de ciertas poblaciones locales.

---

[26] Str. XV.1.15.

[27] Sol. 53.4. En concreto, se dice que dicha travesía duraba veinte días, era realizada en embarcaciones de papiro y tenía su punto de partida en la zona de la India habitada por los prasios, cuyo reino se encontraba en la zona del Ganges, su capital era Pataliputra, y allí estuvo Megástenes como embajador de Seleuco I; desde luego, desconcierta encontrar esta información sobre los prasios en un fragmento que se piensa procede de Onesícrito. De todas maneras, el propio Solino se encarga de destacar que en época romana el tiempo de navegación se había reducido a únicamente siete días, en lo que coincidía, sobre todo, con el testimonio de Plinio.

[28] Str. XV.1.14.

[29] Plin. *NH.* VI.82.

[30] Herrmann, *RE* IV A.2 (1932), s.v. 'Taprobane' (2260-2272).

[31] Casson 1989. Por cierto, que en *PME* 61 también es mencionada Taprobane o Palaisimundu, como productora de perlas, gemas transparentes, vestidos de algodón y caparazones de tortuga.

[32] Según la opinión de Marcotte 2016: 34.

[33] Fussman 1991: 31-38; Robin 1991: 1-30. Como opinión discordante, véase Arnaud 2012: 27-61.

Asimismo, es una fuente fundamental para conocer qué productos eran importados y exportados en cada puerto, ofrece algunos nombres locales y, además, es comentada de forma somera la situación política en cada punto nodal de la región, en especial cuando las circunstancias políticas afectan de manera práctica al tráfico comercial.[34]

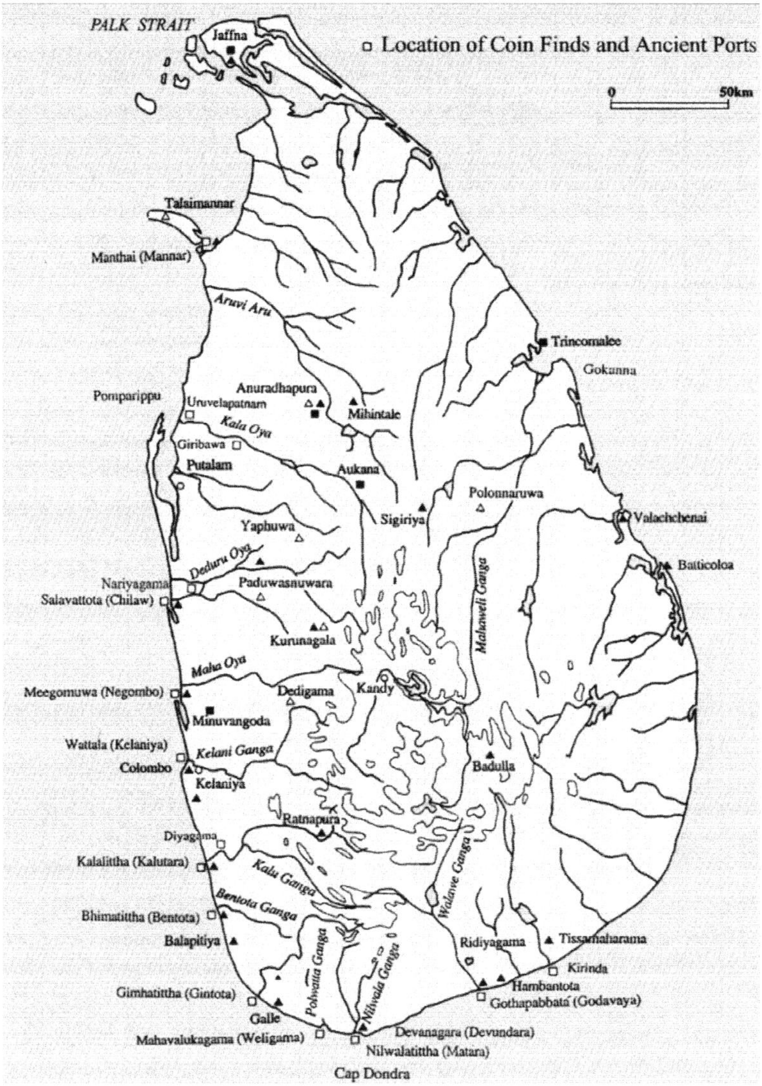

Fig. 1: Mapa de Sri Lanka.
Basado en Bopearachchi / Disanayaka / Perera 2016: 418

[34] Seland 2010.

Si regresamos a los *emporia* mencionados por el *Periplo del mar Eritreo* en la India, habría que comenzar por el de Barbarikon, cuya metrópoli era Minnagar, que pertenecía a los monarcas indo-partos.[35]

Un poco al sur del anterior, pero también en la India noroccidental, estaba el *emporion* de Barygaza,[36] su metrópolis era Minnagara, un topónimo que crea cierta confusión con el anterior, pero se trata de dos ciudades diferentes, en esta ocasión Minnagara era gobernada por los Sakas, una dinastía de origen indo-escita.

Mucho más hacia el sur, el *Periplo* menciona el puerto de Muziris, perteneciente al reino de Kêprobotos[37] o Chera, en la costa malabar o Limyrikê, que recibe mucha atención en esta obra, además de en la *Historia Natural* de Plinio,[38] en un famoso papiro egipcio,[39] en la *Tabula Peutingeriana*[40] e incluso en la poesía tamil.

El otro gran *emporion* de la India suroccidental era Nelkynda, a unos 500 estadios de Muziris, aunque pertenecía a un reino diferente, el de Pandyon (también conocido como 'Pandya'). Nelkynda también estaba cerca de un río, y a unos veinte estadios del mar.[41] Finalmente, el *Periplo* indica que los reyes que gobernaban ambos *emporia* residían en el interior, como era lo habitual en la India.[42]

En el caso de Sri Lanka, los arqueólogos han demostrado que dicho modelo de *emporion* dependiente de un centro político situado lejos de la costa pero conectado con ella a través de un curso fluvial funcionaba plenamente durante la época antigua.[43] No es casualidad que la gran mayoría de los *emporia* cingaleses se encontrasen en los estuarios de los ríos.[44] A esto hay que añadir que la propia red fluvial de Sri Lanka ofrece facilidades a ese tipo de organización político-comercial, ya que presenta un esquema radial al tener sus fuentes en las alturas que dominan la parte centro-sur del país (que van de 1.000 a 2.500 metros de altitud); se sabe que desde tiempos antiguos la isla era circunnavegada debido a la existencia de una serie de islotes y bancos de arena en el golfo de Mannar (concretamente en el Puente de Adán, la parte más cercana al subcontinente), que constituían un peligro para los barcos de gran tonelaje, por lo que las naves procedentes de los puertos de la India sudoriental navegaban a los largo de la costa oriental de Sri Lanka hasta llegar a los *emporia* situados al sur y al oeste de la isla.

---

[35] *PME* 38-39; Casson 1989: 189; Kevran 1999: 70-153.

[36] *PME* 41; Casson 1989: 198; Seland 2010: 53; McLaughlin 2014: 157-171. Otra ciudad vinculada con el *emporion* de Barygaza es Ozênê (identificada con Ujjain): *PME* 48-49.

[37] *PME* 54; McLaughlin 2014: 172-195.

[38] Plin. *NH*. VI.104-105.

[39] *P. Vindọb*. G40822.

[40] *Tab. Peut*. Seg. 12; Rathmann 2017: 98-99.

[41] *PME* 54. Es asimismo mencionado en Plin. *NH*. VI.105, donde una lambda uncial es convertida por error en una "A" mayúscula.

[42] *PME* 55.

[43] Bopearachchi 2008: 5.

[44] Bopearachchi 1999: 5-22, esp.7.

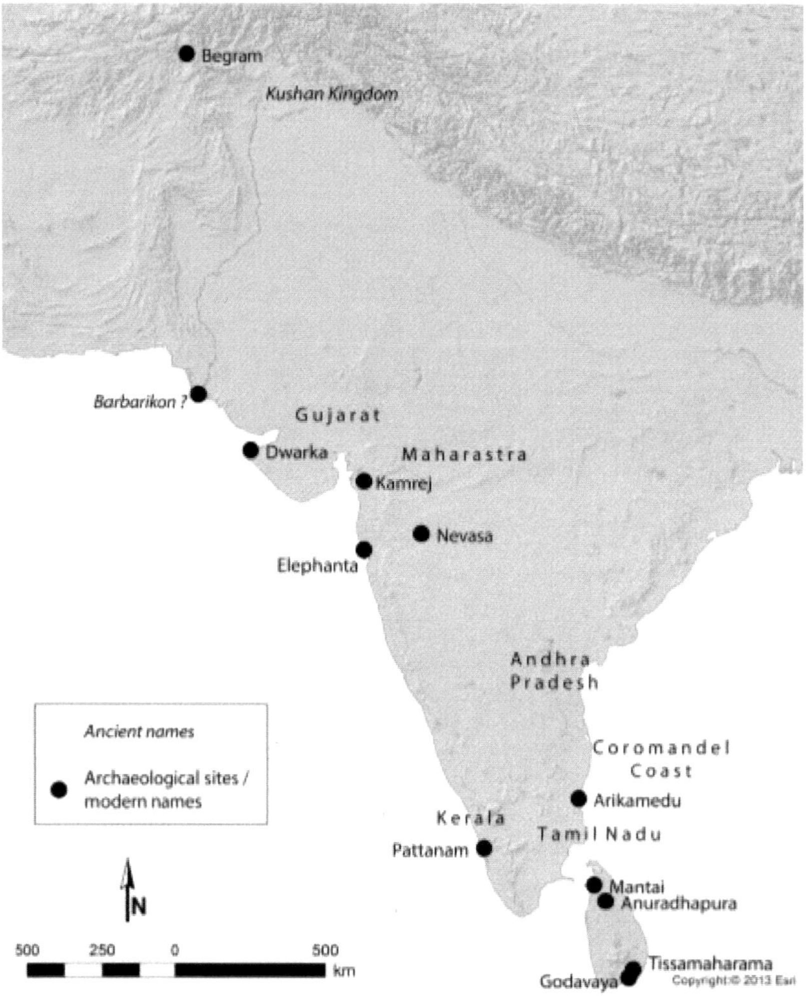

FIG. 2: EMPORIA DE LA INDIA Y TAPROBANE. BASADO EN SELAND 2010: 48

Durante los últimos años, ha tenido cierta repercusión en ambientes dedicados al estudio de las relaciones comerciales entre Occidente y la región del Índico el descubrimiento de un pecio cerca del estuario del río Walawe, en el yacimiento de Godavaya, al sur de la isla, donde se encontraban los puertos más activos.[45] Su estudio comenzó en 1994 a través de una colaboración entre el Instituto Arqueológico Alemán (DAI) y la Universidad de Bonn, y se han recuperado objetos como piedras

[45] Ray 2003: 201-203; Bopearachchi / Disanayaka / Perera 2016: 411-434, esp. 416; Kessler 2016: 435-458.

de moler, bancos ceremoniales también de piedra, recipientes de la denominada "cerámica negra y roja" (*Black and Red Ware*), [46] barras de hierro y de cobre, además de lingotes de vidrio purificado. La tipología de la cerámica encontrada, así como el análisis del C14 de los objetos de madera, han arrojado fechas del siglo II a. C., por lo que este pecio debe ser considerado el más antiguo encontrado hasta la actualidad en el océano Índico.[47]

Las investigaciones preliminares de los lingotes de vidrio permiten ver que dicho material tenía un origen en la India meridional, y está vinculado especialmente con los yacimientos de Manikollai y Appur, que todavía no han sido objeto de una excavación sistemática.[48]

En un yacimiento llamado Ridiyagama, una antigua zona de extracción de piedra preciosas situada a unos doce kilómetros río arriba de la desembocadura del mismo río Walawe,[49] se han encontrado diversos materiales (cerámica negra y roja, terracotas, escorias de cobre, carboncillos, monedas romanas) que ofrecen una cronología que abarca desde el siglo IV a. C. hasta el VII d. C.[50]

En Kelaniya, unos siete kilómetros río arriba del estuario del río Kelani, han aparecido fragmentos de cerámica negra y roja fechados en el siglo VI a. C.,[51] todo lo cual apunta a la existencia temprana de relaciones comerciales entre la India meridional (Tamil Nadu) y la isla de Sri Lanka; si bien la mayor parte de los yacimientos atestiguan la presencia de unos materiales importados de la India en fechas sensiblemente superiores a la época en que tuvo lugar la llegada de los griegos a la India.

De modo que podríamos concluir, teniendo en cuenta el estado del conocimiento de los restos arqueológicos, que no era del todo imposible un contacto indirecto entre el noroeste de la India (zona conquistada por el ejército de Alejandro e incorporada a su imperio) y la isla conocida como Taprobane. El problema es que ese contacto indirecto tenía que pasar, de forma prácticamente inevitable, por los reinos de la India sudoriental, con quienes los habitantes de Sri Lanka tenían un contacto relativamente fluido en el siglo IV a. C.[52] En todo caso, no consideramos posible que Onesícrito hubiese tenido la oportunidad de navegar a Taprobane y de haber permanecido allí el tiempo necesario como para informarse debidamente de todas las cuestiones que planteó en los fragmentos conocidos de su obra. Sin duda, durante el plazo temporal que media entre julio y septiembre/octubre del año 325 a. C. debió estar ocupado en los preparativos de la flota que comandó Nearco de Creta hasta la Susiana.

---

[46] Procedente de la India meridional y que fue introducida en Sri Lanka hacia el siglo V a. C.

[47] Bopearachchi / Disanayaka / Perera 2016: 419-425. En concreto, los análisis de C14 aplicados a los objetos de madera arrojan fechas entre el siglo II a. C. y el I d. C.

[48] Bopearachchi / Disanayaka / Perera 2016: 424-425, 432.

[49] Ray 2003: 202.

[50] Bopearachchi 1999: 13-16, 2008: 7 n. 20.

[51] Bopearachchi 1999: 10-13, 2008: 8.

[52] Véanse las interesantes conclusiones de Bopearachchi 1999: 20-22.

ALEJANDRO FUERA DE ESCENA: EL SILENCIO DE DIONISIO PERIEGETA

FRANCISCO JAVIER GÓMEZ ESPELOSÍN
(Universidad de Alcalá)

La descripción de la tierra habitada de Dionisio Periegeta, un poema en hexámetros que ofrece una panorámica global y aérea del orbe habitado, constituye ciertamente una obra singular, si bien se halla perfectamente incardinada dentro de toda la tradición poética y geográfica anterior.[1] Aunque su mirada abarca los tres continentes tradicionales, Asia ocupa un lugar destacado en esta visión sinóptica del mundo dado que se le dedica a su descripción casi la mitad del poema, 545 versos, que contrastan claramente con los 273 que ocupan conjuntamente Libia y Europa, a pesar de su menor tamaño con respecto a los otros dos continentes juntos, tal y como afirma el propio Dionisio.[2] El continente asiático era ciertamente el más cargado de significaciones y de referentes imaginarios, y en el que la seducción y el exotismo de la alteridad alcanzaban su máxima expresión, así como donde se encontraban los pueblos más numerosos y más diferentes y los lugares más diversos y más apartados, tal y como señaló en su día Christian Jacob.[3] Asia era también el territorio predilecto de una divinidad como Dioniso que desempeña en todo el poema un papel fundamental.[4] Todo ello dentro de un complejo literario en el que priman de manera primordial las alusiones y las evocaciones que suscitan los términos geográficos que en la forma de un catálogo disperso y desordenado configuran la descripción de la ecúmene.[5]

El descubrimiento de Asia aparece indisolublemente vinculado a la figura de Alejandro, que con su conquista del imperio persa abrió por primera vez al cono-

---

[1] Al respecto, Jacob 1990; Ilyushechkina 2010; Lightfoot 2014.

[2] Dionys.Per. 627.

[3] Jacob 1990: 37-38.

[4] Sobre el papel de Dioniso en el poema, Counillon 2001; Lightfoot 2014: 164-166.

[5] Jacob 1990: 39.

cimiento geográfico griego toda la inmensidad del continente asiático, que se había visto reducido hasta entonces a un esquema aparentemente mucho más manejable y difuso donde los testimonios de primera mano no eran precisamente abundantes.[6] Una notoria expansión de los conocimientos tuvo lugar a raíz de la difusión de los relatos surgidos como consecuencia de la expedición, tanto aquellos de carácter escrito que fueron obra de algunos de los que participaron en la aventura, como aquellos otros, seguramente mucho más dispersos pero acumulativamente más difundidos, que a través del testimonio oral de los veteranos y aquellos otros componentes de la marcha que retornaron a sus patrias de origen contribuyeron a difundir toda clase de informaciones a los medios griegos, una parte de las cuales acabaron filtrándose también en diferentes géneros de la literatura posterior. Muchos de estos relatos escritos confluyeron en centros del saber como la biblioteca de Alejandría, donde proporcionaron el material necesario a una obra como la de Eratóstenes que, sin necesidad de moverse de su lugar de estudio, pudo manejar a su antojo un flujo considerable de noticias y relatos acerca de las regiones asiáticas procedentes tanto los que participaron en la conquista como de otros viajeros helenísticos posteriores que como Patrocles, Megástenes, Daímaco y otros incrementaron todavía más los conocimientos acerca toda esta parte del orbe.[7] Tanto Polibio como después Estrabón continuaron atribuyendo a Alejandro el mérito indiscutible de haber hecho transitable y accesible esta parte del orbe a pesar de que desde entonces había ido aumentando el cúmulo de evidencias surgidas posteriormente.[8]

Parecía así casi imposible evitar o marginar la memoria, al menos latente, del conquistador macedonio en cualquier descripción del continente asiático, por apresurada y sintética que fuera, dado que la gran mayor parte de las informaciones disponibles, los nombres de lugares y pueblos o algunos de sus principales referentes geográficos procedían en última instancia del testimonio de primera mano de los denominados historiadores de Alejandro, que, aun con todas sus limitaciones y prejuicios a favor de la gesta heroica de su protagonista, describieron de manera más o menos intensa y detallada los escenarios de la conquista como resultado de su propia experiencia personal durante su recorrido por la zona.[9] No sabemos si Dionisio pudo utilizar o no de forma directa las obras de estos historiadores, que quizá todavía se hallaban disponibles en la biblioteca alejandrina en su tiempo, o si tuvo acceso a ellos a través de la obra de Eratóstenes que previamente los había utilizado como fuente de información preferente para la confección de su geografía a pesar de las

---

[6] Sobre el descubrimiento de Asia por Alejandro, Bunbury 1879: 407-524; Cary / Warmington 1929: 142-149; Van Paassen 1957: 263-288; Thomson 1965: 123-136; Pédech 1976: 75-83; Roller 2015: 90-104. Sobre la significación geográfica de la conquista, Gehrke 2015; Stevens 2016.

[7] Al respecto, Berger 1903: 384-440; Geus 2002: 260-288; Roller 2010: 15-30. Sobre las capacidades de Alejandría en este aspecto, Jacob 1999.

[8] Plb. III.59.3; Str. I.2.1.

[9] Sobre la importancia de dicha contribución, Van Paassen 1957: 267-269.

acusaciones de parcialidad y adulación que les atribuye.[10] El carácter compilatorio y ecléctico del poema, en el que se amontonan, a veces en un cierto desorden y confusión, topónimos y etnónimos de todo tipo y procedencia invitan a pensar en una utilización de esta clase de fuentes a través de intermediarios diversos que conducen a repertorios más generales como los de Eratóstenes o Posidonio.[11]

Las huellas del paso de Alejandro por Asia en el poema de Dionisio parecen a primera vista inexistentes, dado que su nombre no aparece mencionado en ningún momento en el curso de la obra. Es cierto que tampoco lo hacen otras figuras históricas, ni siquiera romanas a pesar de que el autor declara de forma solemne su pertenencia a este imperio proclamando a Roma 'la sede de sus soberanos y la madre de todas las ciudades'.[12] Ni siquiera el nombre de Adriano figura de forma explícita en el texto a pesar de que fue durante su reinado cuando Dionisio compuso su obra, limitando su aparición a un acróstico que solo se descubrió en el curso del siglo XIX.[13] Escasean igualmente las referencias históricas que se reducen a algunas acciones romanas como la exterminación de los nasamones en tiempos de Domiciano o la victoria conseguida por Trajano contra los partos.[14] El contexto general del poema remite esencialmente a referentes de carácter mítico a la vista de la importancia que adquieren los itinerarios de los grandes viajes heroicos como los de Jasón, Ulises, Heracles o Dioniso,[15] relegando al silencio o a la alusión mejor o peor fundamentada a los protagonistas históricos más destacados.

La mayoría de las posibles alusiones a la actividad de Alejandro permanecen casi siempre vinculadas a la ambigüedad significativa de ciertos topónimos cuya estrecha asociación con la conquista del monarca macedonio parece casi incuestionable. Sin embargo, su entrada como referentes ya tópicos dentro de la tradición literaria posterior, donde ocupan ya su lugar respectivo junto a otros topónimos y etnónimos de la zona que pueden derivar de otros testimonios ajenos al relato de la expedición y constituyen ya un complejo difícil de separar en función de sus procedencias originales, nos obliga a ser enormemente cautos a la hora de encontrar tales referentes provistos de esta clara intencionalidad. Tan solo algunas expresiones calificativas permiten a veces dilucidar la cuestión de forma más plausible, como la calificación de 'navegable para las naves' que se hace del río Hidaspes, una acción que remite

---

[10] Jacob 1999: 30-32.

[11] Sobre las fuentes de Dionisio, Counillon 2013; Lightfoot 2014: 27-45. En particular sobre el uso de los historiadores de Alejandro, Lightfoot 2014: 153, 175.

[12] Dionys.Per. 355-356. Sobre Dionisio y Roma, Bowie 2004; Lightfoot 2014: 176-178.

[13] El acróstico en Dionys.Per. 513-532. Jacob 1991 cree encontrar el reflejo de los viajes emprendidos por el emperador en el curso del poema. En contra se muestra Lightfoot 2014: 176 n.174, donde argumenta acerca la significativa ausencia de referentes tan señalados desde el punto de vista adrianeo como Hadrianoutherai en Misia o Antinópolis en Egipto o el escaso espacio dedicado a Grecia donde tuvo lugar una actividad destacada por parte de un emperador filoheleno como Adriano.

[14] Dionys.Per. 208-210 (nasamones), 1050-1052 (partos).

[15] Al respecto, Jacob 1990: 44-51.

casi de forma segura al paso de la flota macedonia por sus aguas en el momento del retorno de la expedición durante su descenso del Indo.[16]

También aparece claramente asociado a la campaña del monarca macedonio un lugar emblemático como las denominadas Puertas del Caspio, convertido en un punto clave en el desarrollo de la expedición que sirvió además de punto de partida para muchas de las mediciones realizadas en el curso de la conquista posterior.[17] Su mención en el poema se decanta claramente a favor del paso atravesado en su día por Alejandro en la región situada al sur del mar Caspio cuando iba en persecución de Darío, frente a la ambigüedad existente en la tradición posterior a la hora de su precisa localización, con su alternativa posición situada en la zona del Cáucaso que adquirió además un mayor protagonismo con algunas campañas romanas por la zona.[18] La expresión que se utiliza para calificarlas, 'las claves de la tierra asiática' (*kleídes gaíes Asiétidos*), indica efectivamente la importancia que adquirió dicho enclave en la tradición posterior como punto de referencia inevitable a la hora de describir siquiera de forma general la topografía de Asia. Su importancia y la capacidad evocativa del término iban estrechamente ligadas a la memoria de Alejandro, dado que fue a partir de aquel punto tan significativo y emblemático cuando inició una nueva etapa de la conquista, adentrándose en un espacio nuevo y desconocido que le conduciría hasta los confines extremos del imperio persa.[19]

Las regiones situadas en torno al Caspio y la condición o concepción del propio mar aparecen también claramente asociadas al paso de Alejandro por toda la zona. La descripción de dicho mar como un golfo septentrional del océano exterior, en claro contraste con la imagen difundida por Heródoto o Aristóteles, que lo consideraban un mar interior, derivaba en buena medida de las aspiraciones ecuménicas del conquistador macedonio que, vistas así las cosas, habría conseguido alcanzar las costas del océano septentrional cuyas aguas penetraban tierra adentro a través del supuesto golfo hircanio, tal y como debieron proclamarlo al menos sus principales portavoces propagandísticos. Esta curiosa percepción del mar centroasiático fue aparentemente confirmada por exploraciones ulteriores como la de Patrocles y perduró durante bastante tiempo en la tradición geográfica posterior ya con independencia de las pretensiones de Alejandro, quien, por otro lado, no estaba del todo convencido de que la realidad geográfica se ajustara del todo a dicha teoría y de hecho envió en sus últimos días una expedición hacia la zona con el objetivo de comprobar *in situ* la veracidad de dichas suposiciones.[20] Sin embargo, de nuevo la calificación que se

---

[16] Dionys.Per. 1138.

[17] Plin. *NH.* VI.45. Sobre las Puertas del Caspio, Anderson 1928; Standish 1980; Prontera 2012.

[18] Dionys.Per. 1034-1038.

[19] Acerca del papel fundamental como límite geográfico que dicho punto geográfico desempeñó en la leyenda posterior de Alejandro, Stoneman 1994; 2008: 77-83.

[20] Sobre el tópico de alcanzar los límites de orbe, Bichler 2011: 324-326. Sobre las pretensiones de Alejandro, Str. 11.7.4. Bosworth 1988: 109; Demandt 2009: 218-220. Sobre la percepción del Caspio en la geografía

hace de sus aguas como un ámbito de navegación difícil (*póros ameílichos*), seguramente reflejo de un *tópos* que aparece también en autores anteriores como Mela (*minus nauigabile*),[21] podría quizá remitir también a la descripción inicial del mar realizada por algunos de los historiadores de Alejandro, que dejaron constancia de la presencia de grandes serpientes en sus aguas,[22] un aspecto que con las consabidas exageraciones y deformaciones resultaría fácilmente extrapolable como un elemento más de los llamados terrores del océano, que circularon por la tradición posterior, tal y como aparece reflejado después en un autor como Avieno.[23]

La topografía y etnografía de las inmediaciones del Caspio se halla igualmente relacionada con los ecos de la campaña de Alejandro en la zona a través de la mención de una serie de pueblos situados en ella, si bien algunos de ellos eran ya conocidos desde mucho tiempo antes.[24] Este es el caso particularmente de los mardos, que hasta el momento de la conquista macedonia tan solo aparecen mencionados como parte de los contingentes militares persas. Sin embargo, durante la campaña asiática fueron el objeto específico de una campaña por parte de Alejandro durante el curso de la cual tuvo lugar el rapto del caballo preferido del rey, Bucéfalo, lo que suscitó la ira del monarca que amenazó con devastar por completo su territorio.[25] Fue precisamente la actuación de Alejandro en esta zona la que condicionó la aparición y mención de los mardos en algunas campañas romanas posteriores, que trasladaban su ubicación a la región de Armenia.[26] De hecho, en el pasaje de Dionisio aparecen asociados a ellos otros pueblos como los hircanos y los tapiros, que se hallan también estrechamente relacionados con las campañas del conquistador macedonio en esta zona.[27] Aunque se asume que la fuente de información más probable de esta parte del poema sea Eratóstenes,[28] la importancia que tuvieron los historiadores de Alejandro en la construcción de la geografía del estudioso alejandrino conserva casi intacto el poder de resonancia que ejercían tales nombres a la hora de recordar la actuación del monarca macedonio en la zona.

Otros pueblos limítrofes como los corasmios y los sogdianos que figuran un poco más adelante en el texto, aparecen también vinculados estrechamente a las campañas

---

posterior, Str. XI.6, 1; Mela III.38; Plin. *NH.* VI.36; Gardiner / Garden 1987; McPhail-Hannah 2008-2011. En general, véase Pyankov 2014. Sobre la expedición de Heráclides al Caspio, véase Arr. *An.* VII.16.1.

21 Mela III.38.

22 D.S. XVII.75.3; Curt. VI.4.18.

23 Además del citado pasaje de Mela, cf. Hor. *Od.* II.9.2; Avien. *Or. Mar.* 102. Sobre la visión negativa del océano, Evans 2005.

24 Dionys.Per. 732-734.

25 D.S. XVII.76; Arr. *An.* III.24.1-3; Curt. VI.5.11-21. Arr. *An.* V.19.6 sitúa el rapto de Bucéfalo en el curso de la campaña contra los uxios.

26 Gregoratti 2014; Bosworth 1980: 351-352: «it was presumably the campaigns of Alexander which revealed their existence to the Greek World».

27 Arr. *An.* III.23.1.

28 Tsavari 1990: 87 (Frg. III B, 68-70 Berger = Str. XI.6.1, 11.5, 7.1).

de Alejandro, así como los dos ríos principales de toda esta región centroasiática, el Oxo y el Yaxartes.[29] Indudablemente la confusa topografía de la zona que presenta Dionisio nada tiene que ver con la descripción algo más detallada que figuraba en los historiadores de Alejandro que utilizaron los dos cursos fluviales como ejes definitorios de las dos grandes regiones, Bactria y Sogdiana, que conformaban las denominadas satrapías superiores y se convirtieron en el escenario más complicado y difícil de toda la campaña oriental. La precisión geográfica no era el punto fuerte del poeta pero posiblemente la selección de los términos utilizados posee ciertamente un poder evocador importante por los hechos que aparecen vinculados a ellos dentro de la memoria colectiva que podía conformar su auditorio.[30] La ubicación de los sacas al otro lado del Yaxartes y su destreza como arqueros podría igualmente apuntar a la campaña que Alejandro llevó a cabo contra ellos después de atravesar el río en su persecución.

Una significación particular adquiere también el nombre del Cáucaso, aplicado en esta ocasión a la cadena montañosa del Hindu Kush, que según el testimonio de Estrabón utilizaron los historiadores de Alejandro con la idea de ensalzar las hazañas del monarca macedonio a un nivel mítico y heroico, asimilando el mítico topónimo que delimitaba el orbe por su vertiente oriental a la cadena montañosa que separaba la India de Asia central.[31] Dionisio utiliza el término en dos ocasiones para hacer referencia a la cordillera a pesar de la emergencia ocasional del nombre Parpaniso que recuerda indudablemente al de Paropamisos con el que los habitantes del lugar la designaban, al menos a una de sus partes.[32] Incluso el propio Arriano, que demuestra ser bien consciente de la maniobra propagandística que implicaba trasladar hacia oriente la cadena montañosa situada en el istmo caucásico más occidental, se decanta también por la utilización más generalizada del término mítico a la hora de describir la campaña en aquella zona. La poderosa resonancia mítica del término en sí se trasfiere a toda la tradición conservada y revela su tremendo poder evocador en este sentido, a pesar de todas las justificaciones de carácter metodológico que Arriano parece alegar para su uso.[33] Incluso la calificación de 'ventoso' (*enemoeís*) que le adjudica Dionisio podría quizá reflejar, aunque sea de forma lejana, las condiciones climáticas adversas que debió afrontar la expedición durante su paso a través de la cordillera además de ser el resultado natural de su orientación hacia el norte, que es destacada en algunos de los testimonios.[34]

La experiencia de Alejandro en la India dejó sin duda su huella en la imagen geográfica del país que aparece reflejada en el poema de Dioniso a pesar de la con-

---

[29] Dionys.Per. 746-749, 1064.

[30] Sobre el poder de esta memoria evocativa en las menciones de carácter geográfico, véase Lightfoot 2014: 113.

[31] Dionys.Per. 1092 y 1134. Sobre la maniobra propagandística a favor de Alejandro, véase Str. XI.5.5; Arr. *An.* V.3.3, *Ind.* 2.3-4.

[32] Arr. *An.* V.3.3.

[33] Arr. *An.* V.5.3.

[34] D.S. XVII.82.2; Curt. VII.3.7.

fusa mezcolanza que impera en el conjunto a causa de la inserción de otra clase de testimonios posteriores. El carácter inmenso del Indo (*apeirésios*), que es convenientemente subrayado en el poema, podría así recordar efectivamente la primera impresión del río contemplada desde la perspectiva de los expedicionarios macedonios que llegaron ante él, provocando que lo calificaran como el más grande de todos los ríos que habían atravesado hasta entonces en el curso de la campaña.[35] Solo el conocimiento del Ganges, primero a través de testimonios orales durante el propio curso de la expedición[36] y después mediante testimonios posteriores como el de Megástenes, condicionó a la baja esta primera sensación de la contemplación del Indo, a pesar de que superaba con creces a cualquiera de los cursos fluviales europeos.

Como se ha señalado antes, la calificación 'navegable para las naves' (*plotós neésin*) con la que se designa al Hidaspes, hace indudablemente referencia a la construcción de la flota macedonia en esta región junto a las orillas del río y a su posterior utilización en el descenso del río hacia la desembocadura en el océano, una vez decidida la retirada a orillas del Hífasis.[37] Esta impresión podría verse reforzada además por la alusión a la confluencia del río con el Acesines, un punto de la navegación fluvial que se convirtió en un auténtico quebradero de cabeza para los macedonios por la violencia del cauce que provocaba el choque entre las embarcaciones.[38] También la caracterización del río Acesines, 'que se precipita desde promontorios rocosos' (*apó skopélon surómenos*), podría recordar la descripción que hacía Arriano del mismo río, remitiendo la procedencia de su información al respecto al relato de Tolomeo, que según afirma el propio Arriano era además el único de los ríos de la India que describió el historiador de Alejandro, con una corriente muy fuerte que arrastraba grandes y puntiagudas piedras contra las que se chocaban y se estrellaban las naves macedonias.[39]

La mención de la isla de Taprobane, descubierta también su existencia, aunque indudablemente desde la distancia, en el curso de la expedición macedonia, constituye también otra posibilidad en este sentido.[40] La isla fue dada a conocer en el relato de Onesícrito que al parecer proporcionaba información sobre su tamaño y su posición meridional, destacando especialmente la presencia de monstruos anfibios en el mar alrededor de la isla, semejantes a bueyes, a caballos y a otros animales terrestres.[41] La expresión utilizada por Dioniso para referirse a este tipo de bestias marinas como 'ganados del mar Eritreo' (*Eruthaíou Botá póntou*) parece resumir la comparación más diversificada que ofrecía Onesícrito a este respecto. Destaca tam-

---

35 Arr. *An*. V.4.

36 Bosworth 1996: 186-200.

37 Dionys.Per. 1139.

38 Arr. *An*. VI.4; Curt. IX.4.9-14.

39 Arr. *An*. V.20.8.

40 Dionys.Per. 591-605.

41 *FGrH* 134 F 12 (= Str. XV.1.15); Brown 1949: 93; Karttunen 1997: 215-216.

bién su afirmación sobre la isla como 'madre de los elefantes nacidos en Asia', un tipo de información que procede igualmente en su origen del relato de Onesícrito, si bien se convirtió luego, incrementada con el relato correspondiente de Megástenes en esta dirección, en un verdadero tópico acerca de la isla, tal y como se hacen eco diferentes testimonios.[42]

En el poema podrían evidenciarse también, de manera más o menos directa, algunos ecos del viaje de Nearco a través de las aguas del Índico. La mención de pueblos como los gedrosios y los carmanios, que constituyeron los sucesivos referentes costeros de la navegación del almirante cretense a las órdenes de Alejandro, podría apuntar en esta dirección, pero de manera especial lo hace la alusión a la cercanía de los primeros a las aguas oceánicas donde habitaban grandes cetáceos, que parece un inequívoco recuerdo del célebre episodio del encuentro con las ballenas, cuya repentina irrupción desde el fondo del mar provocó primero la sorpresa y el miedo de los marinos y luego una mayor confianza en su almirante al comprobar que los animales huían despavoridos a causa del ruido originado por el sonido de las trompetas y el entrechocar de los remos, en una acción auspiciada por el almirante macedonio.[43] Un origen similar podría tener también la noticia acerca de la existencia de una isla situada lejos del promontorio de Carmania en la que se hallaba la tumba del rey Eritro que daba nombre a todo el mar y a la región circundante. De hecho, el nombre de Ogiris que Dionisio otorga a la isla coincide con el que figura también en Mela, Plinio y Estebán de Bizancio, una circunstancia que provocó en su día la corrección en la lectura de los códices de Estrabón, que atribuye dicha denominación a los relatos de Nearco y Ortágoras.[44] Curiosamente, la localización de la isla tomando como referente en la costa el promontorio de Carmania figura tan solo en el testimonio de Estrabón, procedente seguramente de Eratóstenes, y en el poema de Dionisio, lo que podría interpretarse como una indicación ulterior de la derivación originaria de dicha información a partir de un periplo por la costa como fue la navegación de Nearco.

La mención de las dos bocas del río Indo en su desembocadura en aguas del océano y la existencia de una isla situada en medio, llamada Patalene, podría tener su origen en esta misma experiencia marítima, si bien parece que la forma del nombre deriva del testimonio de Aristobulo, autor al que remite constantemente Estrabón cuando utiliza sucesivamente el término en el curso de su descripción.[45] Quizá la atribución del nombre a la isla situada entre las dos bocas obedece en este caso a una

---

[42] Karttunen 1997: 339; Lightfoot 2014: 397.

[43] Dionys.Per. 1082-1087. Sobre el episodio de las ballenas, Arr. *Ind.* 30.

[44] Dionys.Per. 606-607. El nombre de Ogiris figura en Mela III.79; Plin. *NH.* VI.153. Los códices de Estrabón presentaban la lectura Tyrine, con la excepción del Epítome que ofrecía Tyrrene. Fue corregida por algunos editores como Salmasius y Kramer siguiendo la pauta que aparece en los textos latinos mencionados y en el propio Dionisio. Jacoby, en cambio, opta por la crux para el pasaje de forma más prudente a la vista de que en Arr. *Ind.* 37.2-3 aparece el nombre de Organa.

[45] Dionys.Per. 1093-1094; Str. XV.1.13, 17.

mala interpretación de la topografía del lugar, algo mejor apreciada y valorada desde la perspectiva marítima de Nearco que circulaba con la flota por allí, cuyo testimonio parece haber quedado reflejado en Arriano, que atribuye el topónimo a una ciudad situada junto al inicio del lugar donde se escindía el curso del río.[46]

Existen también otras posibles alusiones en el curso del poema, si bien en este caso se trata más de términos aislados aunque inevitablemente cargados de significado, en buena medida si no del todo debido a su papel en el curso de la expedición macedonia. Llama así la atención la mención de la ciudad de Isos, si bien el pasaje concreto donde aparece presenta algunos importantes problemas de carácter textual. En los versos 118 y 119 se citan sucesivamente la ciudad y el golfo de Issos como el referente geográfico que parece definir la zona más oriental del Mediterráneo situada entre Cilicia y Chipre, sin que en ningún momento se haga mención o alusión a su condición como escenario de la célebre batalla entre Alejandro y Darío III librada en sus inmediaciones en el otoño del 333 a.C.[47] La ciudad como tal aparece ya mencionada en el curso del *Anábasis* de Jenofonte, en dos ocasiones, en un momento, por tanto, anterior a la celebración allí de la famosa batalla, en una cita donde priman aspectos como la condición fronteriza de la ciudad con Cilicia, un punto clave para indicar el avance de la expedición hacia oriente, o su carácter de comunidad urbana habitada, grande y próspera.[48] Sin embargo, la relevancia de la ciudad dentro de la tradición literaria aparece estrechamente asociada al recuerdo de la batalla, tal y como sucede en la descripción de Mela, y, de hecho, la referencia utilizada en otros momentos del poema para indicar esta delimitación oriental del Mediterráneo toma su punto de partida en la propia región de Panfilia, sin mencionar para nada el nombre de la ciudad.[49] La denominación del golfo cercano a la ciudad aparece ya en Estrabón, si bien su mención se atribuye a Eratóstenes, al que se critica por haber concedido crédito a quien(es) afirmaba(n) que se trataba del punto más oriental del Mediterráneo.[50] Dejando a un lado las dificultades textuales existentes, que ponen en tela de juicio la pertenencia legítima de ambos versos a la estructura original del poema,[51] la existencia dentro de la tradición anterior de su uso como simple delimitador geográfico de la extensión más oriental del Mediterráneo, cuya difusión pudo estar más o menos influida por la celebración de la famosa batalla, nos obliga a pensar que su condición de lugar de memoria asociado estrechamente a la figura

---

[46] Arr. *An.* VI.18.2. De hecho, el relato más detallado y preciso de Nearco describía la existencia de otras islas en la zona.

[47] Dionys.Per. 118-119.

[48] X. *An.* I.2.24, 4.1.

[49] Dionys.Per. 46, 508.

[50] Str. I.3.2, II.5.25.

[51] Existen dificultades con ambos versos desde un punto de vista textual, especialmente con el primero de ellos que rompe por completo el acróstico entre los versos 112-134: Amato 2004: 3; Lightfoot 2014: 289. Su ausencia en las traducciones latinas de Dionisio por parte de Avieno y Prisciano puede resultar significativa acerca de la validez de tales versos.

de Alejandro ni siquiera pudo figurar de forma prevalente en la intención del autor de la interpolación.

Llama también la atención en este mismo sentido la curiosa referencia que se hace a Alejandría como "la ciudad macedonia" que podría hacer alusión tanto a la circunstancia de su fundación por designio de Alejandro como a su condición de capital de los Tolomeos dado el estatus restrictivo que mantuvo la ciudad durante tanto tiempo, reflejado incluso en su propia denominación.[52] Sin embargo, la existencia de paralelos notorios en la primera de las interpretaciones, que hacen inequívocamente hincapié en la figura del monarca fundador,[53] y la importancia de esta situación en la memoria colectiva asociada tanto a la topografía urbana como a su historia[54] sugieren la posibilidad de que la escueta pero significativa alusión de Dionisio a su propia patria natal pueda interpretarse como un cierto guiño sesgado, quizá incluso no inocente, a la persona de su ilustre fundador que condicionó desde entonces, incluido el propio nombre de la ciudad, toda su identidad como tal.

La existencia de referentes geográficos en el poema que pudieran contener la evocación de las acciones de Alejandro podría todavía incrementarse a través de la mención de algunos topónimos significativos, cuyo poder connotativo fundamental conduce inevitablemente hacia las acciones de nuestro protagonista en tal escenario. Este sería el caso del santuario de Amón en el oasis de Siwah, cuya catalogación en el poema como 'rodeado de mucha arena'[55] puede aludir naturalmente a su condición de lugar situado en medio del desierto líbico, una ubicación bien conocida antes del viaje de Alejandro hasta el lugar, pero existe también la posibilidad de que con dicha calificación se haga alusión a las penurias y dificultades que condicionaron el viaje del monarca macedonio hasta alcanzar el santuario, que son pertinentemente reflejadas en toda la tradición conservada,[56] dejando, sin embargo, en un segundo plano el viaje de retorno donde las mismas circunstancias adversas podían resultar ya prescindibles desde un punto de vista narrativo. De hecho, a pesar de que Siwah fue el destino de héroes como Perseo y Heracles, que habrían motivado en parte el deseo de Alejandro de llegar hasta él, Dionisio omite por completo cualquier referencia en este sentido, una laguna quizá también significativa dada la tendencia del autor a reflejar en su descripción las huellas de los itinerarios heroicos por las diferentes partes del orbe.

Este podría ser también el caso de la ciudad de Aspendos, cuya mención en Dionisio parece solamente justificada a causa de los sacrificios de cerdos que allí tenían

---

[52] Dionys.Per. 254.

[53] Lightfoot 2014: 319.

[54] En este sentido, Howe 2014.

[55] Dionys.Per. 212.

[56] Así en Arr. *An.* III.4.1; Curt. IV.7.6; Plu. *Alex.* 26.11; D.S. XVII.49.3, se insiste especialmente en esta circunstancia.

lugar en honor de Afrodita.[57] La ciudad, que parece inicialmente desprovista de una historia relevante que la hiciera figurar como referente dentro de la zona, desempeñó en cambio un papel relativamente destacado durante la conquista macedonia al haber manifestado una cierta resistencia al avance de Alejandro en la región. El episodio ocupa incluso una cierta relevancia en el relato de Arriano que dedica cierta atención a su topografía urbana y al paso por ella del río Eurimedonte y se convierte así en el acontecimiento mejor conocido de la historia de la ciudad.[58] La celebración de la batalla librada tiempo antes por los atenienses contra los persas en el mencionado río, citada oportunamente por Mela que parece además disociar en cierto modo la ciudad del río,[59] no aparece por ningún lado en Dionisio quien, en cambio, vincula entre sí ambos elementos geográficos a la manera en la que aparecen también asociados en las gestas del monarca macedonio.

En otros casos, sin embargo, algunos elementos topográficos significativos en la evocación de la memoria de Alejandro aparecen ahora en Dionisio trasferidos oportunamente a Dionisos que parece ocupar el lugar del monarca macedonio en la gesta india asumiendo por completo la gloria de su conquista y convirtiéndose a la vez en el marcador referencial de toda esta parte de la ecúmene. Se atribuyen así al dios las columnas que marcaban por oriente el final de sus campañas en un espacio cercano al Ganges, un lugar que iba mucho más allá del límite más occidental alcanzado por la conquista de Alejandro, obligado a detenerse en el Hífasis ante la negativa de sus tropas a continuar adelante.[60] La pretensión de Alejandro de haber superado con su acciones de conquista las hazañas anteriores de sus ilustres predecesores, yendo más allá de donde había llegado Heracles e incluso triunfando donde había fracasado antes el héroe, queda así inevitablemente neutralizada al equiparar los límites efectivos de Asia con los confines geográficos alcanzados por Dionisos, más allá de los cuales se abría ya solo el océano exterior, mientras que Alejandro tuvo que renunciar a ir más allá del Hífasis a pesar de que poseía informaciones acerca de los territorios que se extendían en aquella dirección y de sus expectativas de contemplar finalmente el océano en esta parte del orbe. Dionisio traslada hasta allí también la ubicación de Nisa, que fue visitada en su momento por Alejandro en un emplazamiento geográfico mucho más occidental, en una región situada entre los ríos Cofén e Indo.[61] Una ubicación a orillas del Ganges en un lugar donde el dios castigó de forma rotunda a aquellos que profanaron sus ritos que se sitúa contra el resto de la tradición, recordando de nuevo en el pasaje final del poema la erección de las columnas en los confines orientales de la tierra que conmemoraban su glorioso triunfo sobre aquellas gentes.[62]

---

[57] Dionys.Per. 851-853.
[58] Arr. *An.* I.26-27.
[59] Mela I.78.
[60] Dionys.Per. 624-626.
[61] Arr. *An.* V.1.
[62] Dionys.Per. 1152-1160. Al respecto, Lightfoot 2014: 404-406, 501-503.

Allí se traslada también el enclave de Aornos, situado originalmente en el relato secuencial de la conquista junto al Indo, el lugar donde Alejandro hubo de desplegar todo su talento estratégico para conquistar la plaza y superar de este modo el fracaso habido en su día por el propio Heracles.[63] De la gesta realizada, en el poema solo queda el nombre, explicado por la fácil y falsa etimología que lo hacía derivar del término 'inaccesible a las aves', y la condición elevada y el difícil acceso de la roca (*elíbatos*, *dusémbatos*) sin que ni siquiera se la llegue a relacionar con ninguna hazaña del dios.[64] Da la impresión de que toda la geografía oriental del mundo habitado con sus lugares más significativos en la India ha sido trasferida al protagonismo indiscutible de Dionisos que ocupa de este modo el lugar de Alejandro y define además con sus acciones de conquista los límites efectivos de la ecúmene en ambos extremos del orbe, superando así claramente las hazañas de un héroe que redujo su campo de acción a tan solo una sola parte del mismo. Dionisos se convierte de este modo en el verdadero *leitmotiv* de su geografía de Asia, suplantando de este modo las huellas todavía visibles de las conquistas del monarca macedonio, a las que remitía inevitablemente una buena parte de toda la toponimia asiática y que han quedado bien reflejadas en testimonios posteriores como *la Vida de Apolonio* de Filóstrato o la propia Tabula Peutingeriana.[65]

Ciertamente nos vemos obligados a movernos en puras especulaciones a la vista de referentes claros y precisos o alusiones inequívocamente dirigidas hacia un significado determinado, en medio de un juego de resonancias literarias y simbólicas en el que los lectores antiguos y los intérpretes modernos no jugamos con las mismas cartas. El propio carácter esotérico de todo el poema, que esconde incluso el nombre de su autor en un acróstico que había pasado desapercibido hasta el siglo XIX a pesar de la presencia destacada que el poema tiene en la tradición posterior,[66] y el origen de su autor, un alejandrino que tenía a su alcance los numerosos recursos todavía disponibles en su célebre biblioteca, abonan en cierta medida todo este tipo de propuestas arriesgadas. Lo cierto es que Alejandro ha desaparecido por completo de la escena dentro de una imagen del mundo que tiene Asia como el escenario privilegiado de toda la descripción ecuménica a pesar de que la mayoría de los topónimos y etnónimos que configuran este continente remiten inevitablemente a la memoria del conquistador macedonio que fue quien los hizo entrar a muchos de ellos por la puerta grande dentro del imaginario colectivo después de su sorprendente conquista de todos estos territorios.

Llama igualmente la atención que este silencio o marginación de Alejandro por parte de Dionisio contrasta con otras descripciones generales del orbe como la que

63 Arr. *An*. IV.28-30.
64 Dionys.Per. 1150-1151.
65 Sobre el papel de Dioniso en el poema de Dionisio, véase Counillon 2001.
66 Jacob 1990: 13-14.

figura en las *Astronomica* de Manilio, claramente también integrada dentro de la órbita imperial romana, donde sin que la figura de Alejandro acapare tampoco demasiada atención su presencia alusiva se reconoce claramente al menos en la referencia al principado de la casa de Pela.[67] Alejandro figura también en la descripción de Mela, donde se le menciona expresamente como el conquistador de Asia y se asocia su nombre a determinados lugares como el río Gránico, escenario de la primera gran batalla contra los persas, la ciudad de Isos, donde tuvo lugar otra batalla decisiva contra Darío III, o la ciudad fenicia de Tiro por haber modificado su propia morfología física.[68] Alejandro ocupa también su lugar correspondiente dentro de la descripción del orbe contenida en la *Naturalis Historia* de Plinio el Viejo donde aparece convenientemente asociado a sus grandes eventos y fundaciones e incluso se destacan también algunos otros aspectos más colaterales como modificaciones del territorio en ciertos lugares de Asia Menor o su paso o creación de otros establecimientos menos señalados.[69]

Alejandro ha quedado completamente al margen de una obra de aspiraciones ecuménicas, en claro contraste con otros intentos similares, y ni siquiera sus pretensiones de aupar su figura a la categoría mítico-divina parece que fueron suficientes para granjearle un lugar dentro de una obra que tiene el mito y la divinidad como sus ejes estructurales fundamentales. La tentativa extraordinaria para englobar en un mismo texto el mundo de los hombres, el mundo de los mitos, el mundo de los dioses y el poder de los astros a la que alude Christian Jacob[70] para caracterizar sumariamente la obra de Dionisio ha dejado fuera a Alejandro que aspiraba en sus últimos años a ocupar su lugar correspondiente en el nivel más elevado dentro de esta jerarquía. El dominio del orbe se halla ahora en manos de Roma que se ha convertido en el referente fundamental en torno al que gira también el mundo descrito por Dionisio,[71] y la divinidad, particularmente Zeus, es la garante de su orden y estabilidad, o en el caso de Dionisos es quien otorga los dones de la divinidad a los seres humanos y quien, nuevamente en palabras de Christian Jacob, 'balise l'oecumène'.[72] Ni siquiera su emulación primero y su superación después de un héroe como Heracles ni tampoco el haber seguido los pasos de Dionisos a través de Asia reconociendo en determinados lugares las huellas de su presencia o el haber participado activamente en su culto

---

[67] Man. *Astr.* IV.585-744. La alusión aparece en el v. 690. Sobre la geografía de Manilio, véase Abry 2000.

[68] Mela I.66 (Tiro); 70 (Iso); 98 (Gránico); II.34 (conquistador de Asia).

[69] Plin. *NH.* II.185 (Patala); V.62 (fundación de Alejandría); V.76 (asedio de Tiro); VI.40 (puertas del Caspio); II.180 y VI.41 (victoria de Arbela); VI.49 (Alejandría la última); VI.60 (navegación por el Indo); VI.100 (fiestas de Susa); VI.115 (destrucción de Persépolis); IV.75 (paso por la ciudad de Príapo); V.118 (reconstrucción de Esmirna); VI.47 (fundación de Alejandría de Margiana); VI.93 (fundación de Alejandría de Aria); V.134 (Cinedópolis donde Alejandro abandonó a hombres pervertidos); V.107 (anexión de ciudades a Halicarnaso); V.116-117 (excavación de una llanura para unir dos golfos y aislar la ciudad de Eritras).

[70] Jacob 1990: 75.

[71] Lightfoot 2014: 118.

[72] Jacob 1990: 69.

en grandes celebraciones como las bacanales de Nisa o Carmania[73] sirvieron para garantizarle un lugar indiscutible dentro de un mundo en el que los protagonistas humanos habían dejado paso a instancias más duraderas quedando quizá solo en la memoria asociada a determinados topónimos y etnónimos un mínimo recuerdo perdurable.

[73] Sobre el papel de Dionisos en Alejandro, Goukowsky 1981; Bosworth 1996: 98-132; Stoneman 2019: 80-98.

The Western Domain of the Imaginary: Alexander's Description of India

Chiara Di Serio
(University of Rome La Sapienza*)*

The *Epistola Alexandri ad Aristotelem*[1] is an apocryphal letter sent from Alexander to Aristotle and featuring the description of India's wonders. The text is in Latin, but its dating is still uncertain. According to some scholars it goes back to the 4th or 5th century,[2] others prefer dating it before the 7th century.[3] The epistle circulated as a self-standing text and was variously rewritten and translated during the Middle Ages.

However, this document has a very complex history behind it. As Gunderson pointed out,[4] the *Alexander Romance* by Pseudo-Callisthenes contains two «Letters of Wonders». In Book II, there is a letter from Alexander addressed to his mother Olympias and to Aristotle, where he describes his journey to the East and the monstrous creatures he met.[5] In Book III, there is a letter to Olympias where Alexander recounts his journey to the northern region of India, and his arrival at the border pillars, a silver and a golden one, placed there by Herakles.[6]

---

[1] See Walther Boer 1973 edition, to which I will refer throughout this article.

[2] Cracco Ruggini 1965: 17-18.

[3] Walther Boer 1973: II; Bologna 1977: 204; Stoneman 2007: lxxviii.

[4] Gunderson 1980: 76-90.

[5] Ps.-Callisth. II.23, 32-33, 36-41. The numbering is that of the edition of Müller 1846, which is still today a valid instrument of consultation, as it presents a very long version of Pseudo-Callisthenes' text. He used three manuscripts representing the recensions α, β and γ, as Nawotka (2017: 31) points out. In Müller's edition also appears Palladius' *De Gentibus Indiae et Bragmanibus*, which is also in the manuscript A; see Stoneman 2007: LXXVIII. The text reconstructed by Müller is in any case similar to the edition of van Thiel 1974, which contains the manuscript L. The summary of the letter to Olympias and Aristotle can be found in Gunderson 1980: 76-86.

[6] Ps.-Callisth. III.27. See the observations by Gunderson 1980: 86-88.

In addition to these two letters in Book III, there is a 'shortened version'[7] of the *Epistola*, which was possibly already circulating as an autonomous text, and contains the episode of Alexander's encounter with the oracle of the trees of the Sun and the Moon.[8]

In the Armenian recension of the *Alexander Romance*,[9] there is a long version of this letter; this means, as R. Stoneman noted,[10] that it was also part of the oldest α-recension.

Regarding the Latin tradition of the *Alexander Romance*, the epitome by Julius Valerius Polemius[11] features a longer letter than the one in Pseudo-Callisthenes.[12] Anyway, the transmission concerning the Latin version of this document is even more complex, because we possess two different texts: *Epistle I* is the oldest; *Epistle II* appears in the Bamberg Manuscript Hist. 3 (E. III.14) and goes back to the end of the 10th century.[13] Moreover, the content of the letter was concluded in the recensions[14] of Archpriest Leo's *Historia de preliis*.[15]

Apart from the long and complex history of the different versions of the text, here I would like to offer an interpretation of its contents following a line of inquiry that could mainly account for the way in which different narrative models show the representation of India as a symbolic space[16] and an ideal *alterity*.[17] The *Epistola* is based on an ideological conception of India, and the East in general, which was deeply rooted in the culture of the Greek and later of the Roman world,[18] but still largely common during the Middle Ages and beyond. The basic idea in the text, as in many Greek and Roman literary sources that describe Asian countries, is that India is a land filled with wonders, both negative and positive.[19]

---

[7] Gunderson 1980: 35.

[8] Ps.-Callisth. III.17.

[9] Wolohojian 1969.

[10] Stoneman 2007: lxxix.

[11] Now there is another excellent edition of Rosellini 2004.

[12] Iul. Val. III.17 (Rosellini 2004).

[13] Published by Pfister 1910.

[14] See in particular the J_1 recension in the edition of Hilka / Steffens 1979.

[15] In this regard, Steinmann 2012: 22-23 speaks of an *Epistola III*.

[16] To this purpose, see Zaganelli 1997: 103-113.

[17] Zambrini 1985: 826-847.

[18] On such a complex issue, see at least the essay by Karttunen 1987: 43-52.

[19] This motif appears in the first words of the *Epistola* (Walther Boer 1973: 1). In general, on India as a land of 'wonders', see Wittkower 1942: 159-197; Romm 1993: 82-120; Karttunen 1997: 129-252; Stoneman 2008: 67-88. Furthermore, Zumthor 1993: 269-275 also treats India as a wonderland, although with regard to the Medieval period. Remember Pliny's passage (*HN* VII.21): *Praecipue India Aethiopumque tractus miraculis scatent*. See also Max. Tyr. 2.6c: ἐπεδείκυεν Ἀλεξάνδρωι Ταξίλης τὰ θαυμαστὰ τῆς Ἰνδων γῆς, ποταμοὺς μεγίστους, καὶ ὄρνιθας ποικίλους, καὶ εὐώδη φυτά, καὶ εἴ τι ἄλλο ξένον ὀφθαλμοῖς Ἑλληνικοῖς. Very interesting are the observations of Wright (2020: 173-191), who starts from the manuscript of the Arnstein Bible, but goes back to the Greek literary tradition about the monstrous races that inhabit the East.

Over the centuries, a number of «narrative discourses»[20] on the Indian territory were disseminated, and were repeated according to a fixed pattern, whose propagation had the function of defining the identity and superiority of Western civilization.

The first element that emerges from the epistle is that the space Alexander describes to his master Aristotle is a land of conquest. At the beginning, in fact, Alexander states that he won Darius at the Ganges and that he later defeated King Porus.[21] Soon after, he minutely lists the soldiers, the chariots, and the elephants in the army of the Indian sovereign.[22] Throughout the letter, Alexander underlines that his soldiers have to march fully armed and facing all kinds of dangerous animals,[23] in a barren and waterless land.[24] The lack of drinkable water is a recurring theme in the tale, and emphasizes the difficulties that the Macedonians have to face during their advance. This is the background for the episode when Alexander reaches the river of bitter waters that nobody can drink to quench their thirst.[25]

Alexander also offers details of the number of men and means of transport for the equipment he had carried with him in his expedition, thus underlining the size of his military deployment.[26] The army's gradual march into unknown territories to explore and conquer is an ever-present space-time dimension throughout the *Epistola*.[27]

On the symbolic level of Alexander's discourse the occupation of space becomes concrete and visible in the immense number of forces employed.

The letter also highlights the main feature of India: its enormous riches and abundance of gold. The Macedonians seize the huge royal treasure: Porus' palace is full of solid gold, and also hosts a golden vineyard.[28] The soldiers carry the spoils of conquest all the way to the Far East[29] and their weight slows down and further complicates their march.[30]

The presence of gold in the Indian region is a feature that appears in several passages of a very large literature on this topic.[31] Starting from the accounts in Greek

---

[20] The expression «narrative discourses» can be used according to White's definition; read for example the collection of essays in White 1990.

[21] *Epist.*, Walther Boer 1973: 3.

[22] *Epist.*, Walther Boer 1973: 4.

[23] *Epist.*, Walther Boer 1973: 6: *ne serpentes et rabida ferarum genera incideremus.* Walther Boer 1973: 7: *ut nos in exitiabilia serpentium et rabida ferarum beluarum genera ignaros regionum inducerent.*

[24] *Epist.*, Walther Boer 1973: 6.

[25] *Epist.*, Walther Boer 1973: 9-10.

[26] *Epist.*, Walther Boer 1973: 10.

[27] *Epist.*, Walther Boer 1973: 28: *sinistram partem Indiae scrutari institui, ne quid mihi in ignotis subtraheretur locis.* Walther Boer 1973: 37: *supplex orabam numina ut me regem totius orbis terrarum cum sublimis tropeis triumphantem in Macedoniam Olympiadi matri meae remitterent.*

[28] *Epist.*, Walther Boer 1973: 4-5.

[29] According to Herodotus (III.106), India is the Eastern most inhabited country. In the *Epistola,* the same motif occurs with regard to the statues erected for Hercules and Liber in the extreme Eastern territories: *In Orientis autem ultimis oris aurea utraque deorum constituerat simulacra* (Walther Boer 1973: 26).

[30] *Epist.*, Walther Boer 1973: 8.

[31] On this motif, see Wittkover 1942; Karttunen 1997: 129-252.

ethnography,[32] this theme constitutes one of the stereotypes on which the fascination of exoticism towards a geographical *elsewhere* is built. It is part of a codification that portrays India as a land so attractive for its riches, as to arouse the desire to possess them.

In the *Epistola,* the dangers of this march for the soldiers who penetrate so far East is further underlined by the occurring of exceptional weather phenomena, such as the violence of Euros, –the wind lashing at the men and animals in Alexander's company–, the sudden succession of a thick snowfall and a violent rainfall, and lastly the appearing of a black cloud that plunges the camp into darkness for three whole days.[33] Therefore, the march of the Macedonians is not a smooth one, but it seems doomed to fail and will not succeed in reaching the goal that the king had planned.

Alexander's insatiable lust for power is naturally a *topos*, that already emerges from the works of several classical authors, such as Plutarch,[34] Arrian[35] and Strabo.[36]

His ambition takes him to the extreme limits of the then known world, and in the *Epistle* to Aristotle we read that the King wanted to reach «the sea in order to sail the Ocean that surrounds the whole world».[37] The inhabitants of the place he crosses explain to the king that neither Hercules nor Liber dared to go further, for that sea is dark and shallow, and that he would appear so much greater than those superhuman beings if he managed to reach beyond their sacred footsteps.[38] The wish to overreach the limit imposed on mortals is one of the characteristics that make Alexander an extra-human character, across the human and the divine dimensions.[39]

On this point, it is worth to mention the central episode in the letter, when Alexander visits the oracles of the trees of the Sun and the Moon that prophesy he will be the lord of the world, but will not return home alive.[40] The event is well known, as it appears similarly reported in the *Alexander Romance* (III. 17). However, here the emphasis is on king's destiny as the ruler of the world.[41] Be-

---

[32] First of all, Hdt. III.102 tells about ants digging holes and bringing out auriferous sand, then the theme is repeated by Arr. *Ind.* 15.5; Str. XV.1.44; Mela III.52. Photius' summary of Ctesias' work (Phot. *Bibl.* 72.45b) tells of a well in India that is filled with gold each year. Arr. *Ind.* 8.13 reports that the Indus people dig gold from the very ground. Then D.S. II.36 maintains that the soil has mines of all possible metals. Sol. 52. 53-55. describes all the precious stones and metals to be seen in India.

[33] Walther Boer 1973: 34-36.

[34] Plu. *Alex.* 26.

[35] Arr. *An.* VII.1.4.

[36] Str. XV.1.5.

[37] *Epist.*, Walther Boer 1973: 27-28: *Pergebam ad mare tamen volens, si possem, orbi terrarum circumfluum navigare Oceanum* (my translation above).

[38] *Epist.*, Walther Boer 1973: 28.

[39] On the ambiguity of Alexander's double nature that continuously shifts towards immortality, see the interesting passages in Ael. *VH.* II.19, V.12. Cf. Di Serio 2020.

[40] *Epist.*, Walther Boer 1973: 46.

[41] *Epist.*, Walther Boer 1973: 46: *Cogitabam nim si devicto orbe terrarum in patriam triumphans... possem reverti.* Walther Boer 1973: 51: *Tu autem, etsi breve superest tibi tempus, dominus tamen orbis terrarum eris.*

sides, we are told that the Indians called him immortal, because he had travelled so far.[42] Moreover, twice he competes with the divine greatness of Hercules and Liber. When he reaches the altars devoted to them, he wants to see if they are in solid gold and then he makes offerings to gain their favour.[43] But the soldiers fear to say that he might be chased by the gods' wrath, because as a human being he dared to reach beyond Hercules' and Liber's footprints.[44] The letter ends with the king's decision to erect two golden pillars carved with the accounts of his actions, and to raise –beyond the triumphal monuments (*trophea*) devoted to the two superhuman beings– other five similar monuments for himself, made of gold, and taller than ten feet. They will be etched with his victories and travels,[45] «so that immortality be eternal and the memory of us be proof, excellent Aristotle, of courage and action».[46]

It is already known from the Greek tradition that Alexander would emulate Heracles and Dionysus, from whom he was said to descend.[47] The distinctive feature in these tales is that Alexander is presented as a civilizing hero:[48] his function belongs ideologically to the mythical dimension –and is guaranteed by the sacred one– because of the kinship with his two ancestors, who were the first to civilize the Indian subcontinent.[49]

Regarding Alexander's quest of immortality, we are familiar with several accounts on this subject, especially in the different versions of the *Alexander Romance*.[50] The issue is also connected to the motif of his divine origin.[51] This is one of the main features that transform him into a superhuman character, whose fortune is bound to last.

We continue the analysis of the narrative models by discussing the most prevailing topic in Alexander's Indian travel account. The king and his army repeatedly encounter wild animals and monstrous creatures that are systematically described as extraordinary, dangerous and difficult to fight. Several times, the soldiers are faced with snakes

---

[42] *Epist.*, Walther Boer 1973: 53.

[43] *Epist.*, Walther Boer 1973: 27.

[44] *Epist.*, Walther Boer 1973: 35-36.

[45] *Epist.*, Walther Boer 1973: 59.

[46] *Epist.*, Walther Boer 1973: 60: *ut immortalitas esset perpetua et nobis opinio et animi industriae, optime Aristoteles, indicium* (above my translation).

[47] See, for instance, the passages in Plu. *Mor.* 332b; Str. XV.1.6-8; Arr. *Ind.* 5.8-10, *An.* V.26.5.

[48] Zambrini 1982: 782-784.

[49] D. S. II.38.3, III.3.1; Str. XV.1.7-9; Arr. *Ind.* 5.8, *An.* IV.28.2. V.3.4.

[50] One need only think of the Spring of Immortality that we are told about in the *Alexander Romance* (II.39).

[51] As an example, see Plutarch's account of Alexander as descending from Heracles on his father's side and from Aeacus on his mother's side (Plu. *Alex.* 2). According to other traditions, Alexander is the son of Zeus (Plu. *Alex.* 27.9; Curt. IV.7.25-28, VIII.5.5; Iust. XI.11.7) or of Ammon (D.S. XVII.51; Lucianus *DMort.* X.12.2, 13.1, 14.1; Ps.-Callisth. I.30). See Badian 1981; Fredricksmeyer 1991; Clawkwell 1994; Antela-Bernárdez 2007, 2016b; Ogden 2011: 6-28.

and wild beasts.[52] Some of them are animals of immense size,[53] others are terrible and indomitable beasts,[54] others again are hybrid beings with monstrous traits.[55]

The description of such creatures has a prominent position in the *Epistola*, it even seems that the narrator is almost pleased to offer the details of the many prodigious beings that he meets. It is clear how the purpose underlying the text is to magnify the extraordinariness of the places that the Macedonian army is crossing: the further they move from the civilized lands they have left behind, advancing towards the Easternmost borders, the more unreal, imponderable, exceptional their dimension becomes.

There is a long list of Graeco-Roman texts that describe India as a fabulous and marvellous land: among them it is worth mentioning Ctesias[56] and Megasthenes,[57] but also Diodorus Siculus, Strabo, Pliny, Arrian, Curtius Rufus, Aelian and others.[58]

Moreover, among the extraordinary beings that live on the Indian territory and that are described in our document, there are also some fantastic peoples. The Ichthyophagi, for instance, are furry men, nine feet tall, who feed on raw fish and water, as they live mainly in rivers and ponds;[59] the gigantic Cynocephali live in forests,[60]

---

[52] *Epist.*, Walther Boer 1973: 11: *Sed ego sciebam per bestiosa serpentiosaque loca nobis iter esse.* See n. 23. There are even snakes with precious stones on their necks (Walther Boer 1973: 52).

[53] The letter mentions hippos that are larger than elephants (Walther Boer 1973: 13); lions with the size of bulls and wild boars of immense stature (Walther Boer 1973: 19-20); mice that resemble foxes (Walther Boer 1973: 21).

[54] These are throngs of lions, bears, tigers, leopards and lynxes (Walther Boer 1973: 15); innumerable scorpions, cerastes and water snakes (Walther Boer 1973: 16-17); a multitude of aggressive crabs covered with crocodile skin (Walther Boer 1973: 19); threatening nocturnal crows comparable to vultures (Walther Boer 1973: 21).

[55] The letter describes giant reptiles with two or three heads (Walther Boer 1973: 18); bats equipped with human teeth (Walther Boer 1973: 20); a strange dark-colored being, with three horns, called *dentityrannum* (Walther Boer 1973: 20); an extraordinary beast, with a crested back, the breast of a hippopotamus, two heads, one of a lioness, the other of a crocodile (Walther Boer 1973: 29); predatory gryphons (Walther Boer 1973: 54); beasts with lion heads, tails with two claws, measuring six feet (Walther Boer 1973: 54).

[56] On Ctesias, see the edition of Lenfant 2004.

[57] Zambrini 1982, 1985.

[58] Diodorus Siculus quotes information taken from Megasthenes in II.35-42. Strabo writes extensively about India in XV.1, referring to Nearchus, Onesicritus, Aristobulus and Megasthenes. Plinius devotes a long ethnographic section to India in 6.56-95. From Arrian we have the work *Indikè* that illustrates the customs of the Indians partly referring to Megasthenes, Nearchus, Eratosthenes. Curtius Rufus describes India and its inhabitants in VIII.9.2-36. In *De natura animalium*, Aelian has several chapters describing the strange creatures that inhabit there. On Alexander's historians, see Albaladejo Vivero 2005.

[59] In Walther Boer edition (1973: 32) we find *faunos*: *mulieres virosque pilosos in modum ferarum toto corpore vidimus, pedum altos novem. Hos Indi faunos appellant; hi assueti fluminibus nec non et stagno quam terris erant, crudo pisce tantummodo et aquarum haustu viventes*. On this regard, Arr. *Ind.* 29.9-16 writes largely on the customs of the Ichthyophagi: they eat raw fish, or they let it dry to produce flour and bread; some work the land and eat bread with fish; moreover, the most fortunate build their homes with whalebones, while the others use fishbones.

[60] *Epist.*, Walther Boer 1973: 33. We can here remember that in the recensions J^1, J^2, J^3 of *Historia de preliis* (Steffens 1975; Hilka 1977; Ch. 119 in Hilka / Steffens 1979) several Cynocephali assail Alexander and his soldiers and they have to fight against them and kill them. On the Cynocephali, see the study by Lecouteux 1981: 117-129.

and long-haired women resembling nymphs live underwater and eat fish.[61] Moreover, in his journey Alexander meets groups of Indians who live like savages clothed in the skins of wild beasts,[62] and others that rest on the same skins, feed on incense and opobalsam and have no metals except gold.[63]

But these races are also described in older works such as Ctesias' *Indika*, quoted by Photius in his *Bibliotheca*,[64] that is quite relevant for the characterization of Indian folks.[65]

In the *Epistola* the description of the wild and monstrous creatures visually takes on the function of pointing out the exceeding of the 'limit', that is the transgression of the 'norm'. This is the value of Alexander's journey. Monstrosity becomes the symbolic expression of exceptionality, exasperation of *otherness*, represented as imponderable and unreal.[66]

The marks of primitivity, hostility, deformity of the creatures who inhabit the Indian territory are the sign of a well-defined ideological and conceptual design: the making and diffusion of an image of India and of the Far East that must appear in the eyes of the Western culture as the reverse of its own. The fantastic definition of a world 'other' than one's own had for classical civilizations the function of outlining, in a reversed way, the cultural parameters and the values of their identity. Greek, and later Latin,[67] authors show the intention of removing, containing and 'controlling' a different reality that appears prodigious, but at the same time distant, unknown, and therefore dangerous.

The *Epistola Alexandri ad Aristotelem* is the account of a journey toward the unknown, where the time and space dimensions are altered, deformed and expanded in order to create a chaotic landscape where the only cosmic agent is Alexander. His aim is to conquer the Far East and to reach the farthermost point, to sail the Ocean and to get beyond the limits imposed by the deities Hercules and Liber,[68] and therefore to challenge as *hybristes* the established order.

The expansion of the Easternmost border that the king wants to reach –with a notable alteration of the actual historical facts–[69] is the core element of this apocryphal

---

[61] *Epist.*, Walther Boer 1973: 56-57.

[62] *Epist.*, Walther Boer 1973: 41.

[63] *Epist.*, Walther Boer 1973: 49.

[64] Photius quotes the description of the Pygmies, their bodies entirely covered with hair and beard, then of the Cynocephali, that bark like dogs and have no human voices, and then of a race that only drinks milk, finally of people who have eight fingers and eight toes, with huge ears that cover their elbows and their shoulders (Phot. *Bibl.* 72.46b; 47b; 48a; 48b; 49b). Cf. Janni 1978.

[65] It is worth remembering that in Ctesias' lack of truthfulness was reproached by Photius himself (*Bibl.* 72, 50a).

[66] This theme is well developed by Wright 2020: 180-181. The scholar states that «the body of the human monster has historically provided a tangible site for the inscription of transgression» (180).

[67] Hartog 1996: 87-89; Gruen 2011: 1-5.

[68] This idea is repeated at least twice in the *Epistola*: see notes 37 and 38.

[69] Zaganelli 1997: 96-97 remarks that Alexander had in mind to move farther East, but his soldiers refused and forced him to start their way back home, as reported in Plu. *Alex.* 62.2 and Arr. *An.* 5.26-27.

epistle that must have been in circulation as a self-standing text at the time when the first versions of the *Romance* by Pseudo-Callisthenes appeared.[70]

The story implies that Alexander acts as a 'cultural hero' who has to face and oppose the space of un-culture, of a wild, out-of-time world. The Macedonians' war to conquer the East and to rule all over the *oikoumene*[71] (the world then known), beside and beyond the historical facts, symbolically produces a process of 'colonization' of the imaginary that projects the tale of an infinite journey into the mythical sphere. Alexander's itinerary aims at reaching a Land of Elsewhere whose non-existing borders are continually moved forward, farther off, toward the Easternmost limit.

What is the historical framework out of which the exploration described in the letter is to be imagined? It is, of course, conceived according to the perspective of the Western world, first from the Greeks' and then from the Romans' point of view, that defines the *otherness* as an 'object of desire', and as such something to conquer.

Finally, it is worth noting that the *Epistola* had a long fortune in the Middle Ages, was translated several times, in Middle English, Middle Irish, Islandic, French, German and Italian,[72] and provided inspiration or was revised by authors such as Albertus Magnus, James of Vitry, Vincent of Beauvais, Fulcher of Chartres and Marco Polo.[73] All that shows that it was functionally active in all European literatures and that the image of India it conveyed became a long-lasting and influential cultural product.

---

[70] According to Ross 1963: 28, the text of the letter to Aristotle was not originally part of Pseudo-Callisthenes. Some scholars surmise that Julius Valerius used a better and older version of the Greek original containing the letter (Cary 1956: 14-15 and Gunderson 1980: 34).

[71] See, for instance, the passage in Ps.-Callisth. 2.37: Alexander states that many times his companions wanted to go back, but he would not, because he wished to see the world's borders.

[72] See Tardiola 1991: 61 and Bologna 1977: 204-205.

[73] To this purpose, see Bologna 1977: 204-205.

Concluding Remarks

Marc Mendoza & Borja Antela-Bernárdez

Alexander has been one of the main paradigms and models for conquerors and empires for centuries. We agree with Pierre Briant's statement that the most ground-breaking perspective to study Alexander in the recent future would be to focus on how historiography throughout the centuries has described Alexander, and what kind of contemporary worries historians wanted to address through their respective Alexanders.[1] Authors, throughout history, have tried to depict him in many fashions. As Mommsen once wrote, «[t]hose who had lived through historical events, as I have, begin to see that history is neither written nor made without love and hate».[2] Despite there already existed some critical voices with Alexander's authoritarianism even back in Antiquity, the usual image nowadays –both in popular culture and in scholarship– is that Alexander was a superb and generous king, whose «ability to deal decisively and rationally»,[3] with the challenge of a world conquest deserves not only to be remembered, but to be regarded as a useful precedent for our own quests. Rationality is, in fact, an aspect frequently and closely attached to Alexander's decisions.[4] Many scholars have commonly considered Alexander's actions as a result of a rational process, in which the king was always aware of the pros and cons for every alternative, and he infallibly chose the best and most favourable solution. Therefore, there is no room in these reconstructions for uncertainty, even less for failure nor mistake. Alexander appears almost as a kind of omniscient entity, as close to divinity as he is far from error. Thus, any decision he took is explained by these historians as a result of a complex rational process.

---

[1] Briant 1999, 2009; Antela-Bernárdez 2018.

[2] Cf. Borza 1974: 6 n. 7.

[3] Worthington 2015: 108.

[4] Ma 2013.

Certainly, except for some inveterate apologetic authors such as W. W. Tarn, the sources and the scholars are not uniformly uncritical or commendatory towards Alexander throughout their respective works. A kind of turning point is often stressed in relation to Alexander's authority and attitude, usually describing a tyrannical turn, far from the brilliant Romantic King's image. The adoption of Iranian clothing and the Achaemenid court's protocol on one hand, and his claim for divinity on the other, are many times identified as these turning points. The attempts to understand both phenomena rationally often resort to approaches also applied to other great historical characters –those of the traditional history, i.e., kings, politicians, generals…–, mostly explained as a result of the overwhelming power they had gained.

Although this extreme depiction has already been noticed by some critical voices, the academic approaches are still too 'Alexandercentric', forgetting many times the people around him and the impact that Alexander's actions and decisions had in their lives, and vice versa. Like Brecht wrote in his poem 'A Worker reads History': «Young Alexander conquered India/He alone?». Similarly, the huge amount of biographies that have been flooding into the shelves of bookshops around the world for years usually has usually neglected the situation of the conquered and subject peoples under Alexander's yoke.

Throughout the pages of this book, the readers have found a multifocal view of Alexander and the people who lived under his rule and his legend. Besides the aforementioned critical analysis of the previous historiography, another approach that needs a stronger emphasis is the study of Alexander's epoch leaving him aside from the centre of attention. This cannot be easily fulfilled, being the Macedonian such a powerful and pervading presence in his own age and, consequently, the result might be simply perceived as an unsatisfactory trick or a sheer mirage. Surely, this is an enormous and formidable purpose and many scholars will likely claim against its feasibility, but, after all, it is worth trying at least.

In all likelihood, this is the main contribution of this book to Alexander's studies. Certainly, Alexander is mentioned in all the papers, but rather his idea or legacy than the real person. The king's presence is pervading, but his actual figure is left aside, leaving the stage for other hitherto overshadowed supporting actors. The first section (*One king to rule them all*) is a collection of papers that one can clearly attach to the label 'Subjects' from the book's own subtitle. Neither Macedonians nor Greeks were passive actors, but they played a key role in understanding the foundations of Alexander's power and his dreams of conquest. Like Brecht's verses remark, the king did not succeed in the campaign on his own. Although seminal research on this background seems capital to understand Alexander and his realm, not many authors have dared to deal with this crucial topic so far.[5] A close look at the sources[6] and their problematic readings sheds light on how much we still ignore. The chapters by Taietti, Domínguez Monedero, Antela-Bernárdez and Mendoza addressed different aspects of Alexander's dealings with the populations of mainland Greece and Macedon and the effects that the Asian campaign had in those territories and vice versa. Taietti's paper clearly challenged the image of the heroic Alexander, showing him bound to some more mundane issues, which were necessary to assure the very roots of his right to rule, and how the Macedonians framed his functions and policies. The article by Domínguez Monedero stressed the complex situation that the kingdom of Macedonia and its representatives had to deal with in Greece, being the war of Agis far from the so-called 'war of mices', but one of the most important menaces that Alexander's reign had to face. Antela-Bernárdez's contribution represented a thorough analysis of the actual side effects that the campaign of the Macedonian king had in the eastern Mediterranean basin and its inhabitants. Finally, the chapter written by Mendoza set the relevance that Thessaly has in understanding the early steps of Alexander and how deeply the Thessalians influenced the evolution of the campaign and the king's policies.

The second section (*The tides of war*) moved the scenario from one side of the Hellespont to the other. Similarly, the topics of the articles were no longer the 'Subjects', but the 'Conquered'. However, again, these people were not put behind in those papers, but they were put on the front. This is very clearly addressed in Peltonen's contribution, where he explained how some individuals actually thrived under the conquerors. The tradition forged by the ancient Greek sources about the Persians as 'the' enemies is still well established in Western culture, as it can be watched in the fictional representations of some of the main episodes of ancient (Classical) Greek history that arrived at the cinemas a decade and a half ago.[7] The paper by Almagor defied some of these paradigms and reflected on how far the act of destruction was reimagined and turned into an act of creation. The true face of war is far from the heroic and merciful conquest that some described some decades ago. There was a great deal of suffering among the defeated enemies, especially among the populations in the frontier of Alexander's new empire.[8] War and subjugation themselves are forms of violence as well, and imperial powers have proved their expertise in many forms of violence and repression. Communication is, of course, vital to firmly control a land. Mario Agudo dedicated his paper to Alexander's intelligence system and

---

[5] A nice example can be found in some of the papers collected by Howe / Garvin / Wrightson 2015 in honour of Waldemar Heckel, to quote here a good example. Another one could be Gómez Espelosin / Antela-Bernárdez 2016, which is, to a certain point, the clear precedent to the present book.

[6] For a review of what we do really know and not on the League of Corinth, see Osborne / Rhodes 2007: 372-379; Antela-Bernárdez 2022.

[7] Antela-Bernárdez / Prieto 2007; Mendoza 2019b; Lapeña / Antela-Bernárdez 2020.

[8] Burnstein 2015; Antela-Bernárdez 2016c.

the way the Macedonian army strategically made use of it, but also how local actors were either voluntarily or forcedly part of this mechanism. Finally, the chapter by Molina Marín has traced back the influences for Alexander's cultural conception of the world and how they shaped Alexander`s understanding of his historical mission to solve the never-ending struggle described in Herodotus' *History*.

Finally, the book is completed by a third section (*Describing a Brave New World*), that belongs to 'Chroniclers'. Inasmuch as Alexander left a mark in his world, this impact was greatly enlarged by all the accounts that narrated his deed. Borza wrote, long time ago:

> «Yet Alexander's reputation does not rest so much for us on any precise knowledge of his actual exploits as it does on the legend created about him. [...] It is precisely the existence of a legendary romance about Alexander that has created an enormous intellectual problem for anyone who wishes to seek the sober truth about the king's impact. In one sense the problem is psychological as much as scholarly».[9]

The primary sources on Alexander have just survived in fragments, so the real Alexander is hidden by a series of subsequent filters. Our extant sources are relatively late and, consequently, they were likely influenced and shaped by the ever-growing legend of Alexander. Therefore, we scholars are bound to write all of our papers relying on just a few, late authors –chiefly, Diodorus, Curtius, Arrian, Plutarch and Justin–. Fortunately, historical commentaries and studies like those of Bosworth (1980, 1995), Prandi (2013), Atkinson (1980, 1994), among others, have shed a lot of light onto these sources and about the ultimate primary authors behind them, hidden by the 'dust' that time had spilt over them. Thanks to those, the facts and the chances to know the whole history of the Macedonian King have been significantly enlarged. The chapters in this third section are not closely related to the aforementioned most common sources, but they shared a strong geographical perspective. The papers by Albaladejo and Di Serio were focused on the easternmost spaces of the Macedonian expanse. Again, Alexander was virtually absent. Albaladejo's article convincingly proves that Alexander's men never set a foot on Taprobane and this deed has to be attributed to some other later adventurers. In Di Serio's paper, in turn, the historical Alexander was replaced by a literary lookalike, likewise real India was impersonated by a marvellous version of this land. Both contributors addressed the problems and the differences between true knowledge and fiction, both in the genres of Ancient Geography and History, a topic so much related to Alexander's studies.[10] Finally, the paper written by Gómez Espelosín showed even a more extreme example of the concealing of Alexander's real person through his analysis of the poem of Dionysius Periegetes. The Macedonian king becomes the elephant in the room.

---

[9] Borza 1974: 1.

[10] Molina Marín 2022.

Before ending these concluding remarks, we want to add a final note on what we consider a methodological problem: the bound we, as historians and even as part of the so-called Western culture, have developed with Alexander and his deeds. A good example of what we are trying to explain can be found in the works about Alexander and Afghanistan that appeared during the wrongly-named 'War on Terror' and the Western invasion of Afghanistan.[11] Our views were always on the side of Alexander, who is our brilliant hero, and he supposedly deserved to impose his will over the ancient 'Afghan' peoples, just like what could be heard, watched and read in modern media those days in relation to the modern invaders. Therefore, the ever-lasting motif of 'us against them', already found in Herodotus, was still in vogue. Nevertheless, modern historians, as members of an academic and scientific discipline, should defend their own neutrality. «History will judge us» is said, but, at the end of the day, the real statement is very different: 'we, the historians, will judge the past-although we decide not to judge Alexander, but to promote him'. History cannot judge contemporary facts, so we simply move our focus to those from other ages, like Antiquity. Then, we judge long-gone people and events, but, deep down, our appraisals are actually a reflection of our own times and what we have to face in our lives. Thus, challenging and examining Alexander's methods and legitimacy to conquer faraway places like Afghanistan is, in fact, a form of opening a broader discussion about modern methods and justifications of conquest or waging war. Here, it is where the problems begin. For example, Badian and Bosworth, to quote some of the most eminent names, led a new way to approach Alexander, critical and unapologetic. They both claim for the right of Alexander to be understood within his own times' views. However, their stances cannot be completely told apart from the worldwide decolonisation processes that went on for the decades that followed WWII. Nevertheless, historians usually tend to favour Alexander, even when we are trying to criticise him. Moreover, we are acquiescent to some of his behaviours and acts that we later describe as unacceptable in other people of his times.[12]

Scholars on Alexander usually have to face historians working on other periods or topics in Antiquity that often consider, –and they let us know it with a frankness that it is not always enjoyable–, that there is nothing new to say about the famous Macedonian king. Nevertheless, this is not what we have found while taking part in discussions, like the one from where this book results. As mentioned before, Alexander's scholarship deserves to free itself from the tyranny of the facts (i.e, the traditional history of politics and warfare's accounts). The way to accomplish this is, in our opinion, one: a systematic historiographical approach. Alexander's studies is a field where tons of works are published every year and it is absolutely impossible to be fully updated –even if you just read the studies published in English–. Thus,

---

[11] Cf. Antela-Bernárdez 2014.

[12] Antela-Bernárdez 2020b, 2021a.

knowing the threads that are cyclically repeated or the influences that can be traced back to the historians' own backgrounds and shaped their views of the Macedonian king, will probably offer us a richer perspective of what is, what should not be, and to what topics we must address our work in the future concerning Alexander's scholarship.[13]

The quest for Alexander is not just a simple list of noteworthy facts of his life nor even a sheer academic biography, with no other points of view than the hero's. History has a great responsibility in the challenge of changing the world. A well-known tradition on the historical perception of Alexander is that he was the starting point and the responsible for a new age for humanity.[14] True or not, what we can really find in his history is a chance for a deep consideration about how power (military, colonial, cultural...) must be observed and analysed, from all across the years and centuries, in order to let us guess how a better world should be. Due to the main influence of Alexander in many past and present human civilizations, to study the impact of his conquest is, indeed, one opportunity to question ourselves, and those around us, of how we can deconstruct our perceptions of right and wrong, getting distance from what other times thought about those models, and choosing for our own age the critical perceptions needed to imagine, with empathy, and pursuit new models with which observe the people who lived around Alexander, and how they lived under his overwhelming authority.

---

[13] An attempt to follow Briant's call for a systematic historiographical scholarship on Alexander has been done in Mendoza / Antela-Bernárdez 2022.

[14] Antela-Bernárdez 2000; Bosworth 2009.

Bibliography

Abry, J. H. 2000: «Une carte du monde à l'époque d'Auguste. Manilius, Astronomiques, IV, 585-817», in *L'espace et ses représentations*, Lyon: 83-106.

Aguilera, C. 1988: *Historia de la Comunicación y de la prensa*, Madrid.

Albaladejo Vivero, M. 2005: *La India en la literatura griega. Uno studio etnografico*, Alcalá de Henares.

Alessandri, S. 1994: «Le ambascerie ad Alessandro del 323 a.C.: il problema storiografico», in S. Alessandrì (ed.), *HISTORIE. Studi offerti dagli allievi a G. Nenci per il suo 70º compleanno*, Galatina: 21-36.

Allen, B. 2005: «Alexander the Great: Or the Terrible?», *The Hudson Review* 58: 220-230.

Almagor, E. 2011: «Plutarch on the End of the Persian Empire», *GLB* 16: 3-16.

Alvar, J. 2000: «Alejandro, explorador y hombre de ciencia», in J. Alvar / J. M. Blázquez (eds.), *Alejandro Magno. Hombre y mito*, Madrid: 83-98.

Amato, E. 2004: «Note esegetiche e testuali alla *Descriptio orbis* di Dionisio di Alessandria (III)», *GFA* 7: 1-9.

Amaya Trujillo, J. 2010: «Historia y comunicación social: apuntes para un diálogo inconcluso. Aproximación crítica al campo de estudios históricos en comunicación», *Comunicación y sociedad* 13: 149-171.

Ameling, W. 1988: «Alexander und Achilleus. Eine Bestandsaufnahme», in W. Will / J. Heinrichs (eds.), *Zu Alexander der Große: Festschrift G. Wirth, vol. II*, Amsterdam: 657-692.

Anderson, A. R. 1928: «Alexander at the Caspian Gates», *TAPhA* 59: 130-163.

André, J. / Filliozat, J. 1980: *Pline l'Ancien. Histoire Naturelle. Libre VI, 2e partie*, Paris.

Andreotti, R. 1950: «Il problema di Alessandro Magno nella storiografia dell'ultimo decennio», *Historia* 1: 583-600.

Andrews, K. R. 1971: *The Concept of Corporate Strategy*, Homewood.

Andronikos, M. 1980: «The royal tomb at Vergina and the problem of the dead», *AAA* 13: 156-167 (in Greek), 168-178.

Anson, E. M. 1985: «Macedonia's alleged Constitutionalism», *CJ* 80: 303-316.

— 2004: *Eumenes of Cardia: A Greek among Macedonians*, Boston.

— 2009: «Philip II and the Transformation of Macedonia: A Reappraisal», in T. Howe / J. Reames (eds), *Macedonian Legacies: Studies in Ancient Macedonian History and Culture in Honor of Eugene N. Borza*, Claremont: 17-30.

— 2013: *Alexander the Great: Themes and Issues*, London.

Antela-Bernárdez, B. 2000: «J. G. Droysen e o primeiro *Alexandre* científico», *Gallaecia* 19: 219-250.

— 2005: *Alexandre Magno e Atenas*, Santiago de Compostela.

— 2007: «Alejandro Magno o la demostración de la divinidad», *Faventia* 29: 89-103.

— 2014: «World is not enough. Alexander the Great in Sogdiana: A study in Historiography», in B. Antela-Bernárdez / J. Vidal (eds.), *Central Asia in Antiquity: Interdisciplinary Approaches*, Oxford: 77-84.

— 2016a: «Leócrates contra Atenas. Memoria del conflicto y carestía en Atenas entre 338 y 330 a.C.», *Aevum* 90: 71-82.

— 2016b: «Like Gods among Men. The Use of Religion and Mythical Issues during Alexander's Campaign», in K. Ulanowski (ed.), *The Religious Aspects of War in the Ancient Near East, Greece, and Rome*, Leiden–Boston: 235-255.

— 2016c: «Tracia, Sogdiana, India. Alejandro Magno y las políticas de frontera», in F. J. Gómez Espelosín / B. Antela-Bernárdez (eds.), *El imperio de Alejandro. Aspectos geográficos e historiográficos*, Alcalá de Henares: 117-155.

— 2018: «Alejandro de Babilonia. Del Imperio macedonio al modelo de estado helenístico», in J. Pascual / B. Antela Bernárdez / D. Gómez Castro (coords.), *Cambio y pervivencia: el mundo griego en el siglo IV a.C.*, Madrid: 179-188.

— 2020a: «El tercer hombre. Leócrates, Harpalo y el oscuro Amintas», *Aevum* 94: 39-48.

— 2020b: «*Terrible* Olympias. Another Study in Method», *Karanos* 3: 103-129.

— 2021a: *Apología de Olimpia del Épiro*, Madrid.

— 2021b: «Antigenes' Syndrome», in R. Martínez Lacy / N. Sekunda (eds.), *Hellenistic Warfare IV*, México DC [in print].

— 2022: «Alexander and the Greeks», in D. Ogden (ed.), *Cambridge Companion to Alexander the Great*, Cambridge [in print].

Antela-Bernárdez, B. / Prieto, A. 2007: «Alejandro magno en el cine», in M. J. Castillo Pascual *et al.* (eds.), *Imagines. La Antigüedad en las artes escénicas y visuals*, Logroño: 263-282.

Antela-Bernárdez, B. / Sierra Martín, C. 2016a: «La Divinización de Alejandro a través de la medicina», *QUCC* 113: 115-138.

— 2016b: «Alejandro y la Anábasis de la Medicina Griega», *Athenaeum* 104: 397-417.

Arena, E. 2004: «Filippo II e gli Anfissei in un'iscrizione delfica fra Terza e Quarta Guerra Sacra (IG IX, 1, 2, 775)», *MEP* 7-8: 211-226.

— 2013: «Alessandro basileus nella documentazione epigrafica: la dedica del tempio di Atena a Priene (I.Priene 156)», *Historia* 62: 48-80.

Arnaud, P. 2012: «Le Periplus Maris Erythraei: une oeuvre de compilation aux preoccupations géographiques», *Topoi* (Lyon) *Supplément* 11: 27-61.

Atkinson, J. E. 1980: *A Commentary on Q. Curtius Rufus' Historiae Alexandri Magni. Books 3 and 4*, Amsterdam.
— 1981: «Macedon and Athenian Politics in the period 338 to 323 B.C.», *AC* 24: 37-48.
— 1994: *A commentary on Q. Curtius Rufus' Historiae Alexandri Magni: Books 5 to 7, 2*, Amsterdam.
Atkinson, J. E. / Yardley, J. 2009: *Curtius Rufus. Histories of Alexander the Great. Book 10*, Oxford.
Auberger, J. 2001: *Historiens d'Alexandre*, Paris.
Aymard, A. 1948: «Le protocole royal grec et son évolution», *REA* 50: 232-263.
Babbitt, F. C. 1927: *Plutarch. Moralia: Volume I*, London.
Badian, E. 1958a: «The Eunuch Bagoas», *CQ* 8: 144-157.
— 1958b: «Alexander the Great and the Unity of Mankind», *Historia* 7: 425-444.
— 1958c: «Alexander the Great and the Creation of an Empire», *History Today* 8: 369-376, 494-502.
— 1960: «The Death of Parmenio», *TAPhA* 91: 324-338.
— 1961: «Harpalus», *JHS* 81: 16-43.
— 1965a: «The Date of Clitarchus», *PACA* 8: 5-11.
— 1965b: «The Administration of the Empire», *G&R* 12: 166-182.
— 1967: «Agis III», *Hermes* 95: 170-192.
— 1971: «Alexander the Great 1948-67», *CW* 65: 37-56, 77-83.
— 1976: «Some recent interpretations of Alexander», in A. B. Bosworth / E. Badian (eds.), *Alexandre le Grand: Image et réalité*, Genève: 279-311.
— 1981: «The Deification of Alexander the Great», in H. J. Dell (ed.), *Ancient Macedonian studies in honor of Charles F. Edson*, Thessaloniki: 27-71.
— 1982: «Greeks and Macedonians», *Studies in the History of Art* 10: 33-51.
— 1985: «Alexander in Iran», in I. Gershevitch (ed.), *The Cambridge history of Iran. Vol. 2: The Median and Achaemenian periods*, London: 420-501.
— 1989: «History from 'square brackets'», *ZPE* 79: 59-70.
— 1993: «Alexander and Philippoi», *ZPE* 95: 131-139.
— 1994a: «A Reply to Professor Hammond's Article», *ZPE* 100: 388-390.
— 1994b: «Agis III: revisions and reflections», in I. Worthington (ed.), *Ventures into Greek History*, Oxford: 258-293.
— 1996: «Alexander the Great between the two thrones and Heaven: Variations on an old theme», in A. Small (ed.), *Subject and ruler: The cult of the ruling power in Classical Antiquity*, Ann Arbor: 11-26.
— 2000: «Darius III», *HSCP* 100: 241-267.
Balcer, J. M. 1978: «Alexander's Burning of Persepolis», *IA* 13: 119-133.
Baldry, H. C. 1965: *The Unity of Mankind in Greek thought*, Cambridge.
Barr-Sharrar, B. 2008: *The Derveni Krater: Masterpiece of Classical Greek metalwork*, Princeton.
Baynham, E. 1994: «Antipater: manager of kings», in I. Worthington (ed.), *Ventures into Greek History*, Oxford: 331-356.

— 2003: «The Ancient Evidence for Alexander the Great», in J. Roisman (ed.), *Brill's Companion to Alexander the Great*, Leiden: 3-29.

Baynham, E. / Ryan, T. 2018: «*The Unmanly Ruler*: Bagoas, Alexander's Eunuch Lover, Mary Renault's The Persian Boy, and Alexander Reception», in K. Moore (ed.), *Brill's Companion to the Reception of Alexander the Great*, Leiden: 615-640.

Bearzot, C. S. 1987: «La tradizione su Parmenione negli storici di Alessandro», *Aevum* 6: 89-104.

Benuzzi, F. 2019: «Eratosthenes' *Studia Aristophanica*: The Case of Schol. Ar. *Nub.* 967aα-β, bα-β Holwerda», in R. Berardi / N. Bruno / L. Fizzarotti (eds.), *On the Track of the Books: Scribes, Libraries and Textual Transmission*, Berlin: 125-142.

Berger, H. 1903: *Geschichte der wissenschaftlichen Erdkunde der Griechen*, Leipzig.

Bernard, P. 1972: «Campagne de Fouilles à Aï Khanoum», *CRAI* 116: 605-632.

— 1997: «Les origines thessaliennes de l'Arménie vues par deux historiens thessaliens de la génération d'Alexandre», *Topoi* (Lyon) *Supplément* 1: 131-216.

Berve, H. 1926: *Das Alexanderreich auf prosopographischer Grundlage*, 2 vols, München.

Bianchetti, S. 2014: «Taprobane nella tradizione cartografica antica», in S. Bianchetti / V. Bucciantini (eds.), *Tracce di presenza greca fra Etiopia ed India. Atti del convegno internazionale 21-22 Maggio 2012*, Florence: 24-25.

Bichler, R. 2011: «Die Fahrt zu den Grenzen der Erde. Von Herodotos bis zur Alexander-Historiographie», *Gymnasium* 118: 315-344.

— 2015, «The 'Revolution' of Alexander the Great: Old and New in the World's View», in S. Bianchetti / M. Cataudella / H. J. Gehrke (eds.), *Brill's Companion to Ancient Geography*, Leiden: 78-97.

Bielawski, J. 1964: «Lettres d'Aristote à Alexandre le Grand en version arabe», *Rocznik Orientlistyczny* 27: 7-34.

— 1965: «Lettres d'Aristote à Alexandre et lettres d'Alexandre à Aristote en version arabe», *Rocznik Orientlistyczny* 28: 7-12.

Biffi, N. 2005: *L'Estremo Oriente di Strabone: libro XV della Geografia*, Bari.

Bigwood, J. M. 1993: «Aristotle and the elephant again», *AJPh* 114: 537-555.

Billows, R. A. 1990: *Antigonos the One-eyed and the creation of the Hellenistic state*, Berkeley.

Bloedow, E. F. 1995: «'That Great Puzzle in the History of Alexander': Back into 'The 'Primal Pit of Historical Murk'», in C. Schubert / K. Brodersen (eds.), *Rom und der Griechische Osten, Festschrift Hatto Schmitt*, Stuttgart: 20-41.

Bodson, L. 1991: «Alexander the Great and the scientific exploration of the oriental part of his empire. An overview of the background, trends and results», *AncSoc* 22: 127-138.

Bologna, C. (ed.) 1977: *Liber Monstrorum de diversis generibus. Libro delle mirabili difformità*, Milano.

Bopearachchi, O. 1999: «Sites portuaires et emporia de l'ancien Sri Lanka: nouvelles données archéologiques», *Arts Asiatiques* 54: 5-22.

— 2008: *Tamil Traders in Sri Lanka and Sinhalese Traders in Tamil Nadu*, Colombo.
Bopearachchi, O. / Disanayaka, S. / Perera, N. 2016: «The Oldest Shipwreck in the Indian Ocean», in M. F. Boussac / J. F. Salles / J. P. Yon (eds.), *Ports of the Ancient Indian Ocean*, Delhi: 411-434.
Borza, E. N. 1971: «The End of Agis' Revolt», *CPh* 66: 231-235.
— 1972: «Fire from Heaven: Alexander at Persepolis», *CPh* 67: 233-245.
— 1974: *The impact of Alexander the Great*, Hinsdale.
— 1990: *In the Shadow of Olympos. The Emergence of Macedon*, Princeton.
— 1991 (2012²): «Ethnicity and Cultural Policy at Alexander's Court», *AncW* 22: 21-25 [Repr. in I. Worthington (ed.), *Alexander the Great. A Reader*, London–New York: 313-318].
Borza, E. N. / Palagia, O. 2007: «The chronology of the royal Macedonian tombs at Vergina», *JdI* 122: 81-125.
Bose, P. S. 2004: *Alexander the Great's art of strategy. The timeless leadership lessons of history's greatest empire builder*, London–New York.
Bosschart, R. 2009: *Alexander's women: The Sysigambis letter*, Charleston.
Bosworth, A. B. 1971: «The Death of Alexander the Great: Rumour and Propaganda», *CQ* 21: 112-136.
— 1975: «The Mission of Amphoterus and the Outbreak of Agis' War», *Phoenix* 29: 27-43.
— 1976: «Errors in Arrian», *CQ* 26: 117-139.
— 1980a: *A Historical Commentary on Arrian's History of Alexander. Vol. 1: Books I- III*, Oxford.
— 1980b: «Alexander and the Iranians», *JHS* 100: 1-21.
— 1986: «Alexander the Great and the Decline of Macedon», *JHS* 106: 1-12.
— 1988a: *From Arrian to Alexander. Studies in Historical Interpretation*, Oxford.
— 1988b: *Conquest and Empire. The Reign of Alexander the Great*, Cambridge.
— 1994²: «Alexander the Great Part I: The events of the reign», *CAH* VI: 791-845.
— 1995: *A historical commentary on Arrian's History of Alexander Vol. 2: Books IV-V*, Oxford.
— 1996: *Alexander and the East. The Tragedy of triumph*, Oxford.
— 2000a: «Introduction», in A. B. Bosworth / E. J. Baynham (eds.), *Alexander the Great in Fact and Fiction*, Oxford: 1-22.
— 2000b: «Ptolemy and the Will of Alexander», in A. B. Bosworth / E. Baynham (eds.), *Alexander the Great in fact and fiction*, Oxford: 207-241.
— 2002: *The Legacy of Alexander. Politics, Warfare, and Propaganda under the Successors*, Oxford.
— 2003: «Plus ça change: Ancient Historians and their sources», *ClAnt* 22: 167-197.
— 2005: *Alejandro Magno*, Madrid.

— 2009: «Johan Gustav Droysen, Alexander the Great and the creation of the Hellenistic Age», in P. Weathley / R. Hannah (eds.), *Alexander & His Successors. Essays from the Antipodes*, Claremont: 1-29.

Bourguet, É. 1932: *Les comptes du IVe siècle*, Paris.

Bowden, H. 2014: *Alexander the Great. A Very Short Introduction*, Oxford.

Bowie, E. 2004; «Denys d'Alexandrie: un poète grec dans l'empire romain», *REA* 106: 177-185.

Boyd, T. D. 1978: «The arch and the vault in Greek architecture», *AJA* 82: 83-100.

Briant, P. 1974: *Alexandre le Grand*, Paris.

— 1999: «L'histoire de l'empire achéménide aujourd'hui : l'historien et ses documents» *Annales. Histoire, Sciences Sociales*, 1127-1136.

— 2002: *From Cyrus to Alexander: A History of the Persian Empire*, Winona Lake.

— 2009: «Alexander and the Persian Empire, between «decline» and «renovation». History and historiography», in W. Heckel / L. Trittle (eds.), *Alexander the Great: a new History*, Oxford: 171-188.

— 2010: *Alexander the Great and his Empire: A Short Introduction*, Princeton.

— 2012: *Alejandro Magno*, Madrid.

— 2015: *Darius in the Shadow of Alexander*, London.

— 2017: *The First European - A History of Alexander in the Age of Empire*, Harvard.

Brice, L. L. 2015: «Military Unrest in the Age of Philip and Alexander», in T. Howe / E. E. Garvin / G. Wrightson (eds.), *Greece, Macedon, and Persia. Studies in Social, Political and Military History in Honour of Waldemar Heckel*, Oxford: 69-76.

Brosius, M. 2003: «Alexander and the Persians», in J. Roisman (ed.), *Brill's Companion to Alexander the Great*, Leiden: 169-193.

Brown, T. S. 1949: *Onesicritus. A Study in Hellenistic Hist*oriography, Berkeley–Los Ángeles.

Brunt, P. A. 1976: *Arrian. Anabasis of Alexander I: Books 1-4*, Cambridge.

— 1983: *Arrian. Anabasis of Alexander II: Books 5-7, Indica*, Cambridge.

— 2003: «The Aims of Alexander», in I. Worthington (ed.), *Alexander the Great. A Reader*, London: 45-53.

Bucciantini, V. 2015: *Studio su Nearco di Creta: dalla descrizione geografica alla narrazione storica*, Alessandria.

Bunbury, E. H. 1879: *A History of Ancient Geography among the Greeks and Romans*, London.

Burliga, B. 2014: «Xenophon's Cyrus, Alexander φιλόκυρος. How carefully did Alexander the Great study the Cyropaedia?», *Miscellanea Anthropologica et Sociologica* 15: 134-146.

Burn, A. R. 1952: «Notes on Alexander's Campaigns, 332-330», *JHS* 72: 81-91.

Burstein, M. S. 1974: «Sceptre or Thunderbolt: Plutarch, Moralia 338B», *California Studies in Classical Antiquity* 7: 89-92.

— 2000: «Ptolemaic exploration and Hellenistic ethnography», *AncW* 31: 31-37.

— 2007: «The Gardener Became a King – Or Did He? The Case of Abdalonymus of Sidon», in W. Heckel / L. A. Tritle / P. Wheatley (eds.), *Alexander's Empire: Formulation to Decay*, Michigan: 139-149

— 2008: «Alexander's Organization of Egypt: A Note on the Career of Cleomenes of Naucratis», in T. Howe / J. Reames (eds.), *Macedonian Legacies. Studies in Ancient Macedonian History and Culture in Honor of Eugene N. Borza*, Claremont: 183-195.

— 2015: «Alexander's Unintended Legacy: Borders», in T. Howe / E. E. Garvin / G. Wrightson (eds.), *Greece, Macedon and Persia. Studies in Social, Political and Military History in Honour of Waldemar Heckel*, Oxford: 118-126.

Calder III, W. M. 1981: «Diadem and barrel-vault: A note», *AJA* 85: 334-335.

— 1983: «Golden diadems again», *AJA* 87: 102-103.

Carney, E. D 1991: «What's in a name? The emergence of a title for royal women in the Hellenistic period», in S. B. Pomeroy (ed.), *Women's history and Ancient History*, Chapel Hill: 154-172.

— 1996: «Alexander and Persian Women», *AJPh* 117: 563-583.

— 2000a: *Women and monarchy in Macedonia*, Norman.

— 2000b: «Artifice and Alexander History», in A. B. Bosworth / E. J. Baynham (eds.), *Alexander the Great in Fact and Fiction*, Oxford: 263-285.

— 2008: «The Role of the «Basilikoi Paides» at the Argead Court», in T. Howe / J. Reames (eds.), *Macedonian Legacies: Studies in Ancient Macedonian History and Culture in Honor of Eugene N. Borza*, Claremont: 145-164.

— 2015: *King and Court in Ancient Macedonia. Rivalry, Treason, and Conspiracy*, Swansea.

Cartledge, P. 2004: *Alexander the Great: The Hunt for a New Past*, London.

Cartledge, P. / Spawforth, A. 2002: *Hellenistic and Roman Sparta. A Tale of Two cities*, London.

Cary, G. 1956: *The Medieval Alexander*, Cambridge.

Cary, M. / Warmington, E. H. 1929: *The Ancient Explorers*, London.

Cassio, A. C. 1985: «Old Persian *Marīka-*, Eupolis, *Marikas* and Aristophanes, *Knights*», *CQ* 35: 38-42.

Casson, L. 1989: *The Periplus Maris Erythraei. Text with Introduction, Translation, and Commentary*, Princeton.

Cawkwell, G. L. 1969: «The Crowning of Demosthenes», *CQ* 19: 163-180.

— 1994: «The Deification of Alexander the Great: a note», in I. Worthington (ed.), *Ventures into Greek History*, Oxford: 293-306.

Chaplin, J. D. 2011: «Conversations in History: Arrian and Herodotus, Parmenio and Alexander», *GRBS* 51: 613-633.

Chugg, A. M. 2012: *Alexander's Lovers*, Austin.

Cloché, P. 1933: «Isocrate et la politique lacédémonienne», *REA* 35: 129-145.

Cohen, S. J. D. 1982: «Alexander the Great and Jaddus the High Priest According to Josephus», *AJS* 7: 41-68.

Collart, P. 1937: *Philippes villes de Macedóine, depuis ses origines jusqu'à la fin de l'époque romaine*, Paris.

Counillon, P. 2001: «Dionysos dans la Description de la Terre habitée de Denys d'Alexandrie», in I. Zinguer (ed), *Dionysos: origines et résurgences*, Paris: 105-114.

— 2013, «Denys le Periégète et ses sources», *GeogrAnt* 22: 91-98.

Cracco Ruggini, L. 1965: «Sulla cristianizzazione della cultura pagana: il mito greco e latino di Alessandro dall'età antonina al medioevo», *Athenaeum* 43: 3-80.

Curzon, G. N. 1892: *Persia and the Persian Question*, 2 vols, London.

De Siena, A. A. 2001: «Medea e Medos, eponimi della Media», in G. Traina (ed.), *Studi sull'XI libro dei Geōgrafikà di Strabone*, Galatina: 85–94.

Demandt, A. 2009: *Alexander der Grosse. Leben und Legende*, München.

Desanges, J. 2012: «L'excursus de Pline l'Ancien sur la navigation de mousson et la datation de ses sources», *Topoi* (Lyon) *Supplément* 11: 63-73.

Di Serio, C. 2020: «La dimensione mitica di Alessandro nel *De Alexandri Magni fortuna aut virtute*», in J. A. Clúa Serena (ed.), *Mythologica Plutarchea. Estudios sobre los mitos en Plutarco*, Madrid: 137-146 [in print].

Dilke, O. A. W. 1985: *Greek and Roman maps*.

Domínguez Monedero, A. J. 2014: «Filipo II, Alejandro III de Macedonia y Alejandro I el Moloso. La unidad de acción de sus políticas expansionistas», *Polifemo* 14: 203-236.

— 2016a: «Alejandro Magno y las ciudades griegas de Asia Menor: entre conquista y liberación»., in F. J. Gómez Espelosín / B. Antela Bernárdez (eds.), *El Imperio de Alejandro. Aspectos geográficos e historiográficos*, Alcalá de Henares: 76-113.

— 2016b: «La muerte de Alejandro Magno: ¿muerte natural o crimen perfecto?», in E. Fernández de Mier / J. Cortés Martín (eds.), *¿Pero quién mató a...? Muertes enigmáticas en el Mundo Antiguo*, Madrid: 13-33.

Dover, K. J. 1968a: *Aristophanes, Clouds*, Oxford.

— 1968b: *Lysias and the Corpus Lysiacum*, Berkeley–Los Angeles.

Dreyer, B. 2009: «Heroes, Cults and Divinity», in W. Heckel / L. Tritle (eds.), *Alexander the Great: A New History*, Malden: 218-234.

Droysen, J. G. 1877-1880 [1933-1998]: *Geschichte des Hellenismus*, 3 vols, Gotha–Hamburg Darmstad.

Dusinberre, E. R. M. 2005: «Herzfeld in Persepolis», in A. C. Gunter / S. R. Hauser (eds.), *Ernst Herzfeld and the Development of Near Eastern Studies, 1900-1950*, Leiden: 137-180.

Eddy, S. K. 1961: *The King Is Dead*, Lincoln.

Edmunds, L. 1971: «Alexander's Religiosity», *GRBS* 12: 363-391.

Edson, C. F. 1970: «Early Macedonia», in *AM* 1, Thessaloniki: 17-44.

Edwards, V. 1938: *Group Leader's Guide to Propaganda Analysis*, New York.

Ehrenberg, V 1938: «Pothos», in V. Ehrenberg: *Alexander and the Greeks*, Oxford: 52-61.

EHRHARDT, C. 1967: «Two Notes on Philip of Macedon's First Interventions in Thessaly», *CQ* 17: 296-301.

ELEFTHERATOU, S. 2016: «Δωδώνη και Ακρόπολη», in S. Eleftheratou / K. Soueref (eds.), *Δωδώνη. Το μαντείο των ήχων*, Athina: 191-192.

ENGELS, D. 1980: «Alexander's Intelligence System», *CQ* 30: 327-340.

ENGELS, J. 2010: «Macedonians and Greeks», in J. Roisman / I. Worthington (eds.), *A companion to Ancient Macedonia*, Oxford: 81-98.

ENGEN, D. T. 2010: *Honor and profit. Athenian trade policy and the economy and society of Greece, 415-307 B.C.E*, Ann Harbor.

ERRINGTON, M. 1974: «Macedonian 'Royal Style'», *JHS* 94: 20-37.

— 1983: «The historiographical origins of Macedonian Staatsrecht», in *AM* 3, Thessaloniki: 89-101.

— 1986: *Geschichte des Makedoniens. Von den Anfängen bis zum Untergang des Königreiches*, München.

— 1998: «Neue epigraphische Belege für Makedonien zur Zeit Alexanders des Grossen», in W. Will (ed.), *Alexander der Grosse: Eine Welteroberung und ihr Hintergrund*, Bonn: 77-90.

ÉTIENNE, R. 2002: «La Macédoine entre l'Orient et l'Occident: essai sur l'identité macédonienne au IVe s. av. J.-C.», in C. Muller / F. Prost (eds.), *Identités et cultures dans le monde méditerranéen antique*, Paris: 253-275.

EVANS, R. 2005: «The Cruel Sea? Ocean as Boundary Marker and Transgressor in Pliny´s Roman Geography», *Antichthon* 39: 105-119.

FARAGUNA, M. 1992: *Atene nell'età di Alessandro: Problemi politici, economici, finanziari*, Roma.

— 2003: «Alexander and the Greeks», in J. Roisman (ed.), *Brill's Companion to Alexander the Great*, Leiden: 99-130.

FERGUSSON, J. 1851: *Palaces of Ninevah and Persepolis Restored*, London.

FERNÁNDEZ NIETO, F. J. 2002: «Agis III, Anfótero y el PÓLEMOS XENIKÓS de Creta», *Athenaeum* 90: 111-124.

FLACELIÈRE, R. 1962: «Élève d'Aristote», in J. Romains (ed.), *Alexandre le Grand*, Paris: 41-50.

FLOWER, M. 1988: «Agesilaus of Sparta and the origins of the ruler cult», *CQ* 38: 123-134.

— 2000: «Alexander the Great and Panhellenism», in A. B. Bosworth / E. J. Baynham (eds.), *Alexander the Great in Fact and Fiction*, Oxford: 95-135.

— 2007: «Not great man history: Reconceptualizing a course on Alcxander the Great», *CW* 100.4: 417-23.

FOWLER, R. L. 2000: *Early Greek Mythography*, Oxford.

FRANKS, H. M. 2012: *Hunters, heroes, kings. The Frieze of Tomb II at Vergina*, Princeton.

FRASER, P. M. 1994: «The world of Theophrastus», in S. Hornblower (ed.), *Greek Historiography*, Oxford: 167-191.

FREDRICKSMEYER, E. A. 1958: *The Religion of Alexander the Great*, [PhD Diss.] University of Wisconsin.

— 1979: «Divine honors for Philip II», *TAPhA* 109: 39-61.

— 1981: «Again the so-called tomb of Philip II», *AJA* 85: 330-334.

— 1982: «On the final aims of Philip II», in W. L. Adams / E. N. Borza (eds.), *Philip II, Alexander the Great and the Macedonian heritage*, Washington: 85-98.

— 1991: «Alexander, Zeus Ammon, and the Conquest of Asia», *TAPhA* 121: 199-214.

— 2000: «Alexander the Great and the Kingship of Asia», in A. B. Bosworth / E. J. Baynham (eds.), *Alexander the Great in Fact and Fiction*, Oxford: 36-66.

— 2003: «Alexander's Religion and Divinity», in J. Roisman (ed.), *Brill's Companion to Alexander the Great*, Leiden: 253-278.

FREEMAN, P. 2011: *Alexander the Great*, New York.

FULLER, J. F. C. 1960: *The Generalship of Alexander the Great*, New Brunswick.

FUSSMAN, G. 2001: «Le Périple et l'histoire politique de l'Inde», *Journal Asiatique* 279: 31-38.

GABRIEL, R. A. 2015: *The Madness of Alexander the Great and the Myth of Military Genius*, Barnsley.

GALDÓN, G. 2004: «Prólogo», in AAVV, *Gestión de la Comunicación en las organizaciones*, Barcelona: 25-28.

GANDETO, J. S. G. 2002: *Ancient Macedonians: Differences between the ancient Macedonians and the Greeks*, Lincoln.

GARCÍA GALINDO, J. A. 1996: «La historia de la comunicación social: algunas propuestas en torno a la investigación científica y la docencia universitaria», in J. L. Gómez Mompart (ed.), *Metodologías para la Historia de la Comunicación Social: I Encuentro de la Asociación de Historiadores de la Comunicación*, Bellaterra: 37-40.

GARDINER-GARDEN, J. R. 1987: *Greek Conceptions of Inner Asian Geography and Ethnography from Ephoros to Eratosthenes*, Bloomington.

GARDNER, P. / POOLE, R. S. 1883: *Catalogue of Greek coins: Thessaly to Aetolia*, London.

GARNSEY, P. 1988: *Famine and Food Supply in the Graeco-Roman World*, Cambridge.

GEHRKE, H. J. 2015: «The revolution of Alexander the Great», in S. Bianchetti /– H.-J. Gehrke / M. R. Cataudella (eds.), *Brill's companion to ancient geography: The inhabited world in Greek and Roman tradition*, Leiden: 78-97.

GEUS, K. 2002: *Eratosthenes von Kyrene. Studien zur hellenistischen Kultur-und Wissenschaftsgeschichte*, München.

GILLIS, D. 1977-1978: «Imitatio Alexandri: The license to kill», *CRDAC* 9: 45-65.

GODLEY, A. D. 1982: *Herodotus, with an English Translation*, Cambridge.

GÓMEZ ESPELOSÍN, F. J. / ANTELA-BERNÁRDEZ, B. (eds.) 2016: *El imperio de Alejandro. Aspectos geográficos e historiográficos*, Alcalá.

Goukowsky, P. 1976: *Diodore de Sicile, Bibliothèque historique. Livre XVII*, Paris.
— 1978: *Essai sur les origines du mythe d'Alexandre, vol. I*, Nancy.
— 1981, *Essai sur les origins du mythe d'Alexandre, vol. II. Alexandre et Dionysos*, Nancy.
Grainger, J. 2007: *Alexander the Great Failure: The Collapse of the Macedonian Empire*, London.
— 2019: *Antipater's Dynasty*, Barnsley.
Green, P. 1991: *Alexander of Macedon 356-323 BC: A Historical Biography*, Berkeley, –London.
Greenwalt, W. S. 2010: «Argead Dunasteia during the Reigns of Philip II and Alexander III. Aristotle Reconsidered», in E. Carney / D. Ogden (eds.), *Philip II and Alexander the Great. Father and Son, Lives and Afterlives*, Oxford: 151-163.
— 2015: «Thracian and Macedonian kingship», in J. Valeva (ed.), *A Companion to Ancient Thrace*, Chichester: 337-51.
Gregoratti, L. 2014: «The Mardians: A Note», *Anabasis* 5: 76-85.
Griffith, G. T. 1970: «Philip of Macedon's Early Interventions in Thessaly (358-352 B.C.)», *CQ* 20: 67-80.
Grote, G. 1856: *A History of Greece*, 12 vols, London.
Gruen, E. S. 2011: *Rethinking the Other in Antiquity*, Princeton–Oxford.
Guarducci, M. 2008: *Η Ελληνική επιγραφική, από τις αρχές ως την ύστερη αυτοκρατορική περίοδο*, Athina (Transl. K. Kouremenos).
Gunderson, L. L. 1980: *Alexander's Letter to Aristotle about India*, Meisenheim am Glan.
Guzmán Guerra, A. 1982: *Arriano. Anábasis de Alejandro Magno*, 2 vols, Madrid.
— 1986: *Plutarco - Diodoro: Alejandro Magno*, Madrid.
Hallock, R. T. 1969: *Persepolis Fortification Tablets*, Chicago.
Hamilton, C. D. 1982: «Philip II and Archidamus», in W. L. Adams / E. N. Borza (eds.), *Philip II, Alexander the Great and the Macedonian Heritage*, Washington: 61-83.
Hamilton, J. R. 1961a: «Cleitarchus and Aristobulus», *Historia* 10: 448-458.
— 1961b: «The Letters in Plutarch's Alexander», *PACA* 4, 9-20.
— 1969 [2002]: *Plutarch: Alexander. A Commentary*, Oxford.
— 1973: *Alexander the Great*, London.
Hammond, N. G. L. 1980: *Alexander the Great. King, commander and statesman*, London.
— 1982: «The evidence for the identity of the Royal Tombs at Vergina», in W. L. Adams / E. N. Borza (eds.), *Philip II, Alexander the Great and the Macedonian heritage*, Washington: 111-127.
— 1983: *Three historians of Alexander the Great: The so-called Vulgate authors: Diodorus, Justin, and Curtius*, Cambridge.
— 1986: «The Kingdom of Asia and the Persian Throne», *Antichthon* 20: 73-85.
— 1988a: «The King and the Land in the Macedonian Kingdom», *CQ* 38: 382-391.

— 1988b: «The Royal Journal of Alexander», *Historia* 37: 129-150.
— 1989: *The Macedonian State. Origins, Institutions and History*, Oxford.
— 1990a: «Inscriptions concerning Philippoi and Calindoea in the Reign of Alexander the Great», *ZPE* 82: 167-175.
— 1990b: «Royal Pages, Personal Pages, and Boys trained in the Macedonian manner during the period of the Temenid Monarchy», *Historia* 39: 261-290.
— 1992a: «The Archaeological and Literary Evidence for the Burning of the Persepolis Palace», *CQ* 42: 358-386.
— 1992b: *Alejandro Magno. Rey, general y estadista*, Madrid.
— 1993a: *Sources for Alexander the Great. An Analysis of Plutarch's «Life» and Arrian's «Anabasis Alexandrou»*, Cambridge.
— 1993b: «A Note on E. Badian, 'Alexander and Philippoi', *ZPE* 95 (1993) 131-139», *ZPE* 100: 385-387.
— 1997: *The Genius of Alexander the Great*, London.
— 1999: «Speeches in Arrian's *Indica* and *Anabasis*», *CQ* 49: 238-253.
— 2000: «The Continuity of Macedonian Institutions and the Macedonian Kingdoms of the Hellenistic Era», *Historia* 49: 141-160.
Hammond, N. G. L. / Griffith, G. T. 1979: *A History of Macedonia, vol. II: 550-336 B.C.*, Oxford.
Hammond, N. G. L. / Walbank, F. W. 1995: *Ιστορία της Μακεδονίας Γ' (336-167 π. Χ.)*. Thessaloniki (Transl. A. Kosmatopoulos).
Hansen, M. H. 1974: *The Sovereignty of the People's Court in Athens in the Fourth Century BC and the Public Action against Unconstitutional Proposals*, Odense.
Hanson, V. D. 1998: «Alexander the Killer», *MHQ* 10: 8-19.
Harrison, T. 2007: «Respectable in its Ruins: Achaemenid Persia, Ancient and Modern», in L. Hardwick / C. Stray (eds.), *A Companion to Classical Receptions*, Malden: 50-61.
Hartog, F. 1996: *Mémoire d'Ulysse. Récits sur la frontière en Grèce ancienne*, Paris.
Hasnas, J. 2012: «Reflections on corporate moral responsibility and the problem solving technique of Alexander the Great», *Journal of Business Ethics* 107: 183-195.
Hatzopoulos, M. B. 1986: «Succession and Regency in classical Macedonia», in *AM* 4, Thessaloniki: 279-292.
— 1987: «Bulletin Épigraphique. Macédoine», *REG* 100: 421-440.
— 1988: «Bulletin Épigraphique. Macédoine», *REG* 101: 433-450.
— 1990: «Bulletin Épigraphique. Macédoine», *REG* 103: 520-530.
— 1991: «Bulletin Épigraphique. Macédoine», *REG* 104: 497-505.
— 1993: «Bulletin Épigraphique. Macédoine», *REG* 106: 516-519.
— 1994: «Thessalie et Macédoine: Affinités et Convergences», in *La Thessalie. Quinze Ans de Recherches Archéologiques 1975-1990. Bilan et Perspectives*, Athina: 249-254.
— 1996: *Macedonian institutions under the kings*, 2 vols, Athina.
— 1997: «Alexandre en Perse: la revanche et l'empire», *ZPE* 116: 41-52.

— 2011: «Macedonia and the Macedonians», in R. Lane Fox (ed.), *Brill's Companion to Ancient Macedon. Studies in the Archaeology and History of Macedon, 650 BC-300 AD*, Leiden–Boston: 43-49.
Hatzopoulos, M. B. / Loukopoulou, L. D. 1992: *Recherches sur les marches orientales des Temenides (Anthemonte - Kalindoia)*, Athina.
Hazzard, R. A. 1992: «Did Ptolemy I Get His Surname from the Rhodians?», *ZPE* 93: 52-56.
Heckel, W. 1988: *The Last Days and Testament of Alexander the Great: A prosopographic study*, Stuttgart.
— 1992: *The Marshals of Alexander's Empire*, London.
— 2004: «What's new in Alexander studies», *Amphora* 3: 10-12.
— 2006: *Who's who in the age of Alexander the Great. Prosopography of Alexander's empire*, Oxford.
— 2007: *The Conquests of Alexander the Great*, Cambridge.
— 2009: «Alexander's Conquest of Asia», in W. Heckel / L. A. Tritle (eds.), *Alexander the Great. A New History*, Malden: 26-52.
— 2015a: «Alexander, Achilles, and Heracles: Between Myth and History», in P. Wheatley /– E. Baynham (eds.), *East and West in the World Empire of Alexander. Essays in Honour of Brian Bosworth*, Oxford: 21-33.
— 2015b: «Alexander the Great and the fate of the enemy: Quantifying, Qualifying and Categorizing Atrocities», in W. Heckel / S. Müller / G. Wrightson (eds.), *The Many Faces of War in the Ancient World*, Cambridge: 233-268.
— 2020: *In the Path of Conquest: Resistance to Alexander the Great*, Oxford.
Helly, B. 1995: *L'État thessalien: Aleuas Le Roux, les Trétrades et les Tagoi*, Lyon.
Helly, B. / Te Riele, G.-J. / van Rossum, J. A. 1979: «La Liste des Gymnasiarques de Phères pour les années 330-189 av. J.-C.», in *La Thessalie. Actes de la Table-Ronde, 21-24 Juillet 1975, Lyon*, Lyon: 220-255.
Henkelman, W. F. M. 2008: *The Other Gods Who Are: Studies in Elamite-Iranian Acculturation based on the Persepolis Fortification Texts*, Leiden.
Herrmann, A. 1932: *RE* IV A.2, s.v. 'Taprobane', cols. 2260-2272.
Herzfeld, E. 1935: *Archaeological History of Iran*, Oxford.
Heuss, A. 1954: «Alexander der Grosse und die politische Ideologie des Altertums», *A&A* 4: 65-104
Hilka, A. (ed.) 1977: *Historia Alexandri Magni (Historia de preliis). Rezension J^2 (Orosius - Rezension). Teil II*, Meisenheim am Glan.
Hilka, A. / Steffens, K. (eds.) 1979: *Historia Alexandri Magni (Historia de preliis): Resenzion J_1*, Meisenheim am Glan.
Hoffmann, O. 1906: *Die Makedonen, ihre Sprache und ihr Volkstum*, Göttingen.
Holt, F. L. 1988: *Alexander the Great and Bactria. The formation of a Greek frontier in Central Asia*, Leiden.
— 1999: «Alexander the Great today: In the interests of historical accuracy», *AHB* 13: 111-117.

— 2006: *Into the Land of Bones: Alexander the Great in Afghanistan*, Berkeley.
— 2016: *The Treasures of Alexander the Great*, Oxford.
Howe, T. 2014: «Founding Alexandria: Alexander the Great and the Politics of Memory», in P. Bosman (ed.), *Alexander in Africa*, Pretoria: 72-91.
— 2016: «Alexander and «Afghan insurgency»: A Reassessment», in T. Howe / L. L. Brice (eds.), *Brill's Companion to Insurgency and Terrorism in the Ancient Mediterranean*, Leiden: 151-183.
— 2020: «Friendship is Golden: Harpalus, Alexander and Athens», in M. D'Agostini / E. M. Anson / F. PownalL (eds.), *Affective Relations and Personal Bonds in Hellenistic Antiquity. Studies in Honor of Elizabeth D. Carney*, Oxford: 195-212.
Howe, T. / Garvin, E. E. / Wrightson, G. (eds.) 2015: *Greece, Macedon and Persia. Studies in Social, Political and Military History in Honour of Waldemar Heckel*, Oxford.
Howe, T. / Müller, S. 2012: «Mission Accomplished: Alexander at the Hyphasis», *AHB* 26: 21-38.
Ilyushechkina, E. 2010: *Studien zu Dionysius von Alexandria*, Groningen.
Jacob, C. 1981: «L´oeil et la mémoire: sur la Périègese de la Terre habitée de Denys», in C. Jacob / F. Lestringant (eds.), *Arts et légendes d´espaces. Figures du voyage et rhétoriques du monde*, Paris: 23-97.
— 1990: *La description de la terre habitée de Denys d´Alexandrie ou la leçon de géographie*, Paris.
— 1991: «*Theós Hermés epí Hadrianou*: la mise en scène du pouvoir impérial dans la *Description de la Terre habitée* de Denys d´Alexandrie», *CCG* 2: 43-53.
— 1999: «Mapping in the Mind: The Earth from Ancient Alexandria», in D. Cosgrove (ed.), *Mappings*, London: 24-49.
Jacoby, F. 1921: *RE* XI.1, s.v. 'Kleitarchos (2)', cols. 622-654.
— 1930: *Die Fragmente der griechischen Historiker II D*, Berlin.
Jamzadeh, P. 2012: *Alexander Histories and Iranian Reflections: Remnants of Propaganda and Resistance*, Leiden.
Janni, P. 1978: *Etnografia e mito. La storia dei Pigmei*, Roma.
Kakarikos, K. 2015: «Interaction Phenomena in Ancient Greek Compounds: Cases of the Morphology–Phonology Interface», *Studies in Greek Linguistics* 35: 248-260.
Kanatsoules, D. 1958-1959: «Antipatros als Feldherr und Staatsmann in der Zeit Philipps und Alexanders des Grossen», *Hellenika* 16: 14-64.
— 1964: *Η Ιστορία της Μακεδονίας μέχρι του Μεγάλου Κωνσταντίνου*, Thessaloniki.
— 1976: *Η Μακεδονία από αρχαιοτήτων χρόνων μέχρι της ανόδου του Φιλίππου Β'*, Thessaloniki.
Kantzia, C. 1980: «... τιμος Αβδαλων μου /[Σιδ] νος βασιλ ως: A Bilingual Greco-Phoenician Inscription from Kos», *ArchDelt* 35: 1-16.
Karttunen, K. 1987: «The country of Fabulous Beasts and Naked Philosophers. India in Classical and Medieval Literature», *Arctos* 21: 43-52.
— 1997: *India and the Hellenistic world*, Helsinki.

Kessler, O. 2016: «Environment, Infrastructure and Nature of Ports in Ancient Sri Lanka. Archaeological Evidence from the Port, Monastery, Town and Shipwreck of Godavaya (*Godapavata Pattana*)», in M. F. Boussac / J. F. Salles / J. P. Yon (eds.), *Ports of the Ancient Indian Ocean*, Delhi: 435-458.

Kevran, M. 1999: «Multiple Ports at the Mouth of the River Indus: Barbarike, Deb, Daybul, Lahori Bandal, DiulSinde», in H. P. Ray (ed.), *Archaeology of Seafaring*, Delhi: 70-153.

Kholod, M. M. 2020: «On the Titulature of Alexander the Great. The Title of basileus», in K. Tampedach / A. Meeus (eds), *The Legitimation of Conquest: Monarchical Representation and the Art of Government in the Empire of Alexander the Great*, Stuttgart: 219-241.

King, C. J. 2017: *Ancient Macedonia*, London.

Kingsley, B. M. 1981: «The Cap that Survived Alexander», *AJA* 85: 39-46.

— 1984: «The Kausia Diadematophoros», *AJA* 88: 66-68.

— 1991: «Alexander's Kausia and Macedonian tradition», *CA* 10: 59-76.

Kornemann, E. 1935: *Die Alexandergeschichte des Königs Ptolemaios I. von Ägypten. Versuch einer Rekonstruktion*, Leipzig–Berlin.

Kremmydas, C. 2013: «Alexander the Great, Athens, and the Rhetoric of the Persian Wars», in C. Carey / M. Edwards (eds.), *Marathon – 2,500 Years Proceedings of the Marathon Conference*, London: 199-213.

Kurke, L. B. 2004: *The wisdom of Alexander the Great: Enduring leadership lessons from the man who created an empire*, New York.

Landucci Gattinoni, F. 1994: «I mercenari nella poltica ateniese dell'età di Alessandro. Parte I: Soldati e ufficiali mercenari ateniesi al servizio della Persia», *AncSoc* 25: 33-61.

— 2013: «Gli Spartani e la Macedonia in età classica e protoellenistica», *Aristonothos* 8: 265-285.

Lane Fox, R. 1973: *Alexander the Great*, London.

Lapeña, O. / Antela-Bernárdez, B. 2020: *Alejandro magno en las pantallas*, Bellaterra.

Le Rider, G. 1996: *Monnayage et finances de Philippe II: Un état de la question*, Paris.

Lecouteux, C. 1981: «Les cynocéphales. Étude d'une tradition tératologique de l'Antiquité au XIIe s.», *Cahiers de Civilisation médiévale* 24: 117-129.

Lehmann, P. W. 1980: «The so-called tomb of Philip II: A different interpretation», *AJA* 84: 527-531.

Lenfant, D. 2004: *Ctésias de Cnide. La Perse. L'Inde. Autres Fragments*, Paris.

Leroy, P. O. 2016: *Strabon. Géographie. Tome XII. Livre XV. L'Inde, l'Ariane et la Perse*, París.

Lewis, D. 1977: *Sparta and Persia*, Leiden.

Lightfoot, J. L. 2014: *Dionysius Periegetes Description of the Known World*, Oxford.

Lindsay Adams, W. 1986: «Macedonian Kingship and the right of petition», in *AM* 4, Thessaloniki: 43-52.

— 1996: «In the Wake of Alexander the Great: The Impact of Conquest in the Aegean World», *AncW* 27: 29-37.

Lock, R. A. 1972: «The date of Agis III's war in Greece», *Antichthon* 6: 10-27.

Luschey, H. 1968: «Iran und der Western vom Kyros bis Khosrow», *AMI* 1: 15-38.

Ma, J. 2013: «Alexander's Decision-making as a Historical Problem», *Revue des Etudes Militaires Anciennes* 6, 113-125.

Mahaffy, J 1887: *The Empire of Alexander the Great*, New York.

Maitland, J. 2015: «ΜΗΝΙΝ ΑΕΙΔΕ ΘΕΑ: Alexander the Great and the Anger of Achilles», in P. Wheatley / E. Baynham (eds.), *East and West in the World Empire of Alexander: Essays in Honour of Brian Bosworth*, Oxford: 1-20.

Marcotte, D. 2016: «Le Périple de la mer Érythrée et les informateurs de Ptolémée. Géographie et traditions textuelles», *Journal Asiatique* 304: 33-46.

Marcus, R. 1937: *Josephus: Jewish Antiquities. Books 9-11*, Cambridge.

Mari, M. 2002: *Al di là dell'Olimpo: Macedoni e grandi santuari della Grecia dall'età arcaica al primo ellenismo*, Athina.

— 2018: «Powers in Dialogue: The Letters and diagrammata of the Macedonian Kings to Local Communities», in P. Ceccarelli / L. Doering / Th. Fögen / I. Gildenhard (eds.), *Letters & Communities. Studies in the socio-political dimensions of ancient epistolography*, Oxford: 121-146.

— 2020: «Alexander, the King of the Macedonians», in K. Tampedach / A. Meeus (eds), *The Legitimation of Conquest: Monarchical Representation and the Art of Government in the Empire of Alexander the Great*, Stuttgart: 197-217.

Marinatos, S. 1970: «Mycenaean Elements within the Royal House of Macedonia», *AM* 1, Thessaloniki:: 45-52.

Mariotta, G. 2017: «Una spedizione di Onesicrito nello Sri Lanka?», *Sileno* 43: 113-120.

Markwart, J. 1928: «Le berceau des Arméniens», *REArm* 8: 211-232.

Martín Serrano, M. 1982: *Teoría de la Comunicación. Epistemología y Análisis de la Referencia*, Madrid.

Martin, T. R. 1981: «Diodorus on Philip II and Thessaly in the 350s B. C.», *CPh* 76: 188-201.

— 1982: «A Phantom Fragment of Theopompus and Philip II's First Campaign in Thessaly», *HSPh* 86: 55-78.

McLaughlin, R. 2014: *The Roman Empire and the Indian Ocean. The ancient world economy and the kingdoms of Africa, Arabia and India*, Barnsley.

McPhail, C. / Hannah, R. 2008-2011: «Eratosthenes´Perception of the Caspian Sea: A Gulf or an Inland Sea?», *Orbis Terrarum* 10: 155-172.

McQueen, E. I. 1978: «Some notes on the anti-Macedonian movement in the Peloponnese in 331 B.C.», *Historia* 27: 40-64.

Mederer, E. 1936: *Die Alexanderlegenden bei den ältesten Historikern*, Stuttgart.
Mendels, D. 1984: «Aetolia 331-301: Frustration, political power and survival», *Historia* 33: 129-180.
Mendoza, M. 2017: «Stasanor of Soloi and the government of Bactria during the wars of the Diadochi», *Anabasis* 8: 44-70.
— 2019a: *La impiedad de Alejandro*, Alcalá de Henares.
Mendoza, M. 2019b. «El ejército persa en el cine», in B. Antela-Bernárdez / J. Vidal (eds.), *La guerra de la Antigüedad en el cine*, Zaragoza: 81-127.
Mendoza, M. 2020. «Cleómenes de Náucratis: realidad, fuentes e historiografía», *Trabajos de Egiptología* 11: 215-224.
Mendoza, M. / Antela-Bernárdez, B. (eds.) 2022: *Historiographical Alexander. Alexander the Great and the Historians in XIXth and XXth Centuries*, Coimbra [in print].
Mills, K. R. 1998: *Colonial Spanish America: A Documentary History*, California.
Milns, R. D. 1968: *Alexander the Great*, London.
— 1999: «The Effects of Alexander's Campaigns on Food Prices», in *AM* 6, Thessaloniki: 763-769.
Mitchel, F. 1965: «Athens in the Time of Alexander», *G&R* 12: 189-204.
Molina Marín, A. I. 2011: *Geographica. Ciencia del espacio y tradición narrativa de Homero a Cosmas Indicopleustes*, Murcia.
— 2017a:«Póthos y musas. El anhelo de los reyes de Macedonia», *Minerva* 30: 13-34.
— 2017b: «Under the shadow of Eratosthenes: Strabo and the Alexander historians», in D. Dueck (ed.), *The Routledge Companion to Strabo*, London: 294-305.
— 2018: *Alejandro Magno (1916-2015). Un siglo de estudios sobre Macedonia antigua*, Zaragoza.
Molina Marín, A. I. 2022: «Geography, science, knowledge of the world and Alexander's expedition», in D. Ogden (ed.), *Cambridge Companion to Alexander the Great*, Cambridge [in print].
Momigliano, A. 1979: «Flavius Josephus and Alexander's Visit to Jerusalem», *Athenaeum* 57: 442-448.
Mørkholm, O. 1991: *Early Hellenistic coinage: from the accession of Alexander to the Peace of Apamea (336-188 B.C.)*, Cambridge.
Morrison, G. 2001: «Alexander, Combat Psychology, and Persepolis», *Antichthon* 35: 30-44.
Mousavi, A. 2012: *Persepolis: Discovery and Afterlife of a World Wonder*, Berlin.
Müller, C. (ed.) 1846: *Arriani Anabasis et Indica ex optimo codice Parisino emendavit et varietatem ejus libri retulit Fr. Dübner. Reliqua Arriani et scriptorum de rebus Alexandri M. Fragmenta collegit, Pseudo Callisthenis historiam fabulosam ex tribus codicibus nunc primum edidit, Itinerarium Alexandri et indices adiecit C. Müller*, Paris.
Müller, S. 2011: «Die frühen Perserkönige im kulturellen Gedächtnis der Makedonen und in der Propaganda Alexanders d. Gr.», *Gymnasium* 118: 105-133.

NAGLE, D. B. 1996: «The Cultural Context of Alexander's Speech at Opis», *TAPhA* 126, 151-172.

NAWOTKA, K. 2003a: «Alexander the Great in Persepolis», *AAntHung* 43: 67-76.

— 2003b: «Freedom of Greek Cities in Asia Minor in the Age of Alexander the Great», *Klio* 85: 15-41.

— 2010: *Alexander the Great*, Newcastle upon Tyne.

— 2017: *The Alexander Romance by Ps.-Callistenes. A Historical Commentary*, Leiden–Boston.

NÖLDEKE, T. 1887: *Aufsätze zur persischen Geschichte*, Leipzig.

O'BRIEN, J. M. 1992: *Alexander the Great: The Invincible Enemy*, London.

OGDEN, D. 2009: «Alexander's Sex Life», in W. Heckel / L. A. Tritle (eds.), *Alexander the Great. A New History*, Chichester: 203-218.

— 2011: *Alexander the Great. Myth, Genesis and Sexuality*, Exeter.

OLBRYCHT, M. J. 2008: «Curtius Rufus, the Macedonian Mutiny at Opis and Alexander's Iranian Policy in 324 BC», in J. Pigoń (ed.), *The Children of Herodotus. Greek and Roman Historiography and Related Genres*, Newcastle upon Tyne: 231-252.

— 2011: «First Iranian Military Units in the Army of Alexander the Great», *Anabasis* 2: 67-84.

— 2014: «'An Admirer of Persian Ways': Alexander the Great's Reforms in Parthia-Hyrcania and the Iranian Heritage», in T. Daryaee / A. Mousavi / K. Rezakhani (eds.), *Excavating an Empire, Achaemenid Persia in Longue Durée*, Costa Mesa: 37-62.

— 2015: «The Epigonoi – The Iranian Phalanx of Alexander the Great», in W. Heckel / S. Müller / G. Wrightson (eds.), *The Many Faces of War in the Ancient World*, Newcastle upon Tyne: 196-212.

OMIDSALAR, M. 2008: «Jamšid. ii. In Persian Literature», *Enc. Iran.* 14: 522-528.

OVERTOOM, N. 2013: «Six Polybian Themes Concerning Alexander the Great», *CW* 106: 571-593.

PALAGIA, O. 2002: «Ο Ζεύς Νάιος και Διώνη στην Ακρόπολη της Αθήνας», in *Αφιέρωμα στη μνήμη του γλύπτη Στέλιου Τριάντη*, Athina: 71-180.

— 2009: «Review: *The Derveni Krater*, by Beryl Barr-Sharrarr», *AntJ* 89: 432-433.

PARIBENI, R. 1947: *La Macedonia sino ad Alessandro Magno*, Milano.

PARKE, H. W. 1977: *Festivals of the Athenians*, London.

PEARSON, L. 1955: «The Diary and Letters of Alexander», *Historia* 3: 429-455.

— 1960: *The Lost Histories of Alexander the Great*, New York–London.

PÉDECH, P. 1976: *La géographie des grecs*, Paris.

PELTONEN, J. 2019: *Alexander the Great in the Roman Empire, 150 BC to AD 600*, London.

PEJENAUTE RUBIO, F. 2008: *Quinto Curcio Rufo: Historia de Alejandro Magno*, Madrid.

PERRIN, B. 1919: *Plutarch's Lives*, Cambridge.

PFISTER, F. 1910: *Kleine Texte zum Alexanderroman*, Heidelberg.

PIZARROSO QUINTERO, A. 1993: *Historia de la propaganda. Notas para un estudio de la propaganda política y de guerra*, Madrid.

— 1996: «La situación actual en España de los estudios de Historia de la Comunicación Social: problemas y perspectivas», in J. L. Gómez Mompart (ed.), *Metodologías para la Historia de la Comunicación Social: I Encuentro de la Asociación de Historiadores de la Comunicación*, Bellaterra: 87-94.

Poddighe, E. 2009: «Alexander and the Greeks. The Corinthian League», in W. Heckel / L. A. Tritle (eds.), *Alexander the Great. A New History*, Oxford: 99-120.

Pope, A. U. 1957: «Persepolis as a Ritual City», *Archaeology* 10: 123-130.

Potter, D. S. 1984: «IG II2 399; evidence for Athenian involvement in the War of Agis III», *ABSA* 79: 229-235.

Prandi, L. 1996: *Fortuna e realtà dell'opera di Clitarco*, Stuttgart.

— 2013: *Diodoro Siculo: Biblioteca storica, Libro XVII, Commento storico*, Milano.

Prestianni-Giallombardo, A. M. 1986: «Il diadema di Vergina e l'iconografia di Filippo II», in *AM* 4, Thessaloniki: 497-509.

Price, M. J. 1991: *The Coinage of in the Name of Alexander the Great and Philip Arrhidaeus*, 2 vols, London.

Pridik, E. 1893: *De Alexandri Magni Epistularum Commercio*, Dorpat.

Prontera, F. 2012: «Le Porte Caspie: dalla topografia alla geografia», in R. Bargnesi / R. Scuderi (eds.), *Il Paesaggio e l'esperienza. Scritti di antichità offerti a Pierluigi Tozzi in occasione del suo 75º compleanno*, Pavia: 129-134.

Pyankov, I. V. 2014: «The Oxus and the Caspian Sea in the Ancient Geography of the Classical World», in A. V. Podossinov (ed.), *Periphery of the Classical World in Ancient Geography and Cartography*, Leuven: 59-66.

Radet, G. 1925: *Notes critiques sur l'histoire d'Alexandre*, Bordeaux.

— 1931: *Alexandre le Grand*, Paris.

Radt, S. 2008: «Miscellanea Kleinigkeiten zu Plutarch», *Mnemosyne* 61: 634-646.

Ralli, A. 2008: «Compound Markers and Parametric Variation. Language Typology and Universals», *STUF (Language Typology and Universals)* 61: 19-38.

Rathmann, M. 2017: *Tabula Peutingeriana. Die einzige Weltkarte aus der Antike*², Darmstadt.

Ravazzolo, C. 1998: «Clitarco e il suo tempo», *Patavium* 6: 31-44.

Ray, H. P. 2003: *The Archaeology of Seafaring in Ancient South Asia*, Cambridge.

Razmjou, S. 2005: «Ernst Herzfeld and the Study of Graffiti at Persepolis», in A. C. Gunter / S. R. Hauser (eds.), *Ernst Herzfeld and the Development of Near Eastern Studies, 1900-1950*, Leiden: 315-341.

Rhodes, P. J. / Osborne, R. 2007 [2003]: *Greek historical inscriptions, 404-323 BC*, Oxford.

Ritter, H.-W. 1965: *Diadem und Königsherrschaft. Untersuchungen zu Zeremonien und Rechtsgrundlagen des Herrschaftsantritts bei den Persern, bei Alexander dem Grossen und im Hellenismus*, München.

Roaf, M. 1983: «Sculptures and Sculptors at Persepolis», *Iran* 21: 1-164.

Robert, L. 1968: «De Delphes à l'Oxus. Inscriptions grecques nouvelles de la Bactriane», *CRAI* 112: 416-457.

ROBIN, C. 1991: «L'Arabie du sud et la date du Périple de la mer Érythrée», *JA* 279: 1-30.
ROBINSON, C. A., JR 1945: «Alexander the Great and Parmenio», *AJA* 49: 422-424.
— 1949: «Review: Alexander the Great by W. W. Tarn», *AJPh* 70: 192-202.
— 1957: «The extraordinary ideas of Alexander the Great», *AHR* 62: 326-344.
ROBSON, J. C. 1929: *Arrian: Anabasis of Alexander the great*, Cambridge.
ROEBUCK, C. 1948: «The settlements of Philip II with the Greek States in 338 B.C.», *CPh* 43: 73-92.
ROISMAN, J. 2012a: *Alexander's Veterans and the Early Wars of the Successors*, Austin.
— 2012b: «Royal Power, Law and Justice in Ancient Macedonia», *AHB* 26: 131-148.
ROLFE, J. C. 1946: *Quintus Curtius. History of Alexander II: Books VI-X*, London.
— 1962: *Quintus Curtius. History of Alexander*, 2 vols, London.
ROLLER, D. W. 2010: *Eratosthenes' Geography*, Princeton–Oxford.
— 2015: *Ancient Geography. The Discovery of the World in Classical Greece and Rome*, London.
ROMM, J. S. 1989: «Aristotle's elephant and the myth of Alexander's scientific patronage», *AJPh* 10: 566-575.
— 1992: *The Edges of the Earth in Ancient Thought. Geography, Exploration, and Fiction*, Princeton.
— 2010: «Alexander's Policy of Perso-Macedonian Fusion», in *The Landmark Arrian – The Campaigns of Alexander*, New York: 380-387.
ROOT, M. 1979: *The King and Kingship in Achaemenid Art*, Leiden.
ROSELLINI, M. (ed.) 2004: *Res gestae Alexandri Macedonis*, München–Leipzig.
ROSS, D. J. A. 1963: *Alexander Historiatus. A Guide to Medieval Illustrated Alexander Literature*, London.
RUIZ ACOSTA, M. J. 1997: «La historia de la comunicación social en el ámbito universitario: objeto, fundamentos y problemas», *Comunicación y sociedad* 10: 185-202.
RUSSO, L. 2004: *The forgotten revolution: how the science was born in the 300 BC and why it had to be reborn*, Berlin–New York.
RUZICKA, S. 1988: «War in the Aegean, 333-331 B.C.: A Reconsideration», *Phoenix* 42: 131-151.
SACHS, A. / HUNGER, H. 1988-1996: *Astronomical Diaries and Related Texts from Babylon*, Vienna.
SALLMANN, K. G. 1971: *Die Geographie des älteren Plinius in ihrem Verhältnis zu Varro. Versuch einer Quellenanalyse*, Berlin–New York.
SANCISI-WEERDENBURG, H. 1993: «Alexander and Persepolis», in J. Carlson (ed.), *Alexander the Great: Reality and Myth*, Rome: 177-188.
SANDERS, L. J. 1991: «Dionysius of Syracuse and the origins of the ruler cult in the Greek world», *Historia* 40: 275-287.
SAVILL, A. F 1955: *Alexander the Great and his time*, London.

Sawada, N. 2010: «Social customs and institutions: Aspects of Macedonian elite society», in J. Roisman / I. Worthington (eds.), *A companion to ancient Macedonia*, Oxford: 392-408.

Schachermeyr, F. 1973: *Alexander der Grosse: Das Problem seiner Personlichkeit und seines Wirkens*, Vienna.

Schmidt, E. F. 1953: *Persepolis I: Structures, Reliefs, Inscriptions*, Chicago

— 1970: *Persepolis III: The Royal Tombs and Other Monuments*, Chicago.

Schwartz, D. R. 2008: *2 Maccabees*, Berlin.

Schwenk, J. 1985: *Athens in the Age of Alexander. The dated laws and decrees of the 'Lykourgan Era' 338-322 B.C.*, Chicago.

Scott, G. 1938: «Persepolis», *G&R* 7: 65-75.

Seibert, J. 2004-2005: «Alexander der Große in Persepolis (Takht-e Ĵamšīd), Iranistik», *Deutschsprachige Zeitschrift für iranistische Studien* 6: 5-105.

Seland, E. H. 2010: *Ports and Political Power in the Periplus: Complex Societies and Maritime Trade on the Indian Ocean in the First Century AD*, Oxford.

Shahbazi, A. S. 1977: «From Pārsa to Taxt-e Jamšid», *AMI* 9: 197-207.

Shea, J. 1997: *Macedonia and Greece: The struggle to define a new Balkan nation*, London.

Sheedy, K. E. 2007: *Alexander and the Hellenistic kingdoms: Coins, image and the creation of identity: the Westmoreland collection*, Sydney.

Sisti, F. 2001: *Anabasi di Alessandro. Vol. 1: Libri I-III*, Milano.

Sisti, F. / Zambrini, A. 2004: *Anabasi di Alessandro. Vol. 2: Libri IV-VII*, Milano.

Smyth, H. W. 1920: *Greek Grammar*, Cambridge.

Sordi, M. 1956: «La Dracma di Aleuas e l'origine di un tipo monetario di Alessandro Magno», *AIIN* 3, 9-22 [Repr. 2002: *Scritti di storia greca*, Milano: 159-173].

— 1958: *La lega tessala fino ad Alessandro Magno*, Roma.

— 1984: «Alessandro e l'Anfizionia nel 336/5», in M. Sordi (ed.), *Alessandro Magno: Tra storia e mito*, Milano: 9-13.

Sotelo Enríquez, C. 2004: «Historia de la gestión de la comunicación en las organizaciones», in *Gestión de la Comunicación en las organizaciones*, Barcelona: 35-56.

Squillace, G. 1998-2001: «Filippo triskaidekatos theos nella proposta di Demade del 338 a.C. (nota ad Apsin., Tech. Rhet. IX 470 Walz)», *MStudStor* 11: 31-46.

— 2000: «L'ultimo intervento di Filipo II in Tessaglia nella propaganda macedone e antimacedone», *Aevum* 74: 81-94.

— 2010: «Consensus Strategies under Philip and Alexander – The Revenge Theme», in E. Baynham / D. Ogden (eds.), *Philip II and Alexander the Great: Father and son, lives and afterlives*, Oxford: 69-80.

Standish, J. F. 1980: «The Caspian Gates», *G&R* 17: 17-24.

Steffens, K. (ed.) 1975: *Die Historia de preliis Alexandri Magni. Rezension J^3*, Meiseheim am Glan.

STEINMANN, M. 2012: *Alexander der Grosse und die «nackten Weisen" Indiens*, Berlin.

STEVENS, K. 2016: «From Herodotus to a Hellenistic World? The Eastern Geographies of Aristotle and Theophrastus», in E. Barker / S. Bouzarovski / C. Pellin / L. Isaksen (eds.), *New Worlds from Old Texts. Revisiting Ancient Space and Place*, Oxford: 121-152.

STEWART, A. 1993: *Faces of power: Alexander's image and Hellenistic politics*, Berkeley.

STONEMAN, R. 1994: «Romantic Ethnography: Central Asia and India in the Alexander Romance», *AncW* 25: 93-107.

— 1997: *Alexander the Great*, London.

— (ed.) 2007: *Il Romanzo di Alessandro. Vol. I*, Milano.

— 2008: *Alexander the Great. A Life in Legend*, New Haven–London.

— 2019: *The Greek Experience of India: From Alexander to the Indo-Greeks*, Princeton.

STRASBURGER, H. 1939: *RE* XVIII.1, s.v. 'Onesikritos', cols. 460-467.

STROOTMAN, R. 2007: *The Hellenistic Royal Court. Court Culture, Ceremonial and Ideology in Greece, Egypt and the Near East, 336-30 BCE*, [PhDiss.] University of Utrecht.

— 2010-2011: «Alexander's Thessalian Cavalry», *Talanta* 42-43: 51-67.

SZNYCER, M. 1980: «La partie phénicienne de l'inscription bilingue Greco-phenicienne de Cos», *ArchDelt* 35: 17-30.

TAIETTI, G. D. M. 2016: «Alexander the Great as a Herodotean Persian King», in K. Nawotka / A. Wojciechowska (eds.), *Alexander the Great and the East. History, Art, Tradition*, Wiesbaden: 159-178.

TARDIOLA, G. 1991: *Le meraviglie dell'India*, Roma.

TARN, W. 1933: «Alexander the Great and the Unity of Mankind», *PEA* 19: 123-166.

— 1948: *Alexander the Great*, 2 vols, Cambridge.

TATAKI, A. B. 1998: *Macedonians abroad: A contribution to the prosopography of Ancient Macedonia*, Athina.

THOMSON, J. O. 1965: *History of Ancient Geography*, New York.

TIMOTEO ÁLVAREZ, J. 1978: «Elementos para un nuevo modelo de análisis histórico de la Historia del Periodismo a la «Historia Total», en *Estudios de Historia Moderna y Contemporánea. Homenaje a D. Jesús Pabón*, Madrid: 399-424.

TORRES ESBARRANCH, J. J.; GUZMÁN HERMIDA, J. 2012: *Diodoro Sículo: Biblioteca Histórica. Libros XV-XVII*, Madrid.

TRONSON, A. 1984: «Satyrus the Peripatetic and the Marriages of Philip II», *JHS* 104: 116-126.

TROPPER, A. D. 2013: *Simeon the Righteous in Rabbinic Literature: A Legend Reinvented*, Leiden.

TSAVARI, I. 1990: *Dionisíou Alexandréos Oikouménes Periégesis. Kritiké ékdose*, Ioanina.

Tuplin, C. J. 1996: *Achaemenid Studies*, Stuttgart.
— 1998: «The Seasonal Migration of Achaemenid Kings», *AchHist* 11: 63-114.
— 2014: «The Sick Man of Asia? Fourth Century Historians on the End of the Achaemenids», in G. Parmeggiani (ed.), *Between Thucydides and Polybius. The Golden Age of Greek Historiography*, Cambridge: 211-238.
Urso, G. 1998: *Taranto e gli xenikoì strategoí*, Roma.
Van Paassen, C. 1957: *The Classical Tradition of Geography*, Groningen.
Van Thiel, H. (ed.) 1974: *Leben und Taten Alexanders von Makedonien. Der griechische Alexanderroman nach der Handschrift L*, Darmstadt.
Vatin, C. 1984: «Lettre addressée a la cite de Philippes par les ambassadeurs auprès d'Alexandre», in A. G. Kalogeropoulou (ed.), *Πρακτικά του Η' Διεθνούς Συνεδρίου Ελληνικής και Λατινικής Επιγραφικής (Athens 3-9 October 1982)*, Athina: 259-270.
Verdejo Manchado, J. / Antela-Bernárdez, B. 2021: «IG II[2] 1623, 276-285. Athens versus Pirates: Between Recovery, Need and Patriotism», *Klio* 103: 1-17.
Vokotopoulou, I. 1986: «Η επιγραφή των Καλινδοίων», in *AM* 4, Thessaloniki: 87-114.
Voutiras, E. 1993: «Η Λατρεία του Ασκληπιού στην Αρχαία Μακεδονία», in *AM* 5, Thessaloniki: 251-265.
Wackernagel, J. 1926: «Griechische Miszellen, 1: Persepolis», *Glotta* 16: 36-44.
Walbank, F. W. 1979: *A Historical Commentary on Polybius, vol. III: Commentary on Books XIX-XL*, Oxford.
Walsh, J. 2015: «Antipater and the Lamian War: A study in 4th Century Macedonian Counterinsurgency Doctrine», *AHB* 29: 1-27.
Walther Boer, W. (ed.) 1973: *Epistola Alexandri ad Aristotelem ad codicum fidem edidit et commentario critico instruxit W. W. B*, Meisenheim am Glan.
Wardman, A. E. 1955: «Plutarch and Alexander», *CQ* 5: 96-107.
Weber, G. 2009: «The Court of Alexander the Great as social system», in W. Heckel / L. A. Trittle (eds.), *Alexander the Great. A New history*, Oxford: 83-98.
Webster, P. 2001: *Pétain's Crime: The Full Story of French Collaboration in the Holocaust*, London.
Weerakkody, D. P. M. 1997: *Taprobanê: ancient Sri Lanka as known to Greeks and Romans*, Turnhout.
Westlake, H. D. 1935: *Thessaly in the fourth century B.C*, London.
Wheeler, M. 1968: *Flames over Persepolis: Turning-point in History*, London.
White, H. 1990: *The Content of the Form: Narrative Discourse and Historical Representation*, Baltimore–London.
Wiesehöfer, J. 2001: *Ancient Persia from 550 BC to 650 AD*, London–New York.
— 2016: «Fourth Century Revolts against Persia: The Test Case of Sidon (348-345 BCE)», in T. Howe / L. L. Brice (eds.), *Brill's Companion to Insurgency and Terrorism in the Ancient Mediterranean*, Leiden: 93-112.
Wilcken, U. 1932: *Alexander the Great*, London.

WIRTH, G. 1971: «Alexander zwischen Gaugamela und Persepolis», *Historia* 20: 617-632.

WITTKOWER, R. 1942: «Marvels of the East», *JWI* 5: 159-197.

WOLOHOJIAN, A. M. 1969: *The Romance of Alexander the Great by Pseudo-Callisthenes*, New York–London.

WOOD, M. 1997: *In the footsteps of Alexander the Great: A journey from Greece to Asia*, London.

WORTHINGTON, I. 1999: «How «Great» was Alexander?», *AHB* 13: 39-59.

— 2003: «Alexander, Philip, and the Macedonian Background», in J. Roisman (ed.), *Brill's Companion to Alexander the Great*, Leiden–Boston: 69-98.

— 2014: *By the Spear. Philip II, Alexander the Great, and the Rise and Fall of the Macedonian Empire*, Oxford.

— 2015: 'From East to West: Alexander and the Exiles Decree', in P. Weatlhley / E. Baynham (eds.), *East and West in the World Empire of Alexander*, Oxford: 93-108.

WRIGHT, A. 2020: «Monstrous Strangers at the Edge of the World. The Monstrous Races», in J. A. Weinstock (ed.), *The Monster Theory Reader*, Minneapolis: 173-191.

WÜRST, F. R. 1953: «Die Rede Alexanders des Grossen in Opis, Arrian VII. 9-10», *Historia* 2: 177-188.

YARDLEY, J. / HECKEL, W. 1997: *Justin: Epitome of the Philippic history of Pompeius Trogus. Volume I. Books 11-12: Alexander the Great*, Oxford.

YENNE, B. 2010: *Alexander the Great: Lessons from history's undefeated general*, New York.

ZAGANELLI, G. 1997: *L'Oriente incognito medieval*, Soveria Mannelli.

ZAMBRINI, A. 1982: «Gli *Indiká* di Megastene», *ASNP*, 12: 71-149.

— 1985: «Gli *Indiká* di Megastene. II», *ASNP*, 15: 781-853.

— 2007: «The Historians of Alexander the Great», in J. Marincola (ed.), *A Companion to Greek and Roman Historiography*, Oxford: 210-220.

ZUMETIKOS, A. M. 1894: *De Alexandri Olympiadisque Epistularum fontibus et reliquiis*, Berlin.

ZUMTHOR, P. 1993: *La mesure du monde*, Paris.